The Translator

SEAMUS HEANEY is the author of many volumes of poetry, criticism, and translation. One of the leading poets of his generation, he was awarded the Nobel Prize in Literature in 1995 and the Whitbread Prize in 2000 for his translation of *Beowulf.*

The Editor

DANIEL DONOGHUE is Professor of English at Harvard University. He is the author of *Style in Old English Poetry: The Test of the Auxiliary*, *Lady Godiva: A History of a Legend*, and many articles on Old and Middle English literature.

A NORTON CRITICAL EDITION

BEOWULF
A VERSE TRANSLATION

AUTHORITATIVE TEXT

CONTEXTS

CRITICISM

Translated by

SEAMUS HEANEY

HARVARD UNIVERSITY

Edited by

DANIEL DONOGHUE

HARVARD UNIVERSITY

W • W • NORTON & COMPANY • *New York* • *London*

This title is printed on permanent paper containing 30 percent post-consumer waste recycled fiber.

Printed in the United States of America.
First Edition.

The text of this book is composed in Fairfield Medium
with the display set in Bernhard Modern.
Composition by Binghamton Valley Composition.
Manufacturing by the Maple-Vail Book Manufacturing Group.
Book design by Antonina Krass.

Library of Congress Cataloging-in-Publication Data
Beowulf—a verse translation : authoritative text, contexts, criticism / translated by Seamus Heaney ; edited by Daniel Donoghue.
p. cm.—(A Norton critical edition)
Includes bibliographical references.

ISBN 0-393-97580-0 (pbk.)

1. Epic poetry, English (Old)—Modernized versions. 2. Epic poetry, English (Old)—History and criticism. 3. Epic poetry, English (Old) 4. Scandinavia—Poetry. 5. Monsters—Poetry. 6. Dragons—Poetry. 7. Heroes—Poetry. 8. Beowulf. I. Heaney, Seamus. II. Donoghue, Daniel, 1956– III. Series.
PR1583 .H43 2001
829'.3—dc21

W. W. Norton & Company, Inc.
500 Fifth Avenue, New York, N.Y. 10110
www.wwnorton.com

W. W. Norton & Company Ltd.
15 Carlisle Street, London W1D 3BS

9 0

Contents

Illustrations

Preface

This Norton Critical Edition differs from others because the literary text at its center carries a double identity. The Old English *Beowulf* is a verse narrative that survives in a manuscript transcribed around the year 1000, but the version printed here is Seamus Heaney's poetic translation from the cusp of the year 2000. Both deserve to be read as literary texts, but the fact that one translates the other sets up an intriguing dynamic involving interpretation, poetic invention, and fidelity to the source text.

Over sixty translations of *Beowulf* have appeared since the early nineteenth century, but none has caught the reading public's attention as much as Heaney's. Given this translation's reception, it is remarkable how little Heaney's *Beowulf* concedes to the contemporary reader. A moment's thought will reveal extensive differences between the poem's medieval and current audiences, yet Heaney does not provide a new or updated version of an old story but the old story itself. Obscure allusions, abrupt transitions, and words lost because of damage to the manuscript remain as problematic as they ever were. No episodes or characters are added or dropped. Even when Heaney's verse line adopts a different rhythm (ll. 1070–1159), the correspondence with the Old English remains close. Both the old poem and the new poem end on line 3182.

What sets Heaney's apart from other translations, however, is the language. His "Introduction" explains how, when he was searching for the "enabling note" to give the right voice to his project, he made the surprising turn to the speech of some older relatives in Ulster. It was a bold choice, but it enables him to make a clean break with the scholarly glossaries, which have a way of insinuating their formal, literary, and slightly archaic language into most *Beowulf* translations. The choice of a rural Ulster dialect carries ideological and political consequences that will be discussed elsewhere. Of more immediate concern is the odd fact that the translation requires footnotes to gloss its language, even for the intended audience. Most of the words in question are Hibernicisms, that is, usages characteristic of the English spoken in Ireland—or more specifically the English Heaney recalls from his Ulster relatives. Not all of the words are Irish in origin; some go back to Scandinavian languages and others to Old English. Perhaps the overriding lesson to be learned from the language that Heaney fashions is that all dialects have an equal claim on the remote origins of English because they all have a parallel history. The voice of the Scullions is as adequate to the task as Received Pronunciation or any other variety of English. On a more practical level, the simple task of looking up a glossed word may remind the reader that an older *Beowulf* stands behind Heaney's poem.

Beowulf is a poem of many dimensions. Over the years it has been assigned to the genres epic, heroic narrative, and folk-tale, and it incorporates a variety of other poetic forms such as creation hymn, elegy, gnomic verse, and heroic boast. While it is clear that the *Beowulf* poet was drawing from traditional sources, it is equally clear that most of those sources were oral and are thus unavailable today. The great exception is the Bible, which provides the story of Cain and Abel and Noah's flood. So the material in the "Contexts" section, immediately after the poem, includes explanatory material (such as genealogies of the various royal families) and analogues (such as an episode from a fourteenth-century Icelandic saga).

The "Translator's Introduction" and the final essay in this volume address the process of translation and situate Heaney's *Beowulf* within the trajectory of his career as a poet. While the other critical essays were written with the Old English poem in mind, they work well with Heaney's translation. Most of the *Beowulf* criticism that has accumulated over the years pays close attention to the language of the poem, but because the readers of this volume are not expected to know Old English, the essays selected do not rely on sustained close readings and instead address broad themes. Each piece includes its own literal prose translations, which can provide an interesting point of comparison with Heaney's, because every translation is also an interpretation.

The opening sentence of the "Translator's Introduction" indicates a period of about 350 years for the composition of *Beowulf*, "some time between the middle of the seventh and the end of the tenth century of the first millennium." The interval is so extensive that, if accepted at face value, it would frustrate any attempt to historicize the poem, because Anglo-Saxon England was anything but a static society from the years 650 to 1000—an interval equivalent to that from John Milton to the present day. The range reflects the current lack of consensus among *Beowulf* scholars and signals that (for the purposes of his translation) Heaney prefers to remain noncommital about the issue. For much of the twentieth century, there was a rough consensus favoring an earlier date of composition, often expressed as "early-eighth century," but since about 1980 the issue has undergone intensive scrutiny, which has in some cases cast doubt on the earlier certainties and in others found new advocates for specific periods within the larger span. The critical essays included in this volume reflect the shift away from the earlier consensus: the older essays confidently assume an early date of composition, while the more recent ones are more circumspect on the matter.

J. R. R. Tolkien's "*Beowulf*: The Monsters and the Critics" has been the most influential reading of the poem since it was published over fifty years ago. Arguing against a clumsy historicism in earlier *Beowulf* criticism, Tolkien makes a spirited case for the artistic merits of the poem. Today even those who take issue with Tolkien or who feel that the field has moved on have to reckon with the essay's influence. Jane Chance's essay offers a foil to Tolkien, both in its attention to Grendel's mother (whom Tolkien ignores) and in its gendered reading of Beowulf's struggle with her. What it shares with Tolkien is an admiration for the poem's artistry. John Leyerle compares the interlace motif prevalent in early insular art with the nonlinear strands of narrative in *Beowulf* to shed light on its aesthetic principles.

Beowulf is usually seen as a fictional character who moves in a world of myth and legend, but Roberta Frank's essay reminds us that the poem shows a sophisticated historical vision that avoids anachronism and even extends a sense of the past to its characters. The essays by Fred C. Robinson and Thomas Hill complement one another in addressing the poem's religious affiliations. Previous generations of scholars erected a simplistic pagan vs. Christian dichotomy and argued for one or the other as dominant. Both Robinson and Hill, on the other hand, assume that the narrative voice is Christian, but they offer readings that are more nuanced than the older dichotomies. Leslie Webster provides a different kind of context for *Beowulf* by using archaeology to explore the material culture of the poem.

While the other essays focus on the Old English *Beowulf*, my essay suggests that Heaney's turn to *Beowulf* is in many ways a return to the language that has always informed his poetry. His *Beowulf* self-consciously reverses the movement of colonization by using an Irish dialect to appropriate a foundational text of English literary history, but over and above the linguistic politics it is also a gesture of deep respect from one master poet to another across the expanse of a millennium.

DANIEL DONOGHUE

Acknowledgments

Although the author of *Beowulf* is no longer around to receive expressions of gratitude, I have the rare privilege of thanking the poet's shoulder-companion in this volume, Seamus Heaney, for his magnificent translation and for his encouragement in this project. J. R. R. Tolkien is no longer around either, but it is my happy duty to thank the other authors of the critical essays: John Leyerle, Jane Chance, Roberta Frank, Thomas Hill, Fred C. Robinson, and Leslie Webster. Special thanks are also due to my colleague Joseph Harris and to Al David, Rob Fulk, Kevin Kiernan, Bruce Mitchell, and Fred C. Robinson (again) for varying amounts of practical advice, encouragement, material help, and prose; my gratitude also to Carol Bemis, Rolf Bremmer, Chick Chickering, Terry Dolan, Mike Drout, Anthony Adams, Nick Howe, and Jason Puskar for more advice, opinions, and assistance. For two years my students, bless their hearts, have willingly submitted themselves to a range of critical approaches that went into the shaping of this edition.

This book is dedicated to my hearth-companions: Ann, Nathaniel, Kevin, and Hannah.

Old English Language and Poetics

Many students are surprised to learn that English poetry is older than prose—older by many centuries. We are accustomed to think of prose as naturally prior because of our personal experience: being simpler, prose is something we learn to write in the early days of our schooling. Poetry seems more challenging to read, and most of us never learn to compose it. We are also accustomed to think of prose as little more than a transcription of speech. But it is not. Written prose has its own conventions, which did not emerge in English until well after the conversion of the Anglo-Saxons around 700 C.E. and the subsequent introduction of the Latin system of writing. For centuries before that time, Germanic tribes all over Europe had fashioned a sophisticated practice of poetry, which was learned and passed on by memory. Several passages in *Beowulf* describe how an Anglo-Saxon *scop* (pronounced "shop") either improvised a poem or recounted a traditional story in verse, and the presence of an official *scop* in Hrothgar's court gives an idea of how highly valued they were in society. By the time Latin letters were introduced to England, the Anglo-Saxons were already in possession of a vigorous tradition of oral poetry. The familiarity of the conventions helps explain why, when clerics began to write down poems, they felt little need to indicate where clauses or verse lines ended. Any reader, it seems, would bring that knowledge to the task. To our eyes, the poems are lineated as if they were prose.

The words not only look foreign in the manuscript (written in a script called Anglo-Saxon square minuscule), they also sound strange to the ear. The reason is not simply that the sounds of individual words are different: *Þæt wæs god cyning* is recognizable as "That was a good king." And the reason is not found in the use of alliteration or compound words, which are still everyday features of English. The pronunciation, spelling, and word endings of Old English take some time to understand, but even at that stage the syntax and rhythm of *Beowulf* can resist comprehension. Many people find this residue of strangeness intriguing, as if a parallel poetic world opens up that forces them to reconsider the received wisdom. Generations of admirers (like Longfellow, Tennyson, Auden, and Heaney) have been attracted to *Beowulf*'s faintly disorienting strangeness within an otherwise familiar English tradition.

Since about the thirteenth century, the dominant verse pattern in English has been built on the iambic foot, which is immediately recognizable from just a brief example, such as these lines from a Wordsworth poem:

```
x     /  x   /   x  / x    /
I wandered lonely as a cloud
  x      /     x   /      x   /      x      /
that floats on high o'er vales and hills.
```

The syllables are drawn into the iambic rhythm to the extent that even the humble "as" gets carried along by a stress that it would rarely have in normal speech, and "o'er" is reduced to one syllable to keep the count right. The iambic regularity sets up a "prosodic contract" with the reader, so that even if another kind of foot is substituted, the rhythm plays off the underlying expectation of regularly alternating syllables. To those who have become habituated to the iambic rhythm, it can come to seem natural, but it is a highly conventionalized artifice, against which free verse and other metrical innovations of modernism and postmodernism have defined themselves.

The Old English prosodic contract works from equally arbitrary but entirely different principles. It is almost as though the Germanic innovators of this prosody (some time before the fifth century) selected a limited number of phrasings from their ordinary speech and formalized those rhythms as the basic units of the poetic line. Other rhythms were excluded. So rather than elevate a regularly repeating pattern (like the iamb), they pieced together phrasal units from already-familiar rhythms. Two such phrases, called half-lines, combine to form an Old English verse line. In pairing them together a premium is placed on variety, so that the same rhythm is rarely repeated in both halves of the line (thus ruling out an iambic line), and two successive lines are rarely alike. The paired half-lines are linked by alliteration on the stressd syllables, as in the *g*-sounds of

```
1          2              3              4
Grendel gongan,   Godes yrre bær.
```

In translating this line Heaney preserves the alliterating pattern in

```
1                2                         3        4
God-cursed Grendel came greedily loping.
```

Each half-line typically has two primary stresses that qualify for alliteration, which add up to four per line, as numbered above. The con-

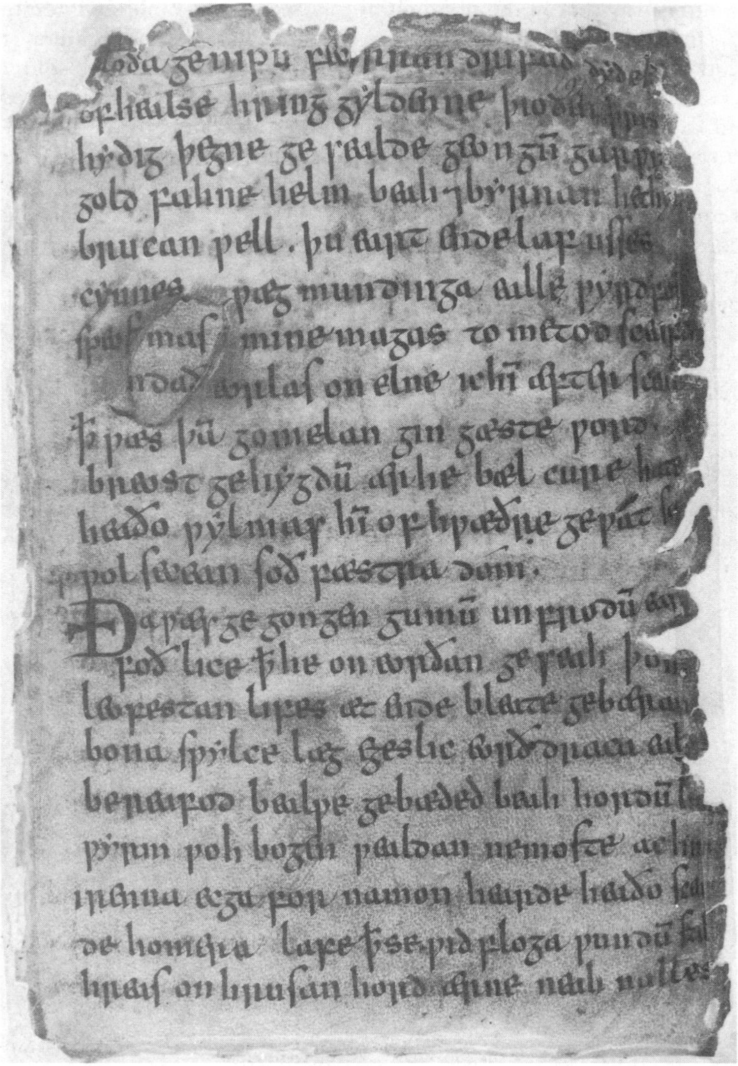

Figure 1. The *Beowulf* Manuscript: Cotton Vitellius A. xv, folio 191r. By permission of the British Library. Note the hole in the top half, which was likely caused by a blemish in the animal's skin from which the vellum was made. Letters from the next folio can be seen through it. The folio's ragged, distorted edge is the result of damage from a fire in 1731.

ventions say that in the first half of the line either 1 and 2 alliterate (as in this line), or just 1 by itself; in the latter half 3 always alliterates and 4 never does. One final source of variety: the alliterating sound is rarely repeated from one line to the next. Thus if one line alliterates on [b], the next line will alliterate on any sound but [b]. Other features that cannot be discussed here, such as syllable length, also come into play. Taken together, the metrical constraints favor an economy of expression within the half-lines so that each syllable is carefully weighed. Compound words, for example, not only create vivid juxtapositions, but their conciseness as a single word (as opposed to a phrase) offers a metrically compact element that is useful in constructing half-lines: "earth-dragon" is shorter than "dragon of the earth," but it has the same number of stressed syllables.

The following passage from *Beowulf* shows the intricate interplay of these features.[1] It is based on a transcription from the folio reproduced here, beginning with the large Ð (a letter known to the Anglo-Saxons as "eth"). For reasons that will become clear later, the gloss given above the lines makes little concession to Modern English syntax:

Then it came about to the man un-aged
Ða wæs gegongen   gumun unfrodum

with difficulty that he on earth saw
earfoðlice   þæt he on eorðan geseah

the most beloved of life at end
þone leofestan   lifes æt ende 2823

wretchedly faring. Killer likewise lay
bleate gebæran.   Bona swylce læg

terrible earthdragon of life bereft
egeslic eorð-draca   ealdre bereafod

by aggression afflicted. Ring-hoards longer
bealwe gebæded.   Beah-hordum leng 2826

dragon coiled to possess was not allowed,
wyrm woh-bogen   wealdan ne moste,

1. This passage is given a thematic and rhetorical interpretation in Donoghue, "The Philologer Poet: Seamus Heaney and the Translation of *Beowulf*," pp. 245–46, below.

but him of iron the edges took
ac him irenna ecga fornamon

hard battle-sharp of hammers remnant
hearde heaðo-scear[p]e homera lafe, 2829

so that the wide-flier because of wounds quiet
x x / \ x / x / x
þæt se wid-floga wundum stille

fell to earth the hoard-cave near.
/ x / x / \ x /
hreas on hrusan hord-ærne neah. 2821–31

No pair of half-lines duplicates the rhythm, yet each conforms to one of the established patterns found throughout the poem. Similarly, the alliterating sounds of each line are not repeated in its neighbors. By way of illustration, the last two lines are scanned using the conventional notations for an unstressed syllable [x], full stress [/], and the kind of secondary stress [\] found in the latter half of compounds like *wid-floga*. Taken together, these conventions give each line of Old English verse a precisely modulated but endlessly variable rhythmic and alliterating contour. The very features that the Anglo-Saxons found aesthetically pleasing can make the poetry seem foreign today. Where the iambic line sets up the expectation of regularity, the Old English line insists on rhythmic variety. Where end-rhyme puts the most prominent aural feature at the end of the verse, alliteration creates a dynamic across the middle of the line.

The syntax can seem baffling. The order of words is sometimes called "free," but "free" must not be understood as a kind of linguistic liberty where words can be scattered around without constraint. For the phrase *lifes æt ende* (line 2823) another idiomatic word order might be *æt lifes ende*, which snaps into focus as "at life's end," but as such it would be unmetrical. The line reads *lifes æt ende* not because of some syntactic whim but because the meter requires *lifes*, which takes the alliteration, to precede the unstressed syllable of *æt*. Other half-lines, such as *wealdan ne moste*, are poetic formulas that had a practical usefulness as prefabricated elements in the construction of verse.

Another syntactic feature, called "variation" or "apposition," is also a pervasive rhetorical device. In the sentence beginning on line 2824, for example, two separate nouns refer to the dragon, and they in turn are modified by two separate phrases. By way of illustration, they can be reconfigured to align the parallel elements:

Bona egeslic eorð-draca	swylce læg	ealdre bereafod bealwe gebæded

A literal translation:

the killer terrible earthdragon	likewise lay	bereft of life afflicted by aggression

It is a construction in which separate words have the same referent and the same syntactic function within a clause, but they are placed as parallel elements without any formal linking—not even a conjunction like "and."[2] At times the effect of apposition is simply cumulative, so that the additional information supplied by successive words fills out the first reference, such as "the killer, the terrible earthdragon." On other occasions, however, there can be more subtle rhetorical effects. The dead dragon, for example, is "bereft of life, afflicted by aggression," where the Old English word *bealwe*, means "aggression," but it also carries connotations of "evil." One way to read this apposed element then, is to be alert to the clue that the dragon's death was justified because its violence was evil. This meaning is not explicit, but rather an interpretive possibility available to readers attentive to the connotations of *bealwe*.

One of the rhetorical advantages of apposition is its openendedness: the aggression in this case can be both Beowulf's (with less emphasis on evil) or the dragon's. The same passage has another set of parallel epithets in "edges of iron" and "the hard, battle-sharp remnants of hammers," both of which are descriptive phrases for "sword." In fact, the half-line *homera lafe* "remnants of hammers" is an instance of a highly compressed and enigmatic figure of speech known as a kenning. Kennings are especially characteristic of Old English (and Old Norse), and their spare allusiveness lends itself to the economy of the alliterative line. If one were to expand *homera lafe* into a more prosaic expression, it might be "what remains after the blacksmith's hammers have finished their work"; that is, "a sword."

The principle of apposition can be extended in two directions. In the lexicon, the effort to give multiple perspectives and the requirements of alliteration lead to a proliferation of synonyms. Common concepts like "horse," "hall," and "man" may have over a dozen variants, a number that does not include the many possible compounds. Some of these words, like *guma* "man" (in the first line of the pas-

2. For a lucid account of apposition, see Fred C. Robinson, *Beowulf and the Appositive Style* (Knoxville: U of Tennessee P, 1985).

sage), are found only in poetry, and were part of a specialized lexicon which would also include poetic compounds and kennings. In any language, however, true synonyms are very rare, and the Old English synonyms for a word like "man" had connotations which in many (perhaps most) cases are lost to us.

The absence of conjunctions that characterizes apposition leads to the second direction: the syntax of sentences. Old English poetry is sparing in its use of subordinating conjunctions like "although," "while," "because," and "if." The sentences in the passage under discussion are typical: the most adventurous conjunctions are "so that" and "but." But in the same way that apposed elements within a sentence can suggest nuances, the sparing use of conjunctions can induce the reader to make interpretive connections between clauses.

This brief survey has identified a number of areas where the language of *Beowulf* seems to diverge from contemporary English. The most pronounced case might be apposition. Today the repetition of words and phrases with the same referent, even the kind of "elegant variation" once favored by some Victorian writers, is actively discouraged. A student paper that included passages like "the killer, the terrible earth-dragon, deprived of life, afflicted by evil aggression" would be savaged in red ink. In the case of *homera lafe* and the other variations on sword, Heaney restructures the syntax into an epithet followed by descriptive adjectives, "Hard-edged blades, hammered out / and keenly filed," where "hammered out" is itself a kind of remnant (*laf*) of the original kenning. But he does not always rephrase apposition out of existence. By preserving it on occasion, Heaney's translation reminds the reader that another tradition lies behind his text. In addition, there are other areas where the old conventions resist an easy assimilation. Old English favors metrical variety over iambic regularity; alliteration within the line to rhyme at the end; a specialized vocabulary that includes compounds and kennings; and a sparing use of subordinating conjunctions. Within each half-line there is a strict economy of syllables and word order. In units larger than the half-line, however, the clauses have an elasticity that allows them to grow very long. Much of the "feel" of Old English verse results from the tension between the constraint of one and the expansiveness of the other. Just how Seamus Heaney finds the right pitch between the two is described in his "Introduction."

Because the Anglo-Saxons left no *ars poetica*, the principles outlined here are a scholarly reconstruction from some 32,000 lines of Old English verse that survive in written form. Even though there is much still to learn, it is clear that Old English verse was complex. And conversely, Anglo-Saxon audiences were sophisticated in their ability to understand how poets manipulated the conventions. It is wrong to assume that because the material conditions of Anglo-

Saxon society were primitive by today's standards, everything else about it was underdeveloped as well. Such an assumption flies in the face of what we know about many oral cultures, some of which are still active today. Even without an Anglo-Saxon *ars poetica* we know that oral poetry was a primary art form in their culture. After the introduction of writing some poets were able to fuse the oral and literary traditions into profoundly powerful compositions like *Beowulf*.

Translator's Introduction

And now this is 'an inheritance'—
Upright, rudimentary, unshiftably planked
In the long ago, yet willable forward

Again and again and again.

1 Beowulf: The Poem

The poem called *Beowulf* was composed some time between the middle of the seventh and the end of the tenth century of the first millennium, in the language that is today called Anglo-Saxon or Old English. It is a heroic narrative, more than three thousand lines long, concerning the deeds of a Scandinavian prince, also called Beowulf, and it stands as one of the foundation works of poetry in English. The fact that the English language has changed so much in the last thousand years means, however, that the poem is now generally read in translation and mostly in English courses at schools and universities. This has contributed to the impression that it was written (as Osip Mandelstam said of *The Divine Comedy*) "on official paper," which is unfortunate, since what we are dealing with is a work of the greatest imaginative vitality, a masterpiece where the structuring of the tale is as elaborate as the beautiful contrivances of its language. Its narrative elements may belong to a previous age but as a work of art it lives in its own continuous present, equal to our knowledge of reality in the present time.

The poem was written in England but the events it describes are set in Scandinavia, in a "once upon a time" that is partly historical. Its hero, Beowulf, is the biggest presence among the warriors in the land of the Geats, a territory situated in what is now southern Sweden, and early in the poem Beowulf crosses the sea to the land of the Danes in order to rid their country of a man-eating monster called Grendel. From this expedition (which involves him in a second contest with Grendel's mother) he returns in triumph and eventually rules for fifty years as king of his homeland. Then a dragon begins to terrorize the countryside and Beowulf must confront it. In a final climactic encounter, he does manage to slay the dragon, but he also meets his own death and enters the legends of his people as a warrior of high renown.

We know about the poem more or less by chance, because it exists in one manuscript only. This unique copy (now in the British Library) barely survived a fire in the eighteenth century and was then transcribed and titled, retranscribed and edited, translated and adapted, interpreted and taught, until it has become an acknowledged classic. For decades it has been a set book on English syllabuses at university level all over the world. The fact that many English departments require it to be studied in the original continues to generate resistance, most notably at Oxford University, where the pros and cons of the inclusion of part of it as a compulsory element in the English course have been debated regularly in recent years.

For generations of undergraduates, academic study of the poem was often just a matter of construing the meaning, getting a grip on the grammar and vocabulary of Anglo-Saxon, and being able to recognize, translate, and comment upon random extracts that were presented in the examinations. For generations of scholars too the interest had been textual and philological; then there developed a body of research into analogues and sources, a quest for stories and episodes in the folklore and legends of the Nordic peoples that would parallel or foreshadow episodes in *Beowulf*. Scholars were also preoccupied with fixing the exact time and place of the poem's composition, paying minute attention to linguistic, stylistic, and scribal details. More generally, they tried to establish the history and genealogy of the dynasties of Swedes, Geats, and Danes to which the poet makes constant allusion; and they devoted themselves to a consideration of the world-view behind the poem, asking to what extent (if at all) the newly established Christian religion, which was fundamental to the poet's intellectual formation, displaced him from his imaginative at-homeness in the world of his poem—a pagan Germanic society governed by a heroic code of honor, one where the attainment of a name for warrior-prowess among the living overwhelms any concern about the soul's destiny in the afterlife.

However, when it comes to considering *Beowulf* as a work of literature, one publication stands out. In 1936, the Oxford scholar and teacher J. R. R. Tolkien published an epoch-making paper entitled "*Beowulf*: The Monsters and the Critics," which took for granted the poem's integrity and distinction as a work of art and proceeded to show in what this integrity and distinction inhered. Tolkien assumed that the poet had felt his way through the inherited material—the fabulous elements and the traditional accounts of an heroic past—and by a combination of creative intuition and conscious structuring had arrived at a unity of effect and a balanced order. He assumed, in other words, that the *Beowulf* poet was an imaginative writer rather than some kind of back-formation derived from nineteenth-century folklore and philology. Tolkien's brilliant literary treatment changed the way the poem was valued and initiated a new era—and new terms—of appreciation.

It is impossible to attain a full understanding and estimate of *Beowulf* without recourse to this immense body of commentary and elucidation. Nevertheless, readers coming to the poem for the first time are likely to experience something other than mere discomfiture when faced with the strangeness of the names and the immediate lack of known reference points. An English-speaker new to *The Iliad* or *The Odyssey* or *The Aeneid* will probably at least have heard of Troy and Helen, or of Penelope and the Cyclops, or of Dido and the Golden Bough. These epics may be in Greek and Latin, yet the classical heritage has entered the cultural memory enshrined in English so thoroughly that their worlds are more familiar than that of the first native epic, even though it was composed centuries after them. Achilles rings a bell, but not *Scyld Scēfing*. Ithaca leads the mind in a certain direction, but not *Heorot*. The Sibyl of Cumae will stir certain associations, but not bad Queen Modthryth. * * *

Still, in spite of the sensation of being caught between a "shield-wall" of opaque references and a "word-hoard" that is old and strange, such readers are also bound to feel a certain "shock of the new." This is because the poem possesses a mythic potency. Like Shield Sheafson (as *Scyld Scēfing* is known in this translation), it arrives from somewhere beyond the known bourne of our experience, and having fulfilled its purpose (again like Shield) it passes once more into the beyond. In the intervening time, the poet conjures up a work as remote as Shield's funeral boat borne toward the horizon, as commanding as the horn-pronged gables of King Hrothgar's hall, as solid and dazzling as Beowulf's funeral pyre that is set ablaze at the end. These opening and closing scenes retain a haunting presence in the mind; they are set pieces but they have the life-marking power of certain dreams. They are like the pillars of the gate of horn, through which the wise dreams of true art can still be said to pass.

What happens in between is what W. B. Yeats would have called a phantasmagoria. Three agons—three struggles in which the preternatural force-for-evil of the hero's enemies comes springing at him in demonic shapes; three encounters with what the critical literature and the textbook glossaries call "the monsters"—in three archetypal sites of fear: the barricaded night-house, the infested underwater current and the reptile-haunted rocks of a wilderness. If we think of the poem in this way, its place in world art becomes clearer and more secure. We can conceive of it re-presented and transformed in performance in a *bunraku* theater in Japan, where the puppetry and the poetry are mutually supportive, a mixture of technicolor spectacle and ritual chant. Or we can equally envisage it as an animated cartoon (and there has been at least one shot at this already), full of mutating graphics and minatory stereophonics. We can avoid, at any rate, the slightly cardboard effect that the word "monster" tends to introduce, and give the poem a fresh chance to sweep "in off the moors, down through the mist-bands" of Anglo-Saxon England, forward into the global village of the third millennium.

Nevertheless, the dream element and overall power to haunt come at a certain readerly price. The poem abounds in passages that will leave an unprepared audience bewildered. Just when the narrative seems ready to take another step ahead, it sidesteps. For a moment it is as if we have been channel-surfed into another poem, and at two points in this translation I indicate that we are in fact participating in a poem-within-our-poem not only by the use of italics, but by a slight quickening of pace and shortening of metrical rein. The passages comprise lines 883–914 and 1070–158,* and on each occasion a minstrel has begun to chant a poem as part of the celebration of Beowulf's achievements. In the former case, the minstrel expresses his praise by telling the story of Sigemund's victory over a dragon, which both parallels Beowulf's triumph over Grendel and prefigures his fatal encounter with the *wyrm* in his old age. In the latter—the most famous of what were once called the "digressions" in the poem, the one dealing with a fight between Danes and Frisians at the stronghold of Finn, the Frisian king—the song the minstrel sings has a less obvious bearing on the immediate situation of the hero, but its import is nevertheless central to both the historical and imaginative worlds of the poem.

The "Finnsburg episode" immerses us in a society that is at once honor-bound and blood-stained, presided over by the laws of the blood-feud, where the kin of a person slain are bound to exact a price for the death, either by slaying the killer or by receiving satisfaction in the form of *wergild* (the "man-price"), a legally fixed compensation. The claustrophobic and doomladen atmosphere of this interlude gives the reader an intense intimation of what *wyrd*, or fate, meant not only to the characters in the Finn story but to those participating in the main action of *Beowulf* itself. All conceive of themselves as hooped within the great wheel of necessity, in thrall to a code of loyalty and bravery, bound to seek glory in the eye of the warrior world. The little nations are grouped around their lord; the greater nations spoil for war and menace the little ones; a lord dies, defenselessness ensues; the enemy strikes; vengeance for the dead becomes an ethic for the living, bloodshed begets further bloodshed;

* Line numbers given in the Translator's Introduction refer to this translation, not to the Old English text.

the wheel turns, the generations tread and tread and tread—which is what I meant above when I said that the import of the Finnsburg passage is central to the historical and imaginative worlds of the poem as a whole.

One way of reading *Beowulf* is to think of it as three agons in the hero's life, but another way would be to regard it as a poem that contemplates the destinies of three peoples by tracing their interweaving histories in the story of the central character. First we meet the Danes—variously known as the Shieldings (after Shield Sheafson, the founder of their line), the Ingwins, the Spear-Danes, the Bright-Danes, the West-Danes, and so on—a people in the full summer of their power, symbolized by the high hall built by King Hrothgar, one "meant to be a wonder of the world." The threat to this superb people comes from within their own borders, from marshes beyond the pale, from the bottom of the haunted mere where "Cain's clan," in the shape of Grendel and his troll-dam, trawl and scavenge and bide their time. But it also comes from without, from the Heathobards, for example, whom the Danes have defeated in battle and from whom they can therefore expect retaliatory war (see lines 2020–69).

Beowulf actually predicts this turn of events when he goes back to his own country after saving the Danes (for the time being, at any rate) by staving off the two "reavers from hell." In the hall of his "ring-giver," Hygelac, lord of the Geats, the hero discourses about his adventures in a securely fortified cliff-top enclosure. But this security is only temporary, for it is the destiny of the Geat people to be left lordless in the end. Hygelac's alliances eventually involve him in deadly war with the Swedish king, Ongentheow, and even though he does not personally deliver the fatal stroke (two of his thanes are responsible for this—see lines 2484–89 and then the lengthier reprise of this incident at lines 2922–3003), he is known in the poem as "Ongentheow's killer." Hence it comes to pass that after the death of Beowulf, who eventually succeeds Hygelac, the Geats experience a great foreboding and the poem closes in a mood of somber expectation. A world is passing away, the Swedes and others are massing on the borders to attack, and there is no lord or hero to rally the defence.

The Swedes, therefore, are the third nation whose history and destiny are woven into the narrative, and even though no part of the main action is set in their territory, they and their kings constantly stalk the horizon of dread within which the main protagonists pursue their conflicts and allegiances. The Swedish dimension gradually becomes an important element in the poem's emotional and imaginative geography, a geography that entails, it should be said, no very clear map-sense of the world, more an apprehension of menaced borders, of danger gathering beyond the mere and the marshes, of *mearc-stapas* "prowling the moors, huge marauders / from some other world."

Within these phantasmal boundaries, each lord's hall is an actual and a symbolic refuge. Here are heat and light, rank and ceremony, human solidarity and culture; the *duguþ* share the mead-benches with the *geogoþ*, the veterans with their tales of warrior-kings and hero-saviors from the past rub shoulders with young braves—*þegnas, eorlas*, thanes, retainers—keen to win such renown in the future. The prospect of gaining a glorious name in the *wæl-ræs* (the rush of battle-slaughter), the pride of defending one's lord and bearing heroic witness to the integrity of the bond between him and his hall-companions—a bond sealed in the *glēo* and *gidd* of peace-time feasting and ring-giving—this is what gave drive and sanction to the Germanic warrior-culture enshrined in *Beowulf*.

Heorot and Hygelac's hall are the hubs of this value system upon which the poem's action turns. But there is another, outer rim of value, a circumference of understanding within which the heroic world is occasionally viewed as from a distance and recognized for what it is, an earlier state of consciousness and culture, one that has not been altogether shed but that has now been comprehended as part of another pattern. And this circumference and pattern arise, of course, from the poet's Christianity and from his perspective as an Englishman looking back at places and legends that his ancestors knew before they made their migration from continental Europe to their new home on the island of the Britons. As a consequence of his doctrinal certitude, which is as composed as it is ardent, the poet can view the story-time of his poem with a certain historical detachment and even censure the ways of those who lived *in illo tempore*:

> Sometimes at pagan shrines they vowed
> offerings to idols, swore oaths
> that the killer of souls might come to their aid
> and save the people. That was their way,
> their heathenish hope; deep in their hearts
> they remembered hell. (175–80)

At the same time, as a result of his inherited vernacular culture and the imaginative sympathy that distinguishes him as an artist, the poet can lend the full weight of his rhetorical power to Beowulf as he utters the first principles of the northern warrior's honor-code:

> It is always better
> to avenge dear ones than to indulge in mourning.
> For every one of us, living in this world
> means waiting for our end. Let whoever can
> win glory before death. When a warrior is gone,
> that will be his best and only bulwark. (1384–89)

In an age when "the instability of the human subject" is constantly argued for if not presumed, there should be no problem with a poem that is woven from two such different psychic fabrics. In fact, *Beowulf* perfectly answers the early modern conception of a work of creative imagination as one in which conflicting realities find accommodation within a new order; and this reconciliation occurs, it seems to me, most poignantly and most profoundly in the poem's third section, once the dragon enters the picture and the hero in old age must gather his powers for the final climactic ordeal. From the moment Beowulf advances under the crags, into the comfortless arena bounded by the rock-wall, the reader knows he is one of those "marked by fate." The poetry is imbued with a strong intuition of *wyrd* hovering close, "unknowable but certain," and yet, because it is imagined within a consciousness that has learned to expect that the soul will find an ultimate home "among the steadfast ones," this primal human emotion has been transmuted into something less "zero at the bone," more metaphysically tempered.

A similar transposition from a plane of regard that is, as it were, helmeted and hall-bound to one that sees things in a slightly more heavenly light is discernible in the different ways the poet imagines gold. Gold is a constant element, gleaming solidly in underground vaults, on the breasts of queens or the arms and regalia of warriors on the mead-benches. It is loaded into boats as spoil, handed out in bent bars as hall-gifts, buried in the earth as treasure, persisting underground as an affirmation of a people's glorious past and an elegy for it. It pervades the ethos of the poem and adds luster to its diction. And yet the bullion with which Waels's son Sigemund weighs down the hold after an earlier dragon-slaying triumph (in the old days, long before Beowulf's time) is a more trustworthy substance than that which is secured behind the walls of Beowulf's barrow. By the end of the poem, gold has suffered a radiation from the Christian vision. It is not that it yet equals riches in the medieval sense of worldly corruption, just that its status as the ore of all value has been put in doubt. It is *lǣne*, transitory, passing from hand to hand, and its changed status is registered as a symptom of the changed world. Once the dragon is disturbed, the melancholy and sense of displacement that pervade the last movement of the poem enter the hoard as a disabling and ominous light. And the dragon himself, as a genius of the older order, is bathed in this light, so that even as he begins to stir, the reader has a premonition that the days of his empery are numbered.

Nevertheless, the dragon has a wonderful inevitability about him and a unique glamor. It is not that the other monsters are lacking in presence and aura; it is more that they remain, for all their power to terrorize, creatures of the physical world. Grendel comes alive in the reader's imagination as a kind of dog-breath in the dark, a fear of collision with some hard-boned and immensely strong android frame, a mixture of Caliban and hoplite. And while his mother too has a definite brute-bearing about her, a creature of slouch and lunge on land if seal-swift in the water, she nevertheless retains a certain non-strangeness. As antagonists of a hero being tested, Grendel and his mother possess an appropriate head-on strength. The poet may need them as figures who do the devil's work, but the poem needs them more as figures who call up and show off Beowulf's physical strength and his superb gifts as a warrior. They are the right enemies for a young glory-hunter, instigators of the formal boast, worthy trophies to be carried back from the grim testing-ground—Grendel's hand is ripped off and nailed up, his head severed and paraded in Heorot. It is all consonant with the surge of youth and the compulsion to win fame "as wide as the wind's home, / as the sea around cliffs," utterly a manifestation of the Germanic heroic code.

Enter then, fifty years later, the dragon—from his dry-stone vault, from a nest where he is heaped in coils around the body-heated gold. Once he is wakened, there is something glorious in the way he manifests himself, a Fourth of July effulgence fireworking its path across the night sky; and yet, because of the centuries he has spent dormant in the tumulus, there is a foundedness as well as a lambency about him. He is at once a stratum of the earth and a streamer in the air, no painted dragon but a figure of real oneiric power, one that can easily survive the prejudice that arises at the very mention of the word "dragon." Whether in medieval art or modern Disney cartoons, the dragon can strike us as far less horrific than he is meant to be, but in the final movement of *Beowulf* he lodges himself in the imagination as *wyrd* rather than *wyrm*, more a destiny than a set of reptilian vertebrae.

Grendel and his mother enter Beowulf's life from the outside, accidentally, challenges which in other circumstances he might not have taken up, enemies from whom he might have been distracted or deflected. The dragon, on the other hand, is a given of his home ground, abiding in his under-earth as in his understanding, waiting for the meeting, the watcher at the ford, the questioner who sits so sly, the "lion-limb," as Gerard Manley Hopkins might have called him, against whom Beowulf's body and soul must measure themselves. Dragon equals shadow-line, the psalmist's valley of the shadow of death, the embodiment of a knowledge deeply ingrained in the species—the knowledge, that is, of the price to be paid for physical and spiritual survival.

It has often been observed that all the scriptural references in *Beowulf* are to the Old Testament. The poet is more in sympathy with the tragic, waiting, unredeemed phase of things than with any transcendental promise. Beowulf's mood as he gets ready to fight the dragon—who could be read as a projection of Beowulf's own chthonic wisdom refined in the crucible of experience—recalls the mood of other tragic heroes: Oedipus at Colonus, Lear at his "ripeness is all" extremity, Hamlet in the last illuminations of his "prophetic soul":

> no easy bargain
> would be made in that place by any man.
> The veteran king sat down on the cliff-top.
> He wished good luck to the Geats who had shared
> his hearth and his gold. He was sad at heart,
> unsettled yet ready, sensing his death.
> His fate hovered near, unknowable but certain. (2415–21)

Here the poet attains a level of insight that approaches the visionary. The subjective and the inevitable are in perfect balance, what is solidly established is bathed in an element that is completely sixth-sensed, and indeed the whole, slow-motion, constantly self-deferring approach to the hero's death and funeral continues to be like this. Beowulf's soul may not yet have fled "to its destined place among the steadfast ones," but there is already a beyond-the-grave aspect to him, a revenant quality about his resoluteness. This is not just metrical narrative full of anthropological interest and typical heroic-age motifs; it is poetry of a high order, in which passages of great lyric intensity—such as the "Lay of the Last Survivor" (lines 2247–66) and, even more remarkably, the so-called "Father's Lament" (2444–62)—rise like emanations from some fissure in the bedrock of the human capacity to endure:

> It was like the misery endured by an old man
> who has lived to see his son's body
> swing on the gallows. He begins to keen
> and weep for his boy, watching the raven
> gloat where he hangs; he can be of no help.
> The wisdom of age is worthless to him.
> Morning after morning, he wakes to remember
> that his child is gone; he has no interest
> in living on until another heir
> is born in the hall . . .
> Alone with his longing, he lies down on his bed
> and sings a lament; everything seems too large,
> the steadings and the fields. (2444–53, 2460–62)

Such passages mark an ultimate stage in poetic attainment; they are the imaginative equivalent of Beowulf's spiritual state at the end, when he tells his men that "doom of battle will bear [their] lord away," in the same way that the sea-journeys so vividly described in lines 210–28 and lines 1903–24 are the equivalent of his exultant prime.

At these moments of lyric intensity, the keel of the poetry is deeply set in the element of sensation while the mind's lookout sways metrically and far-sightedly in the element of pure comprehension—which is to say that the elevation of *Beowulf* is always, paradoxically, buoyantly down-to-earth. And nowhere is this more obviously and memorably the case than in the account of the hero's funeral with which the poem ends. Here the inexorable and the elegiac combine in a description of the funeral pyre being got ready, the body being burnt and the barrow being constructed—a scene at once immemorial and oddly contemporary. The Geat woman who cries out in dread as the flames consume the body of her dead lord could come straight from a late-twentieth-century news report, from Rwanda or Kosovo; her keen is a nightmare glimpse into the minds of people who have survived traumatic, even monstrous events and who are now being exposed to a comfortless future. We immediately recognize her predicament and the pitch of her grief and find ourselves the better for having them expressed with such adequacy, dignity and unforgiving truth:

> On a height they kindled the hugest of all
> funeral fires; fumes of woodsmoke
> billowed darkly up, the blaze roared
> and drowned out their weeping, wind died down
> and flames wrought havoc in the hot bone-house,
> burning it to the core. They were disconsolate
> and wailed aloud for their lord's decease.
> A Geat woman too sang out in grief;
> with hair bound up, she unburdened herself
> of her worst fears, a wild litany
> of nightmare and lament: her nation invaded,
> enemies on the rampage, bodies in piles,
> slavery and abasement. Heaven swallowed the smoke.
> (3143–55)

2 About This Translation

When I was an undergraduate at Queen's University, Belfast, I studied *Beowulf* and other Anglo-Saxon poems and developed not only a feel for the language, but a fondness for the melancholy and fortitude that characterized the poetry. Consequently, when an invitation to translate the poem arrived from the editors of *The Norton Anthology of English Literature*, I was tempted to try my hand. While I had no great expertise in Old English, I had a strong desire to get back to the first stratum of the language and to "assay the hoard" (line 2509). This was during the middle years of the 1980s, when I had begun a regular teaching job at Harvard and was opening my ear to the unmoored speech of some contemporary American poetry. Saying yes to the *Beowulf* commission would be (I argued with myself) a kind of aural antidote, a way of ensuring that my linguistic anchor would stay lodged on the Anglo-Saxon sea-floor. So I undertook to do it.

Very soon, however, I hesitated. It was labor-intensive work, scriptorium-slow. I proceeded dutifully like a sixth-former at homework. I would set myself twenty lines a day, write out my glossary of hard words in longhand, try to pick a way through the syntax, get the run of the meaning established in my head and then hope that the lines could be turned into metrical shape and raised to the power of verse. Often, however, the whole attempt to turn it into modern English seemed to me like trying to bring down a megalith with a toy hammer. What had been so attractive in the first place, the hand-built, rock-sure feel of the thing, began to defeat me. I turned to other work, the commissioning editors did not pursue me, and the project went into abeyance.

Even so, I had an instinct that it should not be let go. An understanding I had worked out for myself concerning my own linguistic and literary origins made me reluctant to abandon the task. I had noticed, for example, that without any conscious intent on my part certain lines in the first poem in my first book conformed to the requirements of Anglo-Saxon metrics. These lines were made up of two balancing halves, each half containing two stressed syllables—"The spade sinks into gravelly ground: / My father digging. I look down . . ."—and in the case of the second line there was alliteration linking "digging" and "down" across the caesura. Part of me, in other words, had been writing Anglo-Saxon from the start.

This was not surprising, given that the poet who had first formed my ear was Gerard Manley Hopkins. Hopkins was a chip off the Old English block, and the earliest lines I published when I was a student were as much pastiche Anglo-Saxon as they were pastiche Hopkins: "Starling thatch-watches and sudden swallow / Straight breaks to mud-nest, home-rest rafter," and so on. I have written about all this elsewhere and about the relation of my Hopkins ventriloquism to the speech patterns of Ulster—especially as these were caricatured by the poet W. R. Rodgers. Ulster people, according to Rodgers, are "an abrupt people / who like the spiky consonants of speech / and think the soft ones cissy," and get a kick out of "anything that gives or takes attack / like Micks, Teagues, tinkers' gets, Vatican."

Joseph Brodsky once said that poets' biographies are present in the sounds they make and I suppose all I am saying is that I consider *Beowulf* to be part of my voice-right. And yet to persuade myself that

I was born into its language and that its language was born into me took a while: for somebody who grew up in the political and cultural conditions of Lord Brookeborough's Northern Ireland, it could hardly have been otherwise.

Sprung from an Irish nationalist background and educated at a Northern Irish Catholic school, I had learned the Irish language and lived within a cultural and ideological frame that regarded it as the language that I should by rights have been speaking but I had been robbed of. I have also written, for example, about the thrill I experienced when I stumbled upon the word *lachtar* in my Irish-English dictionary, and found that this word, which my aunt had always used when speaking of a flock of chicks, was in fact an Irish language word, and more than that, an Irish word associated in particular with County Derry. Yet here it was, surviving in my aunt's English speech generations after her forebears and mine had ceased to speak Irish. For a long time, therefore, the little word was—to borrow a simile from Joyce—like a rapier point of consciousness pricking me with an awareness of language-loss and cultural dispossession, and tempting me into binary thinking about language. I tended to conceive of English and Irish as adversarial tongues, as either/or conditions rather than both/and, and this was an attitude that for a long time hampered the development of a more confident and creative way of dealing with the whole vexed question—the question, that is, of the relationship between nationality, language, history, and literary tradition in Ireland.

Luckily, I glimpsed the possibility of release from this kind of cultural determination early on, in my first arts year at Queen's University, Belfast, when we were lectured on the history of the English Language by Professor John Braidwood. Braidwood could not help informing us, for example, that the word "whiskey" is the same word as the Irish and Scots Gaelic word *uisce*, meaning water, and that the River Usk in Britain is therefore to some extent the River Uisce (or Whiskey); and so in my mind the stream was suddenly turned into a kind of linguistic river of rivers issuing from a pristine Celto-British Land of Cockaigne, a riverrun of Finnegans Wakespeak pouring out of the cleft rock of some prepolitical, prelapsarian, ur-philological Big Rock Candy Mountain—and all of this had a wonderfully sweetening effect upon me. The Irish/English duality, the Celtic/Saxon antithesis were momentarily collapsed and in the resulting etymological eddy a gleam of recognition flashed through the synapses and I glimpsed an elsewhere of potential that seemed at the same time to be a somewhere being remembered. The place on the language map where the Usk and the *uisce* and the whiskey coincided was definitely a place where the spirit might find a loophole, an escape route from what John Montague has called "the partitioned intellect," away into some unpartitioned linguistic country, a region where one's language would not be simply a badge of ethnicity or a matter of cultural preference or an official imposition, but an entry into further language. And I eventually came upon one of these loopholes in *Beowulf* itself.

What happened was that I found in the glossary to C. L. Wrenn's edition of the poem the Old English word meaning "to suffer," the word *þolian*; and although at first it looked completely strange with its *thorn* symbol instead of the familiar *th*, I gradually realized that it was not strange at all, for it was the word that older and less educated people would have used in the country where I grew up. "They'll just have to learn to thole," my aunt would say about some family who had suffered an unforeseen bereavement. And now suddenly here was "thole" in the official textual world, mediated through the apparatus of a scholarly edition, a little bleeper to remind me that my aunt's language was not just a self-enclosed family possession but an historical heritage, one that involved the journey *þolian* had made north into Scotland and then across into Ulster with the planters, and then across from the planters to the locals who had originally spoken Irish, and then farther across again when the Scots Irish emigrated to the American South in the eighteenth century. When I read in John Crowe Ransom the line, "Sweet ladies, long may ye bloom, and toughly I hope ye may thole," my heart lifted again, the world widened, something was furthered. The farflungness of the word, the phenomenological pleasure of finding it variously transformed by Ransom's modernity and *Beowulf*'s venerability made me feel vaguely something for which again I only found the words years later. What I was experiencing as I kept meeting up with *thole* on its multicultural odyssey was the feeling that Osip Mandelstam once defined as a "nostalgia for world culture." And this was a nostalgia I didn't even know I suffered until I experienced its fulfilment in this little epiphany. It was as if, on the analogy of baptism by desire, I had undergone something like illumination by philology. And even though I did not know it at the time, I had by then reached the point where I was ready to translate *Beowulf*. *Þolian* had opened my right of way.

So, in a sense, the decision to accept Norton's invitation was taken thirty-five years before the invitation was actually issued. But between one's sense of readiness to take on a subject and the actual inscription of the first lines, there is always a problematical hiatus. To put it another way: from the point of view of the writer, words in a poem need what the Polish poet Anna Swir once called "the equivalent of a biological right to life." The erotics of composition are essential to the process, some prereflective excitation and orientation, some sense that your own little verse-craft can dock safe and sound at the big quay of the language. And this is as true for translators as it is for poets attempting original work.

It is one thing to find lexical meanings for the words and to have some feel for how the meter might go, but it is quite another thing to find the tuning fork that will give you the note and pitch for the overall music of the work. Without some melody sensed or promised, it is simply impossible for a poet to establish the translator's right of way into and through a text. I was therefore lucky to hear this enabling note almost straight away, a familiar local voice, one that had belonged to relatives of my father, people whom I had once described (punning on their surname) as "big-voiced scullions."

I called them "big-voiced" because when the men of the family spoke, the words they uttered came across with a weighty distinctness, phonetic units as separate and defined as delph platters displayed on a dresser shelf. A simple sentence such as "We cut the corn today" took on immense dignity when one of the Scullions spoke it. They had a kind of Native American solemnity of utterance, as if they were announcing verdicts rather than making small talk. And when I came to ask myself how I wanted *Beowulf* to sound in my version, I realized I wanted it to be speakable by one of those relatives. I therefore tried to frame the famous opening lines in cadences that would have suited their voices, but that still echoed with the sound and sense of the Anglo-Saxon:

> Hwæt wē Gār-Dena   in gēar-dagum
> þēod-cyninga   þrym gefrūnon,
> hū þā æþelingas   ellen fremedon.

Conventional renderings of *hwæt*, the first word of the poem, tend towards the archaic literary, with "lo," "hark," "behold," "attend" and—more colloquially—"listen" being some of the solutions offered previously. But in Hiberno-English Scullion-speak, the particle "so" came naturally to the rescue, because in that idiom "so" operates as an expression that obliterates all previous discourse and narrative, and at the same time functions as an exclamation calling for immediate attention. So, "so" it was:

> So. The Spear-Danes in days gone by
> and the kings who ruled them had courage and greatness.
> We have heard of those princes' heroic campaigns.

I came to the task of translating *Beowulf* with a prejudice in favor of forthright delivery. I remembered the voice of the poem as being attractively direct, even though the diction was ornate and the narrative method at times oblique. What I had always loved was a kind of foursquareness about the utterance, a feeling of living inside a constantly indicative mood, in the presence of an understanding that assumes you share an awareness of the perilous nature of life and are yet capable of seeing it steadily and, when necessary, sternly. There is an undeluded quality about the *Beowulf* poet's sense of the world that gives his lines immense emotional credibility and allows him to make general observations about life that are far too grounded in experience and reticence to be called "moralizing." These so-called "gnomic" parts of the poem have the cadence and force of earned wisdom, and their combination of cogency and verity was again something that I could remember from the speech I heard as a youngster in the Scullion kitchen. When I translate lines 24–25 as "Behavior that's admired / is the path to power among people everywhere," I am attending as much to the grain of my original vernacular as to the content of the Anglo-Saxon lines. But then the evidence suggests that this middle ground between oral tradition and the demands of written practice was also the ground occupied by the *Beowulf* poet. The style of the poem is hospitable to the kind of formulaic phrases that are the stock-in-trade of oral bards, and yet it is marked too by the self-consciousness of an artist convinced that "we must labor to be beautiful."

In one area, my own labors have been less than thorough-going. I have not followed the strict metrical rules that bound the Anglo-Saxon *scop*. I have been guided by the fundamental pattern of four stresses to the line, but I allow myself several transgressions. For example, I don't always employ alliteration, and sometimes I alliterate only in one half of the line. When these breaches occur, it is because I prefer to let the natural "sound of sense" prevail over the demands of the convention: I have been reluctant to force an artificial shape or an unusual word choice just for the sake of correctness.

In general, the alliteration varies from the shadowy to the substantial, from the properly to the improperly distributed. Substantial and proper are such lines as

> The *fórtunes* of wár   *fávored* Hróthgar (line 64)
> the híghest in the *lánd*,   would *lénd* advíce (line 172)
> and *find fríendship*   in the *Fáther's* embráce (line 188)

Here the caesura is definite, there are two stresses in each half of the line, and the first stressed syllable of the second half alliterates with the first or the second or both of the stressed syllables in the first half. The main deviation from this is one that other translators have allowed themselves—the freedom, that is, to alliterate on the fourth stressed syllable, a practice that breaks the rule but that nevertheless does bind the line together:

> We have héard of those *prínces'*   heróic cam*páigns* (line 3)
> and he *crós*sed óver   into the Lórd's *kéeping* (line 27)

In the course of the translation, such deviations, distortions, syncopations, and extensions do occur; what I was after first and foremost was a narrative line that sounded as if it meant business and I was prepared to sacrifice other things in pursuit of this directness of utterance.

The appositional nature of the Old English syntax, for example, is somewhat slighted here, as is the *Beowulf* poet's resourcefulness with synonyms and (to a lesser extent) his genius for compound-making, kennings, and all sorts of variation. Usually—as at line 1209, where I render *ȳða ful* as "frothing wave-vat," and at line 1523, where *beado-lēoma* becomes "battle-torch"—I try to match the poet's analogy-seeking habit at its most original; and I use all the common coinages for the lord of the nation, variously referred to as "ring-giver," "treasure-giver," "his people's shield" or "shepherd" or "helmet." I have been less faithful, however, to the way the poet rings the changes when it comes to compounds meaning a sword or a spear, or a battle or any bloody encounter with foes. Old English abounds in vigorous, evocative and specifically poetic words for these things, but I have tended to follow modern usage and in the main have called a sword a sword.

There was one area, however, where a certain strangeness in the diction came naturally. In those instances where a local Ulster word seemed either poetically or historically right, I felt free to use it. For example, at lines 324 and 2988 I use the word "graith" for "harness," and at 3026 "hoked" for "rooted about," because the local term seemed in each case to have special body and force. Then, for reasons of historical suggestiveness, I have in several instances used the word "bawn" to refer to Hrothgar's hall. In Elizabethan English, "bawn" (from the Irish *bó-dhún*, a fort for cattle) referred specifically to the fortified dwellings that the English planters built in Ireland to keep the dispossessed natives at bay, so it seemed the proper term to apply to the embattled keep where Hrothgar waits and watches. Indeed, every time I read the lovely interlude that tells of the minstrel singing in Heorot just before the first attacks of Grendel, I cannot help thinking of Edmund Spenser in Kilcolman Castle, reading the early cantos of *The Faerie Queene* to Sir Walter Raleigh, just before the Irish would burn the castle and drive Spenser out of Munster back to the Elizabethan court. Putting a bawn into *Beowulf* seems one way for an Irish poet to come to terms with that complex history of conquest and colony, absorption and resistance, integrity and antagonism, a history that has to be clearly acknowledged by all concerned in order to render it ever more "willable forward / again and again and again."

SEAMUS HEANEY

The Text of
BEOWULF
A VERSE TRANSLATION

Beowulf

[Prologue: The Rise of the Danes]

So. The Spear-Danes[1] in days gone by
and the kings who ruled them had courage and greatness.
We have heard of those princes' heroic campaigns.
There was Shield Sheafson,[2] scourge of many tribes,
a wrecker of mead-benches, rampaging among foes.
This terror of the hall-troops had come far.
A foundling to start with, he would flourish later on
as his powers waxed and his worth was proved.
In the end each clan on the outlying coasts
beyond the whale-road[3] had to yield to him
and begin to pay tribute. That was one good king.
Afterward a boy-child was born to Shield,
a cub in the yard, a comfort sent
by God to that nation. He knew what they had tholed,[4]
the long times and troubles they'd come through
without a leader; so the Lord of Life,
the glorious Almighty, made this man renowned.
Shield had fathered a famous son:
Beow's name was known through the north.
And a young prince must be prudent like that,
giving freely while his father lives
so that afterward in age when fighting starts
steadfast companions will stand by him
and hold the line. Behavior that's admired
is the path to power among people everywhere.

1. The Danes are identified by a variety of names, all referring to the same tribe: Spear-Danes, East-Danes, Victory-Shieldings, etc. See "The Kingdoms and Tribes of *Beowulf*," p. 96, below.
2. The poem up to line 52 recounts the story of Shield, who arrived as a "foundling to start with," but as an adult established the Danish royal family. For the pronunciation of Old English names, see the glossary, pp. 248–50, below; for the legend of Shield, see pp. 93–94, below.
3. "Whale-road" is a literal translation of the Old English *hron-rad*, an example of a compressed figure of speech known as a kenning. Other kennings for "ocean" are "swan's road" (line 200) and "gannet's bath" (line 1861).
4. Suffered, endured [*Translator's note*]. Heaney takes advantage of the fact that the Old English *þolian*, while long obsolete in Standard English, survived in the Ulster dialect of his parents. See the "Translator's Introduction," p. xxxv, above.

Shield was still thriving when his time came
and he crossed over into the Lord's keeping.
His warrior band did what he bade them
when he laid down the law among the Danes:
they shouldered him out to the sea's flood,
the chief they revered who had long ruled them.
A ring-whorled prow rode in the harbor,
ice-clad, outbound, a craft for a prince.
They stretched their beloved lord in his boat,
laid out by the mast, amidships,
the great ring-giver. Far-fetched treasures
were piled upon him, and precious gear.
I never heard before of a ship so well furbished
with battle-tackle, bladed weapons
and coats of mail. The massed treasure
was loaded on top of him: it would travel far
on out into the ocean's sway.
They decked his body no less bountifully
with offerings than those first ones did
who cast him away when he was a child
and launched him alone out over the waves.
And they set a gold standard up
high above his head and let him drift
to wind and tide, bewailing him
and mourning their loss. No man can tell,
no wise man in hall or weathered veteran
knows for certain who salvaged that load.
Then it fell to Beow to keep the forts.
He was well regarded and ruled the Danes
for a long time after his father took leave
of his life on earth. And then his heir,
the great Halfdane,[5] held sway
for as long as he lived, their elder and warlord.
He was four times a father, this fighter prince:
one by one they entered the world,
Heorogar, Hrothgar, the good Halga,
and a daughter, I have heard, who was Onela's queen,
a balm in bed to the battle-scarred Swede.
The fortunes of war favored Hrothgar.
Friends and kinsmen flocked to his ranks,
young followers, a force that grew
to be a mighty army. So his mind turned
to hall-building: he handed down orders
for men to work on a great mead-hall

5. According to an early source, Halfdane's mother was Swedish.

meant to be a wonder of the world forever;
it would be his throne-room and there he would dispense
his God-given goods to young and old—
but not the common land or people's lives.[6]
Far and wide through the world, I have heard,
orders for work to adorn that wallstead
were sent to many peoples. And soon it stood there
finished and ready, in full view,
the hall of halls. Heorot was the name[7]
he had settled on it, whose utterance was law.
Nor did he renege, but doled out rings
and torques at the table. The hall towered,
its gables wide and high and awaiting
a barbarous burning.[8] That doom abided,
but in time it would come: the killer instinct
unleashed among in-laws, the blood-lust rampant.

[Heorot Is Attacked]

Then a powerful demon, a prowler through the dark,
nursed a hard grievance. It harrowed him
to hear the din of the loud banquet
every day in the hall, the harp being struck
and the clear song of a skilled poet
telling with mastery of man's beginnings,
how the Almighty had made the earth
a gleaming plain girdled with waters;
in His splendor He set the sun and the moon
to be earth's lamplight, lanterns for men,
and filled the broad lap of the world
with branches and leaves; and quickened life
in every other thing that moved.
So times were pleasant for the people there
until finally one, a fiend out of hell,
began to work his evil in the world.
Grendel was the name of this grim demon
haunting the marches, marauding round the heath
and the desolate fens; he had dwelt for a time

6. Even a powerful king could not dispose of land used in common or unlawfully kill his subjects.
7. Heorot means "hart" or "stag," a symbol of royalty.
8. An allusion to the future destruction of the hall as a result of a feud between the Danes and the Heatho-Bards. Upon his arrival back among the Geats, Beowulf brings the news that Hrothgar plans to give his daughter Freawaru in marriage to Ingeld, the Heatho-Bard king, to settle the feud (lines 2020–69). He predicts, however, that hostilities will flare up again, leading (by implication) to the burning of Heorot.

in misery among the banished monsters,
Cain's clan, whom the Creator had outlawed
and condemned as outcasts.[9] For the killing of Abel
the Eternal Lord had exacted a price:
Cain got no good from committing that murder
because the Almighty made him anathema,
and out of the curse of his exile there sprang
ogres and elves and evil phantoms
and the giants too who strove with God
time and again until He gave them their reward.
  So, after nightfall, Grendel set out
for the lofty house, to see how the Ring-Danes
were settling into it after their drink,
and there he came upon them, a company of the best
asleep from their feasting, insensible to pain
and human sorrow. Suddenly then
the God-cursed brute was creating havoc:
greedy and grim, he grabbed thirty men
from their resting places and rushed to his lair,
flushed up and inflamed from the raid,
blundering back with the butchered corpses.
  Then as dawn brightened and the day broke,
Grendel's powers of destruction were plain:
their wassail was over, they wept to heaven
and mourned under morning. Their mighty prince,
the storied leader, sat stricken and helpless,
humiliated by the loss of his guard,
bewildered and stunned, staring aghast
at the demon's trail, in deep distress.
He was numb with grief, but got no respite
for one night later merciless Grendel
struck again with more gruesome murders.
Malignant by nature, he never showed remorse.
It was easy then to meet with a man
shifting himself to a safer distance
to bed in the bothies,[1] for who could be blind
to the evidence of his eyes, the obviousness
of the hall-watcher's hate? Whoever escaped
kept a weather-eye open and moved away.
  So Grendel ruled in defiance of right,
one against all, until the greatest house
in the world stood empty, a deserted wallstead.
For twelve winters, seasons of woe,
the lord of the Shieldings suffered under

9. See Genesis 4.1–16, pp. 84–85, below.
1. The Irish word *bothóg* means "hut" or "shanty," often for unmarried workers on a farm. Grendel occupies Heorot, the seat of Danish culture, and ignores the outlying buildings.

his load of sorrow; and so, before long,
the news was known over the whole world.
Sad lays were sung about the beset king,
the vicious raids and ravages of Grendel,
his long and unrelenting feud,
nothing but war; how he would never
parley or make peace with any Dane
nor stop his death-dealing nor pay the death-price.[2]
No counselor could ever expect
fair reparation from those rabid hands.
All were endangered; young and old
were hunted down by that dark death-shadow
who lurked and swooped in the long nights
on the misty moors; nobody knows
where these reavers from hell roam on their errands.
  So Grendel waged his lonely war,
inflicting constant cruelties on the people,
atrocious hurt. He took over Heorot,
haunted the glittering hall after dark,
but the throne itself, the treasure-seat,
he was kept from approaching; he was the Lord's outcast.
  These were hard times, heartbreaking
for the prince of the Shieldings; powerful counselors,
the highest in the land, would lend advice,
plotting how best the bold defenders
might resist and beat off sudden attacks.
Sometimes at pagan shrines they vowed
offerings to idols, swore oaths
that the killer of souls[3] might come to their aid
and save the people. That was their way,
their heathenish hope; deep in their hearts
they remembered hell. The Almighty Judge
of good deeds and bad, the Lord God,
Head of the Heavens and High King of the World,
was unknown to them. Oh, cursed is he
who in time of trouble has to thrust his soul
in the fire's embrace, forfeiting help;
he has nowhere to turn. But blessed is he
who after death can approach the Lord
and find friendship in the Father's embrace.

2. According to Anglo-Saxon law, a murder or any unlawful killing could be resolved by the payment of a substantial fine to the family of the victim. It was the society's means of preventing the cycles of feuds from beginning.
3. I.e., the devil. Christians identified the old pagan gods with devils.

[The Hero Comes to Heorot]

So that troubled time continued, woe
that never stopped, steady affliction
for Halfdane's son, too hard an ordeal.
There was panic after dark, people endured
raids in the night, riven by the terror.
When he heard about Grendel, Hygelac's thane[4]
was on home ground, over in Geatland.
There was no one else like him alive.
In his day, he was the mightiest man on earth,
highborn and powerful. He ordered a boat
that would ply the waves. He announced his plan:
to sail the swan's road and seek out that king,
the famous prince who needed defenders.
Nobody tried to keep him from going,
no elder denied him, dear as he was to them.
Instead, they inspected omens and spurred
his ambition to go, whilst he moved about
like the leader he was, enlisting men,
the best he could find; with fourteen others
the warrior boarded the boat as captain,
a canny pilot along coast and currents.
Time went by, the boat was on water,
in close under the cliffs.
Men climbed eagerly up the gangplank,
sand churned in surf, warriors loaded
a cargo of weapons, shining war-gear
in the vessel's hold, then heaved out,
away with a will in their wood-wreathed ship.
Over the waves, with the wind behind her
and foam at her neck, she flew like a bird
until her curved prow had covered the distance,
and on the following day, at the due hour,
those seafarers sighted land,
sunlit cliffs, sheer crags
and looming headlands, the landfall they sought.[5]
It was the end of their voyage and the Geats vaulted
over the side, out on to the sand,
and moored their ship. There was a clash of mail
and a thresh of gear. They thanked God

4. I.e., Beowulf. His name is withheld until he reveals it in dialogue on line 343. In Old English poetry "thane" means "warrior, follower of the king," though in Anglo-Saxon society it designated a specific, relatively high rank.

5. They journey from the south coast of what is now Sweden to the Danish island of Zealand (Sjælland), where Heorot was located.

for that easy crossing on a calm sea.
  When the watchman on the wall, the Shieldings' lookout
whose job it was to guard the sea-cliffs,
saw shields glittering on the gangplank
and battle-equipment being unloaded
he had to find out who and what
the arrivals were. So he rode to the shore,
this horseman of Hrothgar's, and challenged them
in formal terms, flourishing his spear:
"What kind of men are you who arrive
rigged out for combat in your coats of mail,
sailing here over the sea-lanes
in your steep-hulled boat? I have been stationed
as lookout on this coast for a long time.
My job is to watch the waves for raiders,
any danger to the Danish shore.
Never before has a force under arms
disembarked so openly—not bothering to ask
if the sentries allowed them safe passage
or the clan had consented. Nor have I seen
a mightier man-at-arms on this earth
than the one standing here: unless I am mistaken,
he is truly noble. This is no mere
hanger-on in a hero's armor.
So now, before you fare inland
as interlopers, I have to be informed
about who you are and where you hail from.
Outsiders from across the water,
I say it again: the sooner you tell
where you come from and why, the better."
  The leader of the troop unlocked his word-hoard;
the distinguished one delivered this answer:
"We belong by birth to the Geat people
and owe allegiance to Lord Hygelac.
In his day, my father was a famous man,
a noble warrior-lord named Ecgtheow.
He outlasted many a long winter
and went on his way. All over the world
men wise in counsel continue to remember him.
We come in good faith to find your lord
and nation's shield, the son of Halfdane.
Give us the right advice and direction.
We have arrived here on a great errand
to the lord of the Danes, and I believe therefore
there should be nothing hidden or withheld between us.
So tell us if what we have heard is true
about this threat, whatever it is,

this danger abroad in the dark nights,
this corpse-maker mongering death
in the Shieldings' country. I come to proffer
my wholehearted help and counsel.
I can show the wise Hrothgar a way
to defeat his enemy and find respite—
if any respite is to reach him, ever.
I can calm the turmoil and terror in his mind.
Otherwise, he must endure woes
and live with grief for as long as his hall
stands at the horizon on its high ground."
  Undaunted, sitting astride his horse,
the coast-guard answered: "Anyone with gumption[6]
and a sharp mind will take the measure
of two things: what's said and what's done.
I believe what you have told me, that you are a troop
loyal to our king. So come ahead
with your arms and your gear, and I will guide you.
What's more, I'll order my own comrades
on their word of honor to watch your boat
down there on the strand—keep her safe
in her fresh tar, until the time comes
for her curved prow to preen on the waves
and bear this hero back to Geatland.
May one so valiant and venturesome
come unharmed through the clash of battle."
  So they went on their way. The ship rode the water,
broad-beamed, bound by its hawser
and anchored fast. Boar-shapes[7] flashed
above their cheek-guards, the brightly forged
work of goldsmiths, watching over
those stern-faced men. They marched in step,
hurrying on till the timbered hall
rose before them, radiant with gold.
Nobody on earth knew of another
building like it. Majesty lodged there,
its light shone over many lands.
So their gallant escort guided them
to that dazzling stronghold and indicated
the shortest way to it; then the noble warrior
wheeled on his horse and spoke these words:
"It is time for me to go. May the Almighty

6. A Scottish colloquialism sometimes heard in American English, meaning "resourcefulness, initiative."
7. Helmets decorated with images of boars have been found at a number of archaeological sites. It is thought that boars were valued for their aggressiveness and possibly for religious reasons. For armor and its decoration, see pp. 216–21, below.

Father keep you and in His kindness
watch over your exploits. I'm away to the sea,
back on alert against enemy raiders."
  It was a paved track, a path that kept them
in marching order. Their mail-shirts glinted,
hard and hand-linked; the high-gloss iron
of their armor rang. So they duly arrived
in their grim war-graith[8] and gear at the hall,
and, weary from the sea, stacked wide shields
of the toughest hardwood against the wall,
then collapsed on the benches; battle-dress
and weapons clashed. They collected their spears
in a seafarers' stook, a stand of grayish
tapering ash. And the troops themselves
were as good as their weapons.
                                        Then a proud warrior
questioned the men concerning their origins:
"Where do you come from, carrying these
decorated shields and shirts of mail,
these cheek-hinged helmets and javelins?
I am Hrothgar's herald and officer.
I have never seen so impressive or large
an assembly of strangers. Stoutness of heart,
bravery not banishment, must have brought you to Hrothgar."
  The man whose name was known for courage,
the Geat leader, resolute in his helmet,
answered in return: "We are retainers
from Hygelac's band. Beowulf is my name.
If your lord and master, the most renowned
son of Halfdane, will hear me out
and graciously allow me to greet him in person,
I am ready and willing to report my errand."
  Wulfgar replied, a Wendel chief
renowned as a warrior, well known for his wisdom
and the temper of his mind: "I will take this message,
in accordance with your wish, to our noble king,
our dear lord, friend of the Danes,
the giver of rings. I will go and ask him
about your coming here, then hurry back
with whatever reply it pleases him to give."
  With that he turned to where Hrothgar sat,
an old man among retainers;
the valiant follower stood foursquare
in front of his king: he knew the courtesies.
Wulfgar addressed his dear lord:

8. "Graith" is a dialectal word for harness or gear. See the "Translator's Introduction," p. xxxviii.

"People from Geatland have put ashore.
They have sailed far over the wide sea.
They call the chief in charge of their band
by the name of Beowulf. They beg, my lord,
an audience with you, exchange of words
and formal greeting. Most gracious Hrothgar,
do not refuse them, but grant them a reply.
From their arms and appointment, they appear well born
and worthy of respect, especially the one
who has led them this far: he is formidable indeed."
Hrothgar, protector of Shieldings, replied:
"I used to know him when he was a young boy.
His father before him was called Ecgtheow.
Hrethel the Geat[9] gave Ecgtheow
his daughter in marriage. This man is their son,
here to follow up an old friendship.
A crew of seamen who sailed for me once
with a gift-cargo across to Geatland
returned with marvelous tales about him:
a thane, they declared, with the strength of thirty
in the grip of each hand. Now Holy God
has, in His goodness, guided him here
to the West-Danes, to defend us from Grendel.
This is my hope; and for his heroism
I will recompense him with a rich treasure.
Go immediately, bid him and the Geats
he has in attendance to assemble and enter.
Say, moreover, when you speak to them,
they are welcome to Denmark."
At the door of the hall,
Wulfgar duly delivered the message:
"My lord, the conquering king of the Danes,
bids me announce that he knows your ancestry;
also that he welcomes you here to Heorot
and salutes your arrival from across the sea.
You are free now to move forward
to meet Hrothgar in helmets and armor,
but shields must stay here and spears be stacked
until the outcome of the audience is clear."
The hero arose, surrounded closely
by his powerful thanes. A party remained
under orders to keep watch on the arms;
the rest proceeded, led by their prince
under Heorot's roof. And standing on the hearth
in webbed links that the smith had woven,

9. Hygelac's father and Beowulf's grandfather.

the fine-forged mesh of his gleaming mail-shirt,
resolute in his helmet, Beowulf spoke:
"Greetings to Hrothgar. I am Hygelac's kinsman,
one of his hall-troop. When I was younger,
I had great triumphs. Then news of Grendel,
hard to ignore, reached me at home:
sailors brought stories of the plight you suffer
in this legendary hall, how it lies deserted,
empty and useless once the evening light
hides itself under heaven's dome.
So every elder and experienced councilman
among my people supported my resolve
to come here to you, King Hrothgar,
because all knew of my awesome strength.
They had seen me boltered[1] in the blood of enemies
when I battled and bound five beasts,
raided a troll-nest and in the night-sea
slaughtered sea-brutes. I have suffered extremes
and avenged the Geats (their enemies brought it
upon themselves; I devastated them).
Now I mean to be a match for Grendel,
settle the outcome in single combat.
And so, my request, O king of Bright-Danes,
dear prince of the Shieldings, friend of the people
and their ring of defense, my one request
is that you won't refuse me, who have come this far,
the privilege of purifying Heorot,
with my own men to help me, and nobody else.
I have heard moreover that the monster scorns
in his reckless way to use weapons;
therefore, to heighten Hygelac's fame
and gladden his heart, I hereby renounce
sword and the shelter of the broad shield,
the heavy war-board: hand-to-hand
is how it will be, a life-and-death
fight with the fiend. Whichever one death fells
must deem it a just judgment by God.
If Grendel wins, it will be a gruesome day;
he will glut himself on the Geats in the war-hall,
swoop without fear on that flower of manhood
as on others before. Then my face won't be there
to be covered in death: he will carry me away
as he goes to ground, gorged and bloodied;
he will run gloating with my raw corpse
and feed on it alone, in a cruel frenzy

1. The *Oxford English Dictionary* defines blood-boltered as "clotted or clogged with blood, *esp*. having the hair matted with blood."

fouling his moor-nest. No need then
to lament for long or lay out my body:[2]
if the battle takes me, send back
this breast-webbing that Weland[3] fashioned
and Hrethel gave me, to Lord Hygelac.
Fate goes ever as fate must."[4]
Hrothgar, the helmet of Shieldings, spoke:
"Beowulf, my friend, you have traveled here
to favor us with help and to fight for us.
There was a feud one time, begun by your father.
With his own hands he had killed Heatholaf
who was a Wulfing; so war was looming
and his people, in fear of it, forced him to leave.
He came away then over rolling waves
to the South-Danes here, the sons of honor.
I was then in the first flush of kingship,
establishing my sway over the rich strongholds
of this heroic land. Heorogar,
my older brother and the better man,
also a son of Halfdane's, had died.
Finally I healed the feud by paying:
I shipped a treasure-trove to the Wulfings,
and Ecgtheow acknowledged me with oaths of allegiance.
"It bothers me to have to burden anyone
with all the grief that Grendel has caused
and the havoc he has wreaked upon us in Heorot,
our humiliations. My household guard
are on the wane, fate sweeps them away
into Grendel's clutches—but God can easily
halt these raids and harrowing attacks!
"Time and again, when the goblets passed
and seasoned fighters got flushed with beer
they would pledge themselves to protect Heorot[5]
and wait for Grendel with their whetted swords.
But when dawn broke and day crept in
over each empty, blood-spattered bench,
the floor of the mead-hall where they had feasted
would be slick with slaughter. And so they died,
faithful retainers, and my following dwindled.
Now take your place at the table, relish
the triumph of heroes to your heart's content."

2. There can be no funeral because no corpse will be left behind.
3. The mythical Germanic blacksmith; thus a chain-mail shirt of superior workmanship.
4. One of many gnomic or proverbial expressions.
5. Hrothgar refers to a formal speech-act made by a warrior in front of his peers, sealed by ceremonial drinking, which pledges him to a course of action.

[Feast at Heorot]

Then a bench was cleared in that banquet hall
so the Geats could have room to be together
and the party sat, proud in their bearing,
strong and stalwart. An attendant stood by
with a decorated pitcher, pouring bright
helpings of mead. And the minstrel sang,
filling Heorot with his head-clearing voice,
gladdening that great rally of Geats and Danes.
From where he crouched at the king's feet,
Unferth, a son of Ecglaf's, spoke
contrary words. Beowulf's coming,
his sea-braving, made him sick with envy:
he could not brook or abide the fact
that anyone else alive under heaven
might enjoy greater regard than he did:
"Are you the Beowulf who took on Breca
in a swimming match on the open sea,
risking the water just to prove that you could win?
It was sheer vanity made you venture out
on the main deep. And no matter who tried,
friend or foe, to deflect the pair of you,
neither would back down: the sea-test obsessed you.
You waded in, embracing water,
taking its measure, mastering currents,
riding on the swell. The ocean swayed,
winter went wild in the waves, but you vied
for seven nights; and then he outswam you,
came ashore the stronger contender.
He was cast up safe and sound one morning
among the Heatho-Reams, then made his way
to where he belonged in Bronding country,
home again, sure of his ground
in strongroom and bawn.[6] So Breca made good
his boast upon you and was proved right.
No matter, therefore, how you may have fared
in every bout and battle until now,
this time you'll be worsted; no one has ever
outlasted an entire night against Grendel."
Beowulf, Ecgtheow's son, replied:
"Well, friend Unferth, you have had your say

6. Fortified outwork of a court or castle. The word was used by English planters in Ulster to describe fortified dwellings they erected on lands confiscated from the Irish [*Translator's note*]. See also p. xxxviii.

about Breca and me. But it was mostly beer
that was doing the talking. The truth is this:
when the going was heavy in those high waves,
I was the strongest swimmer of all.
We'd been children together and we grew up
daring ourselves to outdo each other,
boasting and urging each other to risk
our lives on the sea. And so it turned out.
Each of us swam holding a sword,
a naked, hard-proofed blade for protection
against the whale-beasts. But Breca could never
move out farther or faster from me
than I could manage to move from him.
Shoulder to shoulder, we struggled on
for five nights, until the long flow
and pitch of the waves, the perishing cold,
night falling and winds from the north
drove us apart. The deep boiled up
and its wallowing sent the sea-brutes wild.
My armor helped me to hold out;
my hard-ringed chain-mail, hand-forged and linked,
a fine, close-fitting filigree of gold,
kept me safe when some ocean creature
pulled me to the bottom. Pinioned fast
and swathed in its grip, I was granted one
final chance: my sword plunged
and the ordeal was over. Through my own hands,
the fury of battle had finished off the sea-beast.
"Time and again, foul things attacked me,
lurking and stalking, but I lashed out,
gave as good as I got with my sword.
My flesh was not for feasting on,
there would be no monsters gnawing and gloating
over their banquet at the bottom of the sea.
Instead, in the morning, mangled and sleeping
the sleep of the sword, they slopped and floated
like the ocean's leavings. From now on
sailors would be safe, the deep-sea raids
were over for good. Light came from the east,
bright guarantee of God, and the waves
went quiet; I could see headlands
and buffeted cliffs. Often, for undaunted courage,
fate spares the man it has not already marked.
However it occurred, my sword had killed
nine sea-monsters. Such night dangers
and hard ordeals I have never heard of
nor of a man more desolate in surging waves.

But worn out as I was, I survived,
came through with my life. The ocean lifted
and laid me ashore, I landed safe
on the coast of Finland.
Now I cannot recall
any fight you entered, Unferth,
that bears comparison. I don't boast when I say
that neither you nor Breca were ever much
celebrated for swordsmanship
or for facing danger on the field of battle.
You killed your own kith and kin,
so for all your cleverness and quick tongue,
you will suffer damnation in the depths of hell.
The fact is, Unferth, if you were truly
as keen or courageous as you claim to be
Grendel would never have got away with
such unchecked atrocity, attacks on your king,
havoc in Heorot and horrors everywhere.
But he knows he need never be in dread
of your blade making a mizzle of his blood
or of a vengeance arriving ever from this quarter—
from the Victory-Shieldings, the shoulderers of the spear.
He knows he can trample down you Danes
to his heart's content, humiliate and murder
without fear of reprisal. But he will find me different.
I will show him how Geats shape to kill
in the heat of battle. Then whoever wants to
may go bravely to mead, when the morning light,
scarfed in sun-dazzle, shines forth from the south
and brings another daybreak to the world."
Then the gray-haired treasure-giver was glad;
far-famed in battle, the prince of Bright-Danes
and keeper of his people counted on Beowulf,
on the warrior's steadfastness and his word.
So the laughter started, the din got louder
and the crowd was happy. Wealhtheow came in,
Hrothgar's queen, observing the courtesies.
Adorned in her gold, she graciously saluted
the men in the hall, then handed the cup
first to Hrothgar, their homeland's guardian,
urging him to drink deep and enjoy it
because he was dear to them. And he drank it down
like the warlord he was, with festive cheer.
So the Helming woman went on her rounds,
queenly and dignified, decked out in rings,
offering the goblet to all ranks,
treating the household and the assembled troop,

until it was Beowulf's turn to take it from her hand.
With measured words she welcomed the Geat
and thanked God for granting her wish
that a deliverer she could believe in would arrive
to ease their afflictions. He accepted the cup,
a daunting man, dangerous in action
and eager for it always. He addressed Wealhtheow;
Beowulf, son of Ecgtheow, said:
"I had a fixed purpose when I put to sea.
As I sat in the boat with my band of men,
I meant to perform to the uttermost
what your people wanted or perish in the attempt,
in the fiend's clutches. And I shall fulfill that purpose,
prove myself with a proud deed
or meet my death here in the mead-hall."
This formal boast by Beowulf the Geat
pleased the lady well and she went to sit
by Hrothgar, regal and arrayed with gold.
  Then it was like old times in the echoing hall,
proud talk and the people happy,
loud and excited; until soon enough
Halfdane's heir had to be away
to his night's rest. He realized
that the demon was going to descend on the hall,
that he had plotted all day, from dawn light
until darkness gathered again over the world
and stealthy night-shapes came stealing forth
under the cloud-murk. The company stood
as the two leaders took leave of each other:
Hrothgar wished Beowulf health and good luck,
named him hall-warden and announced as follows:
"Never, since my hand could hold a shield
have I entrusted or given control
of the Danes' hall to anyone but you.
Ward and guard it, for it is the greatest of houses.
Be on your mettle now, keep in mind your fame,
beware of the enemy. There's nothing you wish for
that won't be yours if you win through alive."

[The Fight with Grendel]

  Hrothgar departed then with his house-guard.
The lord of the Shieldings, their shelter in war,
left the mead-hall to lie with Wealhtheow,
his queen and bedmate. The King of Glory
(as people learned) had posted a lookout

who was a match for Grendel, a guard against monsters,
special protection to the Danish prince.
And the Geat placed complete trust
in his strength of limb and the Lord's favor.
He began to remove his iron breast-mail,
took off the helmet and handed his attendant
the patterned sword, a smith's masterpiece,
ordering him to keep the equipment guarded.
And before he bedded down, Beowulf,
that prince of goodness, proudly asserted:
"When it comes to fighting, I count myself
as dangerous any day as Grendel.
So it won't be a cutting edge I'll wield
to mow him down, easily as I might.
He has no idea of the arts of war,
of shield or sword-play, although he does possess
a wild strength. No weapons, therefore,
for either this night: unarmed he shall face me
if face me he dares. And may the Divine Lord
in His wisdom grant the glory of victory
to whichever side He sees fit."
Then down the brave man lay with his bolster
under his head and his whole company
of sea-rovers at rest beside him.
None of them expected he would ever see
his homeland again or get back
to his native place and the people who reared him.
They knew too well the way it was before,
how often the Danes had fallen prey
to death in the mead-hall. But the Lord was weaving
a victory on His war-loom for the Weather-Geats.
Through the strength of one they all prevailed;
they would crush their enemy and come through
in triumph and gladness. The truth is clear:
Almighty God rules over mankind
and always has.
Then out of the night
came the shadow-stalker, stealthy and swift.
The hall-guards were slack, asleep at their posts,
all except one; it was widely understood
that as long as God disallowed it,
the fiend could not bear them to his shadow-bourne.
One man, however, was in fighting mood,
awake and on edge, spoiling for action.
In off the moors, down through the mist-bands
God-cursed Grendel came greedily loping.
The bane of the race of men roamed forth,

hunting for a prey in the high hall.
Under the cloud-murk he moved toward it
until it shone above him, a sheer keep
of fortified gold. Nor was that the first time
he had scouted the grounds of Hrothgar's dwelling—
although never in his life, before or since,
did he find harder fortune or hall-defenders.
Spurned and joyless, he journeyed on ahead
and arrived at the bawn.[7] The iron-braced door
turned on its hinge when his hands touched it.
Then his rage boiled over, he ripped open
the mouth of the building, maddening for blood,
pacing the length of the patterned floor
with his loathsome tread, while a baleful light,
flame more than light, flared from his eyes.
He saw many men in the mansion, sleeping,
a ranked company of kinsmen and warriors
quartered together. And his glee was demonic,
picturing the mayhem: before morning
he would rip life from limb and devour them,
feed on their flesh; but his fate that night
was due to change, his days of ravening
had come to an end.
                                    Mighty and canny,
Hygelac's kinsman was keenly watching
for the first move the monster would make.
Nor did the creature keep him waiting
but struck suddenly and started in;
he grabbed and mauled a man on his bench,
bit into his bone-lappings, bolted down his blood
and gorged on him in lumps, leaving the body
utterly lifeless, eaten up
hand and foot. Venturing closer,
his talon was raised to attack Beowulf
where he lay on the bed, he was bearing in
with open claw when the alert hero's
comeback and armlock forestalled him utterly.
The captain of evil discovered himself
in a handgrip harder than anything
he had ever encountered in any man
on the face of the earth. Every bone in his body
quailed and recoiled, but he could not escape.
He was desperate to flee to his den and hide
with the devil's litter, for in all his days
he had never been clamped or cornered like this.

7. See the note for line 523.

Then Hygelac's trusty retainer recalled
his bedtime speech, sprang to his feet
and got a firm hold. Fingers were bursting,
the monster back-tracking, the man overpowering.
The dread of the land was desperate to escape,
to take a roundabout road and flee
to his lair in the fens. The latching power
in his fingers weakened; it was the worst trip
the terror-monger had taken to Heorot.
And now the timbers trembled and sang,
a hall-session[8] that harrowed every Dane
inside the stockade: stumbling in fury,
the two contenders crashed through the building.
The hall clattered and hammered, but somehow
survived the onslaught and kept standing:
it was handsomely structured, a sturdy frame
braced with the best of blacksmith's work
inside and out. The story goes
that as the pair struggled, mead-benches were smashed
and sprung off the floor, gold fittings and all.
Before then, no Shielding elder would believe
there was any power or person upon earth
capable of wrecking their horn-rigged hall
unless the burning embrace of a fire
engulf it in flame. Then an extraordinary
wail arose, and bewildering fear
came over the Danes. Everyone felt it
who heard that cry as it echoed off the wall,
a God-cursed scream and strain of catastrophe,
the howl of the loser, the lament of the hell-serf
keening his wound. He was overwhelmed,
manacled tight by the man who of all men
was foremost and strongest in the days of this life.
   But the earl-troop's leader was not inclined
to allow his caller to depart alive:
he did not consider that life of much account
to anyone anywhere. Time and again,
Beowulf's warriors worked to defend
their lord's life, laying about them
as best they could, with their ancestral blades.
Stalwart in action, they kept striking out
on every side, seeking to cut
straight to the soul. When they joined the struggle
there was something they could not have known at the time,
that no blade on earth, no blacksmith's art

8. In Hiberno-English the word "session" (*seissiún* in Irish) can mean a gathering where musicians and singers perform for their own enjoyment [*Translator's note*].

could ever damage their demon opponent.
He had conjured the harm from the cutting edge
of every weapon.[9] But his going away
out of this world and the days of his life
would be agony to him, and his alien spirit
would travel far into fiends' keeping.
Then he who had harrowed the hearts of men
with pain and affliction in former times
and had given offense also to God
found that his bodily powers failed him.
Hygelac's kinsman kept him helplessly
locked in a handgrip. As long as either lived,
he was hateful to the other. The monster's whole
body was in pain; a tremendous wound
appeared on his shoulder. Sinews split
and the bone-lappings burst. Beowulf was granted
the glory of winning; Grendel was driven
under the fen-banks, fatally hurt,
to his desolate lair. His days were numbered,
the end of his life was coming over him,
he knew it for certain; and one bloody clash
had fulfilled the dearest wishes of the Danes.
The man who had lately landed among them,
proud and sure, had purged the hall,
kept it from harm; he was happy with his nightwork
and the courage he had shown. The Geat captain
had boldly fulfilled his boast to the Danes:
he had healed and relieved a huge distress,
unremitting humiliations,
the hard fate they'd been forced to undergo,
no small affliction. Clear proof of this
could be seen in the hand the hero displayed
high up near the roof: the whole of Grendel's
shoulder and arm, his awesome grasp.

[Celebration at Heorot]

Then morning came and many a warrior
gathered, as I've heard, around the gift-hall,
clan-chiefs flocking from far and near
down wide-ranging roads, wondering greatly
at the monster's footprints. His fatal departure
was regretted by no one who witnessed his trail,

9. By some unknown sorcery, Grendel (unlike his mother) has been rendered impervious to human weapons.

the ignominious marks of his flight
where he'd skulked away, exhausted in spirit
and beaten in battle, bloodying the path,
hauling his doom to the demons' mere.[1]
The bloodshot water wallowed and surged,
there were loathsome upthrows and overturnings
of waves and gore and wound-slurry.
With his death upon him, he had dived deep
into his marsh-den, drowned out his life
and his heathen soul: hell claimed him there.
Then away they rode, the old retainers
with many a young man following after,
a troop on horseback, in high spirits
on their bay steeds. Beowulf's doings
were praised over and over again.
Nowhere, they said, north or south
between the two seas or under the tall sky
on the broad earth was there anyone better
to raise a shield or to rule a kingdom.
Yet there was no laying of blame on their lord,
the noble Hrothgar; he was a good king.
At times the war-band broke into a gallop,
letting their chestnut horses race
wherever they found the going good
on those well-known tracks. Meanwhile, a thane
of the king's household, a carrier of tales,
a traditional singer deeply schooled
in the lore of the past, linked a new theme
to a strict meter. The man started
to recite with skill, rehearsing Beowulf's
triumphs and feats in well-fashioned lines,
entwining his words.
He told what he'd heard
repeated in songs about Sigemund's exploits,[2]
all of those many feats and marvels,
the struggles and wanderings of Waels's son,
things unknown to anyone
except to Fitela, feuds and foul doings
confided by uncle to nephew when he felt
the urge to speak of them: always they had been
partners in the fight, friends in need.

1. A lake or pond. Grendel and his mother live in a cave that can be reached only through the water.
2. Legends concerning Sigemund circulated throughout the Germanic-speaking regions of medieval Europe. They are most fully recorded in the Icelandic *Volsung's Saga* from the thirteenth century, although Sigemund's fight with the dragon is found only in *Beowulf*. Fitela is Sigemund's nephew; Waels is his father. The Danish poet's comparison between Beowulf and Sigemund is a compliment of the highest order.

They killed giants, their conquering swords
had brought them down.
After his death
Sigemund's glory grew and grew
because of his courage when he killed the dragon,
the guardian of the hoard. Under gray stone
he had dared to enter all by himself
to face the worst without Fitela.
But it came to pass that his sword plunged
right through those radiant scales
and drove into the wall. The dragon died of it.
His daring had given him total possession
of the treasure-hoard his to dispose of
however he liked. He loaded a boat:
Waels's son weighted her hold
with dazzling spoils. The hot dragon melted.
Sigemund's name was known everywhere.
He was utterly valiant and venturesome,
a fence round his fighters, and flourished therefore
after King Heremod's[3] *prowess declined*
and his campaigns slowed down. The king was betrayed,
ambushed in Jutland overpowered
and done away with. The waves of his grief
had beaten him down, made him a burden,
a source of anxiety to his own nobles:
that expedition was often condemned
in those earlier times by experienced men,
men who relied on his lordship for redress,
who presumed that the part of a prince was to thrive
on his father's throne and defend the nation,
the Shielding land where they lived and belonged,
its holdings and strongholds. Such was Beowulf
in the affection of his friends and of everyone alive.
But evil entered into Heremod.
They kept racing each other, urging their mounts
down sandy lanes. The light of day
broke and kept brightening. Bands of retainers
galloped in excitement to the gabled hall
to see the marvel; and the king himself,
guardian of the ring-hoard, goodness in person,
walked in majesty from the women's quarters
with a numerous train, attended by his queen
and her crowd of maidens, across to the mead-hall.
When Hrothgar arrived at the hall, he spoke,
standing on the steps, under the steep eaves,

3. Heremod started off as an admirable Danish hero but became, over the years, a vicious, miserly king who alienated his own people. See also lines 1709–22.

gazing toward the roofwork and Grendel's talon:
"First and foremost, let the Almighty Father
be thanked for this sight. I suffered a long
harrowing by Grendel. But the Heavenly Shepherd
can work His wonders always and everywhere.
Not long since, it seemed I would never
be granted the slightest solace or relief
from any of my burdens: the best of houses
glittered and reeked and ran with blood.
This one worry outweighed all others—
a constant distress to counselors entrusted
with defending the people's forts from assault
by monsters and demons. But now a man,
with the Lord's assistance, has accomplished something
none of us could manage before now
for all our efforts. Whoever she was
who brought forth this flower of manhood,
if she is still alive, that woman can say
that in her labor the Lord of Ages
bestowed a grace on her. So now, Beowulf,
I adopt you in my heart as a dear son.
Nourish and maintain this new connection,
you noblest of men; there'll be nothing you'll want for,
no worldly goods that won't be yours.
I have often honored smaller achievements,
recognized warriors not nearly as worthy,
lavished rewards on the less deserving.
But you have made yourself immortal
by your glorious action. May the God of Ages
continue to keep and requite you well."
Beowulf, son of Ecgtheow, spoke:
"We have gone through with a glorious endeavor
and been much favored in this fight we dared
against the unknown. Nevertheless,
if you could have seen the monster himself
where he lay beaten, I would have been better pleased.
My plan was to pounce, pin him down
in a tight grip and grapple him to death—
have him panting for life, powerless and clasped
in my bare hands, his body in thrall.
But I couldn't stop him from slipping my hold.
The Lord allowed it, my lock on him
wasn't strong enough; he struggled fiercely
and broke and ran. Yet he bought his freedom
at a high price, for he left his hand
and arm and shoulder to show he had been here,
a cold comfort for having come among us.

And now he won't be long for this world.
He has done his worst but the wound will end him.
He is hasped and hooped and hirpling[4] with pain,
limping and looped in it. Like a man outlawed
for wickedness, he must await
the mighty judgment of God in majesty."
  There was less tampering and big talk then
from Unferth the boaster, less of his blather
as the hall-thanes eyed the awful proof
of the hero's prowess, the splayed hand
up under the eaves. Every nail,
claw-scale and spur, every spike
and welt on the hand of that heathen brute
was like barbed steel. Everybody said
there was no honed iron hard enough
to pierce him through, no time-proofed blade
that could cut his brutal, blood-caked claw.
  Then the order was given for all hands
to help to refurbish Heorot immediately:
men and women thronging the wine-hall,
getting it ready. Gold thread shone
in the wall-hangings, woven scenes
that attracted and held the eye's attention.[5]
But iron-braced as the inside of it had been,
that bright room lay in ruins now.
The very doors had been dragged from their hinges.
Only the roof remained unscathed
by the time the guilt-fouled fiend turned tail
in despair of his life. But death is not easily
escaped from by anyone:
all of us with souls, earth-dwellers
and children of men, must make our way
to a destination already ordained
where the body, after the banqueting,
sleeps on its deathbed.
                    Then the due time arrived
for Halfdane's son to proceed to the hall.
The king himself would sit down to feast.
No group ever gathered in greater numbers
or better order around their ring-giver.
The benches filled with famous men
who fell to with relish; round upon round
of mead was passed; those powerful kinsmen,
Hrothgar and Hrothulf, were in high spirits

4. Limping or hobbling.
5. The Anglo-Saxon nobility decorated their halls with tapestries. From what little has survived the centuries, it is clear that some were made with exquisite skill.

in the raftered hall. Inside Heorot
there was nothing but friendship. The Shielding nation
was not yet familiar with feud and betrayal.[6]
Then Halfdane's son presented Beowulf
with a gold standard as a victory gift,
an embroidered banner; also breast-mail
and a helmet; and a sword carried high,
that was both precious object and token of honor.
So Beowulf drank his drink, at ease;
it was hardly a shame to be showered with such gifts
in front of the hall-troops. There haven't been many
moments, I am sure, when men exchanged
four such treasures at so friendly a sitting.
An embossed ridge, a band lapped with wire
arched over the helmet: head-protection
to keep the keen-ground cutting edge
from damaging it when danger threatened
and the man was battling behind his shield.
Next the king ordered eight horses
with gold bridles to be brought through the yard
into the hall. The harness of one
included a saddle of sumptuous design,
the battle-seat where the son of Halfdane
rode when he wished to join the sword-play:
wherever the killing and carnage were the worst,
he would be to the fore, fighting hard.
Then the Danish prince, descendant of Ing,
handed over both the arms and the horses,
urging Beowulf to use them well.
And so their leader, the lord and guard
of coffer and strongroom, with customary grace
bestowed upon Beowulf both sets of gifts.
A fair witness can see how well each one behaved.
The chieftain went on to reward the others:
each man on the bench who had sailed with Beowulf
and risked the voyage received a bounty,
some treasured possession. And compensation,
a price in gold, was settled for the Geat
Grendel had cruelly killed earlier—
as he would have killed more, had not mindful God
and one man's daring prevented that doom.
Past and present, God's will prevails.
Hence, understanding is always best
and a prudent mind. Whoever remains

6. By contrasting the present comity with future "feud and betrayal," these lines seem to intimate that Hrothulf, King Hrothgar's nephew, will later betray Hrothgar's sons and usurp the throne. See also lines 1163–64, 1179–86, 1228.

for long here in this earthly life
will enjoy and endure more than enough.
They sang then and played to please the hero,
words and music for their warrior prince,
harp tunes and tales of adventure:
there were high times on the hall benches,
and the king's poet performed his part
with the saga of Finn and his sons, unfolding
the tale of the fierce attack in Friesland
where Hnaef, king of the Danes, met death.[7]

Hildeburh
had little cause
to credit the Jutes:
son and brother,
she lost them both
on the battlefield.
She, bereft
and blameless, they
foredoomed, cut down
and spear-gored. She,
the woman in shock,
waylaid by grief,
Hoc's daughter—
how could she not
lament her fate
when morning came
and the light broke
on her murdered dears?
And so farewell
delight on earth,
war carried away
Finn's troop of thanes
all but a few.
How then could Finn
hold the line
or fight on
to the end with Hengest,
how save
the rump of his force
from that enemy chief?
So a truce was offered

7. The "saga of Finn," recounted by the court poet, is summarized from the point of view of Hildeburh, who lost her son, her brother, and her husband in the tragedy. The passage achieves its poignancy in part by being allusive and sparing in details. For a reconstruction of the events and a fragment from another poem on the subject, see pp. 89–91, below.

as follows:[8] *first*
separate quarters
to be cleared for the Danes,
hall and throne
to be shared with the Frisians.
Then, second:
every day
at the dole-out of gifts
Finn, son of Folcwald,
should honor the Danes,
bestow with an even
hand to Hengest
and Hengest's men
the wrought-gold rings,
bounty to match
the measure he gave
his own Frisians—
to keep morale
in the beer-hall high.
Both sides then
sealed their agreement.
With oaths to Hengest
Finn swore
openly, solemnly,
that the battle survivors
would be guaranteed
honor and status.
No infringement
by word or deed,
no provocation
would be permitted.
Their own ring-giver
after all
was dead and gone,
they were leaderless,
in forced allegiance
to his murderer.
So if any Frisian
stirred up bad blood
with insinuations
or taunts about this,
the blade of the sword
would arbitrate it.
A funeral pyre

8. The Frisian king Finn offers terms to the Danes, who are now led by Hengest after Hnaef's death.

was then prepared,
effulgent gold
brought out from the hoard.
The pride and prince
of the Shieldings lay
awaiting the flame.
Everywhere
there were blood-plastered
coats of mail.
The pyre was heaped
with boar-shaped helmets
forged in gold,
with the gashed corpses
of wellborn Danes—
many had fallen.
Then Hildeburh
ordered her own
son's body
be burnt with Hnaef's,
the flesh on his bones
to sputter and blaze
beside his uncle's.
The woman wailed
and sang keens,
the warrior went up.
Carcass flame
swirled and fumed,
they stood round the burial
mound and howled
as heads melted,
crusted gashes
spattered and ran
bloody matter.
The glutton element
flamed and consumed
the dead of both sides.
Their great days were gone.
Warriors scattered
to homes and forts
all over Friesland,
fewer now, feeling
loss of friends.
Hengest stayed,
lived out that whole
resentful, blood-sullen
winter with Finn,
homesick and helpless.

No ring-whorled prow
could up then
and away on the sea.
Wind and water
raged with storms,
wave and shingle
were shackled in ice
until another year
appeared in the yard
as it does to this day,
the seasons constant,
the wonder of light
coming over us.
Then winter was gone,
earth's lap grew lovely,
longing woke
in the cooped-up exile
for a voyage home—
but more for vengeance,
some way of bringing
things to a head:
his sword arm hankered
to greet the Jutes.
So he did not balk
once Hunlafing
placed on his lap
Dazzle-the-Duel,
the best sword of all,[9]
whose edges Jutes
knew only too well.
Thus blood was spilled,
the gallant Finn
slain in his home
after Guthlaf and Oslaf[1]
back from their voyage
made old accusation:
the brutal ambush,
the fate they had suffered,
all blamed on Finn.
The wildness in them
had to brim over.

9. The identity of Hunlafing is unknown, but the ceremonial presentation of a famous sword to Hengest seems to be a symbolic gesture prompting revenge. It is unclear whether this action takes place back in Denmark or whether the Danes never left Frisia (Friesland) before renewing the fighting. Famous swords were sometimes given names, such as Beowulf's Naegling and Unferth's Hrunting.
1. This pair may be the same Ordlaf and Guthlaf mentioned in the Finnsburg Fragment, but aside from their Danish affiliation, nothing is known about them.

The hall ran red
with blood of enemies.
Finn was cut down,
the queen brought away
and everything
the Shieldings could find
inside Finn's walls—
the Frisian king's
gold collars and gemstones—
swept off to the ship.
Over sea-lanes then
back to Daneland
the warrior troop
bore that lady home.

The poem was over,
the poet had performed, a pleasant murmur
started on the benches, stewards did the rounds
with wine in splendid jugs, and Wealhtheow came to sit
in her gold crown between two good men,
uncle and nephew, each one of whom
still trusted the other;[2] and the forthright Unferth,
admired by all for his mind and courage
although under a cloud for killing his brothers,
reclined near the king.
The queen spoke:
"Enjoy this drink, my most generous lord;
raise up your goblet, entertain the Geats
duly and gently, discourse with them,
be open-handed, happy and fond.
Relish their company, but recollect as well
all of the boons that have been bestowed on you.
The bright court of Heorot has been cleansed
and now the word is that you want to adopt
this warrior as a son. So, while you may,
bask in your fortune, and then bequeath
kingdom and nation to your kith and kin,
before your decease. I am certain of Hrothulf.
He is noble and will use the young ones well.
He will not let you down. Should you die before him,
he will treat our children truly and fairly.
He will honor, I am sure, our two sons,
repay them in kind, when he recollects
all the good things we gave him once,
the favor and respect he found in his childhood."

2. Hrothgar and Hrothulf; see the note for line 1018.

She turned then to the bench where her boys sat,
Hrethric and Hrothmund, with other nobles' sons,
all the youth together; and that good man,
Beowulf the Geat, sat between the brothers.
  The cup was carried to him, kind words
spoken in welcome and a wealth of wrought gold
graciously bestowed: two arm bangles,
a mail-shirt and rings, and the most resplendent
torque of gold I ever heard tell of
anywhere on earth or under heaven.
There was no hoard like it since Hama snatched
the Brosings' neck-chain and bore it away
with its gems and settings to his shining fort,
away from Eormenric's wiles and hatred,[3]
and thereby ensured his eternal reward.
Hygelac the Geat, grandson of Swerting,
wore this neck-ring on his last raid;[4]
at bay under his banner, he defended the booty,
treasure he had won. Fate swept him away
because of his proud need to provoke
a feud with the Frisians. He fell beneath his shield,
in the same gem-crusted, kingly gear
he had worn when he crossed the frothing wave-vat.
So the dead king fell into Frankish hands.
They took his breast-mail, also his neck-torque,
and punier warriors plundered the slain
when the carnage ended; Geat corpses
covered the field.
                    Applause filled the hall.
Then Wealhtheow pronounced in the presence of the
        company:
"Take delight in this torque, dear Beowulf,
wear it for luck and wear also this mail
from our people's armory: may you prosper in them!
Be acclaimed for strength, for kindly guidance
to these two boys, and your bounty will be sure.
You have won renown: you are known to all men
far and near, now and forever.
Your sway is wide as the wind's home,
as the sea around cliffs. And so, my prince,
I wish you a lifetime's luck and blessings

3. The treasures presented to Beowulf are compared to a legendary necklace once worn by the goddess Freyja in Germanic legend, which later came into the possession of Eormenric, whom legends portray as a treacherous tyrant.
4. Beowulf later gives the necklace to Hygd, Hygelac's queen. Hygelac was to wear it during the ill-fated raid on Frankish territories near the mouth of the Rhine, where he lost his life and the necklace. The raid, which can be dated to *c.* 520 C.E., is alluded to several times in the poem.

to enjoy this treasure. Treat my sons
with tender care, be strong and kind.
Here each comrade is true to the other,
loyal to lord, loving in spirit.
The thanes have one purpose, the people are ready:
having drunk and pledged, the ranks do as I bid."
  She moved then to her place. Men were drinking wine
at that rare feast; how could they know fate,
the grim shape of things to come,
the threat looming over many thanes
as night approached and King Hrothgar prepared
to retire to his quarters? Retainers in great numbers
were posted on guard as so often in the past.
Benches were pushed back, bedding gear and bolsters
spread across the floor, and one man
lay down to his rest, already marked for death.
At their heads they placed their polished timber
battle-shields; and on the bench above them,
each man's kit was kept to hand:
a towering war-helmet, webbed mail-shirt
and great-shafted spear. It was their habit
always and everywhere to be ready for action,
at home or in the camp, in whatever case
and at whatever time the need arose
to rally round their lord. They were a right people.

[Another Attack]

  They went to sleep. And one paid dearly
for his night's ease, as had happened to them often,
ever since Grendel occupied the gold-hall,
committing evil until the end came,
death after his crimes. Then it became clear,
obvious to everyone once the fight was over,
that an avenger lurked and was still alive,
grimly biding time. Grendel's mother,
monstrous hell-bride, brooded on her wrongs.
She had been forced down into fearful waters,
the cold depths, after Cain had killed
his father's son, felled his own
brother with a sword. Branded an outlaw,
marked by having murdered, he moved into the wilds,
shunned company and joy. And from Cain there sprang
misbegotten spirits, among them Grendel,
the banished and accursed, due to come to grips
with that watcher in Heorot waiting to do battle.

The monster wrenched and wrestled with him,
but Beowulf was mindful of his mighty strength,
the wondrous gifts God had showered on him:
he relied for help on the Lord of All,
on His care and favor. So he overcame the foe,
brought down the hell-brute. Broken and bowed,
outcast from all sweetness, the enemy of mankind
made for his death-den. But now his mother
had sallied forth on a savage journey,
grief-racked and ravenous, desperate for revenge.
She came to Heorot. There, inside the hall,
Danes lay asleep, earls who would soon endure
a great reversal, once Grendel's mother
attacked and entered. Her onslaught was less
only by as much as an amazon warrior's
strength is less than an armed man's
when the hefted sword, its hammered edge
and gleaming blade slathered in blood,
razes the sturdy boar-ridge off a helmet.
Then in the hall, hard-honed swords
were grabbed from the bench, many a broad shield
lifted and braced; there was little thought of helmets
or woven mail when they woke in terror.
The hell-dam[5] was in panic, desperate to get out,
in mortal terror the moment she was found.
She had pounced and taken one of the retainers
in a tight hold, then headed for the fen.
To Hrothgar, this man was the most beloved
of the friends he trusted between the two seas.
She had done away with a great warrior,
ambushed him at rest.
Beowulf was elsewhere.
Earlier, after the award of the treasure,
the Geat had been given another lodging.
There was uproar in Heorot. She had snatched their trophy,
Grendel's bloodied hand. It was a fresh blow
to the afflicted bawn. The bargain was hard,
both parties having to pay
with the lives of friends. And the old lord,
the gray-haired warrior, was heartsore and weary
when he heard the news: his highest-placed adviser,
his dearest companion, was dead and gone.
Beowulf was quickly brought to the chamber:
the winner of fights, the arch-warrior,

5. Cf. the expression "the devil and his dam."

came first-footing in with his fellow troops
to where the king in his wisdom waited,
still wondering whether Almighty God
would ever turn the tide of his misfortunes.
So Beowulf entered with his band in attendance
and the wooden floorboards banged and rang
as he advanced, hurrying to address
the prince of the Ingwins, asking if he'd rested
since the urgent summons had come as a surprise.
  Then Hrothgar, the Shieldings' helmet, spoke:
"Rest? What is rest? Sorrow has returned.
Alas for the Danes! Aeschere is dead.
He was Yrmenlaf's elder brother
and a soul-mate to me, a true mentor,
my right-hand man when the ranks clashed
and our boar-crests had to take a battering
in the line of action. Aeschere was everything
the world admires in a wise man and a friend.
Then this roaming killer came in a fury
and slaughtered him in Heorot. Where she is hiding,
glutting on the corpse and glorying in her escape,
I cannot tell; she has taken up the feud
because of last night, when you killed Grendel,
wrestled and racked him in ruinous combat
since for too long he had terrorized us
with his depredations. He died in battle,
paid with his life; and now this powerful
other one arrives, this force for evil
driven to avenge her kinsman's death.
Or so it seems to thanes in their grief,
in the anguish every thane endures
at the loss of a ring-giver, now that the hand
that bestowed so richly has been stilled in death.
  "I have heard it said by my people in hall,
counselors who live in the upland country,
that they have seen two such creatures
prowling the moors, huge marauders
from some other world. One of these things,
as far as anyone ever can discern,
looks like a woman; the other, warped
in the shape of a man, moves beyond the pale
bigger than any man, an unnatural birth
called Grendel by the country people
in former days. They are fatherless creatures,
and their whole ancestry is hidden in a past
of demons and ghosts. They dwell apart
among wolves on the hills, on windswept crags

and treacherous keshes,[6] where cold streams
pour down the mountain and disappear
under mist and moorland.
A few miles from here
a frost-stiffened wood waits and keeps watch
above a mere; the overhanging bank
is a maze of tree-roots mirrored in its surface.
At night there, something uncanny happens:
the water burns. And the mere bottom
has never been sounded by the sons of men.
On its bank, the heather-stepper halts:
the hart in flight from pursuing hounds
will turn to face them with firm-set horns
and die in the wood rather than dive
beneath its surface. That is no good place.
When wind blows up and stormy weather
makes clouds scud and the skies weep,
out of its depths a dirty surge
is pitched toward the heavens. Now help depends
again on you and on you alone.
The gap of danger where the demon waits
is still unknown to you. Seek it if you dare.
I will compensate you for settling the feud
as I did the last time with lavish wealth,
coffers of coiled gold, if you come back."

[Beowulf Fights Grendel's Mother]

Beowulf, son of Ecgtheow, spoke:
"Wise sir, do not grieve. It is always better
to avenge dear ones than to indulge in mourning.
For every one of us, living in this world
means waiting for our end. Let whoever can
win glory before death. When a warrior is gone,
that will be his best and only bulwark.
So arise, my lord, and let us immediately
set forth on the trail of this troll-dam.
I guarantee you: she will not get away,
not to dens under ground nor upland groves
nor the ocean floor. She'll have nowhere to flee to.
Endure your troubles today. Bear up
and be the man I expect you to be."
With that the old lord sprang to his feet
and praised God for Beowulf's pledge.

6. A causeway or bridge across a bog.

Then a bit and halter were brought for his horse
with the plaited mane. The wise king mounted
the royal saddle and rode out in style
with a force of shield-bearers. The forest paths
were marked all over with the monster's tracks,
her trail on the ground wherever she had gone
across the dark moors, dragging away
the body of that thane, Hrothgar's best
counselor and overseer of the country.
So the noble prince proceeded undismayed
up fells and screes,[7] along narrow footpaths
and ways where they were forced into single file,
ledges on cliffs above lairs of water-monsters.
He went in front with a few men,
good judges of the lie of the land,
and suddenly discovered the dismal wood,
mountain trees growing out at an angle
above gray stones: the bloodshot water
surged underneath. It was a sore blow
to all of the Danes, friends of the Shieldings,
a hurt to each and every one
of that noble company when they came upon
Aeschere's head at the foot of the cliff.
  Everybody gazed as the hot gore
kept wallowing up and an urgent war-horn
repeated its notes: the whole party
sat down to watch. The water was infested
with all kinds of reptiles. There were writhing sea-dragons
and monsters slouching on slopes by the cliff,
serpents and wild things such as those that often
surface at dawn to roam the sail-road
and doom the voyage. Down they plunged,
lashing in anger at the loud call
of the battle-bugle. An arrow from the bow
of the Geat chief got one of them
as he surged to the surface: the seasoned shaft
stuck deep in his flank and his freedom in the water
got less and less. It was his last swim.
He was swiftly overwhelmed in the shallows,
prodded by barbed boar-spears,
cornered, beaten, pulled up on the bank,
a strange lake-birth, a loathsome catch
men gazed at in awe.
                Beowulf got ready,
donned his war-gear, indifferent to death;

7. A mountain slope of loose rock.

his mighty, hand-forged, fine-webbed mail
would soon meet with the menace underwater.
It would keep the bone-cage of his body safe:
no enemy's clasp could crush him in it,
no vicious armlock choke his life out.
To guard his head he had a glittering helmet
that was due to be muddied on the mere bottom
and blurred in the upswirl. It was of beaten gold,
princely headgear hooped and hasped
by a weapon-smith who had worked wonders
in days gone by and adorned it with boar-shapes;
since then it had resisted every sword.
And another item lent by Unferth
at that moment of need was of no small importance:
the brehon[8] handed him a hilted weapon,
a rare and ancient sword named Hrunting.
The iron blade with its ill-boding patterns
had been tempered in blood. It had never failed
the hand of anyone who hefted it in battle,
anyone who had fought and faced the worst
in the gap of danger. This was not the first time
it had been called to perform heroic feats.
When he lent that blade to the better swordsman,
Unferth, the strong-built son of Ecglaf,
could hardly have remembered the ranting speech
he had made in his cups. He was not man enough
to face the turmoil of a fight under water
and the risk to his life. So there he lost
fame and repute. It was different for the other
rigged out in his gear, ready to do battle.
Beowulf, son of Ecgtheow, spoke:
"Wisest of kings, now that I have come
to the point of action, I ask you to recall
what we said earlier: that you, son of Halfdane
and gold-friend to retainers, that you, if I should fall
and suffer death while serving your cause,
would act like a father to me afterward.
If this combat kills me, take care
of my young company, my comrades in arms.
And be sure also, my beloved Hrothgar,
to send Hygelac the treasures I received.
Let the lord of the Geats gaze on that gold,
let Hrethel's son take note of it and see
that I found a ring-giver of rare magnificence
and enjoyed the good of his generosity.

8. One of an ancient class of lawyers in Ireland [*Translator's note*].

And Unferth is to have what I inherited:
to that far-famed man I bequeath my own
sharp-honed, wave-sheened wonder-blade.
With Hrunting I shall gain glory or die."
  After these words, the prince of the Weather-Geats
was impatient to be away and plunged suddenly:
without more ado, he dived into the heaving
depths of the lake. It was the best part of a day
before he could see the solid bottom.
  Quickly the one who haunted those waters,
who had scavenged and gone her gluttonous rounds
for a hundred seasons, sensed a human
observing her outlandish lair from above.
So she lunged and clutched and managed to catch him
in her brutal grip; but his body, for all that,
remained unscathed: the mesh of the chain-mail
saved him on the outside. Her savage talons
failed to rip the web of his war-shirt.
Then once she touched bottom, that wolfish swimmer
carried the ring-mailed prince to her court
so that for all his courage he could never use
the weapons he carried; and a bewildering horde
came at him from the depths, droves of sea-beasts
who attacked with tusks and tore at his chain-mail
in a ghastly onslaught. The gallant man
could see he had entered some hellish turn-hole
and yet the water there did not work against him
because the hall-roofing held off
the force of the current; then he saw firelight,
a gleam and flare-up, a glimmer of brightness.
  The hero observed that swamp-thing from hell,
the tarn-hag[9] in all her terrible strength,
then heaved his war-sword and swung his arm:
the decorated blade came down ringing
and singing on her head. But he soon found
his battle-torch extinguished; the shining blade
refused to bite. It spared her and failed
the man in his need. It had gone through many
hand-to-hand fights, had hewed the armor
and helmets of the doomed, but here at last
the fabulous powers of that heirloom failed.
  Hygelac's kinsman kept thinking about
his name and fame: he never lost heart.
Then, in a fury, he flung his sword away.
The keen, inlaid, worm-loop-patterned steel

9. Tarn: a small mountain lake.

was hurled to the ground: he would have to rely
on the might of his arm. So must a man do
who intends to gain enduring glory
in a combat. Life doesn't cost him a thought.
Then the prince of War-Geats, warming to this fight
with Grendel's mother, gripped her shoulder
and laid about him in a battle frenzy:
he pitched his killer opponent to the floor
but she rose quickly and retaliated,
grappled him tightly in her grim embrace.
The sure-footed fighter felt daunted,
the strongest of warriors stumbled and fell.
So she pounced upon him and pulled out
a broad, whetted knife: now she would avenge
her only child. But the mesh of chain-mail
on Beowulf's shoulder shielded his life,
turned the edge and tip of the blade.
The son of Ecgtheow would have surely perished
and the Geats lost their warrior under the wide earth
had the strong links and locks of his war-gear
not helped to save him: holy God
decided the victory. It was easy for the Lord,
the Ruler of Heaven, to redress the balance
once Beowulf got back up on his feet.
  Then he saw a blade that boded well,
a sword in her armory, an ancient heirloom
from the days of the giants, an ideal weapon,
one that any warrior would envy,
but so huge and heavy of itself
only Beowulf could wield it in a battle.
So the Shieldings' hero hard-pressed and enraged,
took a firm hold of the hilt and swung
the blade in an arc, a resolute blow
that bit deep into her neck-bone
and severed it entirely, toppling the doomed
house of her flesh; she fell to the floor.
The sword dripped blood, the swordsman was elated.
  A light appeared and the place brightened
the way the sky does when heaven's candle
is shining clearly. He inspected the vault:
with sword held high, its hilt raised
to guard and threaten, Hygelac's thane
scouted by the wall in Grendel's wake.
Now the weapon was to prove its worth.
The warrior determined to take revenge
for every gross act Grendel had committed—
and not only for that one occasion

when he'd come to slaughter the sleeping troops,
fifteen of Hrothgar's house-guards
surprised on their benches and ruthlessly devoured,
and as many again carried away,
a brutal plunder. Beowulf in his fury
now settled that score: he saw the monster
in his resting place, war-weary and wrecked,
a lifeless corpse, a casualty
of the battle in Heorot. The body gaped
at the stroke dealt to it after death:
Beowulf cut the corpse's head off.
  Immediately the counselors keeping a lookout
with Hrothgar, watching the lake water,
saw a heave-up and surge of waves
and blood in the backwash. They bowed gray heads,
spoke in their sage, experienced way
about the good warrior, how they never again
expected to see that prince returning
in triumph to their king. It was clear to many
that the wolf of the deep had destroyed him forever.
  The ninth hour of the day arrived.
The brave Shieldings abandoned the cliff-top
and the king went home; but sick at heart,
staring at the mere, the strangers held on.
They wished, without hope, to behold their lord,
Beowulf himself.
                Meanwhile, the sword
began to wilt into gory icicles
to slather and thaw. It was a wonderful thing,
the way it all melted as ice melts
when the Father eases the fetters off the frost
and unravels the water-ropes, He who wields power
over time and tide: He is the true Lord.
  The Geat captain saw treasure in abundance
but carried no spoils from those quarters
except for the head and the inlaid hilt
embossed with jewels; its blade had melted
and the scrollwork on it burned, so scalding was the blood
of the poisonous fiend who had perished there.
Then away he swam, the one who had survived
the fall of his enemies, flailing to the surface.
The wide water, the waves and pools,
were no longer infested once the wandering fiend
let go of her life and this unreliable world.
  The seafarers' leader made for land,
resolutely swimming, delighted with his prize,
the mighty load he was lugging to the surface.

His thanes advanced in a troop to meet him,
thanking God and taking great delight
in seeing their prince back safe and sound.
Quickly the hero's helmet and mail-shirt
were loosed and unlaced. The lake settled,
clouds darkened above the bloodshot depths.
With high hearts they headed away
along footpaths and trails through the fields,
roads that they knew, each of them wrestling
with the head they were carrying from the lakeside cliff,
men kingly in their courage and capable
of difficult work. It was a task for four
to hoist Grendel's head on a spear
and bear it under strain to the bright hall.
But soon enough they neared the place,
fourteen Geats in fine fettle,
striding across the outlying ground
in a delighted throng around their leader.
In he came then, the thanes' commander,
the arch-warrior, to address Hrothgar:
his courage was proven, his glory was secure.
Grendel's head was hauled by the hair,
dragged across the floor where the people were drinking,
a horror for both queen and company to behold.
They stared in awe. It was an astonishing sight.

[Another Celebration at Heorot]

Beowulf, son of Ecgtheow, spoke:
"So, son of Halfdane, prince of the Shieldings,
we are glad to bring this booty from the lake.
It is a token of triumph and we tender it to you.
I barely survived the battle under water.
It was hard-fought, a desperate affair
that could have gone badly; if God had not helped me,
the outcome would have been quick and fatal.
Although Hrunting is hard-edged,
I could never bring it to bear in battle.
But the Lord of Men allowed me to behold—
for He often helps the unbefriended—
an ancient sword shining on the wall,
a weapon made for giants, there for the wielding.
Then my moment came in the combat and I struck
the dwellers in that den. Next thing the damascened
sword blade melted; it bloated and it burned
in their rushing blood. I have wrested the hilt

from the enemies' hand, avenged the evil
done to the Danes; it is what was due.
And this I pledge, O prince of the Shieldings:
you can sleep secure with your company of troops
in Heorot Hall. Never need you fear
for a single thane of your sept[1] or nation,
young warriors or old, that laying waste of life
that you and your people endured of yore."
  Then the gold hilt was handed over
to the old lord, a relic from long ago
for the venerable ruler. That rare smithwork
was passed on to the prince of the Danes
when those devils perished; once death removed
that murdering, guilt-steeped, God-cursed fiend,
eliminating his unholy life
and his mother's as well, it was willed to that king
who of all the lavish gift-lords of the north
was the best regarded between the two seas.
  Hrothgar spoke; he examined the hilt,
that relic of old times. It was engraved all over
and showed how war first came into the world
and the flood destroyed the tribe of giants.
They suffered a terrible severance from the Lord;
the Almighty made the waters rise,
drowned them in the deluge for retribution.[2]
In pure gold inlay on the sword-guards
there were rune-markings[3] correctly incised,
stating and recording for whom the sword
had been first made and ornamented
with its scrollworked hilt. Then everyone hushed
as the son of Halfdane spoke this wisdom:
"A protector of his people, pledged to uphold
truth and justice and to respect tradition,
is entitled to affirm that this man
was born to distinction. Beowulf, my friend,
your fame has gone far and wide,
you are known everywhere. In all things you are
    even-tempered,
prudent and resolute. So I stand firm by the promise of
    friendship
we exchanged before. Forever you will be

1. A clan or subgroup of a tribe, especially in Ireland.
2. Near the beginning of the story of Noah, Genesis 6.4 reads, "Now giants were upon the earth in those days. For after the sons of God went in to the daughters of men, and they brought forth children, these are the mighty men of old, men of renown."
3. The rune-markings (Old English *run-stafas*) were a system of writing developed by early Germanic tribes before the introduction of Latin letters following the tribes' conversion to Christianity. In some contexts runes also had associations with mystery, counsel, and magic.

your people's mainstay and your own warriors'
helping hand.
                    Heremod was different,
the way he behaved to Ecgwela's sons.
His rise in the world brought little joy
to the Danish people, only death and destruction.
He vented his rage on men he caroused with,
killed his own comrades, a pariah king
who cut himself off from his own kind,
even though Almighty God had made him
eminent and powerful and marked him from the start
for a happy life. But a change happened,
he grew bloodthirsty, gave no more rings
to honor the Danes. He suffered in the end
for having plagued his people for so long:
his life lost happiness.
                              So learn from this
and understand true values. I who tell you
have wintered into wisdom.
                                   It is a great wonder
how Almighty God in His magnificence
favors our race with rank and scope
and the gift of wisdom; His sway is wide.
Sometimes He allows the mind of a man
of distinguished birth to follow its bent,
grants him fulfillment and felicity on earth
and forts to command in his own country.
He permits him to lord it in many lands
until the man in his unthinkingness
forgets that it will ever end for him.
He indulges his desires; illness and old age
mean nothing to him; his mind is untroubled
by envy or malice or the thought of enemies
with their hate-honed swords. The whole world
conforms to his will, he is kept from the worst
until an element of overweening
enters him and takes hold
while the soul's guard, its sentry, drowses,
grown too distracted. A killer stalks him,
an archer who draws a deadly bow.
And then the man is hit in the heart,
the arrow flies beneath his defenses,
the devious promptings of the demon start.
His old possessions seem paltry to him now.
He covets and resents; dishonors custom
and bestows no gold; and because of good things
that the Heavenly Powers gave him in the past
he ignores the shape of things to come.

Then finally the end arrives
when the body he was lent collapses and falls
prey to its death; ancestral possessions
and the goods he hoarded are inherited by another
who lets them go with a liberal hand.
  "O flower of warriors, beware of that trap.
Choose, dear Beowulf, the better part,
eternal rewards. Do not give way to pride.
For a brief while your strength is in bloom
but it fades quickly; and soon there will follow
illness or the sword to lay you low,
or a sudden fire or surge of water
or jabbing blade or javelin from the air
or repellent age. Your piercing eye
will dim and darken; and death will arrive,
dear warrior, to sweep you away.
  "Just so I ruled the Ring-Danes' country
for fifty years, defended them in wartime
with spear and sword against constant assaults
by many tribes: I came to believe
my enemies had faded from the face of the earth.
Still, what happened was a hard reversal
from bliss to grief. Grendel struck
after lying in wait. He laid waste to the land
and from that moment my mind was in dread
of his depredations. So I praise God
in His heavenly glory that I lived to behold
this head dripping blood and that after such harrowing
I can look upon it in triumph at last.
Take your place, then, with pride and pleasure,
and move to the feast. Tomorrow morning
our treasure will be shared and showered upon you."
  The Geat was elated and gladly obeyed
the old man's bidding; he sat on the bench.
And soon all was restored, the same as before.
Happiness came back, the hall was thronged,
and a banquet set forth; black night fell
and covered them in darkness.
                                        Then the company rose
for the old campaigner: the gray-haired prince
was ready for bed. And a need for rest
came over the brave shield-bearing Geat.
He was a weary seafarer, far from home,
so immediately a house-guard guided him out,
one whose office entailed looking after
whatever a thane on the road in those days
might need or require. It was noble courtesy.

[Beowulf Returns Home]

That great heart rested. The hall towered,
gold-shingled and gabled, and the guest slept in it
until the black raven with raucous glee
announced heaven's joy, and a hurry of brightness
overran the shadows. Warriors rose quickly,
impatient to be off: their own country
was beckoning the nobles; and the bold voyager
longed to be aboard his distant boat.
Then that stalwart fighter ordered Hrunting
to be brought to Unferth, and bade Unferth
take the sword and thanked him for lending it.
He said he had found it a friend in battle
and a powerful help; he put no blame
on the blade's cutting edge. He was a considerate man.
And there the warriors stood in their war-gear,
eager to go, while their honored lord
approached the platform where the other sat.
The undaunted hero addressed Hrothgar.
Beowulf, son of Ecgtheow, spoke:
"Now we who crossed the wide sea
have to inform you that we feel a desire
to return to Hygelac. Here we have been welcomed
and thoroughly entertained. You have treated us well.
If there is any favor on earth I can perform
beyond deeds of arms I have done already,
anything that would merit your affections more,
I shall act, my lord, with alacrity.
If ever I hear from across the ocean
that people on your borders are threatening battle
as attackers have done from time to time,
I shall land with a thousand thanes at my back
to help your cause. Hygelac may be young
to rule a nation, but this much I know
about the king of the Geats: he will come to my aid
and want to support me by word and action
in your hour of need, when honor dictates
that I raise a hedge of spears around you.
Then if Hrethric should think about traveling
as a king's son to the court of the Geats,
he will find many friends. Foreign places
yield more to one who is himself worth meeting."
Hrothgar spoke and answered him:
"The Lord in his wisdom sent you those words
and they came from the heart. I have never heard

so young a man make truer observations.
You are strong in body and mature in mind,
impressive in speech. If it should come to pass
that Hrethel's descendant[4] dies beneath a spear,
if deadly battle or the sword blade or disease
fells the prince who guards your people
and you are still alive, then I firmly believe
the seafaring Geats won't find a man
worthier of acclaim as their king and defender
than you, if only you would undertake
the lordship of your homeland. My liking for you
deepens with time, dear Beowulf.
What you have done is to draw two peoples,
the Geat nation and us neighboring Danes,
into shared peace and a pact of friendship
in spite of hatreds we have harbored in the past.
For as long as I rule this far-flung land
treasures will change hands and each side will treat
the other with gifts; across the gannet's bath,
over the broad sea, whorled prows will bring
presents and tokens. I know your people
are beyond reproach in every respect,
steadfast in the old way with friend or foe."
Then the earls' defender furnished the hero
with twelve treasures and told him to set out,
sail with those gifts safely home
to the people he loved, but to return promptly.
And so the good and gray-haired Dane,
that highborn king, kissed Beowulf
and embraced his neck, then broke down
in sudden tears. Two forebodings
disturbed him in his wisdom, but one was stronger:
nevermore would they meet each other
face to face. And such was his affection
that he could not help being overcome:
his fondness for the man was so deep-founded,
it warmed his heart and wound the heartstrings
tight in his breast.
The embrace ended
and Beowulf, glorious in his gold regalia,
stepped the green earth. Straining at anchor
and ready for boarding, his boat awaited him.
So they went on their journey, and Hrothgar's generosity
was praised repeatedly. He was a peerless king
until old age sapped his strength and did him

4. I.e., Hygelac.

mortal harm, as it has done so many.
  Down to the waves then, dressed in the web
of their chain-mail and war-shirts the young men marched
in high spirits. The coast-guard spied them,
thanes setting forth, the same as before.
His salute this time from the top of the cliff
was far from unmannerly; he galloped to meet them
and as they took ship in their shining gear,
he said how welcome they would be in Geatland.
Then the broad hull was beached on the sand
to be cargoed with treasure, horses and war-gear.
The curved prow motioned; the mast stood high
above Hrothgar's riches in the loaded hold.
  The guard who had watched the boat was given
a sword with gold fittings, and in future days
that present would make him a respected man
at his place on the mead-bench.
                                        Then the keel plunged
and shook in the sea; and they sailed from Denmark.
  Right away the mast was rigged with its sea-shawl;
sail-ropes were tightened, timbers drummed
and stiff winds kept the wave-crosser
skimming ahead; as she heaved forward,
her foamy neck was fleet and buoyant,
a lapped prow loping over currents,
until finally the Geats caught sight of coastline
and familiar cliffs. The keel reared up,
wind lifted it home, it hit on the land.
  The harbor guard came hurrying out
to the rolling water: he had watched the offing
long and hard, on the lookout for those friends.
With the anchor cables, he moored their craft
right where it had beached, in case a backwash
might catch the hull and carry it away.
Then he ordered the prince's treasure-trove
to be carried ashore. It was a short step
from there to where Hrethel's son and heir,
Hygelac the gold-giver, makes his home
on a secure cliff, in the company of retainers.
  The building was magnificent, the king majestic,
ensconced in his hall; and although Hygd, his queen,
was young, a few short years at court,
her mind was thoughtful and her manners sure.
Haereth's daughter behaved generously
and stinted nothing when she distributed
bounty to the Geats.
                                        Great Queen Modthryth

perpetrated terrible wrongs.[5]
If any retainer ever made bold
to look her in the face, if an eye not her lord's[6]
stared at her directly during daylight,
the outcome was sealed: he was kept bound,
in hand-tightened shackles, racked, tortured
until doom was pronounced—death by the sword,
slash of blade, blood-gush, and death-qualms
in an evil display. Even a queen
outstanding in beauty must not overstep like that.
A queen should weave peace, not punish the innocent
with loss of life for imagined insults.
But Hemming's kinsman[7] put a halt to her ways
and drinkers round the table had another tale:
she was less of a bane to people's lives,
less cruel-minded, after she was married
to the brave Offa, a bride arrayed
in her gold finery, given away
by a caring father, ferried to her young prince
over dim seas. In days to come
she would grace the throne and grow famous
for her good deeds and conduct of life,
her high devotion to the hero king
who was the best king, it has been said,
between the two seas or anywhere else
on the face of the earth. Offa was honored
far and wide for his generous ways,
his fighting spirit and his farseeing
defense of his homeland; from him there sprang Eomer,
Garmund's grandson, kinsman of Hemming,
his warriors' mainstay and master of the field.
  Heroic Beowulf and his band of men
crossed the wide strand, striding along
the sandy foreshore; the sun shone,
the world's candle warmed them from the south
as they hastened to where, as they had heard,
the young king, Ongentheow's killer
and his people's protector,[8] was dispensing rings

5. Modthryth's excessive cruelty suggests a negative exemplum to Hygd's virtues, and the abruptness of the transition finds parallels elsewhere in the poem. The origins of the story are obscure, but they seem to combine historical legend with folk-tale motifs. By the end of the passage the story shifts focus to Modthryth's husband, King Offa (of the continental Angles), who changed her ways. It may be an oblique compliment to a later, Anglo-Saxon Offa, who was king of Mercia in the eighth century. Mercian genealogies traced their kings' lineage back to the continental Offa.
6. Either her father before her marriage or Offa afterward.
7. I.e., Offa.
8. I.e., Hygelac. Ongentheow was king of the Swedish tribe, with whom the Geats had a long-running feud. The poem circles back on a number of occasions to their battles, and

inside his bawn. Beowulf's return
was reported to Hygelac as soon as possible,
news that the captain was now in the enclosure,
his battle-brother back from the fray
alive and well, walking to the hall.
Room was quickly made, on the king's orders,
and the troops filed across the cleared floor.
  After Hygelac had offered greetings
to his loyal thane in a lofty speech,
he and his kinsman, that hale survivor,
sat face to face. Haereth's daughter
moved about with the mead-jug in her hand,
taking care of the company, filling the cups
that warriors held out. Then Hygelac began
to put courteous questions to his old comrade
in the high hall. He hankered to know
every tale the Sea-Geats had to tell:
"How did you fare on your foreign voyage,
dear Beowulf, when you abruptly decided
to sail away across the salt water
and fight at Heorot? Did you help Hrothgar
much in the end? Could you ease the prince
of his well-known troubles? Your undertaking
cast my spirits down, I dreaded the outcome
of your expedition and pleaded with you
long and hard to leave the killer be,[9]
let the South-Danes settle their own
blood-feud with Grendel. So God be thanked
I am granted this sight of you, safe and sound."
  Beowulf, son of Ecgtheow, spoke:
"What happened, Lord Hygelac, is hardly a secret
any more among men in this world—
myself and Grendel coming to grips
on the very spot where he visited destruction
on the Victory-Shieldings and violated
life and limb, losses I avenged
so no earthly offspring of Grendel's
need ever boast of that bout before dawn,
no matter how long the last of his evil
family survives.
                    When I first landed
I hastened to the ring-hall and saluted Hrothgar.
Once he discovered why I had come,

one episode reveals that it was Eofer, one of Hygelac's warriors, who actually killed Ongentheow.

9. Note the discrepancy between what Hygelac recalls here and what Beowulf tells Hrothgar at lines 415–18.

the son of Halfdane sent me immediately
to sit with his own sons on the bench.
It was a happy gathering. In my whole life
I have never seen mead enjoyed more
in any hall on earth. Sometimes the queen
herself appeared, peace-pledge between nations,
to hearten the young ones and hand out
a torque to a warrior, then take her place.
Sometimes Hrothgar's daughter distributed
ale to older ranks, in order on the benches:
I heard the company call her Freawaru
as she made her rounds, presenting men
with the gem-studded bowl, young bride-to-be
to the gracious Ingeld,[1] in her gold-trimmed attire.
The friend of the Shieldings favors her betrothal:
the guardian of the kingdom sees good in it
and hopes this woman will heal old wounds
and grievous feuds.
But generally the spear
is prompt to retaliate when a prince is killed,
no matter how admirable the bride may be.

"Think how the Heatho-Bards are bound to feel,
their lord, Ingeld, and his loyal thanes,
when he walks in with that woman to the feast:
Danes are at the table, being entertained,
honored guests in glittering regalia,
burnished ring-mail that was their hosts' birthright,
looted when the Heatho-Bards could no longer wield
their weapons in the shield-clash, when they went down
with their beloved comrades and forfeited their lives.
Then an old spearman will speak while they are drinking,
having glimpsed some heirloom that brings alive
memories of the massacre; his mood will darken
and heart-stricken, in the stress of his emotion,
he will begin to test a young man's temper
and stir up trouble, starting like this:
'Now, my friend, don't you recognize
your father's sword, his favorite weapon,
the one he wore when he went out in his war-mask
to face the Danes on that final day?
After Withergeld[2] died and his men were doomed,
the Shieldings quickly claimed the field;

1. King of a rival tribe called the Heatho-Bards; Ingeld's father, Froda, was killed by the Danes. Beowulf's speculative account here amounts to a prophecy that Freawaru's marriage to Ingeld will never resolve the deep-seated animosity between the two tribes. See the note for line 83.
2. A Heatho-Bard leader in the battle against the Danes.

and now here's a son of one or other
of those same killers coming through our hall
overbearing us, mouthing boasts,
and rigged in armor that by right is yours.'
And so he keeps on, recalling and accusing,
working things up with bitter words
until one of the lady's retainers lies
spattered in blood, split open
on his father's account.[3] The killer knows
the lie of the land and escapes with his life.
Then on both sides the oath-bound lords
will break the peace, a passionate hate
will build up in Ingeld, and love for his bride
will falter in him as the feud rankles.
I therefore suspect the good faith of the Heatho-Bards,
the truth of their friendship and the trustworthiness
of their alliance with the Danes.
But now, my lord,
I shall carry on with my account of Grendel,
the whole story of everything that happened
in the hand-to-hand fight.
After heaven's gem
had gone mildly to earth, that maddened spirit,
the terror of those twilights, came to attack us
where we stood guard, still safe inside the hall.
There deadly violence came down on Hondscio
and he fell as fate ordained, the first to perish,
rigged out for the combat. A comrade from our ranks
had come to grief in Grendel's maw:
he ate up the entire body.
There was blood on his teeth, he was bloated and furious,
all roused up, yet still unready
to leave the hall empty-handed;
renowned for his might, he matched himself against me,
wildly reaching. He had this roomy pouch,
a strange accoutrement, intricately strung
and hung at the ready, a rare patchwork
of devilishly fitted dragon-skins.[4]
I had done him no wrong, yet the raging demon
wanted to cram me and many another
into this bag—but it was not to be
once I got to my feet in a blind fury.
It would take too long to tell how I repaid

3. The young Heatho-Bard, goaded by the veteran, kills the Dane who is now wearing his dead father's armor and sword.
4. This is the only mention of Grendel's "pouch" (Old English *glof*). Its significance is unknown, although it has associations with trolls in Germanic mythology.

the terror of the land for every life he took
and so won credit for you, my king,
and for all your people. And although he got away
to enjoy life's sweetness for a while longer,
his right hand stayed behind him in Heorot,
evidence of his miserable overthrow
as he dived into murk on the mere bottom.
"I got lavish rewards from the lord of the Danes
for my part in the battle, beaten gold
and much else, once morning came
and we took our places at the banquet table.
There was singing and excitement: an old reciter,
a carrier of stories, recalled the early days.
At times some hero made the timbered harp
tremble with sweetness, or related true
and tragic happenings; at times the king
gave the proper turn to some fantastic tale,
or a battle-scarred veteran, bowed with age,
would begin to remember the martial deeds
of his youth and prime and be overcome
as the past welled up in his wintry heart.
"We were happy there the whole day long
and enjoyed our time until another night
descended upon us. Then suddenly
the vehement mother avenged her son
and wreaked destruction. Death had robbed her,
Geats had slain Grendel, so his ghastly dam
struck back and with bare-faced defiance
laid a man low. Thus life departed
from the sage Aeschere, an elder wise in counsel.
But afterward, on the morning following,
the Danes could not burn the dead body
nor lay the remains of the man they loved
on his funeral pyre. She had fled with the corpse
and taken refuge beneath torrents on the mountain.
It was a hard blow for Hrothgar to bear,
harder than any he had undergone before.
And so the heartsore king beseeched me
in your royal name to take my chances
underwater, to win glory
and prove my worth. He promised me rewards.
Hence, as is well known, I went to my encounter
with the terror-monger at the bottom of the tarn.
For a while it was hand-to-hand between us,
then blood went curling along the currents
and I beheaded Grendel's mother in the hall
with a mighty sword. I barely managed

to escape with my life; my time had not yet come.
But Halfdane's heir, the shelter of those earls,
again endowed me with gifts in abundance.
"Thus the king acted with due custom.
I was paid and recompensed completely,
given full measure and the freedom to choose
from Hrothgar's treasures by Hrothgar himself.
These, King Hygelac, I am happy to present
to you as gifts. It is still upon your grace
that all favor depends. I have few kinsmen
who are close, my king, except for your kind self."
Then he ordered the boar-framed standard to be brought,
the battle-topping helmet, the mail-shirt gray as hoar-frost,
and the precious war-sword; and proceeded with his speech:
"When Hrothgar presented this war-gear to me
he instructed me, my lord, to give you some account
of why it signifies his special favor.
He said it had belonged to his older brother,
King Heorogar, who had long kept it,
but that Heorogar had never bequeathed it
to his son Heoroward, that worthy scion,
loyal as he was.
Enjoy it well."
I heard four horses were handed over next.
Beowulf bestowed four bay steeds
to go with the armor, swift gallopers,
all alike. So ought a kinsman act,
instead of plotting and planning in secret
to bring people to grief, or conspiring to arrange
the death of comrades. The warrior king
was uncle to Beowulf and honored by his nephew:
each was concerned for the other's good.
I heard he presented Hygd with a gorget,
the priceless torque that the prince's daughter,
Wealhtheow, had given him; and three horses,
supple creatures brilliantly saddled.
The bright necklace would be luminous on Hygd's breast.
Thus Beowulf bore himself with valor;
he was formidable in battle yet behaved with honor
and took no advantage; never cut down
a comrade who was drunk, kept his temper
and, warrior that he was, watched and controlled
his God-sent strength and his outstanding
natural powers. He had been poorly regarded
for a long time, was taken by the Geats
for less than he was worth:[5] and their lord too

5. No other mention is made of Beowulf's unpromising youth, and it is inconsistent with his own account of the swimming match with Breca.

had never much esteemed him in the mead-hall.
They firmly believed that he lacked force,
that the prince was a weakling; but presently
every affront to his deserving was reversed.
  The battle-famed king, bulwark of his earls,
ordered a gold-chased heirloom of Hrethel's[6]
to be brought in; it was the best example
of a gem-studded sword in the Geat treasury.
This he laid on Beowulf's lap
and then rewarded him with land as well,
seven thousand hides; and a hall and a throne.
Both owned land by birth in that country,
ancestral grounds; but the greater right
and sway were inherited by the higher born.

[The Dragon Wakes]

A lot was to happen in later days
in the fury of battle. Hygelac fell
and the shelter of Heardred's shield proved useless
against the fierce aggression of the Shylfings:[7]
ruthless swordsmen, seasoned campaigners,
they came against him and his conquering nation,
and with cruel force cut him down
so that afterwards
                    the wide kingdom
reverted to Beowulf. He ruled it well
for fifty winters, grew old and wise
as warden of the land
                    until one began
to dominate the dark, a dragon on the prowl
from the steep vaults of a stone-roofed barrow
where he guarded a hoard; there was a hidden passage,
unknown to men, but someone managed
to enter by it and interfere
with the heathen trove. He had handled and removed
a gem-studded goblet; it gained him nothing,
though with a thief's wiles he had outwitted
the sleeping dragon. That drove him into rage,
as the people of that country would soon discover.
  The intruder who broached the dragon's treasure

6. Hygelac's father; Beowulf's grandfather.
7. After Hygelac was killed in the raid on Frisia, his son Heardred became king of the Geats. The Swedish (or Shylfing) king Onela later invades and kills Heardred, after which Beowulf becomes king. Note the abrupt transitions in events (Beowulf becomes king) and time (fifty years pass). For a summary of the Swedish-Geat wars, see pp. 94–95, below.

and moved him to wrath had never meant to.[8]
It was desperation on the part of a slave
fleeing the heavy hand of some master,
guilt-ridden and on the run,
going to ground. But he soon began
to shake with terror; . . . . . . in shock
the wretch . . . .
. . . . panicked and ran
away with the precious . . . . . .
metalwork. There were many other
heirlooms heaped inside the earth-house,
because long ago, with deliberate care,
some forgotten person had deposited the whole
rich inheritance of a highborn race
in this ancient cache. Death had come
and taken them all in times gone by
and the only one left to tell their tale,
the last of their line, could look forward to nothing
but the same fate for himself: he foresaw that his joy
in the treasure would be brief.
A newly constructed
barrow stood waiting, on a wide headland
close to the waves, its entryway secured.
Into it the keeper of the hoard had carried
all the goods and golden ware
worth preserving. His words were few:
"Now, earth, hold what earls once held
and heroes can no more; it was mined from you first
by honorable men. My own people
have been ruined in war; one by one
they went down to death, looked their last
on sweet life in the hall. I am left with nobody
to bear a sword or to burnish plated goblets,
put a sheen on the cup. The companies have departed.
The hard helmet, hasped with gold,
will be stripped of its hoops; and the helmet-shiner
who should polish the metal of the war-mask sleeps;
the coat of mail that came through all fights,
through shield-collapse and cut of sword,
decays with the warrior. Nor may webbed mail
range far and wide on the warlord's back
beside his mustered troops. No trembling harp,
no tuned timber, no tumbling hawk
swerving through the hall, no swift horse

8. The manuscript folio for this passage shows extensive damage, perhaps from rainwater, which leaves some words completely illegible, while others have been reconstructed by editorial conjecture.

pawing the courtyard. Pillage and slaughter
have emptied the earth of entire peoples."
And so he mourned as he moved about the world,
deserted and alone, lamenting his unhappiness
day and night, until death's flood
brimmed up in his heart.
Then an old harrower of the dark
happened to find the hoard open,
the burning one who hunts out barrows,
the slick-skinned dragon, threatening the night sky
with streamers of fire. People on the farms
are in dread of him. He is driven to hunt out
hoards under ground, to guard heathen gold
through age-long vigils, though to little avail.
For three centuries, this scourge of the people
had stood guard on that stoutly protected
underground treasury, until the intruder
unleashed its fury; he hurried to his lord
with the gold-plated cup and made his plea
to be reinstated. Then the vault was rifled,
the ring-hoard robbed, and the wretched man
had his request granted. His master gazed
on that find from the past for the first time.
When the dragon awoke, trouble flared again.
He rippled down the rock, writhing with anger
when he saw the footprints of the prowler who had stolen
too close to his dreaming head.
So may a man not marked by fate
easily escape exile and woe
by the grace of God.
The hoard-guardian
scorched the ground as he scoured and hunted
for the trespasser who had troubled his sleep.
Hot and savage, he kept circling and circling
the outside of the mound. No man appeared
in that desert waste, but he worked himself up
by imagining battle; then back in he'd go
in search of the cup, only to discover
signs that someone had stumbled upon
the golden treasures. So the guardian of the mound,
the hoard-watcher, waited for the gloaming
with fierce impatience; his pent-up fury
at the loss of the vessel made him long to hit back
and lash out in flames. Then, to his delight,
the day waned and he could wait no longer
behind the wall, but hurtled forth
in a fiery blaze. The first to suffer

were the people on the land, but before long
it was their treasure-giver who would come to grief.
The dragon began to belch out flames
and burn bright homesteads; there was a hot glow
that scared everyone, for the vile sky-winger
would leave nothing alive in his wake.
Everywhere the havoc he wrought was in evidence.
Far and near, the Geat nation
bore the brunt of his brutal assaults
and virulent hate. Then back to the hoard
he would dart before daybreak, to hide in his den.
He had swinged the land, swathed it in flame,
in fire and burning, and now he felt secure
in the vaults of his barrow; but his trust was unavailing.
Then Beowulf was given bad news,
the hard truth: his own home,
the best of buildings, had been burned to a cinder,
the throne-room of the Geats. It threw the hero
into deep anguish and darkened his mood:
the wise man thought he must have thwarted
ancient ordinance of the eternal Lord,
broken His commandment. His mind was in turmoil,
unaccustomed anxiety and gloom
confused his brain; the fire-dragon
had razed the coastal region and reduced
forts and earthworks to dust and ashes,
so the war-king planned and plotted his revenge.
The warriors' protector, prince of the hall-troop,
ordered a marvelous all-iron shield
from his smithy works. He well knew
that linden boards would let him down
and timber burn. After many trials,
he was destined to face the end of his days,
in this mortal world, as was the dragon,
for all his long leasehold on the treasure.
Yet the prince of the rings was too proud
to line up with a large army
against the sky-plague. He had scant regard
for the dragon as a threat, no dread at all
of its courage or strength, for he had kept going
often in the past, through perils and ordeals
of every sort, after he had purged
Hrothgar's hall, triumphed in Heorot
and beaten Grendel. He outgrappled the monster
and his evil kin.
One of his cruelest
hand-to-hand encounters had happened

when Hygelac, king of the Geats, was killed
in Friesland: the people's friend and lord,
Hrethel's son, slaked a swordblade's
thirst for blood. But Beowulf's prodigious
gifts as a swimmer guaranteed his safety:
he arrived at the shore, shouldering thirty
battle-dresses, the booty he had won.
There was little for the Hetware[9] to be happy about
as they shielded their faces and fighting on the ground
began in earnest. With Beowulf against them,
few could hope to return home.
Across the wide sea, desolate and alone,
the son of Ecgtheow swam back to his people.
There Hygd offered him throne and authority
as lord of the ring-hoard: with Hygelac dead,
she had no belief in her son's ability
to defend their homeland against foreign invaders.
Yet there was no way the weakened nation
could get Beowulf to give in and agree
to be elevated over Heardred as his lord
or to undertake the office of kingship.
But he did provide support for the prince,
honored and minded him until he matured
as the ruler of Geatland.
Then over sea-roads
exiles arrived, sons of Ohthere.[1]
They had rebelled against the best of all
the sea-kings in Sweden, the one who held sway
in the Shylfing nation, their renowned prince,
lord of the mead-hall. That marked the end
for Hygelac's son: his hospitality
was mortally rewarded with wounds from a sword.
Heardred lay slaughtered and Onela returned
to the land of Sweden, leaving Beowulf
to ascend the throne, to sit in majesty
and rule over the Geats. He was a good king.
In days to come, he contrived to avenge
the fall of his prince; he befriended Eadgils
when Eadgils was friendless, aiding his cause
with weapons and warriors over the wide sea,
sending him men. The feud was settled
on a comfortless campaign when he killed Onela.
And so the son of Ecgtheow had survived

9. A tribe within the larger kingdom of the Franks.
1. After Ohthere's death his brother Onela became king of the Swedes. Ohthere's sons Eadgils and Eanmund went into exile and found refuge with the Geats. See the summary on pp. 94–95, below.

every extreme, excelling himself
in daring and in danger, until the day arrived
when he had to come face to face with the dragon.
The lord of the Geats took eleven comrades
and went in a rage to reconnoiter.
By then he had discovered the cause of the affliction
being visited on the people. The precious cup
had come to him from the hand of the finder,
the one who had started all this strife
and was now added as a thirteenth to their number.
They press-ganged and compelled this poor creature
to be their guide. Against his will
he led them to the earth-vault he alone knew,
an underground barrow near the sea-billows
and heaving waves, heaped inside
with exquisite metalwork. The one who stood guard
was dangerous and watchful, warden of the trove
buried under earth: no easy bargain
would be made in that place by any man.
  The veteran king sat down on the cliff-top.
He wished good luck to the Geats who had shared
his hearth and his gold. He was sad at heart,
unsettled yet ready, sensing his death.
His fate hovered near, unknowable but certain:
it would soon claim his coffered soul,
part life from limb. Before long
the prince's spirit would spin free from his body.
  Beowulf, son of Ecgtheow, spoke:
"Many a skirmish I survived when I was young
and many times of war: I remember them well.
At seven, I was fostered out by my father,
left in the charge of my people's lord.
King Hrethel kept me and took care of me,
was openhanded, behaved like a kinsman.
While I was his ward, he treated me no worse
as a wean[2] about the place than one of his own boys,
Herebeald and Haethcyn, or my own Hygelac.
For the eldest, Herebeald, an unexpected
deathbed was laid out, through a brother's doing,
when Haethcyn bent his horn-tipped bow
and loosed the arrow that destroyed his life.
He shot wide and buried a shaft
in the flesh and blood of his own brother.
That offense was beyond redress, a wrongfooting
of the heart's affections; for who could avenge

2. A young child [*Translator's note*].

the prince's life or pay his death-price?[3]
It was like the misery endured by an old man
who has lived to see his son's body
swing on the gallows. He begins to keen
and weep for his boy, watching the raven
gloat where he hangs: he can be of no help.
The wisdom of age is worthless to him.
Morning after morning, he wakes to remember
that his child is gone; he has no interest
in living on until another heir
is born in the hall, now that his first-born
has entered death's dominion forever.
He gazes sorrowfully at his son's dwelling,
the banquet hall bereft of all delight,
the windswept hearthstone; the horsemen are sleeping,
the warriors under ground; what was is no more.
No tunes from the harp, no cheer raised in the yard.
Alone with his longing, he lies down on his bed
and sings a lament; everything seems too large,
the steadings and the fields.
Such was the feeling
of loss endured by the lord of the Geats
after Herebeald's death. He was helplessly placed
to set to rights the wrong committed,
could not punish the killer in accordance with the law
of the blood-feud, although he felt no love for him.
Heartsore, wearied, he turned away
from life's joys, chose God's light
and departed, leaving buildings and lands
to his sons, as a man of substance will.
"Then over the wide sea Swedes and Geats
battled and feuded and fought without quarter.
Hostilities broke out when Hrethel died.[4]
Ongentheow's sons were unrelenting,
refusing to make peace, campaigning violently
from coast to coast, constantly setting up
terrible ambushes around Hreosnahill.
My own kith and kin avenged
these evil events, as everybody knows,
but the price was high: one of them paid
with his life. Haethcyn, lord of the Geats,
met his fate there and fell in the battle.
Then, as I have heard, Hygelac's sword

3. Even an accidental homicide demanded vengeance or compensation, but neither option is open to King Hrethel because two sons were involved. Unable to act, he succumbs to his grief.
4. See pp. 94–95, Phases 1 and 2.

was raised in the morning against Ongentheow,
his brother's killer. When Eofor cleft
the old Swede's helmet, halved it open,
he fell, death-pale: his feud-calloused hand
could not stave off the fatal stroke.
"The treasures that Hygelac lavished on me
I paid for when I fought, as fortune allowed me,
with my glittering sword. He gave me land
and the security land brings, so he had no call
to go looking for some lesser champion,
some mercenary from among the Gifthas
or the Spear-Danes or the men of Sweden.
I marched ahead of him, always there
at the front of the line; and I shall fight like that
for as long as I live, as long as this sword
shall last, which has stood me in good stead
late and soon, ever since I killed
Dayraven the Frank in front of the two armies.
He brought back no looted breastplate
to the Frisian king but fell in battle,
their standard-bearer, highborn and brave.
No sword blade sent him to his death:
my bare hands stilled his heartbeats
and wrecked the bone-house. Now blade and hand,
sword and sword-stroke, will assay the hoard."

[Beowulf Attacks the Dragon]

Beowulf spoke, made a formal boast
for the last time: "I risked my life
often when I was young. Now I am old,
but as king of the people I shall pursue this fight
for the glory of winning, if the evil one will only
abandon his earth-fort and face me in the open."
Then he addressed each dear companion
one final time, those fighters in their helmets,
resolute and highborn: "I would rather not
use a weapon if I knew another way
to grapple with the dragon and make good my boast
as I did against Grendel in days gone by.
But I shall be meeting molten venom
in the fire he breathes, so I go forth
in mail-shirt and shield. I won't shift a foot
when I meet the cave-guard: what occurs on the wall
between the two of us will turn out as fate,
overseer of men, decides. I am resolved.

I scorn further words against this sky-borne foe.
"Men-at-arms, remain here on the barrow,
safe in your armor, to see which one of us
is better in the end at bearing wounds
in a deadly fray. This fight is not yours,
nor is it up to any man except me
to measure his strength against the monster
or to prove his worth. I shall win the gold
by my courage, or else mortal combat,
doom of battle, will bear your lord away."
Then he drew himself up beside his shield.
The fabled warrior in his war-shirt and helmet
trusted in his own strength entirely
and went under the crag. No coward path.
Hard by the rock face that hale veteran,
a good man who had gone repeatedly
into combat and danger and come through,
saw a stone arch and a gushing stream
that burst from the barrow, blazing and wafting
a deadly heat. It would be hard to survive
unscathed near the hoard, to hold firm
against the dragon in those flaming depths.
Then he gave a shout. The lord of the Geats
unburdened his breast and broke out
in a storm of anger. Under gray stone
his voice challenged and resounded clearly.
Hate was ignited. The hoard-guard recognized
a human voice, the time was over
for peace and parleying. Pouring forth
in a hot battle-fume, the breath of the monster
burst from the rock. There was a rumble under ground.
Down there in the barrow, Beowulf the warrior
lifted his shield: the outlandish thing
writhed and convulsed and viciously
turned on the king, whose keen-edged sword,
an heirloom inherited by ancient right,
was already in his hand. Roused to a fury,
each antagonist struck terror in the other.
Unyielding, the lord of his people loomed
by his tall shield, sure of his ground,
while the serpent looped and unleashed itself.
Swaddled in flames, it came gliding and flexing
and racing toward its fate. Yet his shield defended
the renowned leader's life and limb
for a shorter time than he meant it to:
that final day was the first time
when Beowulf fought and fate denied him

glory in battle. So the king of the Geats
raised his hand and struck hard
at the enameled scales, but scarcely cut through:
the blade flashed and slashed yet the blow
was far less powerful than the hard-pressed king
had need of at that moment. The mound-keeper
went into a spasm and spouted deadly flames:
when he felt the stroke, battle-fire
billowed and spewed. Beowulf was foiled
of a glorious victory. The glittering sword,
infallible before that day,
failed when he unsheathed it, as it never should have.
For the son of Ecgtheow, it was no easy thing
to have to give ground like that and go
unwillingly to inhabit another home
in a place beyond; so every man must yield
the leasehold of his days.
Before long
the fierce contenders clashed again.
The hoard-guard took heart, inhaled and swelled up
and got a new wind; he who had once ruled
was furled in fire and had to face the worst.
No help or backing was to be had then
from his highborn comrades; that hand-picked troop
broke ranks and ran for their lives
to the safety of the wood. But within one heart
sorrow welled up: in a man of worth
the claims of kinship cannot be denied.
His name was Wiglaf, a son of Weohstan's,
a well-regarded Shylfing warrior
related to Aelfhere.[5] When he saw his lord
tormented by the heat of his scalding helmet,
he remembered the bountiful gifts bestowed on him,
how well he lived among the Waegmundings,
the freehold he inherited from his father[6] before him.
He could not hold back: one hand brandished
the yellow-timbered shield, the other drew his sword—
an ancient blade that was said to have belonged
to Eanmund, the son of Ohthere, the one
Weohstan had slain when he was an exile without friends.
He carried the arms to the victim's kinfolk,
the burnished helmet, the webbed chain-mail

5. Wiglaf is said to be a Swede (Shylfing, line 2603) and a Waegmunding (line 2607), which is also Beowulf's family among the Geats. There is no problem with this dual identity if, for example, the family shifted allegiance at some point or if a marriage united families from two different tribes. Nothing else is known of Aelfhere.

6. I.e., Weohstan.

and that relic of the giants. But Onela returned
the weapons to him, rewarded Weohstan
with Eanmund's war-gear. He ignored the blood-feud,
the fact that Eanmund was his brother's son.[7]
Weohstan kept that war-gear for a lifetime,
the sword and the mail-shirt, until it was the son's turn
to follow his father and perform his part.
Then, in old age, at the end of his days
among the Weather-Geats, he bequeathed to Wiglaf
innumerable weapons.
And now the youth
was to enter the line of battle with his lord,
his first time to be tested as a fighter.
His spirit did not break and the ancestral blade
would keep its edge, as the dragon discovered
as soon as they came together in the combat.
Sad at heart, addressing his companions,
Wiglaf spoke wise and fluent words:
"I remember that time when mead was flowing,
how we pledged loyalty to our lord in the hall,
promised our ring-giver we would be worth our price,
make good the gift of the war-gear,
those swords and helmets, as and when
his need required it. He picked us out
from the army deliberately, honored us and judged us
fit for this action, made me these lavish gifts—
and all because he considered us the best
of his arms-bearing thanes. And now, although
he wanted this challenge to be one he'd face
by himself alone—the shepherd of our land,
a man unequaled in the quest for glory
and a name for daring—now the day has come
when this lord we serve needs sound men
to give him their support. Let us go to him,
help our leader through the hot flame
and dread of the fire. As God is my witness,
I would rather my body were robed in the same
burning blaze as my gold-giver's body
than go back home bearing arms.
That is unthinkable, unless we have first
slain the foe and defended the life
of the prince of the Weather-Geats. I well know

7. Because Weohstan killed King Onela's nephew Eanmund, he might have expected retribution from a less dysfunctional family. But the Swedish royal family was already embroiled in a deadly power struggle, so to say that Onela "ignored the blood-feud" is deeply ironic: he rewarded Weohstan for removing a rival claimant to the throne. See pp. 94–95, Phase 3.

the things he has done for us deserve better.
Should he alone be left exposed
to fall in battle? We must bond together,
shield and helmet, mail-shirt and sword."
Then he waded the dangerous reek[8] and went
under arms to his lord, saying only:
"Go on, dear Beowulf, do everything
you said you would when you were still young
and vowed you would never let your name and fame
be dimmed while you lived. Your deeds are famous,
so stay resolute, my lord, defend your life now
with the whole of your strength. I shall stand by you."
  After those words, a wildness rose
in the dragon again and drove it to attack,
heaving up fire, hunting for enemies,
the humans it loathed. Flames lapped the shield,
charred it to the boss, and the body armor
on the young warrior was useless to him.
But Wiglaf did well under the wide rim
Beowulf shared with him once his own had shattered
in sparks and ashes.
                Inspired again
by the thought of glory, the war-king threw
his whole strength behind a sword stroke
and connected with the skull. And Naegling snapped.
Beowulf's ancient iron-gray sword
let him down in the fight. It was never his fortune
to be helped in combat by the cutting edge
of weapons made of iron. When he wielded a sword,
no matter how blooded and hard-edged the blade,
his hand was too strong, the stroke he dealt
(I have heard) would ruin it. He could reap no advantage.
  Then the bane of that people, the fire-breathing dragon,
was mad to attack for a third time.
When a chance came, he caught the hero
in a rush of flame and clamped sharp fangs
into his neck. Beowulf's body
ran wet with his life-blood: it came welling out.
  Next thing, they say, the noble son of Weohstan
saw the king in danger at his side
and displayed his inborn bravery and strength.
He left the head alone, but his fighting hand
was burned when he came to his kinsman's aid.
He lunged at the enemy lower down
so that his decorated sword sank into its belly

8. The Old English compound *wæl-rec* literally means "slaughter-smoke." Heaney preserves the element "reek" even though today the primary meaning of the noun is "stench."

and the flames grew weaker.
Once again the king
gathered his strength and drew a stabbing knife
he carried on his belt, sharpened for battle.
He stuck it deep in the dragon's flank.
Beowulf dealt it a deadly wound.
They had killed the enemy, courage quelled his life;
that pair of kinsmen, partners in nobility,
had destroyed the foe. So every man should act,
be at hand when needed; but now, for the king,
this would be the last of his many labors
and triumphs in the world.
Then the wound
dealt by the ground-burner earlier began
to scald and swell; Beowulf discovered
deadly poison suppurating inside him,
surges of nausea, and so, in his wisdom
the prince realized his state and struggled
toward a seat on the rampart. He steadied his gaze
on those gigantic stones, saw how the earthwork
was braced with arches built over columns.
And now that thane unequaled for goodness
with his own hands washed his lord's wounds,
swabbed the weary prince with water,
bathed him clean, unbuckled his helmet.
Beowulf spoke: in spite of his wounds,
mortal wounds, he still spoke
for he well knew his days in the world
had been lived out to the end—his allotted time
was drawing to a close, death was very near.
"Now is the time when I would have wanted
to bestow this armor on my own son,
had it been my fortune to have fathered an heir
and live on in his flesh. For fifty years
I ruled this nation. No king
of any neighboring clan would dare
face me with troops, none had the power
to intimidate me. I took what came,
cared for and stood by things in my keeping,
never fomented quarrels, never
swore to a lie. All this consoles me,
doomed as I am and sickening for death;
because of my right ways, the Ruler of mankind
need never blame me when the breath leaves my body
for murder of kinsmen. Go now quickly,
dearest Wiglaf, under the gray stone
where the dragon is laid out, lost to his treasure;

hurry to feast your eyes on the hoard.
Away you go: I want to examine
that ancient gold, gaze my fill
on those garnered jewels; my going will be easier
for having seen the treasure, a less troubled letting-go
of the life and lordship I have long maintained."
  And so, I have heard, the son of Weohstan
quickly obeyed the command of his languishing
war-weary lord; he went in his chain-mail
under the rock-piled roof of the barrow,
exulting in his triumph, and saw beyond the seat
a treasure-trove of astonishing richness,
wall-hangings that were a wonder to behold,
glittering gold spread across the ground,
the old dawn-scorching serpent's den
packed with goblets and vessels from the past,
tarnished and corroding. Rusty helmets
all eaten away. Armbands everywhere,
artfully wrought. How easily treasure
buried in the ground, gold hidden
however skillfully, can escape from any man!
  And he saw too a standard, entirely of gold,
hanging high over the hoard,
a masterpiece of filigree; it glowed with light
so he could make out the ground at his feet
and inspect the valuables. Of the dragon there was no
remaining sign: the sword had dispatched him.
Then, the story goes, a certain man
plundered the hoard in that immemorial howe,[9]
filled his arms with flagons and plates,
anything he wanted; and took the standard also,
most brilliant of banners.
                    Already the blade
of the old king's sharp killing-sword
had done its worst: the one who had for long
minded the hoard, hovering over gold,
unleashing fire, surging forth
midnight after midnight, had been mown down.
  Wiglaf went quickly, keen to get back,
excited by the treasure. Anxiety weighed
on his brave heart—he was hoping he would find
the leader of the Geats alive where he had left him
helpless, earlier, on the open ground.
  So he came to the place, carrying the treasure
and found his lord bleeding profusely,

9. A hollow place in the earth, a depression.

his life at an end; again he began
to swab his body. The beginnings of an utterance
broke out from the king's breast-cage.
The old lord gazed sadly at the gold.
"To the everlasting Lord of all,
to the King of Glory, I give thanks
that I behold this treasure here in front of me,
that I have been allowed to leave my people
so well endowed on the day I die.
Now that I have bartered my last breath
to own this fortune, it is up to you
to look after their needs. I can hold out no longer.
Order my troop to construct a barrow
on a headland on the coast, after my pyre has cooled.
It will loom on the horizon at Hronesness[1]
and be a reminder among my people—
so that in coming times crews under sail
will call it Beowulf's Barrow, as they steer
ships across the wide and shrouded waters."
Then the king in his great-heartedness unclasped
the collar of gold from his neck and gave it
to the young thane, telling him to use
it and the war-shirt and gilded helmet well.
"You are the last of us, the only one left
of the Waegmundings. Fate swept us away,
sent my whole brave highborn clan
to their final doom. Now I must follow them."
That was the warrior's last word.
He had no more to confide. The furious heat
of the pyre would assail him. His soul fled from his breast
to its destined place among the steadfast ones.

[Beowulf's Funeral]

It was hard then on the young hero,
having to watch the one he held so dear
there on the ground, going through
his death agony. The dragon from underearth,
his nightmarish destroyer, lay destroyed as well,
utterly without life. No longer would his snakefolds
ply themselves to safeguard hidden gold.
Hard-edged blades, hammered out
and keenly filed, had finished him

1. Literally, "whale's headland."

so that the sky-roamer lay there rigid,
brought low beside the treasure-lodge.
Never again would he glitter and glide
and show himself off in midnight air,
exulting in his riches: he fell to earth
through the battle-strength in Beowulf's arm.
There were few, indeed, as far as I have heard,
big and brave as they may have been,
few who would have held out if they had had to face
the outpourings of that poison-breather
or gone foraging on the ring-hall floor
and found the deep barrow-dweller
on guard and awake.
The treasure had been won,
bought and paid for by Beowulf's death.
Both had reached the end of the road
through the life they had been lent.
Before long
the battle-dodgers abandoned the wood,
the ones who had let down their lord earlier,
the tail-turners, ten of them together.
When he needed them most, they had made off.
Now they were ashamed and came behind shields,
in their battle outfits, to where the old man lay.
They watched Wiglaf, sitting worn out,
a comrade shoulder to shoulder with his lord,
trying in vain to bring him round with water.
Much as he wanted to, there was no way
he could preserve his lord's life on earth
or alter in the least the Almighty's will.
What God judged right would rule what happened
to every man, as it does to this day.
Then a stern rebuke was bound to come
from the young warrior to the ones who had been cowards.
Wiglaf, son of Weohstan, spoke
disdainfully and in disappointment:
"Anyone ready to admit the truth
will surely realize that the lord of men
who showered you with gifts and gave you the armor
you are standing in—when he would distribute
helmets and mail-shirts to men on the mead-benches,
a prince treating his thanes in hall
to the best he could find, far or near—
was throwing weapons uselessly away.
It would be a sad waste when the war broke out.
Beowulf had little cause to brag
about his armed guard; yet God who ordains

who wins or loses allowed him to strike
with his own blade when bravery was needed.
There was little I could do to protect his life
in the heat of the fray, but I found new strength
welling up when I went to help him.
Then my sword connected and the deadly assaults
of our foe grew weaker, the fire coursed
less strongly from his head. But when the worst happened
too few rallied around the prince.

"So it is good-bye now to all you know and love
on your home ground, the open-handedness,
the giving of war-swords. Every one of you
with freeholds of land, our whole nation,
will be dispossessed, once princes from beyond
get tidings of how you turned and fled
and disgraced yourselves. A warrior will sooner
die than live a life of shame."

Then he ordered the outcome of the fight to be reported
to those camped on the ridge, that crowd of retainers
who had sat all morning, sad at heart,
shield-bearers wondering about
the man they loved: would this day be his last
or would he return? He told the truth
and did not balk, the rider who bore
news to the cliff-top. He addressed them all:
"Now the people's pride and love,
the lord of the Geats, is laid on his deathbed,
brought down by the dragon's attack.
Beside him lies the bane of his life,
dead from knife-wounds. There was no way
Beowulf could manage to get the better
of the monster with his sword. Wiglaf sits
at Beowulf's side, the son of Weohstan,
the living warrior watching by the dead,
keeping weary vigil, holding a wake
for the loved and the loathed.

Now war is looming
over our nation, soon it will be known
to Franks and Frisians, far and wide,
that the king is gone. Hostility has been great
among the Franks since Hygelac sailed forth
at the head of a war-fleet into Friesland:
there the Hetware harried and attacked
and overwhelmed him with great odds.
The leader in his war-gear was laid low,
fell among followers: that lord did not favor
his company with spoils. The Merovingian king

has been an enemy to us ever since.[2]
"Nor do I expect peace or pact-keeping
of any sort from the Swedes. Remember:
at Ravenswood Ongentheow
slaughtered Haethcyn, Hrethel's son,
when the Geat people in their arrogance
first attacked the fierce Shylfings.
The return blow was quickly struck
by Ohthere's father.[3] Old and terrible,
he felled the sea-king and saved his own
aged wife, the mother of Onela
and of Ohthere, bereft of her gold rings.
Then he kept hard on the heels of the foe
and drove them, leaderless, lucky to get away
in a desperate rout into Ravenswood.
His army surrounded the weary remnant
where they nursed their wounds; all through the night
he howled threats at those huddled survivors,
promised to axe their bodies open
when dawn broke, dangle them from gallows
to feed the birds. But at first light
when their spirits were lowest, relief arrived.
They heard the sound of Hygelac's horn,
his trumpet calling as he came to find them,
the hero in pursuit, at hand with troops.
"The bloody swathe that Swedes and Geats
cut through each other was everywhere.
No one could miss their murderous feuding.
Then the old man made his move,
pulled back, barred his people in:
Ongentheow withdrew to higher ground.
Hygelac's pride and prowess as a fighter
were known to the earl; he had no confidence
that he could hold out against that horde of seamen,
defend his wife and the ones he loved
from the shock of the attack. He retreated for shelter
behind the earthwall. Then Hygelac swooped
on the Swedes at bay, his banners swarmed
into their refuge, his Geat forces
drove forward to destroy the camp.
There in his gray hairs, Ongentheow
was cornered, ringed around with swords.
And it came to pass that the king's fate

2. The Merovingians were the royal family of the Frankish kingdom.
3. I.e., Ongentheow. The messenger traces back the animosity of the Swedes to the battle of Ravenswood. See pp. 94–95, below.

was in Eofor's hands,[4] and in his alone.
Wulf, son of Wonred, went for him in anger,
split him open so that blood came spurting
from under his hair. The old hero
still did not flinch, but parried fast,
hit back with a harder stroke:
the king turned and took him on.
Then Wonred's son, the brave Wulf,
could land no blow against the aged lord.
Ongentheow divided his helmet
so that he buckled and bowed his bloodied head
and dropped to the ground. But his doom held off.
Though he was cut deep, he recovered again.
"With his brother down, the undaunted Eofor,
Hygelac's thane, hefted his sword
and smashed murderously at the massive helmet
past the lifted shield. And the king collapsed,
the shepherd of people was sheared of life.
Many then hurried to help Wulf,
bandaged and lifted him, now that they were left
masters of the blood-soaked battle-ground.
One warrior stripped the other,
looted Ongentheow's iron mail-coat,
his hard sword-hilt, his helmet too,
and carried the graith[5] to King Hygelac,
he accepted the prize, promised fairly
that reward would come, and kept his word.
For their bravery in action, when they arrived home,
Eofor and Wulf were overloaded
by Hrethel's son, Hygelac the Geat,
with gifts of land and linked rings
that were worth a fortune. They had won glory,
so there was no gainsaying his generosity.
And he gave Eofor his only daughter
to bide at home with him, an honor and a bond.
"So this bad blood between us and the Swedes,
this vicious feud, I am convinced,
is bound to revive; they will cross our borders
and attack in force when they find out
that Beowulf is dead. In days gone by
when our warriors fell and we were undefended,
he kept our coffers and our kingdom safe.
He worked for the people, but as well as that
he behaved like a hero.
We must hurry now

4. Eofor's killing of Ongentheow is related more sparingly in lines 2486–89.
5. Harness or gear. See line 324.

to take a last look at the king
and launch him, lord and lavisher of rings,
on the funeral road. His royal pyre
will melt no small amount of gold:
heaped there in a hoard, it was bought at heavy cost,
and that pile of rings he paid for at the end
with his own life will go up with the flame,
be furled in fire: treasure no follower
will wear in his memory, nor lovely woman
link and attach as a torque around her neck—
but often, repeatedly, in the path of exile
they shall walk bereft, bowed under woe,
now that their leader's laugh is silenced,
high spirits quenched. Many a spear
dawn-cold to the touch will be taken down
and waved on high; the swept harp
won't waken warriors, but the raven winging
darkly over the doomed will have news,
tidings for the eagle of how he hoked[6] and ate,
how the wolf and he made short work of the dead."
Such was the drift of the dire report
that gallant man delivered. He got little wrong
in what he told and predicted.
The whole troop
rose in tears, then took their way
to the uncanny scene under Earnaness.[7]
There, on the sand, where his soul had left him,
they found him at rest, their ring-giver
from days gone by. The great man
had breathed his last. Beowulf the king
had indeed met with a marvelous death.
But what they saw first was far stranger:
the serpent on the ground, gruesome and vile,
lying facing him. The fire-dragon
was scaresomely[8] burned, scorched all colors.
From head to tail, his entire length
was fifty feet. He had shimmered forth
on the night air once, then winged back
down to his den; but death owned him now,
he would never enter his earth-gallery again.
Beside him stood pitchers and piled-up dishes,
silent flagons, precious swords

6. Rooted about [*Translator's note*]. The gathering of the raven, the eagle, and the wolf in anticipation of a battle, where they can expect to scavenge on the dead flesh afterward, is a common motif in Germanic heroic poetry. It suggests that fate is so strong that even wild animals can sense it.
7. Literally "Eagles' headland," the place of the dragon's barrow.
8. Terrifyingly; a Hibernicism (T. P. Dolan, personal communication).

eaten through with rust, ranged as they had been
while they waited their thousand winters under ground.
That huge cache, gold inherited
from an ancient race, was under a spell—
which meant no one was ever permitted
to enter the ring-hall unless God Himself,
mankind's Keeper, True King of Triumphs,
allowed some person pleasing to Him—
and in His eyes worthy—to open the hoard.
What came about brought to nothing
the hopes of the one who had wrongly hidden
riches under the rock-face. First the dragon slew
that man among men, who in turn made fierce amends
and settled the feud.[9] Famous for his deeds
a warrior may be, but it remains a mystery
where his life will end, when he may no longer
dwell in the mead-hall among his own.
So it was with Beowulf, when he faced the cruelty
and cunning of the mound-guard. He himself was ignorant
of how his departure from the world would happen.
The highborn chiefs who had buried the treasure
declared it until doomsday so accursed
that whoever robbed it would be guilty of wrong
and grimly punished for their transgression,
hasped in hell-bonds in heathen shrines.
Yet Beowulf's gaze at the gold treasure
when he first saw it had not been selfish.
Wiglaf, son of Weohstan, spoke:
"Often when one man follows his own will
many are hurt. This happened to us.
Nothing we advised could ever convince
the prince we loved, our land's guardian,
not to vex the custodian of the gold,
let him lie where he was long accustomed,
lurk there under earth until the end of the world.
He held to his high destiny. The hoard is laid bare,
but at a grave cost; it was too cruel a fate
that forced the king to that encounter.
I have been inside and seen everything
amassed in the vault. I managed to enter
although no great welcome awaited me
under the earthwall. I quickly gathered up
a huge pile of the priceless treasures
handpicked from the hoard and carried them here
where the king could see them. He was still himself,

9. The dragon gave Beowulf a mortal wound before Beowulf killed it.

alive, aware, and in spite of his weakness
he had many requests. He wanted me to greet you
and order the building of a barrow that would crown
the site of his pyre, serve as his memorial,
in a commanding position, since of all men
to have lived and thrived and lorded it on earth
his worth and due as a warrior were the greatest.
Now let us again go quickly
and feast our eyes on that amazing fortune
heaped under the wall. I will show the way
and take you close to those coffers packed with rings
and bars of gold. Let a bier be made
and got ready quickly when we come out
and then let us bring the body of our lord,
the man we loved, to where he will lodge
for a long time in the care of the Almighty."
  Then Weohstan's son, stalwart to the end,
had orders given to owners of dwellings,
many people of importance in the land,
to fetch wood from far and wide
for the good man's pyre:
                                        "Now shall flame consume
our leader in battle, the blaze darken
round him who stood his ground in the steel-hail,
when the arrow-storm shot from bowstrings
pelted the shield-wall. The shaft hit home.
Feather-fledged, it finned the barb in flight."
  Next the wise son of Weohstan
called from among the king's thanes
a group of seven: he selected the best
and entered with them, the eighth of their number,
under the God-cursed roof; one raised
a lighted torch and led the way.
No lots were cast for who should loot the hoard
for it was obvious to them that every bit of it
lay unprotected within the vault,
there for the taking. It was no trouble
to hurry to work and haul out
the priceless store. They pitched the dragon
over the cliff-top, let tide's flow
and backwash take the treasure-minder.
Then coiled gold was loaded on a cart
in great abundance, and the gray-haired leader,
the prince on his bier, borne to Hronesness.
  The Geat people built a pyre for Beowulf,
stacked and decked it until it stood foursquare,
hung with helmets, heavy war-shields

and shining armor, just as he had ordered.
Then his warriors laid him in the middle of it,
mourning a lord far-famed and beloved.
On a height they kindled the hugest of all
funeral fires; fumes of woodsmoke
billowed darkly up, the blaze roared
and drowned out their weeping, wind died down
and flames wrought havoc in the hot bone-house,[1]
burning it to the core. They were disconsolate
and wailed aloud for their lord's decease.
A Geat woman too sang out in grief;
with hair bound up, she unburdened herself
of her worst fears, a wild litany
of nightmare and lament: her nation invaded,
enemies on the rampage, bodies in piles,
slavery and abasement. Heaven swallowed the smoke.
Then the Geat people began to construct
a mound on a headland, high and imposing,
a marker that sailors could see from far away,
and in ten days they had done the work.
It was their hero's memorial; what remained from the fire
they housed inside it, behind a wall
as worthy of him as their workmanship could make it.
And they buried torques in the barrow, and jewels
and a trove of such things as trespassing men
had once dared to drag from the hoard.
They let the ground keep that ancestral treasure,
gold under gravel, gone to earth,
as useless to men now as it ever was.
Then twelve warriors rode around the tomb,
chieftains' sons, champions in battle,
all of them distraught, chanting in dirges,
mourning his loss as a man and a king.
They extolled his heroic nature and exploits
and gave thanks for his greatness; which was the proper thing,
for a man should praise a prince whom he holds dear
and cherish his memory when that moment comes
when he has to be convoyed from his bodily home.
So the Geat people, his hearth-companions,
sorrowed for the lord who had been laid low.
They said that of all the kings upon earth
he was the man most gracious and fair-minded,
kindest to his people and keenest to win fame.

1. A kenning for "body."

CONTEXTS

BRUCE MITCHELL AND FRED C. ROBINSON

The *Beowulf* Manuscript†

§1 *Beowulf* is preserved in a single manuscript in the British Library in London. Since the early seventeenth century it has been known as MS Cotton Vitellius A. XV,[1] or, more informally, simply as 'the *Beowulf* manuscript'. Since the vast majority of Old English manuscripts perished during the Anglo-Saxon period and in the centuries immediately following, it is by lucky chance that this one is still extant. There may once have been many copies of the poem, but only Cotton Vitellius A. XV survives. Palaeographers have determined from characteristics of the scribal hands that wrote the text that the manuscript was copied down in the late tenth century or perhaps the first decade of the eleventh.

§2 Originally the poem *Beowulf* seems to have been the last in a series of narratives about wondrous creatures gathered together to make the book that is Cotton Vitellius A. XV. The first text in the manuscript is a fragmentary homily on St. Christopher in Old English prose. The saint is said to have been twelve fathoms tall and is in other respects quite out of the ordinary, and so he qualifies as a wondrous creature. *The Wonders of the East* and a putative *Letter of Alexander to Aristotle*, both also in Old English prose, follow. Like *The Passion of St. Christopher* these are translations of Latin texts which tell of marvellous creatures and places. *Beowulf* follows *Alexander's Letter*, and the last leaf of *Beowulf* is scuffed in a way that suggests that it was for a time the final page in the collection of narratives. But a fragment of another vernacular poem on the apocryphal Old Testament heroine Judith has been added to the collection following *Beowulf*. It is written by the same scribe who wrote the last portion of *Beowulf*, and so these five texts would appear to have been gathered together in the scriptorium where they were copied out. We may say, then, that *Beowulf* is preserved in a book con-

† From *Beowulf: An Edition*, ed. Bruce Mitchell and Fred C. Robinson (London: Blackwell, 1998) 3–6. Reprinted with the permission of the publisher.

1. 'Cotton' is the name of the collector, Sir Robert Bruce Cotton (1571–1631), who owned and named the manuscript. Cotton kept his manuscripts in bookcases, each of which had a bust of a Roman emperor (or other notable) on top of it. The *Beowulf* manuscript was kept on shelf A of the bookcase surmounted by a bust of Emperor Vitellius. It was the fifteenth book (XV) on shelf A. This volume actually comprises two separate and unrelated manuscripts, *Beowulf* and the four texts accompanying it (all written at about the same period) and a completely unrelated twelfth-century manuscript which Cotton had bound together with it. When one examines the volume in the British Library, it is the later manuscript, beginning with an Old English version of the *Soliloquies* of St. Augustine, that one encounters first, the *Beowulf* manuscript beginning only some ninety leaves into the volume.

taining texts about marvellous creatures combined with a narrative about a heroic woman saving her nation in Old Testament times. Taking note of the contents of the manuscript in which *Beowulf* is found provides us with just about the only context we have for judging what the poem may have meant to its original audience—i.e. it was one of a group of stories about men and monsters.[2]

§3 What do we know about the history of this manuscript? Before it came to rest in the British Library, where it is now displayed as a chief treasure of the English nation, the *Beowulf* manuscript belonged to Sir Robert Bruce Cotton (1571–1631), who kept his library in a building ominously named Ashburnam House. Fire swept through the library in 1731, and the *Beowulf* manuscript was badly singed * * *. Before Cotton owned the manuscript, it had passed through the hands of Lawrence Nowell, a sixteenth-century antiquary who signed his name on the first surviving leaf of the St. Christopher homily, dating the signature 1563. Nowell or a contemporary also wrote the word *feared* (i.e. 'terrified' in sixteenth-century English) over the Old English word *egsode* in 1.6 of *Beowulf*, thus showing that this part of the text was being read with understanding at this time. Before the manuscript came into Nowell's possession it had probably lain in a monastic library since monastic libraries are where most of the manuscripts from Anglo-Saxon England reposed between 1066 and the Reformation. We know that during this period someone took an interest in the *Beowulf* manuscript, for two readers have scribbled a few Middle English translations (or 'modernizations') of Old English words in the interlinear spaces of *The Wonders of the East*. We know nothing about the manuscript's history before this time. Some, it is true, have speculated that *Beowulf* ll. 1357–76 was a source for a somewhat similarly phrased description of hell by a tenth-century homilist,[3] but it is hazardous to assume a direct connection between two similar passages when so much has been lost.

§4 We may be sure that Cotton Vitellius A. XV is not an author's holograph but rather a scribe's copy made from a pre-existing exemplar. Wax tablets rather than vellum and ink would have been what an author would probably use to compose a text, but aside from this there are numerous indications in the manuscript that it is a copy of a copy. Two different scribes wrote out the texts. Scribe A copied *St. Christopher, The Wonders of the East, Alexander's Letter*, and ll. 1–1939 (through the word *scyran*) of *Beowulf*. The remainder of *Beowulf* and all of *Judith* are written in the hand of scribe B.* * * In

2. Andy Orchard, *Pride and Prodigies: Studies in the Monsters of the Beowulf-Manuscript* (Cambridge, 1995) provides a discussion of the monster-theme of Cotton Vitellius A. XV together with text and translations of *The Wonders of the East* and *The Letter of Alexander to Aristotle*.
3. Richard Morris, ed., *The Blickling Homilies*, Early English Text Society O.S. 58, 63, 73 (London, 1880), pp. 208–10.

copying texts scribes were free to follow the spelling of their exemplar or to adapt the spelling to their own habitual practice as they liked. The two scribes of *Beowulf* show different spelling habits in some respects * * *, but they are not very different. It is important to note that their spelling habits change from text to text. Thus scribe B's habit of writing *io* for *eo* is characteristic only of his copying of *Beowulf*; in *Judith* he writes *eo*. This suggests that the *io* spellings were characteristic of his exemplar of *Beowulf* but not of his exemplar of *Judith*. Similarly scribes A and B both frequently use the abbreviation *þōn* for *þonne*, but this abbreviation never occurs in the first two texts copied by A and it occurs only once each in *Alexander's Letter* and *Judith*. From this we can surmise with some confidence that the exemplar of *Beowulf* from which the scribes copied made frequent use of *þōn*. Sometimes metre tells us that the two scribes' way of writing the text of *Beowulf* could not have been the way the original text read. The contracted forms throughout the poem often suggest that our manuscript is a late copy of an earlier text * * * and the scribes' occasional tendency to substitute synonyms for original words which must be restored to provide alliteration (e.g. *hand gripe* 965, *hild plegan* 1073, *side reced* 1981) is a typical copyist's error, as are the instances where the scribes simply confuse similarly formed letters (e.g. *hetlic* 780, *mid* 976, *að* 1107, *speop* 2854, *wræce* 3060).

§ 5 Correcting scribal errors and trying to recover the reading of the poet's original text is the task of every editor of an Old English text, but the editor of *Beowulf* faces yet another challenge. In consequence of the fire that swept through Sir Robert Bruce Cotton's library in 1731, the pages of Cotton Vitellius A. XV containing *Beowulf* were badly scorched, as we have said in §3 above. Some letters of the text were burned away, and over succeeding years more crumbling of the charred edges of the pages and further loss have taken place. Lines 1–19 and 53–73 were copied down and published by Humfrey Wanley in 1705 before the fire took place,[4] and so we have these lines intact (except for *le* of *aldorlease* in l. 15, which was apparently missing before the fire). Another valuable witness to original manuscript reading now lost is the Thorkelin transcripts. Grímur Jónsson Thorkelin (1752–1829), an Icelander living in Copenhagen, began a research trip to England in 1786, and while there he hired a professional copyist to make a complete transcription of the poem *Beowulf* for him. Later Thorkelin himself made a second copy of the manuscript text of the poem. These two transcriptions survive and are of primary importance because at the time Thorkelin's copies

4. *Antiquæ Literaturæ Septentrionalis Liber Alter . . . seu Humphredi Wanleii . . . Catalogus Historico-Criticus* in George Hickes, *Linguarum Vett. Septentrionalium Thesaurus*, vol. 3 (Oxford, 1705), pp. 218–19.

were made the charred manuscript pages had not deteriorated as far as they have today. In 1815 Thorkelin published the first edition of *Beowulf*, using his transcripts as his source for the text. His *editio princeps* is a crude edition with many inaccuracies, but other early scholars (such as N. S. F. Grundtvig, J. M. Kemble, Frederic Madden, and Benjamin Thorpe) made careful collations of Thorkelin's edition with the manuscript, and these often provide further witnesses to the manuscript in an earlier state of preservation.[5] Eventually the progressive deterioration of the manuscript leaves was arrested in August 1845 when Sir Frederic Madden, Keeper of Manuscripts in the British Museum, had the codex rebound and the separate folios inlaid in such a way as to stop the chipping of vellum edges.[6]

* * *

Genesis 4.1–16†

Cain and Abel

4.1 And Adam knew Eve his wife: who conceived and brought forth Cain, saying: I have gotten a man through God.

2 And again she brought forth his brother Abel. And Abel was a shepherd, and Cain a husbandman.

3 And it came to pass after many days, that Cain offered, of the fruits of the earth, gifts to the Lord.

4 Abel also offered of the firstlings of his flock, and of their fat: and the Lord had respect to Abel, and to his offerings.

5 But to Cain and his offerings he had no respect: and Cain was exceeding angry, and his countenance fell.

6 And the Lord said to him: Why art thou angry? and why is thy countenance fallen?

7 If thou do well, shalt thou not receive? but if ill, shall not sin forthwith be present at the door? but the lust thereof shall be under thee, and thou shalt have dominion over it.

8 And Cain said to Abel his brother: Let us go forth abroad. And when they were in the field, Cain rose up against his brother Abel, and slew him.

5. J. R. Hall of the University of Mississippi is currently gathering and evaluating all the early witnesses to the manuscript, and he has kindly made many of his findings available for our use in preparing this edition.
6. Kevin Kiernan, *Beowulf and the Beowulf Manuscript* (New Brunswick, NJ, 1981), p. 69, n.7.

† Given here in the "Douay-Rheims" English translation of the Latin Bible known to the medieval audience of *Beowulf*: *The Holy Bible Translated from the Latin Vulgate* (Baltimore: John Murphy, 1914).

9 And the Lord said to Cain: Where is thy brother Abel? And he
answered, I know not: am I my brother's keeper?
10 And he said to him: What hast thou done? the voice of thy
brother's blood crieth to me from the earth.
11 Now, therefore, cursed shalt thou be upon the earth, which
hath opened her mouth and received the blood of thy brother at thy
hand.
12 When thou shalt till it, it shall not yield to thee its fruit: a
fugitive and a vagabond shalt thou be upon the earth.
13 And Cain said to the Lord: My iniquity is greater than that I
may deserve pardon.
14 Behold thou dost cast me out this day from the face of the
earth, and I shall be hidden from thy face, and I shall be a vagabond
and a fugitive on the earth: every one, therefore, that findeth me,
shall kill me.
15 And the Lord said to him: No, it shall not so be: but whosoever
shall kill Cain, shall be punished sevenfold. And the Lord set a mark
upon Cain, that whosoever found him should not kill him.
16 And Cain went out from the face of the Lord, and dwelt as a
fugitive on the earth, at the east side of Eden.

Hall-Feasts and the Queen†

from an Old English Poem

A king must obtain a queen at a price, with flagons and rings. First of all, both must be generous with gift-giving. War-skills must flourish in a man, and a woman must grow to be beloved among her people, must be cheerful, keep counsel, be generous with horses and treasure; at every banquet, before the troop of warriors, she must first greet the protector of princes, put the first cup right away into the lord's hand, and she must know what advice to give for both of them as masters of the house together.

† "Maxims I," lines 81–92, translated by the Editor of this Norton Critical Edition from *The Exeter Book, The Anglo-Saxon Poetic Records* 3, ed. G. P. Krapp and E. V. K. Dobbie (New York: Columbia UP, 1936) 159–60.

Grettir the Strong and the Trollwoman†

from an Icelandic Saga (c. 1300–1320)

After being declared an outlaw, Grettir steals away and assumes the name "Gest." He offers his help to a woman whose farmstead has been attacked by a trollwoman for the past two years on Christmas Eve.

* * * [T]owards midnight [Grettir] heard a great noise, then a huge trollwoman entered the room. She was holding a trough in one hand and a big knife in the other. She looked around when she was inside and, seeing Gest lying there, made a rush for him. He leapt up to confront her, and they attacked each other ferociously and struggled for a long time in the room. She was stronger but he dodged her cleverly. They smashed everything that was in their way, even the partition which divided the room crossways. She dragged him out through the door and towards the front door, where he made a firm stand against her. She wanted to drag him outside the farmhouse, but could not manage it until they had broken down the entire doorframe and took it with them around their necks. Then she lugged him off down to the river, right up to the chasm. Gest was exhausted, but either had to brace himself or let her hurl him into it. They struggled all night and he felt he had never fought such a powerful beast before. She was pressing him so tightly to her body that he could do nothing with either of his arms except clutch at her waist. When they were on the edge of the chasm he lifted her off her feet and swung her off balance, freeing his right arm. At once he grabbed for the short-sword he was wearing, drew it, swung it at her shoulder and chopped off her right arm. He was released the moment she plunged into the chasm and under the waterfall.

Gest the visitor was left stiff and exhausted and lay on the edge of the cliff for a long time. He went back at daybreak and lay down on the bed, swollen and bruised.

When the farmer's wife came back from the mass she saw the mess in her house, went over to Gest and asked him what had happened there that everything was broken and smashed. He told her about the entire episode, and she found it remarkable and asked him his name. He told her his real name and told her to fetch the priest, saying that he wanted to talk to him. This was done.

When Stein the priest arrived at Sandhaugar he realised at once that it was Grettir Asmundarson who called himself Gest. The priest asked him what he thought might have happened to the men who

† The excerpt from "The Saga of Grettir the Strong" (translation by Bernard Scudder) is reprinted from vol. 2 of *The Complete Sagas of Icelanders* (ed. Viðar Hreinsson et al.), Reykjavík 1997, with the permission of Leifur Eiríksson Publishing.

had vanished, and Grettir said he assumed they had gone into the chasm. The priest said he could not believe his stories without seeing any proof, but Grettir said they would find out for sure later. Then the priest went home. Grettir lay in bed for many days, the farmer's wife treated him very well and Christmas went by.

According to Grettir, the trollwoman plunged into the chasm when she received her wound, but the people of Bardardal claim she turned to stone at daybreak while they were wrestling and died when he chopped off her arm, and is still standing there on the cliff, as a rock in the shape of a woman. The people who lived in the valley hid Grettir there that winter.

One day after Christmas Grettir went to Eyjardalsa, and when he saw the priest he said to him, "I notice that you don't have much faith in my accounts, so I want you to go down to the river with me and see how probable you think it is."

The priest agreed. When they reached the waterfall they saw a cave in the cliff face, which was so sheer that no one could climb it and was almost ten fathoms down to the water. They had taken a rope with them.

The priest said, "It looks way beyond what you can manage, to go down there."

Grettir replied, "There is a way, and all the greater for great men. I shall take a look at what's in the cave while you keep an eye on the rope."

The priest said it was up to him, drove a peg into the top of the cliff and piled rocks around it.

Next, Grettir looped the end of the rope around a rock and lowered it down to the water.

"How do you plan to get down there now?" asked the priest.

"I don't want to be tied to anything when I enter the waterfall," said Grettir. "I have an intuition."

Afterwards he prepared himself to set off. He took off most of his clothes and girded on his short-sword but did not take any other weapons. Then he leapt over the side of the cliff and down into the waterfall. The priest watched the soles of his feet disappear, then had no idea what had become of him. Grettir dived under the waterfall, which was no easy task because to avoid the swirling current he had to dive right down to the bottom before he could resurface on the other side. There was a ledge that he climbed onto. Behind the waterfall, where the river plunged over the side of the cliff, was a huge cave.

He entered the cave and a great log fire was burning there. Grettir saw a giant lying there, monstrous in size and terrible to behold. When Grettir approached it, the giant snatched up a pike and swung a blow at the intruder. Known as a shafted sword, this pike was equally suited for striking or stabbing, and had a wooden shaft. Grettir returned the blow with his short-sword, striking the shaft and chopping through it. The giant tried to reach behind him for a sword that was hanging on the wall of the cave, but as he did so Grettir struck him on the breast, slicing his lower ribs and belly straight off and sending his innards gushing out into the river where they were swept away.

The priest, sitting by the rope, saw some slimy, bloodstained strands floating in the current. He panicked, convinced that Grettir was dead, abandoned the rope and went home. It was evening by then. The priest said that Grettir was certainly dead and described it as a great loss.

To turn to Grettir, he struck a few quick blows at the giant until he was dead, then went inside the cave. He lit a flame and looked around. It is not said how much treasure he found there, but people assume that it was a great hoard. He stayed there into the night, found the bones of two men and put them into a bag. Then he made his way out of the cave, swam back to the rope and shook it, expecting the priest to be there. When he realised that the priest had gone, he had to clamber up it with his hands, and finally made it to the cliff top.

Then he headed back to Eyjardalsa, went to the church porch and left the bag there, which had the bones in it and a rune-stick beautifully carved with this verse:

I entered the black chasm where
the plummeting rock face gaped
with its cold spraying mouth
at the maker of sword showers.
The plunging current pressed hard
at my breast in the trollwoman's hall;
the wife of the god of poets
burdened my shoulders with her hate.

sword-showers: battle

trollwoman's hall: cave?

wife of the god of poets: Idunn, wife of Bragi; a concealed pun on a word for "eddy"

And also this one:

The trollwoman's ugly lover
came at me from his cave,
made his long and bold
struggle with me, for certain.
I snapped his hard-edged pike
away from its shaft—my sword,

ablaze with battle, split
open his breast and black belly.

The runes also stated that Grettir had taken these bones from the cave. When the priest went to church the next morning he found the stick and all the rest, and read the runes. By then, Grettir had gone back to Sandhaugar.

The Frisian Slaughter: Episode and Fragment

Beginning on line 1070, where Heaney's verse adopts a different rhythm, Hrothgar's poet recites a legendary story as part of the celebration following Beowulf's victory over Grendel. It has traditionally been called the Finnsburg Episode, though the *Beowulf* poet calls it *Freswæl* or the Frisian Slaughter. The narrative's oblique allusiveness makes sense only if one assumes that the audience was already familiar with the story, an idea that gains some support from the survival of a fragment of another Old English poem (see below). The events concern a devastating skirmish between the followers of the Frisian king Finn and a Danish party led by Hnaef, who was in Frisia for peaceful purposes, perhaps by invitation. Hnaef had good reason to visit, because his sister Hildeburh was married to Finn. Ideally such a marriage would secure diplomatic ties between two tribes, perhaps to settle a feud but not always for that reason.[1] Sometime during the Danes' visit, a party of Jutes in the service of Finn attack them in their guest-hall and kill Hnaef. At some point Hildeburh's son (not named) is also killed. After extensive fighting and mounting casualties a truce is called and, because winter is coming, terms are negotiated so that Hengest (now the leader of the Danes) is given a hall and his men are treated with the same privileges as Finn's. A funeral pyre is erected for Hnaef, and Hildeburh orders her Frisian son placed beside her Danish brother. When spring arrives, a sword (Heaney's "Dazzle-the-Duel" for the Old English *Hildeleoma*) is laid ceremoniously on Hengest's lap as a reminder of his duty for vengeance. Overcoming his reluctance to renew the bloodshed, Hengest capitulates and leads the Danes against the Frisians. They kill Finn, take Hildeburh, and ransack Finn's hall. Yet another, more descriptive name for the episode might be "Hildeburh's Grief," a perspective the *Beowulf* poet takes pains to emphasize.

One possible explanation for the initial attack is that Jutes in Frisia had an old score to settle with the Danes, which Finn was powerless to stop; another is that Jutes were present in the retinues of *both* the Danes and the Frisians, and an old feud between them flared up, drawing Hnaef's and Finn's men into the fighting against their better judgment and dynastic interests. The generous terms that Finn proposes suggest that he was not in favor of hostilities in the first place and wanted to

1. J. R. R. Tolkien, *Finn and Hengest*, ed. Alan Bliss (Boston: Houghton Mifflin, 1983) 159.

bring them to an honorable end, but either scenario would explain why "Hildeburh / had little cause / to credit the Jutes." In the end the feud stirred up by the Jutes cost her not only her brother and son, but also her husband Finn. She bears the greatest grief of any, but the episode underscores the constant danger of violence erupting in an honor-bound warrior society, despite the most prudent efforts to suppress the imperative for retribution.

A single leaf from a codex once housed in the Lambeth Palace Library contained more lines of poetry concerning the same event. The manuscript survived long enough to be printed in 1705 but was subsequently lost.[2] Because "The Finnsburg Fragment," as it is called, lacks a beginning and end, it is unknown how long the original poem was, but its tone is different from the episode in *Beowulf*. The imagery is visually arresting. In the first lines, for example, as Hnaef looks out of the hall and spots weapons glinting in the moonlight, he uses an expanded antithesis to alert his men about the imminent attack. The Editor's translation printed here follows the Old English text of J. R. R. Tolkien, which indulges in some bold reconstructions.

* * *

The young battle-king Hnaef then spoke: "This is not the dawning in the east, nor is a dragon flying here, nor are gables of this hall burning; on the contrary deadly enemies are carrying war-gear in readiness. Carrion birds sing, the gray-coated wolf howls: spears clang, shield answers shaft. Now that this wandering moon shines under the clouds, evil deeds will arise that will inflict violence on this people. But wake up now, my warriors! Take your coats of mail, contemplate courage, grow enraged in the vanguard, be resolute!"

When many gold-trimmed valiant warriors were getting up from their sleep and buckling their sword, the noble warriors Sigeferth and Eaha advanced to the door and drew their swords, and Ordlaf and Guthlaf went to the other doors, and Hengest himself followed close behind. Yet Garulf still admonished Guthhere that he should not take such a noble life, armed, to the hall door at the first onrush, now that a stern enemy wanted to deprive him of it; but unabashedly the brave hero asked above it all who held the door. "Sigeferth is my name," he said, "I am a Secga prince, a famous adventurer; I have endured much strife, harsh battles; here one of two outcomes you wish to seek for yourself is now ordained for you."

There was the clash of deadly slaughter in the hall: the hollow shield, the body's protector, was to shatter in the hand of brave ones; the hall-floor resounded until Garulf, Guthulf's son, was the first of all the inhabitants to perish—around him the bodies of many virtuous ones. The shadowy dark-brown raven circled. Sword-gleam

2. George Hickes, ed., *Linguarum Vett. Septentrionalium Thesaurus Grammatico-criticus et Archaeologicus,* vol. 3 (Oxford, 1705).

stood out as if all Finnsburg was aflame. I have never heard sixty victory-warriors conduct themselves better, more worthily in a conflict of men, nor did followers and war-comrades ever make a better repayment for their bright mead than his young warriors tendered to Hnaef. For five days they fought so that none of the champions fell; no, they held the doors.

Then a wounded warrior was about to pass away. He said that his chain-mail was broken through, his armor useless, and his helmet was also pierced. Right away then the people's leader asked him how the warriors endured their wounds . . .

ALCUIN

"What has Ingeld to do with Christ?"†

Shortly before the year 800 C.E., an Anglo-Saxon abbot and scholar named Alcuin wrote a letter to a Mercian bishop known to us only by his pen-name "Speratus." Alcuin was one of the foremost scholars of Western Europe and a luminary in the constellation drawn to Charlemagne's court in the late eighth century. By the time of his death (804 C.E.) he had been made abbot of the monastery in Tours, but during all the years he lived on the continent he kept up a steady correspondence with religious institutions in England. Many of Alcuin's letters survive, which, like the one to Speratus, display his command of Latin rhetoric. What is of interest in the passage excerpted below, however, is Alcuin's accusation that Bishop Speratus and his retinue would listen to "pagan song" about pre-Christian Germanic heroes. The old hero specifically mentioned, Hinield, may be the same as the Ingeld who briefly figures in *Beowulf* as a Heatho-Bard betrothed to Hrothgar's daughter Freawaru. Alcuin's accusation suggests that the pagan stories continued circulating well after the Anglo-Saxons converted to Christianity. Such habits help explain how the *Beowulf* poet could make passing allusions to figures such as Sigemund, Ongentheow, Hengest, and Ingeld with some assurance that the audience would be knowledgeable enough to fill in the details. Alcuin's immediate concern, of course, is to discourage such practices as inappropriate for a bishop's household. The contrast between Christ and Ingeld is a rhetorical antithesis that the patristic writers Jerome and Tertullian deployed in various ways and which they in turn probably derived from Paul: "Bear not the yoke with unbelievers. For what participation hath justice with injustice? Or what fellowship hath light with darkness? And what concord hath Christ with Belial? Or what part hath the faithful with the unbeliever? And what agreement

† Translation from Donald A. Bullough, "What has Ingeld to do with Lindisfarne?" *Anglo-Saxon England* 22 (1993): 93–125 at 124. Reprinted with the permission of Cambridge University Press. For discussion, see Fred C. Robinson, *Beowulf and the Appositive Style* (Knoxville: U of Tennessee P, 1985) 8–9 and notes.

hath the temple of God with idols?" (II Corinthians 6:14–16). It is not known how Speratus received Alcuin's admonition, but even two hundred years later the foremost churchmen of England, Abbot Aelfric and Archbishop Wulfstan, felt compelled to renew the condemnation of listening to "heathen songs." The passage printed below includes more than the "Hinield" reference to give a sense of Alcuin's rhetorical style and his pastoral concerns.

* * *

It is surely better that Christ's bishop is more praised for his performance in church than for the pomp of his banquets. What kind of praise is it that your table is loaded so high that it can hardly be lifted and yet Christ is starving at the door? Who will then be saying on the day to be feared, 'Inasmuch as you did it to one of the least of mine you did it to me'. You should certainly have in your retinue an experienced steward, to see to the care of the poor with proper concern. It is better that the poor should eat at your table than entertainers and persons of extravagant behaviour. Avoid those who engage in heavy drinking, as blessed Jerome says, 'like the pit of Hell'. There are two evils here: firstly acting against God's commandment 'Keep a watch on drunkenness and dissipation'; secondly, to seek praise for an action when it is penitence that is called for. Blessed is the man who does not look to deceptions and false enthusiasms. Splendour in dress and the continual pursuit of drunkenness are insanity: in the words of the prophet, 'Shame on you, you mighty wine-drinkers and bold men in mixing your drinks'. Whoever takes pleasure in such things will, as Solomon says, never be wise. May you be the example of all sobriety and self-control.

Let God's words be read at the episcopal dinner-table. It is right that a reader should be heard, not a harpist, patristic discourse, not pagan song. What has Hinield to do with Christ? The house is narrow and has no room for both. The Heavenly King does not wish to have communion with pagan and forgotten kings listed name by name: for the eternal King reigns in Heaven, while the forgotten pagan king wails in Hell. The voices of readers should be heard in your dwellings, not the laughing rabble in the courtyards.

* * *

GREGORY OF TOURS

History of the Franks†

[*Hygelac's Raid into Frisia*]

[Book 3 Chapter 1] After the death of King Clovis, his four sons Theodoric, Chlodomer, Childebert, and Lothar, inherited his kingdom and divided it equally among themselves. By then Theodoric already had a son named Theodobert, graceful and well-trained.

* * *

[Chapter 3] * * * [T]he Danes with their king named Hygelac [Chlochilaicus] crossed the sea in ships and attacked Gaul. Upon landing they ransacked a region of Theodoric's kingdom and took captives. After loading their ships with captives and the rest of the spoils, they were eager to return to their homeland. The king, however, remained on the shore when the ships took to the deep sea, intending to follow them later. When it was announced to Theodoric that his region had been ransacked by foreigners, he sent his son Theodobert to those areas with a strong, well-equipped army. After killing the king [Hygelac], he overwhelmed the enemy in a naval battle and restored all the spoils to the country.

WILLIAM OF MALMESBURY

[Genealogy of the Royal Family of Wessex]‡

The twelfth-century historian William of Malmesbury, drawing on several sources from the Anglo-Saxon period, gives the following genealogy of Æthelwulf, king of Wessex (d. 855 C.E.). What is of interest among the list that traces the West Saxon royal family through Woden and ultimately back to Noah is the presence of several names found in *Beowulf*, such as Finn and Geat, and the sequence Beow, Sceld, and Sceaf. It also includes a short excursus on Sceaf's miraculous arrival on the

† Hygelac's ill-fated raid is mentioned several times in *Beowulf*. Unlike other, historically dubious tales that the poet weaves into the narrative, this story is based on an event that took place around 520 C.E. and was recorded shortly thereafter by the Frankish prelate Gregory of Tours (538–94 C.E.). Translated by the Editor of this Norton Critical Edition from Gregory of Tours, *History of the Franks*; Migne, *Patrologia Latina*, vol. 71, as printed in Klaeber, pp. 267–68.

‡ William of Malmesbury, *Gesta Regum Anglorum*, ed. and trans. R. A. B. Mynors, completed by R. M. Thomson and M. Winterbottom, 2 vols. (Oxford: Clarendon, 1998), bk. 2, para. 116. Reprinted by permission of Oxford University Press.

shores of Denmark. In *Beowulf* it is Shield who arrives as a foundling (l. 4–52), but otherwise the two accounts are remarkably similar.

* * *

Æthelwulf was the son of Ecgberht; Ecgberht of Ealhmund; Ealhmund of Eafa; Eafa of Eoppa; Eoppa of Ingild brother of King Ine and both of them sons of Cenred; Cenred of Ceolwald; Ceolwald of Cutha; Cutha of Cuthwine; Cuthwine of Ceawlin; Ceawlin of Cynric, Cynric * * * of Cerdic, who was the first king of the West Saxons; Cerdic of Elesa; Elesa of Esla; Esla of Gewis; Gewis of Wig; Wig of Freawine; Freawine of Fredegar; Fredegar of Brond; Brond of Bældæg; Bældæg of Woden, from whom, as I have often said, are descended the kings of many nations; Woden was the son of Fridewald; Fridewald of Frealaf; Frealaf of Finn; Finn of Godwulf; Godwulf of Geat; Geat of Tetti; Tetti of Beow; Beow of Sceld; Sceld of Sceaf. (This Sceaf, they say, landed on an island in Germany called Scandza mentioned by Jordanes the historian of the Goths, as a small child in a ship without a crew, sleeping with a sheaf of wheat laid by his head, and hence was called Sheaf. The men of that country welcomed him as something miraculous and brought him up carefully, and on reaching manhood he ruled a town then called *Slaswic* but now Hedeby. The name of that region is Old Anglia, and it was from there that the Angles came to Britain; it lies between the Saxons and the Goths.) Sceaf was the son of Heremod; Heremod of Stermon; Stermon of Hathra; Hathra of Gwala; Gwala of Bedwig; Bedwig of Streph who was, they say, a son of Noah, born in the Ark.

On the Wars between the Swedes and the Geats†

Lying ominously behind the action in the last thousand lines of *Beowulf* are the long-simmering hostilities between the Geats and the Swedes. The poem's references do not follow a chronological order and are allusive enough that it is difficult for a reader today to keep the main players and events straight. The following summary by Alfred David breaks up the events into five phases.

Phase 1: After the death of the Geat patriarch, King Hrethel (lines 2462–70), Ohthere and Onela, the sons of the Swedish king Ongentheow, invade Geat territory and inflict heavy casualties in a battle at Hreosnahill (lines 2472–78).

Phase 2: The Geats invade Sweden under Haethcyn, King Hrethel's son, who has succeeded him. At the battle of Ravenswood, the Geats capture Ongentheow's queen, but Ongentheow counter-

† Reprinted with revisions from *The Norton Anthology of English Literature*, Seventh Edition, ed. M. H. Abrams and Stephen Greenblatt et al. (New York: W. W. Norton, 2000), note 6 on p. 79. Reprinted by permission of W. W. Norton & Company, Inc.

attacks, rescues the queen, and kills Haethcyn. Hygelac, Haethcyn's younger brother, arrives with reinforcements; Ongentheow is killed in savage combat with two of Hygelac's men; and the Swedes are routed (lines 2479–89 and 2922–90).

Phase 3: Eanmund and Eadgils, the sons of Ohthere (presumably dead), are driven into exile by their uncle Onela, who is now king of the Swedes. They are given refuge by Hygelac's son Heardred, who has succeeded his father. Onela invades Geatland and kills Heardred; his retainer Weohstan kills Eanmund; and after the Swedes withdraw, Beowulf becomes king (lines 2204–8 and 2379–90).

Phase 4: Eadgils, supported by Beowulf, invades Sweden and kills Onela (lines 2391–96).

Phase 5 can be anticipated after the events of *Beowulf*. Despite Beowulf's alliance with Eadgils, the unnamed Geatish messenger predicts that "this bad blood between us and the Swedes . . . is bound to revive" (lines 2999–3007). The Swedes will attack the Geats once they learn that Beowulf is dead.

Genealogies of the Royal Families in *Beowulf*

The Danes or **Shieldings** ("Shield's sons")

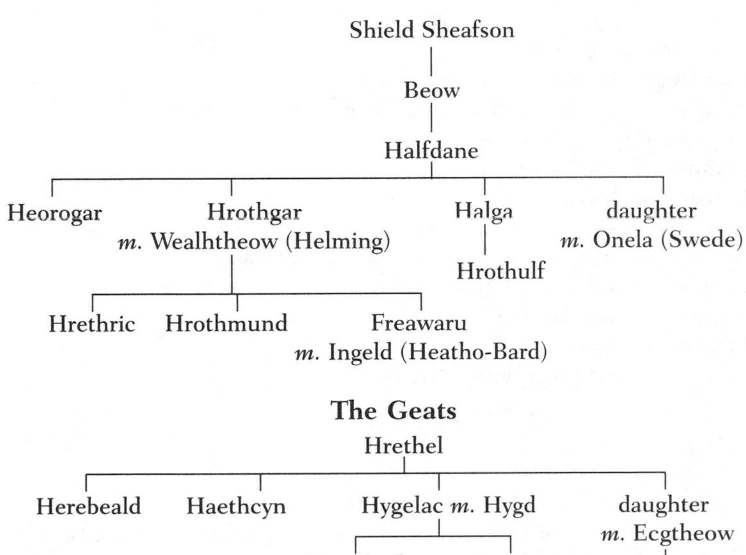

Swedes or **Shylfings** ("Shylf's sons")

Ongentheow
- Ohthere
  - Eanmund
  - Eadgils
- Onela *m.* daughter of Halfdane (Dane)

The Kingdoms and Tribes of *Beowulf*

Many of the kingdoms mentioned in *Beowulf* can be located with some confidence; others involve educated guesses.[1] While the *Beowulf* poet probably did not have a precise knowledge of the geography of early sixth-century Scandinavia, his narrative moves with remarkable assurance among the tribes that populate it.

The poem identifies some kingdoms by several names. The **Danes** are called Bright-Danes, Spear-Danes, Ring-Danes, South-Danes, West-Danes; also the patronymic **Shieldings** ("Shield's sons"), Victory-Shieldings and Ingwins ("Ing's friends"). The **Geats** are called War-Geats, Sea-Geats, Weather-Geats.[2] And the **Swedes** are sometimes called the **Shylfings**, or "Shylf's sons." Smaller tribes can form part of larger kingdoms; Beowulf, for example, is from the Waegmunding family, under the Geatish king. Other tribes are listed below with some of the prominent characters notes in parentheses:

Angles (Offa, Eomer)
Brondings (Beanstan, Breca)
Franks—a large kingdom ruled by the Merovingians
Frisians (Folcwalda, Finn)
Gifthas—a tribe east of the Danes
Heatho-Bards (Ingeld)
Heatho-Reams—in present-day Norway
Hetware—a tribe of the Frankish kingdom (Dayraven)
Jutes—involved in the fighting during the Finn episode
Waegmundings (Beowulf, Ecgtheow, Wiglaf)
Wendel (Wulfgar)
Wulfings=Helmings (Wealhtheow)

1. See Fr. Klaeber's *Beowulf*, p. viii; and Sam Newton, *The Origins of Beowulf* (Woodbridge, Suffolk: D. S. Brewer, 1993), endleaves.
2. The Old English pronunciation of Beowulf's tribe begins with a *y*-sound, roughly "YEAH-ots" run together as one syllable.

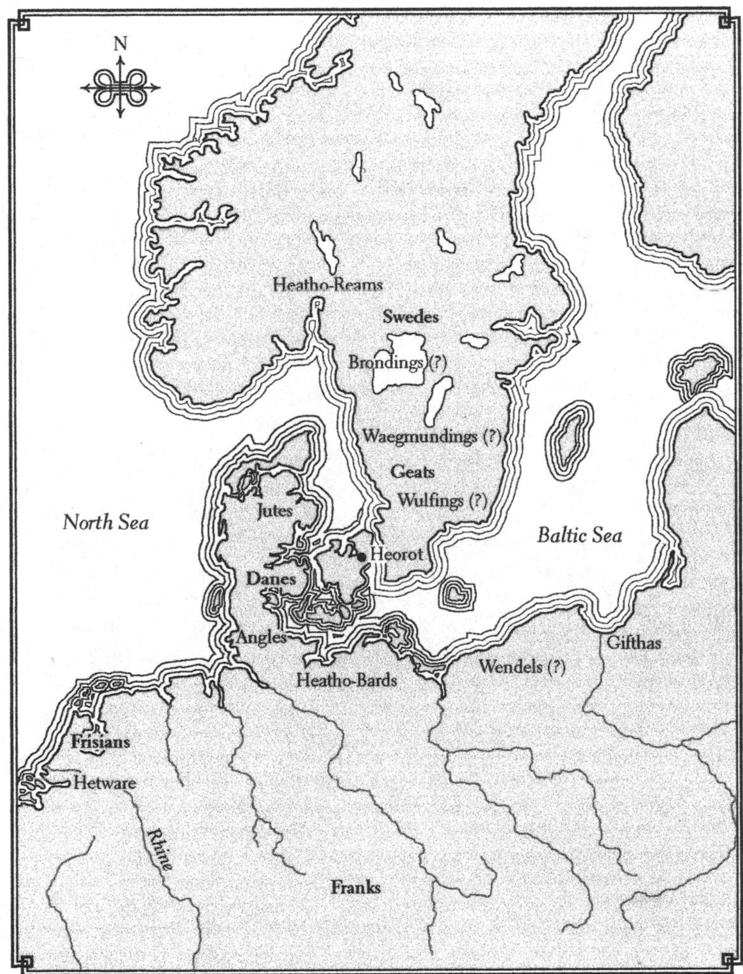

Figure 2. The Scandinavian Setting of *Beowulf*.

R. D. FULK AND JOSEPH HARRIS

Beowulf's Name†

Most contemporary scholars will say that Beowulf's name is probably a kenning (a native Germanic form of metaphorical periphrasis) meaning "bee-wolf," where the wolf or foe of the bee is the honey-seeking bear. This inviting explanation of the hero's rare name arose in 1910 out of Friedrich Panzer's important investigations into the links between *Beowulf*, together with its Nordic analogues, and a type of folktale he calls "the Bear's Son Tale" and connected the hero, who shows some bear-like qualities, to the Bjarki "little bear" of one of the Norse analogues. But the analysis of the elements of the name goes back to Jacob Grimm (1836, hinted at already in 1823), for whom a "bee-wolf" was a woodpecker, a figure, Grimm shows, of more dignity in early myth than modern students might expect. Before Panzer there were several other explanations of the name, some (like Panzer's) coinciding in an essentially allegorical way with the interpreter's understanding of the myth (usually a nature or seasonal myth) underlying the epic, many building on very questionable etymological bases.

The authors of this note believe that an explanation better than the standard one from Grimm via Panzer is to be sought in a normal Germanic theophoric naming-type. (A theophoric name "bears" the name of a god, e.g., Gott-fried, Gott-lieb [which Mozart changed to Amadeus], Trau-gott, Torsten [Thor + "stone"], Jesús.) By contrast names derived from kennings appear to be very scarce indeed, and no good parallel for "bee-wolf," whether meaning woodpecker or bear, has ever been offered. The first element of the hero's name, then, is not *bēo* "bee" but *Bēow*, a pre-Christian god; and the structure of this name is the same as the very common Norse *Þór-ólfr* (from Thor + wolf) or the English *Tiu-wulf* (the god Tiu + wolf, as in *Tiuwulfingaceaster*). Beow appears (in variant spellings Beaw, Beowa, Bedwig, Beowius, etc.) in the upper, divine levels of Anglo-Saxon royal genealogies. In lines 18 and 53, where Heaney and several editors print "Beow," the manuscript reads "Beowulf," a mistake easily attributable to a scribe's confusion or misinterpretation. Metrical reasons support the conclusion that the name of the god Beow once stood in these two passages, but even more conclusive is the fact that Beow/Beowulf of lines 18 and 53 occupies the same gene-

† Based on a forthcoming article by R. D. Fulk and Joseph Harris. Published with permission of the authors.

alogical position as his namesake in the Old English king lists.[1] Outside the genealogies, forms that may or may not belong to the god Beow appear fairly frequently in place names, but only one other appearance of his name has potential relevance to the poem: in a charter (a legal description of a piece of property) of 931 a *Beowan hamm* "Beowa's enclosure" is found in the immediate vicinity of a *Grendles mere* "Grendel's lake." (The relationship between the names Beowulf and Beow cannot be reversed, i.e., Beow cannot be a short form of Beowulf as "bee-wolf" if only because the bee word has no -w- element and a hypocoristic "Beow" would show false division at a relatively early date.) Thus we can only have a "bee-wolf" at the cost of an unlikely disconnection from the Beow of the genealogies and place names and a nearly opaque name-formation.

Beow's own name coincides with the Old English common noun for "barley, grain" and has a firm Germanic etymology; in the genealogies he is a descendent of another apparent vegetation or fertility god, Scēaf (with variants), meaning "sheaf (as of wheat)." The English common noun *bēow* "barley" has its close equivalent (through regular and universally recognized phonological correspondences) in Old Norse *bygg* "barley," and so the Anglo-Saxon deity Beow is inevitably in some sense equivalent to the Norse grain god Byggvir who has a role in the mythological poem *Lokasenna*. The name of Byggvir is of the type known to linguists as a *ja*-stem, and in the parent article of this note we argue (in part following one of the early etymological commentators) that Beow too can be a *ja*-stem. This argument, though difficult, is crucial for reconciling the single occurrence of the name Beowulf in English outside the poem, the form *biu[u]lf* in the Durham *Liber Vitae*, an early ninth-century census of the brothers of a Northumbrian monastery. In the dialect represented by the *Liber Vitae*, the first element can only be "bee" or a *ja*-stem (or *i*-stem) form of the root of *bēow*-; in addition the *ja*-stem derivation explains some of the difficult forms in the genealogies (e.g., *Beowi* and *Bedwig*). The name of Beow/Byggvir has long been thought to be the source of the similar Finnish-Estonian barley god Pekko, and the *ja*-stem hypothesis appears to be no hindrance to this derivation, though the mythological derivation, no less than the philological one, is not uncontroversial.

"Beowulf," we believe, is not an almost unique little allegory but a *name* such as a man might bear—indeed one of the brothers at Durham did. Though rarely attested, it is constructed on a common model

1. For an example of the Old English genealogies see pp. 95–96, above. See also Fr. Klaeber's edition of *Beowulf* and R. W. Chambers's *Beowulf: An Introduction*, both listed in the bibliography [*Editor*].

and is very similar to its closest parallel, the very common *Ingulf* (Ing + wolf) with variants in every Germanic language. The god Ing was, like Beow, known in a euhemerized form to the Anglo-Saxons, and Old Norse sources make it clear that he was or became a hypostasis or (like Byggvir) an adjunct of the most successful fertility god, Freyr. Historical names such as *Inguiomērus* show the same stem morphology necessary for generating Byggvir. Possibly the dearth of human names built on "Byggvir" and the rarity of them with "Beow" is to be explained by the success of names in "Ing." In any case, our aim is to fix the etymology and onomastic type of Beowulf's name, and we suspend judgment on matters of "legend history" (*Sagengeschichte*) raised by the connection with Beow (which so absorbed the early scholars) and by the removal of the name from the Bear's Son complex.

CRITICISM

J. R. R. TOLKIEN

Beowulf: The Monsters and the Critics†

In 1864 the Reverend Oswald Cockayne wrote of the Reverend Doctor Joseph Bosworth, Rawlinsonian Professor of Anglo-Saxon: 'I have tried to lend to others the conviction I have long entertained that Dr. Bosworth is not a man so diligent in his special walk as duly to read the books . . . which have been printed in our old English, or so-called Anglosaxon tongue. He may do very well for a professor.'[1] These words were inspired by dissatisfaction with Bosworth's dictionary, and were doubtless unfair. If Bosworth were still alive, a modern Cockayne would probably accuse him of not reading the 'literature' of his subject, the books written about the books in the so-called Anglo-Saxon tongue. The original books are nearly buried.

Of none is this so true as of *The Beowulf*, as it used to be called. I have, of course, read *The Beowulf*, as have most (but not all) of those who have criticized it. But I fear that, unworthy successor and beneficiary of Joseph Bosworth, I have not been a man so diligent in my special walk as duly to read all that has been printed on, or touching on, this poem. But I have read enough, I think, to venture the opinion that *Beowulfiana* is, while rich in many departments, specially poor in one. It is poor in criticism, criticism that is directed to the understanding of a poem as a poem. It has been said of *Beowulf* itself that its weakness lies in placing the unimportant things at the centre and the important on the outer edges. This is one of the opinions that I wish specially to consider. I think it profoundly untrue of the poem, but strikingly true of the literature about it. *Beowulf* has been used as a quarry of fact and fancy far more assiduously than it has been studied as a work of art.

It is of *Beowulf*, then, as a poem that I wish to speak; and though it may seem presumption that I should try with *swich a lewed mannes wit to pace the wisdom of an heep of lerned men*, in this department there is at least more chance for the *lewed man*. But there is so much that might still be said even under these limitations that I shall confine myself mainly to the *monsters*—Grendel and the Dragon, as they appear in what seems to me the best and most authoritative general criticism in English—and to certain considerations of the structure and conduct of the poem that arise from this theme.

There is an historical explanation of the state of *Beowulfiana* that I have referred to. And that explanation is important, if one would

† From "*Beowulf*: The Monsters and the Critics," Sir Israel Gollancz Memorial Lecture, *Proceedings of the British Academy*, 1936, pp. 245–95. Reprinted by permission of HarperCollins.

1. *The Shrine*, p. 4.

venture to criticize the critics. A sketch of the history of the subject is required. But I will here only attempt, for brevity's sake, to present my view of it allegorically. As it set out upon its adventures among the modern scholars, *Beowulf* was christened by Wanley Poesis—*Poeseos Anglo-Saxonicæ egregium exemplum*. But the fairy godmother later invited to superintend its fortunes was Historia. And she brought with her Philologia, Mythologia, Archaeologia, and Laographia.[2] Excellent ladies. But where was the child's name-sake? Poesis was usually forgotten; occasionally admitted by a side-door; sometimes dismissed upon the door-step. '*The Beowulf*, they said, 'is hardly an affair of yours, and not in any case a protégé that you could be proud of. It is an historical document. Only as such does it interest the superior culture of today.' And it is as an historical document that it has mainly been examined and dissected. Though ideas as to the nature and quality of the history and information embedded in it have changed much since Thorkelin called it *De Danorum Rebus Gestis*, this has remained steadily true. In still recent pronouncements this view is explicit. In 1925 Professor Archibald Strong translated *Beowulf* into verse;[3] but in 1921 he had declared: '*Beowulf* is the picture of a whole civilization, of the Germania which Tacitus describes. The main interest which the poem has for us is thus not a purely literary interest. *Beowulf* is an important historical document.'[4]

I make this preliminary point, because it seems to me that the air has been clouded not only for Strong, but for other more authoritative critics, by the dust of the quarrying researchers. It may well be asked: why should we approach this, or indeed any other poem, mainly as an historical document? Such an attitude is defensible: firstly, if one is not concerned with poetry at all, but seeking information wherever it may be found; secondly, if the so-called poem contains in fact no poetry. I am not concerned with the first case. The historian's search is, of course, perfectly legitimate, even if it does not assist criticism in general at all (for that is not its object), so long as it is not mistaken for criticism. To Professor Birger Ner-

2. Thus in Professor Chambers's great bibliography (in his *Beowulf: An Introduction*) we find a section, § 8. Questions of Literary History, Date, and Authorship; Beowulf in the Light of History, Archaeology, Heroic Legend, Mythology, and Folklore. It is impressive, but there is no section that names Poetry. As certain of the items included show, such consideration as Poetry is accorded at all is buried unnamed in § 8.
3. *Beowulf translated into modern English rhyming verse*, Constable, 1925.
4. *A Short History of English Literature*, Oxford Univ. Press, 1921, pp. 2–3. I choose this example, because it is precisely to general literary histories that we must usually turn for literary judgements on *Beowulf*. The experts in *Beowulfiana* are seldom concerned with such judgements. And it is in the highly compressed histories, such as this, that we discover what the process of digestion makes of the special 'literature' of the experts. Here is the distilled product of Research. This compendium, moreover, is competent, and written by a man who had (unlike some other authors of similar things) read the poem itself with attention.

man as an historian of Swedish origins *Beowulf* is doubtless an important document, but he is not writing a history of English poetry. Of the second case it may be said that to rate a poem, a thing at the least in metrical form, as mainly of historical interest should *in a literary survey* be equivalent to saying that it has no literary merits, and little more need in such a survey then be said about it. But such a judgement on *Beowulf* is false. So far from being a poem so poor that only its accidental historical interest can still recommend it, *Beowulf* is in fact so interesting as poetry, in places poetry so powerful, that this quite overshadows the historical content, and is largely independent even of the most important facts (such as the date and identity of Hygelac) that research has discovered. It is indeed a curious fact that it is one of the peculiar poetic virtues of *Beowulf* that has contributed to its own critical misfortunes. The illusion of historical truth and perspective, that has made *Beowulf* seem such an attractive quarry, is largely a product of art. The author has used an instinctive historical sense—a part indeed of the ancient English temper (and not unconnected with its reputed melancholy), of which *Beowulf* is a supreme expression; but he has used it with a poetical and not an historical object. The lovers of poetry can safely study the art, but the seekers after history must beware lest the glamour of Poesis overcome them.

Nearly all the censure, and most of the praise, that has been bestowed on *The Beowulf* has been due either to the belief that it was something that it was *not*—for example, primitive, pagan, Teutonic, an allegory (political or mythical), or most often, an epic; or to disappointment at the discovery that it was itself and not something that the scholar would have liked better—for example, a heathen heroic lay, a history of Sweden, a manual of Germanic antiquities, or a Nordic *Summa Theologica*.

I would express the whole industry in yet another allegory. A man inherited a field in which was an accumulation of old stone, part of an older hall. Of the old stone some had already been used in building the house in which he actually lived, not far from the old house of his fathers. Of the rest he took some and built a tower. But his friends coming perceived at once (without troubling to climb the steps) that these stones had formerly belonged to a more ancient building. So they pushed the tower over, with no little labour, in order to look for hidden carvings and inscriptions, or to discover whence the man's distant forefathers had obtained their building material. Some suspecting a deposit of coal under the soil began to dig for it, and forgot even the stones. They all said: 'This tower is most interesting.' But they also said (after pushing it over): 'What a muddle it is in!' And even the man's own descendants, who might have been expected to consider what he had been about, were heard to murmur: 'He is such an odd fellow! Imagine his using these old stones just to build a nonsensical tower! Why did not he restore the old house? He had no sense of proportion.' But from the top of that tower the man had been able to look out upon the sea.

I hope I shall show that that allegory is just—even when we consider the more recent and more perceptive critics (whose concern is in intention with literature). To reach these we must pass in rapid flight over the heads of many decades of critics. As we do so a conflicting babel mounts up to us, which I can report as something after this fashion.[5] '*Beowulf* is a half-baked native epic the development of which was killed by Latin learning; it was inspired by emulation of Virgil, and is a product of the education that came in with Christianity; it is feeble and incompetent as a narrative; the rules of narrative are cleverly observed in the manner of the learned epic; it is the confused product of a committee of muddle-headed and probably beer-bemused Anglo-Saxons (this is a Gallic voice); it is a string of pagan lays edited by monks; it is the work of a learned but inaccurate Christian antiquarian; it is a work of genius, rare and surprising in the period, though the genius seems to have been shown principally in doing something much better left undone (this is a very recent voice); it is a wild folk-tale (general chorus); it is a poem of an aristocratic and courtly tradition (same voices); it is a hotchpotch; it is a sociological, anthropological, archaeological document; it is a mythical allegory (very old voices these and generally shouted down, but not so far out as some of the newer cries); it is rude and rough; it is a masterpiece of metrical art; it has no shape at all; it is singularly weak in construction; it is a clever allegory of contemporary politics (old John Earle with some slight support from Mr Girvan, only they look to different periods); its architecture is solid; it is thin and cheap (a solemn voice); it is undeniably weighty (the same voice); it is a national epic; it is a translation from the Danish; it was imported by Frisian traders; it is a burden to English syllabuses; and (final universal chorus of all voices) it is worth studying.'

It is not surprising that it should now be felt that a view, a decision, a conviction are imperatively needed. But it is plainly only in the consideration of *Beowulf* as a poem, with an inherent poetic significance, that any view or conviction can be reached or steadily held. For it is of their nature that the jabberwocks of historical and antiquarian research burble in the tulgy wood of conjecture, flitting from one tum-tum tree to another. Noble animals, whose burbling is on occasion good to hear; but though their eyes of flame may sometimes prove searchlights, their range is short.

5. I include nothing that has not somewhere been said by someone, if not in my exact words; but I do not, of course, attempt to represent all the *dicta*, wise or otherwise, that have been uttered.

None the less, paths of a sort have been opened in the wood. Slowly with the rolling years the obvious (so often the last revelation of analytic study) has been discovered: that we have to deal with a poem by an Englishman using afresh ancient and largely traditional material. At last then, after inquiring so long whence this material came, and what its original or aboriginal nature was (questions that cannot ever be decisively answered), we might also now again inquire what the poet did with it. If we ask that question, then there is still, perhaps, something lacking even in the major critics, the learned and revered masters from whom we humbly derive.

The chief points with which I feel dissatisfied I will now approach by way of W. P. Ker, whose name and memory I honour. He would deserve reverence, of course, even if he still lived and had not *ellor gehworfen on Frean wære*[6] upon a high mountain in the heart of that Europe which he loved: a great scholar, as illuminating himself as a critic, as he was often biting as a critic of the critics. None the less I cannot help feeling that in approaching *Beowulf* he was hampered by the almost inevitable weakness of his greatness: stories and plots must sometimes have seemed triter to him, the much-read, than they did to the old poets and their audiences. The dwarf on the spot sometimes sees things missed by the travelling giant ranging many countries. In considering a period when literature was narrower in range and men possessed a less diversified stock of ideas and themes, one must seek to recapture and esteem the deep pondering and profound feeling that they gave to such as they possessed.

In any case Ker has been potent. For his criticism is masterly, expressed always in words both pungent and weighty, and not least so when it is (as I occasionally venture to think) itself open to criticism. His words and judgements are often quoted, or reappear in various modifications, digested, their source probably sometimes forgotten. It is impossible to avoid quotation of the well-known passage in his *Dark Ages*:

> A reasonable view of the merit of *Beowulf* is not impossible, though rash enthusiasm may have made too much of it, while a correct and sober taste may have too contemptuously refused to attend to Grendel or the Fire-drake. The fault of *Beowulf* is that there is nothing much in the story. The hero is occupied in killing monsters, like Hercules or Theseus. But there are other things in the lives of Hercules and Theseus besides the killing of the Hydra or of Procrustes. Beowulf has nothing else to do, when he has killed Grendel and Grendel's mother in Denmark: he goes home to his own Gautland, until at last the rolling years bring the Fire-drake and his last adventure. It is too sim-

6. "Turned elsewhere into the Lord's protection." Tolkien's invention, patterned after passages in *Beowulf* [*Editor's translation*].

> ple. Yet the three chief episodes are well wrought and well diversified; they are not repetitions, exactly; there is a change of temper between the wrestling with Grendel in the night at Heorot and the descent under water to encounter Grendel's mother; while the sentiment of the Dragon is different again. But the great beauty, the real value, of *Beowulf* is in its dignity of style. In construction it is curiously weak, in a sense preposterous; for while the main story is simplicity itself, the merest commonplace of heroic legend, all about it, in the historic allusions, there are revelations of a whole world of tragedy, plots different in import from that of *Beowulf*, more like the tragic themes of Iceland. Yet with this radical defect, a disproportion that puts the irrelevances in the centre and the serious things on the outer edges, the poem of *Beowulf* is undeniably weighty. The thing itself is cheap; the moral and the spirit of it can only be matched among the noblest authors.[7]

This passage was written more than thirty years ago, but has hardly been surpassed. It remains, in this country at any rate, a potent influence. Yet its primary effect is to state a paradox which one feels has always strained the belief, even of those who accepted it, and has given to *Beowulf* the character of an 'enigmatic poem'. The chief virtue of the passage (not the one for which it is usually esteemed) is that it does accord some attention to the monsters, despite correct and sober taste. But the contrast made between the radical defect of theme and structure, and at the same time the dignity, loftiness in converse, and well-wrought finish, has become a commonplace even of the best criticism, a paradox the strangeness of which has almost been forgotten in the process of swallowing it upon authority.[8] We may compare Professor Chambers in his *Widsith*, p. 79, where he is studying the story of Ingeld, son of Froda, and his feud with the great Scylding house of Denmark, a story introduced in *Beowulf* merely as an allusion.

> Nothing [Chambers says] could better show the disproportion of *Beowulf* which 'puts the irrelevances in the centre and the serious things on the outer edges', than this passing allusion to the story of Ingeld. For in this conflict between plighted

7. *The Dark Ages*, pp. 252–3.
8. None the less Ker modified it in an important particular in *English Literature, Mediæval*, pp. 29–34. In general, though in different words, vaguer and less incisive, he repeats himself. We are still told that 'the story is commonplace and the plan is feeble', or that 'the story is thin and poor'. But we learn also at the end of his notice that: 'Those distracting allusions to things apart from the chief story make up for their want of proportion. They give the impression of reality and weight; the story is not in the air . . . it is part of the solid world.' By the admission of so grave an artistic reason for the procedure of the poem Ker himself began the undermining of his own criticism of its structure. But this line of thought does not seem to have been further pursued. Possibly it was this very thought, working in his mind, that made Ker's notice of *Beowulf* in the small later book, his 'shilling shocker', more vague and hesitant in tone, and so of less influence.

troth and the duty of revenge we have a situation which the old heroic poets loved, and would not have sold for a wilderness of dragons.

I pass over the fact that the allusion has a dramatic purpose in *Beowulf* that is a sufficient defence both of its presence and of its manner. The author of *Beowulf* cannot be held responsible for the fact that we now have only his poem and not others dealing primarily with Ingeld. He was not selling one thing for another, but giving something new. But let us return to the dragon. 'A wilderness of dragons.' There is a sting in this Shylockian plural, the sharper for coming from a critic, who deserves the title of the poet's best friend. It is in the tradition of the Book of St. Albans, from which the poet might retort upon his critics: 'Yea, a desserte of lapwyngs, a shrewednes of apes, a raffull of knaues, and a gagle of gees.'

As for the poem, one dragon, however hot, does not make a summer, or a host; and a man might well exchange for one good dragon what he would not sell for a wilderness. And dragons, real dragons, essential both to the machinery and the ideas of a poem or tale, are actually rare. In northern literature there are only *two* that are significant. If we omit from consideration the vast and vague Encircler of the World, Miðgarðsormr, the doom of the great gods and no matter for heroes, we have but the dragon of the Völsungs, Fáfnir, and Beowulf's bane. It is true that both of these are in *Beowulf*, one in the main story, and the other spoken of by a minstrel praising Beowulf himself. But this is not a wilderness of dragons. Indeed the allusion to the more renowned worm killed by the Wælsing is sufficient indication that the poet selected a dragon of well-founded purpose (or saw its significance in the plot as it had reached him), even as he was careful to compare his hero, Beowulf son of Ecgtheow, to the prince of the heroes of the North, the dragon-slaying Wælsing. He esteemed dragons, as rare as they are dire, as some do still. He liked them—as a poet, not as a sober zoologist; and he had good reason.

But we meet this kind of criticism again. In Chambers's *Beowulf and the Heroic Age*—the most significant single essay on the poem that I know—it is still present. The riddle is still unsolved. The folktale motive stands still like the spectre of old research, dead but unquiet in its grave. We are told again that the main story of *Beowulf* is a *wild folk-tale*. Quite true, of course. It is true of the main story of *King Lear*, unless in that case you would prefer to substitute *silly* for *wild*. But more: we are told that the same sort of stuff is found in Homer, yet there it is kept in its proper place. 'The folk-tale is a good servant', Chambers says, and does not perhaps realize the importance of the admission, made to save the face of Homer and

Virgil; for he continues: 'but a bad master: it has been allowed in *Beowulf* to usurp the place of honour, and to drive into episodes and digressions the things which should be the main stuff of a well-conducted epic.'[9] It is not clear to me why good *conduct* must depend on the main *stuff*. But I will for the moment remark only that, if it is so, *Beowulf* is evidently not a well-conducted epic. It may turn out to be no epic at all. But the puzzle still continues. In the most recent discourse upon this theme it still appears, toned down almost to a melancholy question-mark, as if this paradox had at last begun to afflict with weariness the thought that endeavours to support it. In the final peroration of his notable lecture on *Folk-tale and History in Beowulf*, given last year, Mr. Girvan said:

> Confessedly there is matter for wonder and scope for doubt, but we might be able to answer with complete satisfaction some of the questionings which rise in men's minds over the poet's presentment of his hero, if we could also answer with certainty the question why he chose just this subject, when to our modern judgment there were at hand so many greater, charged with the splendour and tragedy of humanity, and in all respects worthier of a genius as astonishing as it was rare in Anglo-Saxon England.

There is something irritatingly odd about all this. One even dares to wonder if something has not gone wrong with 'our modern judgement', supposing that it is justly represented. Higher praise than is found in the learned critics, whose scholarship enables them to appreciate these things, could hardly be given to the detail, the tone, the style, and indeed to the total effect of *Beowulf*. Yet this poetic talent, we are to understand, has all been squandered on an unprofitable theme: as if Milton had recounted the story of Jack and the Beanstalk in noble verse. Even if Milton had done this (and he might have done worse), we should perhaps pause to consider whether his poetic handling had not had some effect upon the trivial theme; what alchemy had been performed upon the base metal; whether indeed it remained base or trivial when he had finished with it. The high tone, the sense of dignity, alone is evidence in *Beowulf* of the presence of a mind lofty and thoughtful. It is, one would have said, improbable that such a man would write more than three thousand lines (wrought to a high finish) on matter that is really not worth serious attention; that remains thin and cheap when he has finished with it. Or that he should in the selection of his material, in the choice of what to put forward, what to keep subordinate 'upon the outer edges', have shown a puerile simplicity much below the level of the characters he himself draws in his own poem. Any theory that will at least allow us to believe that what he did was of design, and

9. *Foreword* to Strong's translation, p. xxvi: see note 3.

that for that design there is a defence that may still have force, would seem more probable.

It has been too little observed that all the machinery of 'dignity' is to be found elsewhere. Cynewulf, or the author of *Andreas*, or of *Guthlac* (most notably), have a command of dignified verse. In them there is well-wrought language, weighty words, lofty sentiment, precisely that which we are told is the real beauty of *Beowulf*. Yet it cannot, I think, be disputed, that *Beowulf* is more beautiful, that each line there is more significant (even when, as sometimes happens, it is the same line) than in the other long Old English poems. Where then resides the special virtue of *Beowulf*, if the common element (which belongs largely to the language itself, and to a literary tradition) is deducted? It resides, one might guess, in the theme, and the spirit this has infused into the whole. For, in fact, if there were a real discrepancy between theme and style, that style would not be felt as beautiful but as incongruous or false. And that incongruity is present in some measure in all the long Old English poems, save one—*Beowulf*. The paradoxical contrast that has been drawn between matter and manner in *Beowulf* has thus an inherent *literary* improbability.

Why then have the great critics thought otherwise? I must pass rather hastily over the answers to this question. The reasons are various, I think, and would take long to examine. I believe that one reason is that the shadow of research has lain upon criticism. The habit, for instance, of pondering a summarized plot of *Beowulf*, denuded of all that gives it particular force or individual life, has encouraged the notion that its main story is wild, or trivial, or typical, *even after treatment*. Yet all stories, great and small, are one or more of these three things in such nakedness. The comparison of skeleton 'plots' is simply not a critical literary process at all. It has been favoured by research in comparative folk-lore, the objects of which are primarily historical or scientific.[1] Another reason is, I think, that the allusions have attracted curiosity (antiquarian rather than critical) to their elucidation; and this needs so much study and research that attention has been diverted from the poem as a whole, and from the

1. It has also been favoured by the rise of 'English schools', in whose syllabuses *Beowulf* has inevitably some place, and the consequent production of compendious literary histories. For these cater (in fact, if not in intention) for those seeking knowledge about, and ready-made judgements upon, works which they have not the time, or (often enough) the desire, to know at first hand. The small literary value of such summaries is sometimes recognized in the act of giving them. Thus Strong (op. cit.) gives a fairly complete one, but remarks that 'the short summary does scant justice to the poem'. Ker in *E. Lit.* (*Med.*) says: 'So told, in abstract, it is not a particularly interesting story.' He evidently perceived what might be the retort, for he attempts to justify the procedure in this case, adding: 'Told in this way the story of Theseus or Hercules would still have much more in it.' I dissent. But it does not matter, for the comparison of two plots 'told in this way' is no guide whatever to the merits of literary versions told in quite different ways. It is not necessarily the best poem that loses least in précis.

function of the allusions, as shaped and placed, in the poetic economy of *Beowulf* as it is. Yet actually the appreciation of this function is largely independent of such investigations.

But there is also, I suppose, a real question of taste involved: a judgement that the heroic or tragic story on a strictly human plane is by nature superior. Doom is held less literary than ἁμαρτία.[2] The proposition seems to have been passed as self-evident. I dissent, even at the risk of being held incorrect or not sober. But I will not here enter into debate, nor attempt at length a defence of the mythical mode of imagination, and the disentanglement of the confusion between myth and folk-tale into which these judgements appear to have fallen. The myth has other forms than the (now discredited) mythical allegory of nature: the sun, the seasons, the sea, and such things. The term 'folk-tale' is misleading; its very tone of depreciation begs the question. Folk-tales in being, as told—for the 'typical folk-tale', of course, is merely an abstract conception of research nowhere existing—do often contain elements that are thin and cheap, with little even potential virtue; but they also contain much that is far more powerful, and that cannot be sharply separated from myth, being derived from it, or capable in poetic hands of turning into it: that is of becoming largely significant—as a whole, accepted unanalysed. The significance of a myth is not easily to be pinned on paper by analytical reasoning. It is at its best when it is presented by a poet who feels rather than makes explicit what his theme portends; who presents it incarnate in the world of history and geography, as our poet has done. Its defender is thus at a disadvantage: unless he is careful, and speaks in parables, he will kill what he is studying by vivisection, and he will be left with a formal or mechanical allegory, and, what is more, probably with one that will not work. For myth is alive at once and in all its parts, and dies before it can be dissected. It is possible, I think, to be moved by the power of myth and yet to misunderstand the sensation, to ascribe it wholly to something else that is also present: to metrical art, style, or verbal skill. Correct and sober taste may refuse to admit that there can be an interest for *us*—the proud *we* that includes all intelligent living people—in ogres and dragons; we then perceive its puzzlement in face of the odd fact that it has derived great pleasure from a poem that is actually about these unfashionable creatures. Even though it attributes 'genius', as does Mr Girvan, to the author, it cannot admit that the monsters are anything but a sad mistake.

It does not seem plain that ancient taste supports the modern as much as it has been represented to do. I have the author of *Beowulf*,

2. Hamartia, the Aristotelian term for a hero's tragic flaw [*Editor*].

at any rate, on my side: a greater man than most of us. And I cannot myself perceive a period in the North when one kind alone was esteemed: there was room for myth and heroic legend, and for blends of these. As for the dragon: as far as we know anything about these old poets, we know this: the prince of the heroes of the North, supremely memorable—*hans nafn mun uppi meðan veröldin stendr*[3]—was a dragon-slayer. And his most renowned deed, from which in Norse he derived his title Fáfnisbani, was the slaying of the prince of legendary worms. Although there is plainly considerable difference between the later Norse and the ancient English form of the story alluded to in *Beowulf*, already there it had these two primary features: the dragon, and the slaying of him as the chief deed of the greatest of heroes—*he wæs wreccena wide mærost*.[4] A dragon is no idle fancy. Whatever may be his origins, in fact or invention, the dragon in legend is a potent creation of men's imagination, richer in significance than his barrow is in gold. Even to-day (despite the critics) you may find men not ignorant of tragic legend and history, who have heard of heroes and indeed seen them, who yet have been caught by the fascination of the worm. More than one poem in recent years (since *Beowulf* escaped somewhat from the dominion of the students of origins to the students of poetry) has been inspired by the dragon of *Beowulf*, but none that I know of by Ingeld son of Froda. Indeed, I do not think Chambers very happy in his particular choice. He gives battle on dubious ground. In so far as we can now grasp its detail and atmosphere the story of Ingeld the thrice faithless and easily persuaded is chiefly interesting as an episode in a larger theme, as part of a tradition that had acquired legendary, and so dramatically personalized, form concerning moving events in history: the arising of Denmark, and wars in the islands of the North. In itself it is not a supremely potent story. But, of course, as with all tales of any sort, its literary power must have depended mainly upon how it was handled. A poet may have made a great thing of it. Upon this chance must be founded the popularity of Ingeld's legend in England, for which there is some evidence.[5] There is no inherent magical virtue about heroic-tragic stories as such, and apart from the merits of individual treatments. The same heroic plot can yield good and bad poems, and good and bad sagas. The recipe for the central

3. "And his [Sigurd's] name will endure while the world remains," ch. 12, *The Saga of the Volsungs*, trans. Jesse L. Byock (Berkeley: U of California P, 1990), p. 54 [*Editor*].
4. "He was the most famous of exiles," *Beowulf*, lines 898–99 [*Editor's translation*].
5. Namely the use of it in *Beowulf*, both dramatically in depicting the sagacity of Beowulf the hero, and as an essential part of the traditions concerning the Scylding court, which is the legendary background against which the rise of the hero is set—as a later age would have chosen the court of Arthur. Also the probable allusion in Alcuin's letter to Speratus: see Chambers's *Widsith*, p. 78.

situations of such stories, studied in the abstract, is after all as 'simple' and as 'typical' as that of folktales. There are in any case many heroes but very few good dragons.

Beowulf's dragon, if one wishes really to criticize, is not to be blamed for being a dragon, but rather for not being dragon enough, plain pure fairy-story dragon. There are in the poem some vivid touches of the right kind—as *þa se wyrm onwoc, wroht wæs geniwad; stonc æfter stane*, 2285[6]—in which this dragon is real worm, with a bestial life and thought of his own, but the conception, none the less, approaches *draconitas* rather than *draco*: a personification of malice, greed, destruction (the evil side of heroic life), and of the undiscriminating cruelty of fortune that distinguishes not good or bad (the evil aspect of all life). But for *Beowulf*, the poem, that is as it should be. In this poem the balance is nice, but it is preserved. The large symbolism is near the surface, but it does not break through, nor become allegory. Something more significant than a standard hero, a man faced with a foe more evil than any human enemy of house or realm, is before us, and yet incarnate in time, walking in heroic history, and treading the named lands of the North. And this, we are told, is the radical defect of *Beowulf*, that its author, coming in a time rich in the legends of heroic men, has used them afresh in an original fashion, giving us not just one more, but something akin yet different: a measure and interpretation of them all.

We do not deny the worth of the hero by accepting Grendel and the dragon. Let us by all means esteem the old heroes: men caught in the chains of circumstance or of their own character, torn between duties equally sacred, dying with their backs to the wall. But *Beowulf*, I fancy, plays a larger part than is recognized in helping us to esteem them. Heroic lays may have dealt in their own way—we have little enough to judge by—a way more brief and vigorous, perhaps, though perhaps also more harsh and noisy (and less thoughtful), with the actions of heroes caught in circumstances that conformed more or less to the varied but fundamentally simple recipe for an heroic situation. In these (if we had them) we could see the exaltation of undefeated will, which receives doctrinal expression in the words of Byrhtwold at the battle of Maldon.[7] But though with sympathy and patience we might gather, from a line here or a tone there, the background of imagination which gives to this indomitability, this paradox of defeat inevitable yet unacknowledged, its full significance, it is in *Beowulf* that a poet has devoted a whole poem to the theme, and has drawn the struggle in different proportions, so that we may see

6. "When the dragon awoke, strife was renewed; he sniffed along the stone," lines 2287–88 [*Editor's translation*].

7. This expression may well have been actually used by the *eald geneat*, but none the less (or perhaps rather precisely on that account) is probably to be regarded not as new-minted, but as an ancient and honoured *gnome* of long descent.

man at war with the hostile world, and his inevitable overthrow in Time.[8] The particular is on the outer edge, the essential in the centre.

Of course, I do not assert that the poet, if questioned, would have replied in the Anglo-Saxon equivalents of these terms. Had the matter been so explicit to him, his poem would certainly have been the worse. None the less we may still, against his great scene, hung with tapestries woven of ancient tales of ruin, see the *hæleð* walk. When we have read his poem, as a poem, rather than as a collection of episodes, we perceive that he who wrote *hæleð under heofenum* may have meant in dictionary terms 'heroes under heaven', or 'mighty men upon earth', but he and his hearers were thinking of the *eormengrund*, the great earth, ringed with *garsecg*, the shoreless sea, beneath the sky's inaccessible roof; whereon, as in a little circle of light about their halls, men with courage as their stay went forward to that battle with the hostile world and the offspring of the dark which ends for all, even the kings and champions, in defeat. That even this 'geography', once held as a material fact, could now be classed as a mere folk-tale affects its value very little. It transcends astronomy. Not that astronomy has done anything to make the island seem more secure or the outer seas less formidable.

Beowulf is not, then, the hero of an heroic lay, precisely. He has no enmeshed loyalties, nor hapless love. *He is a man, and that for him and many is sufficient tragedy*. It is not an irritating accident that the tone of the poem is so high and its theme so low. It is the theme in its deadly seriousness that begets the dignity of tone: *lif is læne: eal scæceð leoht and lif somod.*[9] So deadly and ineluctable is the underlying thought, that those who in the circle of light, within the besieged hall, are absorbed in work or talk and do not look to the battlements, either do not regard it or recoil. Death comes to the feast, and they say He gibbers: He has no sense of proportion.

I would suggest, then, that the monsters are not an inexplicable blunder of taste; they are essential, fundamentally allied to the underlying ideas of the poem, which give it its lofty tone and high seriousness. The key to the fusion-point of imagination that produced this poem lies, therefore, in those very references to Cain which have often been used as a stick to beat an ass—taken as an evident sign (were any needed) of the muddled heads of early Anglo-Saxons. They could not, it was said, keep Scandinavian bogies and the Scriptures separate in their puzzled brains. The New Testament

8. For the words *hige sceal þe heardra, heorte þe cenre, mod sceal þe mare þe ure mægen lytlað* are not, of course, an exhortation to simple courage. They are not reminders that fortune favours the brave, or that victory may be snatched from defeat by the stubborn. (Such thoughts were familiar, but otherwise expressed: *wyrd oft nereð unfægne eorl, þonne his ellen deah*.) The words of Byrhtwold were made for a man's last and hopeless day.

9. "Life is transitory: all light and life departs together." Tolkien's invention, patterned after Old English gnomic verse [*Editor's translation*].

was beyond their comprehension. I am not, as I have confessed, a man so diligent as duly to read all the books about *Beowulf*, but as far as I am aware the most suggestive approach to this point appears in the essay *Beowulf and the Heroic Age* to which I have already referred.[1] I will quote a small part of it.

> In the epoch of *Beowulf* a Heroic Age more wild and primitive than that of Greece is brought into touch with Christendom, with the Sermon on the Mount, with Catholic theology and ideas of Heaven and Hell. We see the difference, if we compare the wilder things—the folk-tale element—in *Beowulf* with the wilder things of Homer. Take for example the tale of Odysseus and the Cyclops—the No-man trick. Odysseus is struggling with a monstrous and wicked foe, but he is not exactly thought of as struggling with the powers of darkness. Polyphemus, by devouring his guests, acts in a way which is hateful to Zeus and the other gods: yet the Cyclops is himself god-begotten and under divine protection, and the fact that Odysseus has maimed him is a wrong which Poseidon is slow to forgive. But the gigantic foes whom Beowulf has to meet are identified with the foes of God. Grendel and the dragon are constantly referred to in language which is meant to recall the powers of darkness with which Christian men felt themselves to be encompassed. They[2] are the 'inmates of Hell', 'adversaries of God', 'offspring of Cain', 'enemies of mankind'. Consequently, the matter of the main story of *Beowulf*, monstrous as it is, is not so far removed from common mediaeval experience as it seems to us to be from our own. . . . Grendel hardly differs[3] from the fiends of the pit who were always in ambush to waylay a righteous man. And so Beowulf, for all that he moves in the world of the primitive Heroic Age of the Germans, nevertheless is almost a Christian knight.[4]

There are some hints here which are, I think, worth pursuing further. Most important is it to consider how and why the monsters become 'adversaries of God', and so begin to symbolize (and ultimately to become identified with) the powers of evil, even while they remain, as they do still remain in *Beowulf*, mortal denizens of the material world, in it and of it. I accept without argument throughout the attribution of *Beowulf* to the 'age of Bede'—one of the firmer conclusions of a department of research most clearly serviceable to criticism: inquiry into the probable date of the effective composition of the poem as we have it. So regarded *Beowulf* is, of course, an his-

1. *Foreword* to Strong's translation, p. xxviii. See note 3.
2. This is not strictly true. The dragon is not referred to in such terms, which are applied to Grendel and to the primeval giants.
3. He differs in important points, referred to later.
4. I should prefer to say that he moves in a northern heroic age imagined by a Christian, and therefore has a noble and gentle quality, though conceived to be a pagan.

torical document of the first order for the study of the mood and thought of the period and one perhaps too little used for the purpose by professed historians.[5] But it is the mood of the author, the essential cast of his imaginative apprehension of the world, that is my concern, not history for its own sake; I am interested in that time of fusion only as it may help us to understand the poem. And in the poem I think we may observe not confusion, a half-hearted or a muddled business, but a fusion that has occurred *at a given point* of contact between old and new, a product of thought and deep emotion.

One of the most potent elements in that fusion is the Northern courage: the theory of courage, which is the great contribution of early Northern literature. This is not a military judgement. I am not asserting that, if the Trojans could have employed a Northern king and his companions, they would have driven Agamemnon and Achilles into the sea, more decisively than the Greek hexameter routs the alliterative line—though it is not improbable. I refer rather to the central position the creed of unyielding will holds in the North. With due reserve we may turn to the tradition of pagan imagination as it survived in Icelandic. Of English pre-Christian mythology we know practically nothing. But the fundamentally similar heroic temper of ancient England and Scandinavia cannot have been founded on (or perhaps rather, cannot have generated) mythologies divergent on this essential point. 'The Northern Gods', Ker said, 'have an exultant extravagance in their warfare which makes them more like Titans than Olympians; *only they are on the right side, though it is not the side that wins. The winning side is Chaos and Unreason*'—mythologically, the monsters—*'but the gods, who are defeated, think that defeat no refutation*'.[6] And in their war men are their chosen allies, able when heroic to share in this 'absolute resistance, perfect because without hope'. At least in this vision of the final defeat of the humane (and of the divine made in its image), and in the essential hostility of the gods and heroes on the one hand and the monsters on the other, we may suppose that pagan English and Norse imagination agreed.

But in England this imagination was brought into touch with Christendom, and with the Scriptures. The process of 'conversion' was a long one, but some of its effects were doubtless immediate: an alchemy of change (producing ultimately the mediaeval) was at once at work. One does not have to wait until all the native traditions of the older world have been replaced or forgotten; for the minds which

5. It is, for instance, dismissed cursorily, and somewhat contemptuously in the recent (somewhat contemptuous) essay of Dr. Watson, *The Age of Bede* in *Bede, His Life, Times, and Writings*, ed. A. Hamilton Thompson, 1935.
6. *The Dark Ages*, p. 57.

still retain them are changed, and the memories viewed in a different perspective: *at once they become more ancient and remote, and in a sense darker*. It is through such a blending that there was available to a poet who set out to *write* a poem—and in the case of *Beowulf* we may probably use this very word—on a scale and plan unlike a minstrel's lay, both new faith and new learning (or education), and also a body of native tradition (itself requiring to be learned) for the changed mind to contemplate together.[7] The native 'learning' cannot be denied in the case of *Beowulf*. Its display has grievously perturbed the critics, for the author draws upon tradition at will for his own purposes, as a poet of later times might draw upon history or the classics and expect his allusions to be understood (within a certain class of hearers). He was in fact, like Virgil, learned enough in the vernacular department to have an historical perspective, even an antiquarian curiosity. He cast his time into the long-ago, because already the long-ago had a special poetical attraction. He knew much about old days, and though his knowledge—of such things as sea-burial and the funeral pyre, for instance—was rich and poetical rather than accurate with the accuracy of modern archaeology (such as that is), one thing he knew clearly: those days were heathen—heathen, noble, and hopeless.

But if the specifically Christian was suppressed,[8] so also were the old gods. Partly because they had not really existed, and had been always, in the Christian view, only delusions or lies fabricated by the evil one, the *gastbona*, to whom the hopeless turned especially in times of need. Partly because their old names (certainly not forgotten) had been potent, and were connected in memory still, not only with mythology or such fairy-tale matter as we find, say, in *Gylfaginning*, but with active heathendom, religion and *wigweorþung*. Most of all because they were not actually essential to the theme.

The monsters had been the foes of the gods, the captains of men,

7. If we consider the period as a whole. It is not, of course, necessarily true of individuals. These doubtless from the beginning showed many degrees from deep instruction and understanding to disjointed superstition, or blank ignorance.

8. Avoidance of obvious anachronisms (such as are found in *Judith*, for instance, where the heroine refers in her own speeches to Christ and the Trinity), and the absence of all definitely *Christian* names and terms, is natural and plainly intentional. It must be observed that there is a difference between the comments of the author and the things said in reported speech by his characters. The two chief of these, Hrothgar and Beowulf, are again differentiated. Thus the only definitely Scriptural references, to Abel (108) and to Cain (108, 1261), occur where the poet is speaking as commentator. The theory of Grendel's origin is not known to the actors: Hrothgar denies all knowledge of the ancestry of Grendel (1355). The giants (1688 ff.) are, it is true, represented pictorially, and in Scriptural terms. But this suggests rather that the author identified native and Scriptural accounts, and gave his picture Scriptural colour, since of the two accounts Scripture was the truer. And if so it would be closer to that told in remote antiquity when the sword was made, more especially since the *wundorsmiþas* who wrought it were actually giants (1558, 1562, 1679): they would know the true tale. See note 9 [p. 123].

and within Time the monsters would win. In the heroic siege and last defeat men and gods alike had been imagined in the same host. Now the heroic figures, the men of old, *hæleð under heofenum*, remained and still fought on until defeat. For the monsters do not depart, whether the gods go or come. A Christian was (and is) still like his forefathers a mortal hemmed in a hostile world. The monsters remained the enemies of mankind, the infantry of the old war, and became inevitably the enemies of the one God, *ece Dryhten*, the eternal Captain of the new. Even so the vision of the war changes. For it begins to dissolve, even as the contest on the fields of Time thus takes on its largest aspect. The tragedy of the great temporal defeat remains for a while poignant, but ceases to be finally important. It is no defeat, for the end of the world is part of the design of Metod, the Arbiter who is above the mortal world. Beyond there appears a possibility of eternal victory (or eternal defeat), and the real battle is between the soul and its adversaries. So the old monsters became images of the evil spirit or spirits, or rather the evil spirits entered into the monsters and took visible shape in the hideous bodies of the *þyrsas* and *sigelhearwan* of heathen imagination.

But that shift is not complete in *Beowulf*—whatever may have been true of its period in general. Its author is still concerned primarily with *man on earth*, rehandling in a new perspective an ancient theme: that man, each man and all men, and all their works shall die. A theme no Christian need despise. Yet this theme plainly would not be so treated, but for the nearness of a pagan time. The shadow of its despair, if only as a mood, as an intense emotion of regret, is still there. The worth of defeated valour in this world is deeply felt. As the poet looks back into the past, surveying the history of kings and warriors in the old traditions, he sees that all glory (or as we might say 'culture' or 'civilization') ends in night. The solution of that tragedy is not treated—it does not arise out of the material. We get in fact a poem from a pregnant moment of poise, looking back into the pit, by a man learned in old tales who was struggling, as it were, to get a general view of them all, perceiving their common tragedy of inevitable ruin, and yet feeling this more *poetically* because he was himself removed from the direct pressure of its despair. He could view from without, but still feel immediately and from within, the old dogma: despair of the event, combined with faith in the value of doomed resistance. He was still dealing with the great temporal tragedy, and not yet writing an allegorical homily in verse. Grendel inhabits the visible world and eats the flesh and blood of men; he enters their houses by the doors. The dragon wields a physical fire, and covets gold not souls; he is slain with iron in his belly. Beowulf's *byrne* was made by Weland; and the iron shield he bore against the serpent by his own smiths: it was not yet the breastplate of righteousness, nor the shield of faith for the quenching of all the fiery darts of the wicked.

Almost we might say that this poem was (in one direction) inspired by the debate that had long been held and continued after, and that it was one of the chief contributions to the controversy: shall we or shall we not consign the heathen ancestors to perdition? What good will it do posterity to read the battles of Hector? *Quid Hinieldus cum Christo?*[9] The author of *Beowulf* showed forth the permanent value of that *pietas* which treasures the memory of man's struggles in the dark past, man fallen and not yet saved, disgraced but not dethroned. It would seem to have been part of the English temper in its strong sense of tradition, dependent doubtless on dynasties, noble houses, and their code of honour, and strengthened, it may be, by the more inquisitive and less severe Celtic learning, that it should, at least in some quarters and despite grave and Gallic voices, preserve much from the northern past to blend with southern learning, and new faith.

It has been thought that the influence of Latin epic, especially of the *Aeneid*, is perceptible in *Beowulf*, and a necessary explanation, if only in the exciting of emulation, of the development of the long and studied poem in early England. There is, of course, a likeness in places between these greater and lesser things, the *Aeneid* and *Beowulf*, if they are read in conjunction. But the smaller points in which imitation or reminiscence might be perceived are inconclusive, while the real likeness is deeper and due to certain qualities in the authors independent of the question whether the Anglo-Saxon had read Virgil or not. It is this deeper likeness which makes things, that are either the inevitabilities of human poetry or the accidental congruences of all tales, ring alike. We have the great pagan on the threshold of the change of the world; and the great (if lesser) Christian just over the threshold of the great change in his time and place: the backward view: *multa putans sortemque animo miseratus iniquam.*[1]

But we will now return once more to the monsters, and consider especially the difference of their status in the northern and southern mythologies. Of Grendel it is said: *Godes yrre bær.*[2] But the Cyclops is god-begotten and his maiming is an offence against his begetter,

9. "What does Ingeld have to do with Christ?" Alcuin; see pp. 91–92, above [*Editor*].
1. In fact the real resemblance of the *Aeneid* and *Beowulf* lies in the constant presence of a sense of many-storied antiquity, together with its natural accompaniment, stern and noble melancholy. In this they are really akin and together differ from Homer's flatter, if more glittering, surface.
 ["Thinking many things and in his mind pondering their unequal lot," *Aeneid* 6.332—*Editor's translation*.]
2. "He carried God's wrath," line 711 [*Editor's translation*].

the god Poseidon. This radical difference in mythological status is only brought out more sharply by the very closeness of the similarity in conception (in all save mere size) that is seen, if we compare *Beowulf*, 740 ff., with the description of the Cyclops devouring men in *Odyssey*, ix—or still more in *Aeneid*, iii. 622 ff. In Virgil, whatever may be true of the fairy-tale world of the Odyssey, the Cyclops walks veritably in the historic world. He is seen by Aeneas in Sicily, *monstrum horrendum, informe, ingens,*[3] as much a perilous fact as Grendel was in Denmark, *earmsceapen on weres wæstmum . . . næfne he wæs mara þonne ænig man oðer*;[4] as real as Acestes or Hrothgar.[5]

At this point in particular we may regret that we do not know more about pre-Christian English mythology. Yet it is, as I have said, legitimate to suppose that in the matter of the position of the monsters in regard to men and gods the view was fundamentally the same as in later Icelandic. Thus, though all such generalizations are naturally imperfect in detail (since they deal with matter of various origins, constantly reworked, and never even at most more than partially systematized), we may with some truth contrast the 'inhumanness' of the Greek gods, however anthropomorphic, with the 'humanness' of the Northern, however titanic. In the southern myths there is also rumour of wars with giants and great powers not Olympian, the *Titania pubes fulmine deiecti,*[6] rolling like Satan and his satellites in the nethermost Abyss. But this war is differently conceived. It lies in a chaotic past. The ruling gods are not besieged, not in ever-present peril or under future doom.[7] Their offspring on earth may be heroes or fair women; it may also be the other creatures hostile to men. The gods are not the allies of men in their war against these or other monsters. The interest of the gods is in this or that man as part of

3. "A terrible monster, misshapen, huge," *Aeneid*, 3.662 [*Editor's translation*].
4. "Wretchedly shaped in the form of a man . . . except that he was bigger than any other person," lines 1351–53 [*Editor's translation*].
5. I use this illustration following Chambers, because of the close resemblance between Grendel and the Cyclops in kind. But other examples could be adduced: Cacus, for instance, the offspring of Vulcan. One might ponder the contrast between the legends of the torture of Prometheus and of Loki: the one for assisting men, the other for assisting the powers of darkness.
6. "The Titanian youth hurled down by a thunderbolt," *Aeneid* 6.580 [*Editor's translation*].
7. There is actually no final principle in the legendary hostilities contained in classical mythology. For the present purpose that is all that matters: we are not here concerned with remoter mythological origins, in the North or South. The gods, Cronian or Olympian, the Titans, and other great natural powers, and various monsters, even minor local horrors, are not clearly distinguished in origin or ancestry. There could be no permanent policy of war, led by Olympus, to which human courage might be dedicated, among mythological races so promiscuous. Of course, nowhere can absolute rigidity of distinction be expected, because in a sense the foe is always both within and without; the fortress must fall through treachery as well as by assault. Thus Grendel has a perverted human shape, and the giants or *jötnar*, even when (like the Titans) they are of super-divine stature, are parodies of the human-divine form. Even in Norse, where the distinction is most rigid, Loki dwells in Asgarðr, though he is an evil and lying spirit, and fatal monsters come of him. For it is true of man, maker of myths, that Grendel and the Dragon, in their lust, greed, and malice, have a part in him. But mythically conceived the gods do not recognize any bond with *Fenris úlfr*, any more than men with Grendel or the serpent.

their individual schemes, not as part of a great strategy that includes all good men, as the infantry of battle. In Norse, at any rate, the gods are within Time, doomed with their allies to death. Their battle is with the monsters and the outer darkness. They gather heroes for the last defence. Already before euhemerism saved them by embalming them, and they dwindled in antiquarian fancy to the mighty ancestors of northern kings (English and Scandinavian), they had become in their very being the enlarged shadows of great men and warriors upon the walls of the world. When Baldr is slain and goes to Hel he cannot escape thence any more than mortal man.

This may make the southern gods more godlike—more lofty, dread, and inscrutable. They are timeless and do not fear death. Such a mythology may hold the promise of a profounder thought. In any case it was a virtue of the southern mythology that it could not stop where it was. It must go forward to philosophy or relapse into anarchy. For in a sense it had shirked the problem precisely by not having the monsters in the centre—as they are in *Beowulf* to the astonishment of the critics. But such horrors cannot be left permanently unexplained, lurking on the outer edges and under suspicion of being connected with the Government. It is the strength of the northern mythological imagination that it faced this problem, put the monsters in the centre, gave them victory but no honour, and found a potent but terrible solution in naked will and courage. 'As a working theory absolutely impregnable.' So potent is it, that while the older southern imagination has faded for ever into literary ornament, the northern has power, as it were, to revive its spirit even in our own times. It can work, even as it did work with the *goðlauss* viking, without gods: martial heroism as its own end. But we may remember that the poet of *Beowulf* saw clearly: the wages of heroism is death.

For these reasons I think that the passages in *Beowulf* concerning the giants and their war with God, together with the two mentions of Cain (as the ancestor of the giants in general and Grendel in particular) are specially important.

They are directly connected with Scripture, yet they cannot be dissociated from the creatures of northern myth, the ever-watchful foes of the gods (and men). The undoubtedly scriptural Cain is connected with *eotenas* and *ylfe*, which are the *jötnar* and *álfar* of Norse. But this is not due to mere confusion—it is rather an indication of the precise point at which an imagination, pondering old and new, was kindled. At this point new Scripture and old tradition touched and ignited. It is for this reason that these elements of Scripture alone appear in a poem dealing of design with the noble pagan of old days. For they are precisely the elements which bear upon this theme. Man alien in a hostile world, engaged in a struggle which he cannot win while the world lasts, is assured that his foes are the foes also of Dryhten, that his courage noble in itself is also the highest loyalty: so said thyle and clerk.

In *Beowulf* we have, then, an historical poem about the pagan past, or an attempt at one—literal historical fidelity founded on modern research was, of course, not attempted. It is a poem by a learned man writing of old times, who looking back on the heroism and sorrow feels in them something permanent and something symbolical. So far from being a confused semi-pagan—historically unlikely for a man of this sort in the period—he brought probably *first* to his task a knowledge of Christian poetry, especially that of the Cædmon school, and especially *Genesis.*[8] He makes his minstrel sing in Heorot of the Creation of the earth and the lights of Heaven. So excellent is this choice as the theme of the harp that maddened Grendel lurking joyless in the dark without that it matters little whether this is anachronistic or not.[9] *Secondly*, to his task the poet brought a considerable learning in native lays and traditions: only by learning and training could such things be acquired, they were no more born naturally into an Englishman of the seventh or eighth centuries, by simple virtue of being an 'Anglo-Saxon', than ready-made knowledge of poetry and history is inherited at birth by modern children.

It would seem that, in his attempt to depict ancient pre-Christian days, intending to emphasize their nobility, and the desire of the good for truth, he turned naturally when delineating the great King of Heorot to the Old Testament. In the *folces hyrde* of the Danes we have much of the shepherd patriarchs and kings of Israel, servants of the one God, who attribute to His mercy all the good things that come to them in this life. We have in fact a Christian English conception of the noble chief before Christianity, who could lapse (as could Israel) in times of temptation into idolatry.[1] On the other hand, the traditional matter in English, not to mention the living survival of the heroic code and temper among the noble households of

8. The *Genesis* which is preserved for us is a late copy of a damaged original, but is still certainly in its older parts a poem whose composition must be referred to the early period. That *Genesis A* is actually older than *Beowulf* is generally recognized as the most probable reading of such evidence as there is.

9. Actually the poet may have known, what we can guess, that such creation-themes were also ancient in the North. *Völuspá* describes Chaos and the making of the sun and moon, and very similar language occurs in the Old High German fragment known as the *Wessobrunner Gebet*. The song of the minstrel Iopas, who had his knowledge from Atlas, at the end of the first book of the *Aeneid* is also in part a song of origins: *hic canit errantem lunam solisque labores, unde hominum genus et pecudes, unde imber et ignes*. In any case the Anglo-Saxon poet's view throughout was plainly that true, or truer, knowledge was possessed in ancient days (when men were not deceived by the Devil); at least they knew of the one God and Creator, though not of heaven, for that was lost. See note 8, p. 118.

1. It is of Old Testament lapses rather than of any events in England (of which he is not speaking) that the poet is thinking in lines 175 ff., and this colours his manner of allusion to knowledge which he may have derived from native traditions concerning the Danes and the special heathen religious significance of the site of Heorot (*Hleiðrar, æt hærgtrafum*, the tabernacles)—it was possibly a matter that embittered the feud of Danes and Heathobeards. If so, this is another point where old and new have blended* * *.

ancient England, enabled him to draw differently, and in some respects much closer to the actual heathen *hæleð*, the character of Beowulf, especially as a young knight, who used his great gift of *mægen* to earn *dom* and *lof* among men and posterity.

Beowulf is not an actual picture of historic Denmark or Geatland or Sweden about A.D. 500. But it is (if with certain minor defects) on a general view a self-consistent picture, a construction bearing clearly the marks of design and thought. The whole must have succeeded admirably in creating in the minds of the poet's contemporaries the illusion of surveying a past, pagan but noble and fraught with a deep significance—a past that itself had depth and reached backward into a dark antiquity of sorrow. This impression of depth is an effect and a justification of the use of episodes and allusions to old tales, mostly darker, more pagan, and desperate than the foreground.

To a similar antiquarian temper, and a similar use of vernacular learning, is probably due the similar effect of antiquity (and melancholy) in the *Aeneid*—especially felt as soon as Aeneas reaches Italy and the *Saturni gentem . . . sponte sua veterisque dei se more tenentem.*[2] *Ic þa leode wat ge wið feond ge wið freond fæste worhte, æghwæs untæle ealde wisan.*[3] Alas for the lost lore, the annals and old poets that Virgil knew, and only used in the making of a new thing! The criticism that the important matters are put on the outer edges misses this point of artistry, and indeed fails to see why the old things have in *Beowulf* such an appeal: it is the poet himself who made antiquity so appealing. His poem has more value in consequence, and is a greater contribution to early mediaeval thought than the harsh and intolerant view that consigned all the heroes to the devil. We may be thankful that the product of so noble a temper has been preserved by chance (if such it be) from the dragon of destruction.

The general structure of the poem, so viewed, is not really difficult to perceive, if we look to the main points, the strategy, and neglect the many points of minor tactics. We must dismiss, of course, from mind the notion that *Beowulf* is a 'narrative poem', that it tells a tale or intends to tell a tale sequentially. The poem 'lacks steady advance': so Klaeber heads a critical section in his edition.[4] But the poem was not meant to advance, steadily or unsteadily. It is essentially a balance, an opposition of ends and beginnings. In its simplest terms it is a contrasted description of two moments in a great life, rising and setting; an elaboration of the ancient and intensely moving contrast

2. "A race of Saturn . . . ruled by their own will, and guiding themselves by the law of an ancient god," *Aeneid* 7.201–3 [*Editor's translation*].
3. "I know your people / are beyond reproach in every respect, / steadfast in the old way with friend or foe." Heaney, lines 1863–65 [*Editor*].
4. Though only explicitly referred to here and in disagreement, this edition is, of course, of great authority, and all who have used it have learned much from it.

between youth and age, first achievement and final death. It is divided in consequence into two opposed portions, different in matter, manner, and length: A from 1 to 2199 (including an exordium of 52 lines); B from 2200 to 3182 (the end). There is no reason to cavil at this proportion; in any case, for the purpose and the production of the required effect, it proves in practice to be right.

This simple and *static* structure, solid and strong, is in each part much diversified, and capable of enduring this treatment. In the conduct of the presentation of Beowulf's rise to fame on the one hand, and of his kingship and death on the other, criticism can find things to question, especially if it is captious, but also much to praise, if it is attentive. But the only serious weakness, or apparent weakness, is the long recapitulation: the report of Beowulf to Hygelac. This recapitulation is well done. Without serious discrepancy[5] it retells rapidly the events in Heorot, and retouches the account; and it serves to illustrate, since he himself describes his own deeds, yet more vividly the character of a young man, singled out by destiny, as he steps suddenly forth in his full powers. Yet this is perhaps not quite sufficient to justify the repetition. The explanation, if not complete justification, is probably to be sought in different directions.

For one thing, the old tale was not first told or invented by this poet. So much is clear from investigation of the folk-tale analogues. Even the legendary association of the Scylding court with a marauding monster, and with the arrival from abroad of a champion and deliverer was probably already old. The plot was not the poet's; and though he has infused feeling and significance into its crude material, that plot was not a perfect vehicle of the theme or themes that came to hidden life in the poet's mind as he worked upon it. Not an unusual event in literature. For the contrast—youth and death—it would probably have been better, if we had no journeying. If the single nation of the *Geatas* had been the scene, we should have felt the stage not narrower, but symbolically wider. More plainly should we have perceived in one people and their hero all mankind and its heroes. This at any rate I have always myself felt in reading *Beowulf*; but I have also felt that this defect is rectified by the bringing of the tale of Grendel to Geatland. As Beowulf stands in Hygelac's hall and tells his story, he sets his feet firm again in the land of his own people, and is no longer in danger of appearing a mere *wrecca*, an errant

5. I am not concerned with minor discrepancies at any point in the poem. They are no proof of composite authorship, nor even of incompetent authorship. It is very difficult, even in a newly invented tale of any length, to avoid such defects; more so still in rehandling old and oft-told tales. The points that are seized in the study, with a copy that can be indexed and turned to and fro (even if never read straight through as it was meant to be), are usually such as may easily escape an author and still more easily his natural audience. Virgil certainly does not escape such faults, even within the limits of a single book. Modern printed tales, that have presumably had the advantage of proof-correction, can even be observed to hesitate in the heroine's Christian name.

adventurer and slayer of bogies that do not concern him.

There is in fact a double division in the poem: the fundamental one already referred to, and a secondary but important division at line 1887. After that the essentials of the previous part are taken up and compacted, so that all the tragedy of Beowulf is contained between 1888 and the end.[6] But, of course, without the first half we should miss much incidental illustration; we should miss also the dark background of the court of Heorot that loomed as large in glory and doom in ancient northern imagination as the court of Arthur: no vision of the past was complete without it. And (most important) we should lose the direct contrast of youth and age in the persons of Beowulf and Hrothgar which is one of the chief purposes of this section: it ends with the pregnant words *oþ þæt hine yldo benam mægenes wynnum, se þe oft manegum scod.*[7]

In any case we must not view this poem as in intention an exciting narrative or a romantic tale. The very nature of Old English metre is often misjudged. In it there is no single rhythmic pattern progressing from the beginning of a line to the end, and repeated with variation in other lines. The lines do not go according to a tune. They are founded on a balance; an opposition between two halves of roughly equivalent[8] phonetic weight, and significant content, which are more often rhythmically contrasted than similar. They are more like masonry than music. In this fundamental fact of poetic expression I think there is a parallel to the total structure of *Beowulf*. *Beowulf* is indeed the most successful Old English poem because in it the elements, language, metre, theme, structure, are all most nearly in harmony. Judgement of the verse has often gone astray through listening for an accentual rhythm and pattern: and it seems to halt and stumble. Judgement of the theme goes astray through considering it as the narrative handling of a plot: and it seems to halt and stumble. Language and verse, of course, differ from stone or wood or paint, and can be only heard or read in a time-sequence; so that in any poem that deals at all with characters and events some narrative element must be present. We have none the less in *Beowulf* a method and structure that within the limits of the verse-kind approaches rather to sculpture or painting. It is a composition not a tune.

This is clear in the second half. In the struggle with Grendel one can as a reader dismiss the certainty of literary experience that the

6. The least satisfactory arrangement possible is thus to read only lines 1–1887 and not the remainder. This procedure has none the less been, from time to time, directed or encouraged by more than one 'English syllabus'.
7. "Until old age sapped his strength and did him / mortal harm, as it has done so many." Heaney, lines 1886–87 [*Editor*].
8. Equivalent, but not necessarily *equal*, certainly not as such things may be measured by machines.

hero will not in fact perish, and allow oneself to share the hopes and fears of the Geats upon the shore. In the second part the author has no desire whatever that the issue should remain open, even according to literary convention. There is no need to hasten like the messenger, who rode to bear the lamentable news to the waiting people (2892 ff.). They may have hoped, but we are not supposed to. By now we are supposed to have grasped the plan. Disaster is foreboded. Defeat is the theme. Triumph over the foes of man's precarious fortress is over, and we approach slowly and reluctantly the inevitable victory of death.[9]

'In structure', it was said of *Beowulf*, 'it is curiously weak, in a sense preposterous,' though great merits of detail were allowed. In structure actually it is curiously strong, in a sense inevitable, though there are defects of detail. The general design of the poet is not only defensible, it is, I think, admirable. There may have previously existed stirring verse dealing in straightforward manner and even in natural sequence with Beowulf's deeds, or with the fall of Hygelac; or again with the fluctuations of the feud between the houses of Hrethel the Geat and Ongentheow the Swede; or with the tragedy of the Heathobards, and the treason that destroyed the Scylding dynasty. Indeed this must be admitted to be practically certain: it was the existence of such connected legends—connected in the mind, not necessarily dealt with in chronicle fashion or in long semi-historical poems—that permitted the peculiar use of them in *Beowulf*. This poem cannot be criticized or comprehended, if its original audience is imagined in like case to ourselves, possessing only *Beowulf* in splendid isolation. For *Beowulf* was not designed to tell the tale of Hygelac's fall, or for that matter to give the whole biography of Beowulf, still less to write the history of the Geatish kingdom and its downfall. But it used knowledge of these things for its own purpose—to give that sense of perspective, of antiquity with a greater and yet darker antiquity behind. These things are mainly on the outer edges or in the background because they belong there, if they are to function in this way. But in the centre we have an heroic figure of enlarged proportions.

Beowulf is not an 'epic', not even a magnified 'lay'. No terms borrowed from Greek or other literatures exactly fit: there is no reason why they should. Though if we must have a term, we should choose rather 'elegy'. It is an heroic-elegiac poem; and in a sense all its first 3,136 lines are the prelude to a dirge: *him þa gegiredan Geata leode*

9. That the particular bearer of enmity, the Dragon, also dies is important chiefly to Beowulf himself. He was a great man. Not many even in dying can achieve the death of a single worm, or the temporary salvation of their kindred. Within the limits of human life Beowulf neither lived nor died in vain—brave men might say. But there is no hint, indeed there are many to the contrary, that it was a war to end war, or a dragon-fight to end dragons. It is the end of Beowulf, and of the hope of his people.

ad ofer eorðan unwaclicne[1] one of the most moving ever written. But for the universal significance which is given to the fortunes of its hero it is an enhancement and not a detraction, in fact it is necessary, that his final foe should be not some Swedish prince, or treacherous friend, but a dragon: a thing made by imagination for just such a purpose. Nowhere does a dragon come in so precisely where he should. But if the hero falls before a dragon, then certainly he should achieve his early glory by vanquishing a foe of similar order.

There is, I think, no criticism more beside the mark than that which some have made, complaining that it is monsters in both halves that is so disgusting; one they could have stomached more easily. That is nonsense. I can see the point of asking for *no* monsters. I can also see the point of the situation in *Beowulf*. But no point at all in mere reduction of numbers. It would really have been preposterous, if the poet had recounted Beowulf's rise to fame in a 'typical' or 'commonplace' war in Frisia, and then ended him with a dragon. Or if he had told of his cleansing of Heorot, and then brought him to defeat and death in a 'wild' or 'trivial' Swedish invasion! If the dragon is the right end for Beowulf, and I agree with the author that it is, then Grendel is an eminently suitable beginning. They are creatures, *feond mancynnes*, of a similar order and kindred significance. Triumph over the lesser and more nearly human is cancelled by defeat before the older and more elemental. And the conquest of the ogres comes at the right moment: not in earliest youth, though the nicors are referred to in Beowulf's *geogoðfeore* as a presage of the kind of hero we have to deal with; and not during the later period of recognized ability and prowess;[2] but in that first moment, which often comes in great lives, when men look up in surprise and see that a hero has unawares leaped forth. The placing of the dragon is inevitable: a man can but die upon his death-day.

I will conclude by drawing an imaginary contrast. Let us suppose that our poet had chosen a theme more consonant with 'our modern judgement'; the life and death of St Oswald. He might then have made a poem, and told first of Heavenfield, when Oswald as a young prince against all hope won a great victory with a remnant of brave men; and then have passed at once to the lamentable defeat of Oswestry, which seemed to destroy the hope of Christian Northumbria; while all the rest of Oswald's life, and the traditions of the

1. "The Geat people built a pyre for Beowulf, / stacked and decked it until it stood foursquare." Heaney, lines 3137–38 [*Editor*].
2. We do, however, learn incidentally much of this period: it is not strictly true, even of our poem as it is, to say that after the deeds in Heorot Beowulf 'has nothing else to do'. Great heroes, like great saints, should show themselves capable of dealing also with the ordinary things of life, even though they may do so with a strength more than ordinary. We may wish to be assured of this (and the poet has assured us), without demanding that he should put such things in the centre, when they are not the center of his thought.

royal house and its feud with that of Deira might be introduced allusively or omitted. To any one but an historian in search of facts and chronology this would have been a fine thing, an heroic-elegiac poem greater than history. It would be much better than a plain narrative, in verse or prose, however steadily advancing. This mere arrangement would at once give it more significance than a straightforward account of one king's life: the contrast of rising and setting, achievement and death. But even so it would fall far short of *Beowulf*. Poetically it would be greatly enhanced if the poet had taken violent liberties with history and much enlarged the reign of Oswald, making him old and full of years of care and glory when he went forth heavy with foreboding to face the heathen Penda: the contrast of youth and age would add enormously to the original theme, and give it a more universal meaning. But even so it would still fall short of *Beowulf*. To match his theme with the rise and fall of poor 'folk-tale' Beowulf the poet would have been obliged to turn Cadwallon and Penda into giants and demons. It is just because the main foes in *Beowulf* are inhuman that the story is larger and more significant than this imaginary poem of a great king's fall. It glimpses the cosmic and moves with the thought of all men concerning the fate of human life and efforts; it stands amid but above the petty wars of princes, and surpasses the dates and limits of historical periods, however important. At the beginning, and during its process, and most of all at the end, we look down as if from a visionary height upon the house of man in the valley of the world. A light starts—*lixte se leoma ofer landa fela*[3]—and there is a sound of music; but the outer darkness and its hostile offspring lie ever in wait for the torches to fail and the voices to cease. Grendel is maddened by the sound of harps.

And one last point, which those will feel who to-day preserve the ancient *pietas* towards the past: *Beowulf* is not a 'primitive' poem; it is a late one, using the materials (then still plentiful) preserved from a day already changing and passing, a time that has now for ever vanished, swallowed in oblivion; using them for a new purpose, with a wider sweep of imagination, if with a less bitter and concentrated force. When new *Beowulf* was already antiquarian, in a good sense, and it now produces a singular effect. For it is now to us itself ancient; and yet its maker was telling of things already old and weighted with regret, and he expended his art in making keen that touch upon the heart which sorrows have that are both poignant and remote. If the funeral of Beowulf moved once like the echo of an ancient dirge, far-off and hopeless, it is to us as a memory brought over the hills, an echo of an echo. There is not much poetry in the world like this; and though *Beowulf* may not be among the very

3. "Its light shone over many lands." Heaney, line 311 [*Editor*].

greatest poems of our western world and its tradition, it has its own individual character, and peculiar solemnity; it would still have power had it been written in some time or place unknown and without posterity, if it contained no name that could now be recognized or identified by research. Yet it is in fact written in a language that after many centuries has still essential kinship with our own, it was made in this land, and moves in our northern world beneath our northern sky, and for those who are native to that tongue and land, it must ever call with a profound appeal—until the dragon comes.

* * *

JOHN LEYERLE

The Interlace Structure of *Beowulf*†

In the time since Norman Garmonsway* died I have reflected about what I could say that would not embarrass the spirit of the man I wish to honour. He was reticent about himself and I shall be brief. I rarely heard him refer to his distinguished career at King's College, London, for when he spoke of his work, it was always of what lay ahead. His characteristic manner was understatement, like that of the early literature of the north that he knew so well and loved. He was a man who preferred to listen rather than to talk, but he was quick to praise and encourage. He had the virtues of Chaucer's Clerk of Oxenford mixed with a gentle humour.

> Noght o word spak he moore than was neede,
> And that was seyd in forme and reverence,
> And short and quyk and ful of hy sentence;
> Sownynge in moral vertu was his speche,
> And gladly wolde he lerne and gladly teche.

Toronto is a better place for his having lived and worked among us. This paper concerns material he was teaching this year, the relation between early art and poetry in England. I should like to dedicate it to his memory.

† John Leyerle, "The Interlace Structure of *Beowulf*," *University of Toronto Quarterly* 37 (1967): 1–17. Reprinted by permission of the University of Toronto Press Incorporated.

* On February 28, 1967, Norman Garmonsway, Visiting Professor of English at University College in the University of Toronto, died suddenly. This paper, in a slightly different form, was read on March 30 in West Hall of the College in place of a lecture on Canute that Professor Garmonsway was to have delivered on that day.

I

Beowulf is a poem of rapid shifts in subject and time. Events are fragmented into parts and are taken with little regard to chronological order. The details are rich, but the pattern does not present a linear structure, a lack discussed with distaste by many.[1] This lecture will attempt to show that the structure of *Beowulf* is a poetic analogue of the interlace designs common in Anglo-Saxon art of the seventh and eighth centuries. *Beowulf* was composed in the early eighth century in the Midlands or North of England, exactly the time and place where interlace decoration reached a complexity of design and skill in execution never equalled since and, indeed, hardly ever approached. Interlace designs go back to prehistoric Mesopotamia; in one form or another they are characteristic of the art of all races.[2]

The bands may be plaited together to form a braid or rope pattern, a design that appears, for example, on borders of the Franks Casket, a whalebone coffer made in Northumbria about the year 700. Interlace is made when the bands are turned back on themselves to form knots or breaks that interrupt, so to speak, the linear flow of the bands. The south face of the Bewcastle Cross from Cumberland has three panels of knot work; this cross is dated before 710.[3] The bottom panel (Figure 3) has two distinct knots formed by two bands and connected together, a pattern that is identical to that on folio 94^{v} of the Lindisfarne Gospels (Figure 11).[4] There are about a thousand separate pieces of stone surviving from pre-Norman Northumbrian crosses. One need only leaf through W. G. Collingwood's *Northumbrian Crosses of the Pre-Norman Age* (London, 1927) to be struck by the appearance of one interlace design after another, despite the fact that such patterns are relatively difficult to execute in stone, especially when there is any undercutting.

When the bands are cut, the free ends are often elaborated into zoomorphic heads, seen in a very simple stage of development on the Abingdon Brooch (Figure 4) dated in the early seventh century.[5] In more complex designs the stylized heads take on a pronounced

1. For example, see F. P. Magoun, Jr., "*Beowulf* A': A Folk-Variant," *ARV: Tidskrit för Nordisk Folkminnesforskning,* XIV (1958), 95–101, or *Beowulf and the Fight at Finnsburg*, ed. Fr. Klaeber, 3rd edition (Boston, 1950), li–lviii. All quotations are from this edition.
2. For an account of the origin of these designs, see Nils Åberg, *The Occident and the Orient in the Art of the Seventh Century*, Part I, The British Isles, Kungl. Vitterhets Historie och Antikvitets Akademiens Handlingar, Del. 56:1 (Stockholm, 1943). An admirable account of such designs is given by R. L. S. Bruce-Mitford in *Codex Lindisfarnensis*, ed. T. D. Kendrick, *et al.* (Olten and Lausanne, 1956–60), II, iv, vii–x, 197–260.
3. Lawrence Stone, *Sculpture in Britain* ([London], 1955), 13.
4. I wish to thank Professor Michael Sheehan of the Pontifical Institute of Mediaeval Studies at Toronto for helping me assemble the slides used in the lecture and Miss Ann Hutchison of the University of Toronto for help in assembling the prints used to make the plates.
5. Ronald Jessup, *Anglo-Saxon Jewellery* (London, 1950), 116.

Figure 3. The south face of the cross shaft at Bewcastle, Cumberland. Copyright Department of Archaeology, Durham University. Photographed by T. Middlemass.

The Bewcastle Cross stands where it was erected about the year 700 in the churchyard of St Cuthbert at Bewcastle in Cumberland. The top is broken away leaving a truncated shaft 14 feet 6 inches high. The width at the base of the south face is 1 foot 9 inches. For a full discussion and many plates of the cross, see G. Baldwin Brown, *The Arts in Early England*, V (London, 1921), *passim*.

zoomorphic character, often derived from eagles or wolves; the bodies of these creatures extend into curvilinear ribbon trails that form the interlace design. The heads often bite into the bands or back on to a free end, as on the seventh-century Windsor dagger pommel which has an open design with clear separation between the bands (Figure 5). When the bands are drawn together more tightly, the pattern becomes harder to follow, as on the great gold buckle from Sutton Hoo, also of the seventh century (Figure 6). The interlace on the buckle is not symmetrical. The weave is drawn tighter and the zoomorphic heads are less prominent than on the Windsor dagger pommel.

In further development of the zoomorphs, the ribbon trails develop limbs on their serpentine bodies. These limbed lacertines have a coiled and woven appearance and look very like dragons even when they have no wings and have canine heads. The abundant appearance of lacertines in early Anglo-Saxon design may well have reinforced belief in the existence of dragons, thought of as uncommon creatures not met with every day, much as we might think of a hippopotamus or iguana. An example of vigorous treatment of such lacertines may be seen on folio 192^{v} of the Book of Durrow (Figure 7); this manuscript is generally dated in the middle or second half of the seventh century and is often ascribed to Iona. The design is similar to that found on the hilt of the Crundale sword, found in Kent; it dates from the early seventh century (Figure 8). A detail from the seventh-century pins from Witham, Lincolnshire (Figure 9), shows a similar design, although the zoomorphs are distinctly canine. In the lacertine design on folio 110^{v} of the St. Chad Gospels, which were probably written between the Severn and the Welsh marches in the late seventh or early eighth centuries (Figure 10), the zoomorphs are clearly derived from birds, despite the ears. Designs over an entire folio are called carpet pages after their resemblance to woven tapestries. Perhaps the finest carpet pages are found in the Lindisfarne Gospels of about 700; in the later years of the Anglo-Saxon period it was thought to have been the work of angels since no mortal could execute such complex designs so faultlessly. Folio 94^{v} is reproduced in Figure 11. The entire design of the knot work is done with only two ribbons. The generally circular pattern is elaborated with intricate weaving, but the circular knots—which might be thought of as episodes, if I may look forward for a moment—are tied with relatively long straight bands that bind these knots together in the total pattern of the page. With patience and a steady eye one can follow a band through the entire knot-work design of this page. Occasionally the lacertines become recognizable dragons as on the Gandersheim Casket. It is carved from walrus teeth and probably was made at Ely in the second half of the eighth or

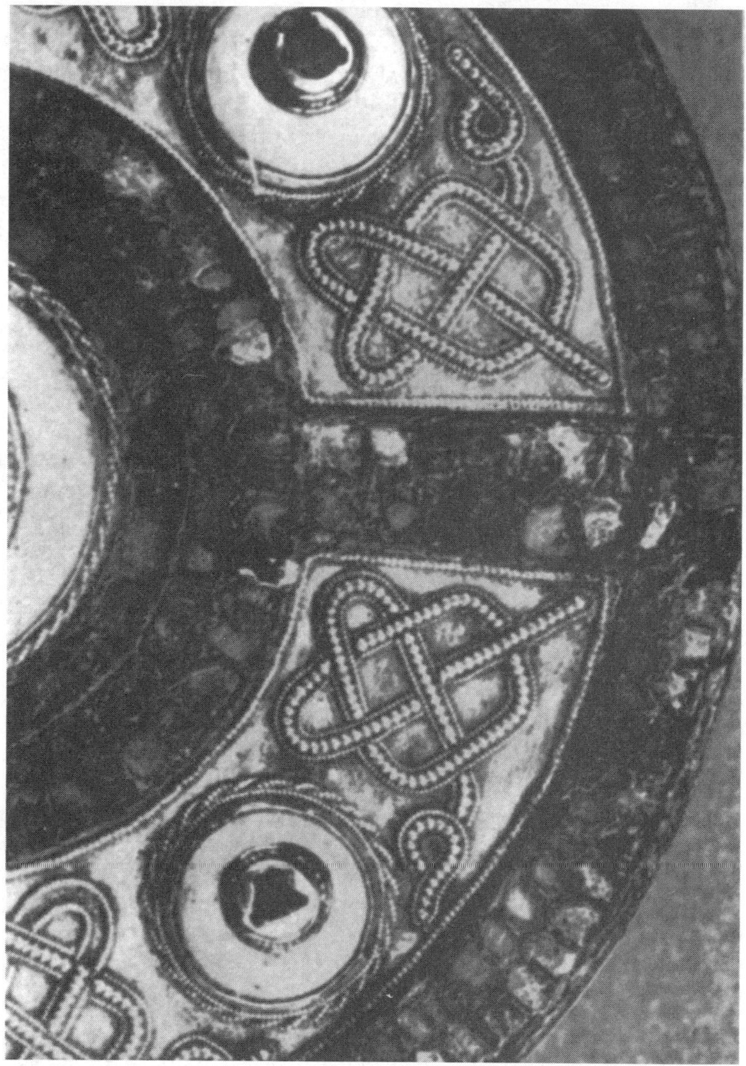

Figure 4. Detail from the Abingdon Brooch. Courtesy of the Victoria and Albert Museum.

This jewel, now in the Victoria and Albert Museum, is one of two composite disc brooches found at Milton near Abingdon, Berkshire, in 1832. It is 3.1 inches in diameter; the detail shown here is about 1.9 inches wide. See Ronald Jessup, *Anglo-Saxon Jewellery* (London, 1950), 116 and Plate XXV (1).

Figure 5. The Windsor dagger pommel. Courtesy of the Ashmolean Museum, Oxford.

The Windsor dagger pommel, now in the Ashmolean Museum, is one of the finest pieces of Anglo-Saxon gold work known. It is only 1.7 inches wide and is shown here greatly enlarged. The panel of gold interlace is .72 inches high by .61 inches wide. See G. Baldwin Brown, *The Arts in Early England*, III (London, 1915) 311 and Plate LVI.

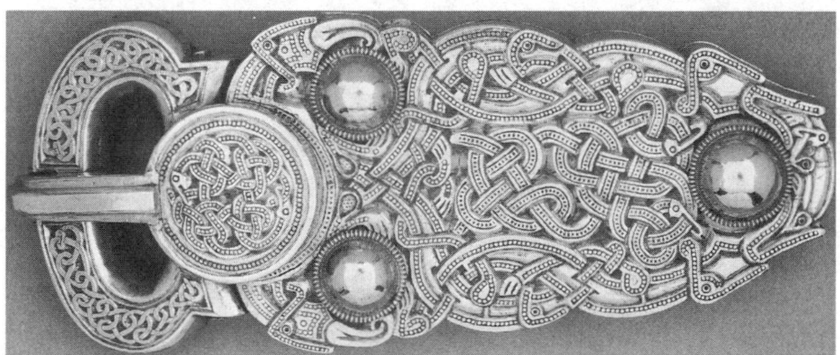

Figure 6. The great gold buckle from Sutton Hoo. Courtesy of the Trustees of The British Museum.

The great gold buckle from Sutton Hoo is 5.5 inches long and weighs nearly 15 ounces. Its value as gold bullion exceeds that of any other object yet dug up in England. See Ronald Jessup, *Anglo-Saxon Jewellery* (London, 1950), 139–40 and Plate XL and Charles Green, *Sutton Hoo* (London, 1963), 79–80 and Plate XX.

Figure 7. Folio 192^{v} of the Book of Durrow. Courtesy of The Board of Trinity College, Dublin.

The Book of Durrow is in Trinity College Dublin Library. The leaves measure about 9.5 by 6.25 inches. During the later middle ages it was at Durrow in Ireland and was thought to have medicinal value. Water was poured over it and given to sick cattle; whatever this treatment did for the livestock it impaired the manuscript, especially the early leaves which were badly damaged. For a full account and facsimile of the manuscript, see *Codex Durmachensis*, ed. A. A. Luce, *et al.* (Olten, Lausanne, and Freiburg, 1960).

Figure 8. The Crundale Sword hilt. Copyright © The British Museum.
This sword hilt, found near Crundale in Kent, is 2.4 inches wide. See G. Baldwin Brown, *The Arts in Early England*, III (London, 1915), 330 and Plate LXIII (4) and T. D. Kendrick, *Anglo-Saxon* Art (London, 1938), 86 and Plate 33; figure 17, XXII, page 82, is a schematic drawing of the hilt.

early ninth century (Figure 12). The casket is small and the skill shown in carving on such miniature scale is impressive.

From the early Anglo-Saxon period there are thousands of interlace designs surviving in illuminations of manuscripts, in carving on bone, ivory and stone, and in metal work for weapons and jewellery. They are so prolific that the seventh and eighth centuries might justly be known as the interlace period. In one artifact after another the complexity and precision of design are as striking as the technical skill of execution. Recognition of this high level of artistic achievement is important for it dispells the widely held view, largely the prejudice of ignorance, that early Anglo-Saxon art is vigorous, but wild and primitive. As the interlace designs show, there is vigour to be sure, but it is controlled with geometric precision and executed with technical competence of very high order. Apart from such direct analogies as the one presented in this lecture, study of Anglo-Saxon art is most useful as an aid to the reassessment of early English literature because it is an important reminder the society was capable of artistic achievements of a high order which can be looked for in the poetry as well.

Figure 9. Detail from the center disc of the Witham Pins. Courtesy of the Trustees of The British Museum.

The Witham Pins, a group of three silver, linked discs, were found at Fiskerton near Lincoln in the River Witham. The detail shown here is about 1.4 inches wide and is greatly enlarged. See the British Museum *Guide to Anglo-Saxon Antiquities* (London, 1923), 98 and T. D. Kendrick, *Anglo-Saxon Art* (London, 1938), 170–1.

II

The pervasive importance of interlace designs in early Anglo-Saxon art establishes the historical possibility that a parallel may be found in poetry of the same culture. The historical probability for the parallel, a rather more important matter, can be established from seventh- and eighth-century Latin writers in England. There is ample evidence that interlace design has literary parallels in both style and structure.

Stylistic interlace is a characteristic of Aldhelm and especially of Alcuin. They weave direct statement and classical tags together to produce verbal braids in which allusive literary references from the past cross and recross with the present subject.[6] The device is self-conscious and the poets describe the technique with the phrases *fingere serta* or *texere serta,* "to fashion or weave intertwinings." *Serta* (related to Sanscrit *sarat*, "thread" and to Greek σειρά, "rope") is from the pass participle of *serere*, "to interweave, entwine, or interlace." The past participle of *texere*, "to weave, braid, interlace," is

6. See Peter Dale Scott, "Alcuin as a Poet," *UTQ*, 33 (1964), 233–57.

Figure 10. A detail from folio 110ᵛ of the St. Chad Gospels. By kind permission of The Conway Library, Courtauld Institute of Art, and the Chapter of Lichfield Cathedral.

The manuscript containing the St. Chad Gospels is in the Lichfield Cathedral Library. The Bishop of Lichfield, the Dean and the Canons swear an oath on this volume to maintain the rights of the Church when they take office. The leaves of the manuscript measure about 9 by 12 inches; the detail shown here measures about 2.25 by 3 inches. Folio 110 was originally the first leaf of the manuscript, but was placed in its present location as early as the ninth century, as is shown by the arrangement of marginal notes. The manuscript is discussed by Canon L. J. Hopkin-James, *The Celtic Gospels* (Oxford, 1934), *passim*. See also *Codex S. Ceaddae Latinus*, ed. F. H. A. Scrivener (Cambridge, 1887) and H. E. Savage, "The Story of St. Chad's Gospels," *Transactions of the Birmingham Archaeological Society*, XLI (1915), 4–21.

Figure 11. Folio 94v of the Lindisfarne Gospels. By permission of The British Museum.

The excellent facsimile of the Lindisfarne Gospels (British Museum MS. Cotton Nero D IV) shows this folio, which measures about 9.6 by 13.5 inches, in colour. See *Codex Lindisfarnensis*, ed. T. D. Kendrick, *et al.* (Olten and Lausanne, 1956–60).

textus, the etymon of our words text and textile. The connection is so obvious that no one thinks of it. In basic meaning, then, a poetic text is a weaving of words to form, in effect, a verbal carpet page.

The passage in *Beowulf* about the scop's praise of Beowulf describes a recital in which a literary past, the exploits of Sigemund and Heremod, is intertwined with the present, Beowulf's killing of Grendel. This episode is extended and might equally be considered

Figure 12. The front of the Gandersheim casket. Courtesy of the Herzog Anton Ulrich Museum, Braunschweig.

The Gandersheim casket, also called the Brunswick casket, in the Herzog Anton Ulrich Museum, Braunschweig, Germany, is 4.8 inches tall by 2.6 inches wide and is carved from walrus teeth. See M. H. Longhurst, *English Ivories* (London, 1926), 127–8 and Plates 13–14 and August Fink, "Zum Gandersheimer Runenkästchen," *Forschungen zur Kunstgeschichte und Christlichen Archäologie*, Vol. III, *Karolingische und Ottonische Kunst* (Wiesbaden, 1957), 277–81.

as an example of simple structural interlace. The scop is said to *wordum wrixlan*, "vary words" (874); the verb *wrixlan* is found elsewhere in this sense, for example in Riddle 8 of the Exeter Book. Klaeber calls such variation "the very soul of the Old English poetical style" (lxv); it involves multiple statement of a subject in several different words or phrases, each of which typically describes a different aspect of the subject. When variation on two or more subjects is combined, the result is stylistic interlace, the interweaving of two or more strands of variation. This may be what Cynewulf refers to in *Elene* when he writes *ic . . . wordcræftum wæf*, "I wove words" (1236–7). An example from *Beowulf* will serve to illustrate stylistic interlace:

No þæt læsest wæs
hondgemot[a] þær mon Hygelac sloh,
syððan Geata cyning guðe ræsum,
freawine folca Freslondum on,
Hreðles eafora hiorodryncum swealt,
bille gebeaten. (2354–9)

Although awkward in modern English, a translation following the original order of phrases shows the stylistic interlace.

That was not the least
of hand-to-hand encounters where Hygelac was killed,
when the king of the Geats in the rush of battle,
the beloved friend of the people, in Frisia,
the son of Hreðel died bloodily,
struck down with the sword.

Hygelac, Geata cyning, freawine folca, and *Hreðles eafora* make one strand; *mon . . . sloh, hiorodryncum swealt*, and *bille gebeaten* make a second strand; *þær, guðe ræsum*, and *Freslondum on* make the third. The three strands are woven together into a stylistic braid. This feature of style is familiar to readers of Anglo-Saxon poetry and is the literary counterpart for interlace designs in art that are decorative rather than structural. Designs on a sword, coffer or cross are decoration applied to an object whose structure arises from other considerations.

At a structural level, literary interlace has a counterpart in tapestries where positional patterning of threads establishes the shape and design of the fabric, whether the medium is thread in textile or words in a text. Unfortunately cloth perishes easily and only a few fragments of Anglo-Saxon tapestry survive although the early English were famous for their weaving and needle work which was referred to on the continent simply as *opus Anglicum* with no other description. Since tapestry examples are lost, decorative interlace must serve here as graphic presentation of the principle of structural interlace, a concept difficult to explain or grasp without such a visual analogue.

Rhetoricians of the classical period distinguished between natural and artificial order, but emphasized the former as being especially effective for oral delivery since they were chiefly concerned with the orator. In the *Scholia Vindobonensia*, an eighth-century commentary on the *Ars Poetica* of Horace, there is a passage on artificial order of great interest to the subject of interlace structure in Anglo-Saxon poetry. The authorship of the *Scholia* is unknown, but its editor attributes it to Alcuin or one of his school.[7] The passage is a comment on four lines of the *Ars Poetica*.

7. *Scholia Vindobonensia ad Horatii Artem Poeticam*, ed. Josephus Zechmeister (Vienna, 1877), iii. I wish to acknowledge my considerable debt to Paula Neuss of the University

Ordinis haec virtus erit et venus, aut ego fallor,
ut iam nunc dicat iam nunc debentia dici,
pleraque differat et praesens in tempus omittat,
hoc amet, hoc spernat promissi carminis auctor. (42–45)

Of order, this will be the excellence and charm, unless I am mistaken, that the author of the long-promised poem shall say at the moment what ought to be said at the moment and shall put off and omit many things for the present, loving this and scorning that.

The commentator was particularly interested in the last line, which he regards as having the force of an independent hortatory subjunctive; he takes *hoc . . . hoc* in the strong sense of "on the one hand . . . on the other" which would have been expressed by *hoc . . . ille* in classical Latin.

> *Hoc*, id est, ut nunc dicat iam debentia dici quantum ad naturalem ordinem; *amet auctor promissi carminis*, id est, amet artificialem ordinem. *Hoc*, id est, contrarium ordinis artificialis, id est, ordinem naturalem *spernat auctor promissi carminis*; hoc breviter dicit. Nam sententia talis est: quicunque promittit se facturum bonum carmen et lucidum habere ordinem, amet artificialem ordinem et spernat naturalem. Omnis ordo aut naturalis aut artificialis est. Naturalis ordo est, si quis narret rem ordine quo gesta est; artificialis ordo est, si quis non incipit a principio rei gestae, sed a medio, ut Virgilius in Aeneide quaedam in futuro dicenda anticipat et quaedam in praesenti dicenda in posterum differt.[8]
>
> *Hoc*, that is, he should say now what ought to have been said before according to natural order; *amet auctor promissi carminis*, that is, should love artificial order. *Hoc*, that is, the opposite of artificial order, that is, *spernat auctor promissi carminis* natural order; Horace says this briefly. For the meaning is as follows: whoever undertakes to make a good poem having clear order should love artificial order and scorn natural order. Every order is either natural or artificial; artificial order is when one does not begin from the beginning of an exploit but from the middle, as does Virgil in the *Aeneid* when he anticipates some things which should have been told later and puts off until later some things which should have been told in the present.

of Kent at Canterbury for research assistance in eighth-century Latin authors and for constructive criticism throughout the work for this lecture.

8. Zechmeister, 4–5, repunctuated.

This comment extends the source into a doctrine on the suitability of artificial order for poetry concerned with martial material (*res gesta*) and takes an epic (the *Aeneid*) as an example. What I have called interlace structure is, in more general terms, complex artificial order, with the word complex in its etymological sense of woven together. Interlace design is a dominant aspect of eighth-century Anglo-Saxon visual art and the *Scholia Vindobonensia* present convincing evidence that the same design principle was applied to narrative poetry.

Alcuin's two lives of St. Willibrord provide instructive examples of natural and artificial order.[9] The prose version begins with an account of Willibrord's parents and gives a chronological account of the Saint's life, death, and the subsequent miracles at his tomb. The poem, on the other hand, plunges *in medias res* with an account of Willibrord's visit to Pippin; the details of the Saint's early life are placed at the end. The poem is in simple artificial order, and in the Preface Alcuin states that it is for private study but that the prose version is for public reading. The same logic is followed in Alcuin's *Disputatio de Rhetorica* which deals only with natural order since it is intended for instruction in public oral discourse.[1] On the basis of this preference for natural order in work intended for oral delivery, an argument might be made that *Beowulf* was meant for private study since it has complex artificial order.

Before I turn to the poem, a brief summary of my argument thus far may be helpful. In the visual arts of the seventh and eighth centuries interlace designs reached an artistic perfection in England that was never equalled again. Interlace appears so regularly on sculpture, jewellery, weapons, and in manuscript illuminations that it is the dominant characteristic of this art. There is clear evidence that a parallel technique of word-weaving was used as a stylistic device in both Latin and Old English poems of the period. Finally there is the specific statement of the *Scholia Vindobonensia* that artificial order was preferred for narrative poetry. Such artificial order I have called interlace structure because the term has historical probability and critical usefulness in reading *Beowulf*.

III

Beowulf is a work of art consistent with the artistic culture that it reflects and from which it came, eighth-century England. It is a lacertine interlace, a complex structure of great technical skill, but it is

9. *De Vita Sancti Willibrordi Archiepiscopi*, ed. B. Krvsch and W. Levison, *MGH, Scriptores Rerum Merov*. (Hanover and Leipzig, 1919), VII, 113–41; this is the prose version. *De Vita Willibrordi Episcopi*, ed. E. Dümmler, *MGH, Poetarum Latinorum Medii Aevi*, I (Berlin, 1881), 207–20.

1. Ed. and trans. Wilbur S. Howell (Princeton, 1941), Section 22.

woven with relatively few strands. When *Beowulf* is read in its own artistic context as an interlace structure, it can be recognized as a literary work parallel to the carpet pages of the Lindisfarne Gospels, having a technical excellence in design and execution that makes it the literary equivalent of that artistic masterpiece.

Examples of narrative threads, intersected by other material, are easy to perceive in the poem once the structural principle is understood. The full account of Hygelac's Frisian expedition is segmented into four episodes, 1202–14, 2354–68, 2501–9 and 2913–21, in which chronology is ignored. The poet interlaces these episodes to achieve juxtapositions impossible in a linear narrative. In the first episode the gift of a precious golden torque to Beowulf for killing Grendel is interrupted by an allusion to its loss years later when Hygelac is killed. Hygelac's death seeking Frisian treasure foreshadows Beowulf's death seeking the dragon's hoard. The transience of gold and its connection with violence are obvious. In the second episode Beowulf's preparations to face the dragon are intersected by another allusion to Hygelac's expedition; each is an example of rash action and each ends in the death of a king. The third episode comes as Beowulf recalls how he went in front of Hygelac

> ana on orde, ond swa to aldre sceall
> sæcce fremman, þenden þis sweord þolað. (2498–99)

> alone in the van and so will I always
> act in battle while this sword holds out.

He had needed no sword to crush Dæghrefn, the slayer of Hygelac; against the dragon his sword Nægling fails. The pattern is the same as for the fights with Grendel whom he had killed with his hands and with Grendel's mother against whom the sword Hrunting fails. Beowulf's trust in a sword against Grendel's mother had nearly cost him his life; against the dragon it does. The last episode comes in the speech of the messenger who states that the fall of Beowulf will bring affliction to the Geats from their enemies. Among them, the messenger warns, are the Frisians seeking revenge for Hygelac's raid years before. Hygelac's death led to the virtual annihilation of his raiding force; Beowulf's death leads to the virtual annihilation of all the Geats. The four Hygelac episodes, like all the narrative elements in the poem, have positional significance; unravel the threads and the whole fabric falls apart. An episode cannot be taken out of context—may I remind you again of the etymology of the word—without impairing the interwoven design. This design reveals the meaning of coincidence, the recurrence of human behaviour, and the circularity of time, partly through the coincidence, recurrence, and circularity of the medium itself—the interlace structure. It allows for the intersection of narrative events without regard for their distance in chronological time and shows the interrelated significances of episodes without the need for any explicit comment by the poet. The significance of the connections is left for the audience to work out for itself. Understatement is thus inherent in interlace structure, a characteristic that fits the heroic temper of the north.

The Hygelac episodes contribute to what I believe is the major theme of *Beowulf*, "the fatal contradiction at the core of heroic society. The hero follows a code that exalts indomitable will and valour in the individual, but society requires a king who acts for the common good, not for his own glory."[2] Only two periods in Beowulf's life are told in linear narrative; they are the few days, perhaps a week, when he fights Grendel and his mother and the last few days when he fights the dragon. This treatment emphasizes Beowulf's heroic grandeur, his glorious deeds, and his predilection for monster-fighting. However, this main narrative is constantly intersected by episodes which present these deeds from a different perspective. The Hygelac episodes show the social consequences of rash action in a king and they become more frequent as the dragon fight develops. Hygelac's Frisian raid was a historical event; the history of this age provides many parallels. In 685 Ecgfrið, King of Northumbria, led a raiding party against the advice of his friends deep into Pictish territory. Caught in mountainous narrows at a place called Nechtanesmere on May 20, he and most of his army were killed, a disaster that ended English ascendency in the north. The main theme of *Beowulf* thus had relevance to a major recent event in the society that most probably produced it. Ecgfrið's brother Aldfrið, a man famed for his learning and skill as a poet, ruled from 685 to 704; Bede says that he re-established his ruined and diminished kingdom nobly,[3] a stable reign that made possible the learning and scholarship of eighth-century Northumbria, the golden age of Bede and Alcuin.

At first the episodes give little more than a hint that Beowulf's heroic susceptibility may have calamitous consequences for his people. The references to Sigemund and Heremod after Beowulf kills Grendel foreshadow Beowulf's later career as king. He kills a dragon, as Sigemund did, and leaves the Geats to suffer national calamity, as Heremod left the Danes to suffer *fyrenðearfe* (14), "terrible distress."[4] In the second part of the poem Beowulf's preparations to fight the dragon are constantly intersected by allusions to the Swedish wars, ominous warnings of the full consequences to the Geats of Beowulf's dragon fight. In this way the poet undercuts Beowulf's

2. John Leyerle, "Beowulf the Hero and the King," *Medium Ævum*, 34 (1965), 89.
3. *Historia Ecclesiastica*, ed. C. Plummer (Oxford, 1896), IV, xxiv, Vol. I, 268. See F. M. Stenton, *Anglo-Saxon England*, 2nd edition (Oxford, 1950), 85–9.
4. See "Beowulf the Hero and the King," 101.

single-minded preoccupation with the dragon by interlacing a stream of more and more pointed episodes about the human threats to his people, a far more serious danger than the dragon poses. Beowulf wins glory by his heroic exploit in killing the dragon, but brings dire affliction on his people, as Wiglaf quite explicitly states.

> Oft sceall eorl monig anes willan
> wræc adreogan, swa us geworden is. (3077–8)

> Often many men must suffer distress
> For the willfulness of one alone, as has happened to us.

Of particular interest to my subject is the way in which the interlace design, in and of itself, makes a contribution to the main theme. Because of the many lines given to the monsters and to Beowulf's preparations to fight them, they are the largest thread in the design, like the zoomorphs on the Windsor dagger pommel or the dragons on the Gandersheim casket. Monster-fighting thus pre-empts the reader's attention just as it pre-empts Beowulf's; the reader gets caught up in the heroic ethos like the hero and easily misses the warnings. In a sense the reader is led to repeat the error, one all too easy in heroic society, hardly noticing that glorious action by a leader often carries a terrible price for his followers.

The monsters are the elongated lacertine elements that thread through the action of the poem making symmetrical patterns characteristic of interlace structure. Beowulf's fights against Grendel's mother and against the monsters in the Breca episode are clear examples. During the swimming match Beowulf, protected by his armour, is dragged to the ocean floor. Fate gives him victory and he kills *niceras nigene* (575), "nine water monsters," with his sword; this prevents them from feasting on him as they intended. After the battle, light comes and the sea grows calm. This is almost a *précis* of the later underwater fight against Grendel's mother; the pattern is the same, though told in greater detail.

Once the probability of parallel design is recognized, the function of some episodes becomes clearer. The Finnesburh lay, for example, is probably a cautionary tale for the Danes and Geats. Beowulf and his Geats visit Hroðgar and his Danes in Heorot to assist in defending the hall against an *eoten*, Grendel. During the first evening they share the hall Unferð issues an insulting challenge to which Beowulf makes a wounding reply stating that Unferð had killed his own brothers. This deed associates him with Cain, the archetypal fratricide, and Cain's descendant, Grendel. The defence of the hall is successful and Grendel is killed. At the victory celebration the scop recites a lay about the visit of Hnæf and his Half-Danes to Finn and his

Frisians in Finnesburh. They fall to quarrelling and slaughter each other. In this episode the word *eoten* occurs three times in the genitive plural form *eotena* and once in the dative plural *eotenum*. These forms are often taken as referring to the Jutes, although no one can say what they are doing there or what part they play. More likely the references are to monsters. At line 1088 the Frisians and Danes surviving from the first battle are said each to control half of the hall *wið eotena bearn*, which probably means "against the giants' kin." Quite possibly the Half-Danes go to Finnesburh to help the Frisians hold their hall against monsters, a situation which would explain why Finn did not burn out the Half-Danes when the fighting started. The hall was their joint protection against the monsters. After the lay Wealhþeow makes two moving pleas (1169–87 and 1216–31) for good faith and firm friendship in Heorot, especially between the Geats and the Danes. She clearly takes the scop's lay as a warning and fears being afflicted like Hildeburh. Just before she speaks, Unferð is described as sitting at Hroðgar's feet; he is a figure of discord as shown by his name, which means "mar-peace", and by his behaviour. The queen might well be concerned lest insults between Dane and Geat be renewed and lead to fighting. From all this emerges an interesting connection. In *Beowulf* monsters are closely associated with the slaying of friends and kinsmen.[5] They function in part as an outward objectification and sign of society beset by internecine slaughter between friend and kin.

The Finnesburh episode and the situation in Heorot are part of another theme that forms a thread of the interlace design of *Beowulf*—visits to a hall. A guest should go to the hall with friendly intent and be given food and entertainment of poetry by his host. Grendel inverts this order. He visits Heorot in rage, angered by the scop's song of creation, and makes food of his unwilling hosts. Hroðgar cannot dispense men's lives in Heorot, but Grendel does little else. He is an *eoten*, or "eater," and swallows up the society he visits almost as if he were an allegorical figure for internecine strife. In a similar way Grendel's mother visits Heorot and devours Æschere; in return Beowulf visits her hall beneath the mere, kills her, and brings back the head of Grendel. The Heaþobard episode concerning Ingeld and the battle that breaks out when the Danes visit his hall is another appearance of this thematic thread. Hroðgar gives his daughter Freawaru to Ingeld in marriage, hoping to end the feud between the two tribes, but an implacable old warrior sees a Dane wearing a sword that once belonged to the father of a young Heaþobard warrior. He incites the youth to revenge and the feud breaks

5. Heremond's story fits this context, too, for he kills his table companions and dies *mid eotenum* (902).

out again; in the end the Heaþobards are decimated and Heorot is burnt. Other hall visits may be noted briefly. A slave visits the hall of the dragon and steals a cup; the dragon burns halls of the Geats in angry retribution, a token of the fate in store for Geatish society soon to be destroyed by war. Beowulf attacks the dragon who dies in the door of his hall fighting in self-defence.

Another theme of the poem is that of women as the bond of kinship. The women often become the bond themselves by marrying into another tribe, like Wealhþeow, Hildeburh, and Freawaru. This tie often has great tension put on it when the woman's blood relations visit the hall of her husband and old enmities between the tribes arise, as happens in the Finnesburh and Heaþobard episodes. The marriage then gives occasion for old wounds to open, even after an interval of years, and produces a result exactly opposite to its intent. On the other hand, women can be implacable in revenge as Grendel's mother is. Þryð (or Modþryð) is also implacable at first in resisting marriage; she causes her would-be husbands to be killed. Afterwards her father sends her over the sea as wife to Offa who checks her savage acts and she becomes a *freoðuwebbe*, "peace-weaver," knitting up her kinsmen rather than refusing all ties. In general the women are *cynna gemyndig*, "intent on kinship," as the poet says of Wealhþeow (613). They preserve the tie of kin or revenge it when given cause.

Another tie that binds society is treasure, especially gold; but, like kinship, it is also a cause of strife. Treasure is not sought for selfish avarice, but to enable a hero to win fame in gaining treasure for his lord and his lord to win fame dispensing it as a *beaga bryttan*, a "dispenser of treasure," from the *gifstol*, "gift throne." The gift and receipt of treasure are a tie between a lord and his retainer, an outward sign of the agreement between them. The strength and security of heroic society depend on the symbolic circulation of treasure. A lord offers support and sustenance to his retainer who agrees in turn to fight unwaveringly for his lord, a bond of contractual force in heroic society. Injury or slaughter of a man had a monetary price and could be atoned by *wergild*, "man payment." The monsters are outside this society; for them treasure is an object to be hoarded under ground. They receive no gifts and do not dispense them. The poet states ironically that none need expect handsome recompense for the slaughter that Grendel inflicts. Hroðgar is the one who pays the *wergild* for the Geat, Hondscio, killed by Grendel in the Danish cause. The relation of the monsters to *gifstolas* presents an interesting parallel in the interlace design. The dragon burns the *gifstol Geata* (2327), an act that implies his disruption of the entire social order of Beowulf's *comitatus*. The full extent of this disruption appears when all but one of Beowulf's chosen retainers desert him in his last battle. Grendel, on the other hand, occupies Heorot, but he is not able to cause complete disruption of Hroðgar's *comitatus*, however ineffective it is against him. The sense of lines 168–9, a much disputed passage, thus seems likely to be that Grendel cannot destroy Hroðgar's *gifstol* (168), thought of as the objectification of the Danish *comitatus*.

The poem is also concerned with a society's gain of treasure as well as its loss. When a king seeks treasure himself, the cost may be ruinous for his people. Hygelac's Frisian raid and Beowulf's dragon fight are examples. Although Grendel's cave is rich in treasure, Beowulf takes away only a golden sword hilt and the severed head of Grendel; his object is to gain revenge, not treasure. Hroðgar's speech to Beowulf after his return contains warnings on pride in heroic exploits and on the ease with which gold can make a man stingy, hoarding his gold like a monster; either way the *comitatus* is apt to suffer. Heremod, who ended *mid eotenum*, is an example. When treasure passes outside the society where it is a bond, it becomes useless. The treasure in Scyld's funeral ship, the golden torque lost in Frisia, the lay of the last survivor, and the dragon's hoard buried with Beowulf are examples. Treasure had some positive force in heroic society, but it casts a baleful glitter in the poem because it is associated with monsters, fighting, the death of kings, and funerals.

These various themes are some of the threads that form the interlace structure of *Beowulf*. Often several are present together, as in the Finnesburh episode or in the final dragon fight. The themes make a complex, tightly knotted lacertine interlace that cannot be untied without losing the design and form of the whole. The tension and force of the poem arise from the way the themes cross and juxtapose. Few comments are needed from the poet because significance comes from the intersections and conjunctions of the design. To the *Beowulf* poet, as to many other writers, the relations between events are more significant than their temporal sequence and he used a structure that gave him great freedom to manipulate time and concentrate on the complex interconnections of events. Although the poem has to be lingered over and gives up its secrets slowly, the principle of its interlace structure helps to reveal the interwoven coherence of the episodes as well as the total design of the poem in all its complex resonances and reverberations of meaning. There are no digressions in *Beowulf*.

The structural interlace of *Beowulf*, like the visual interlace patterns of the same culture, has great technical excellence, but is not to be regarded as an isolated phenomenon. The term is specifically applied to literature in the late middle ages. Robert Manning states in his *Chronicle* (1338) that he writes in a clear and simple style so that he will be readily understood; others, he says, use *quante Inglis* in complicated schemes of *ryme couwee* or *strangere* or *enterlace.*[6] *Entrelacement* was a feature of prose romances, especially those in the Arthurian tradition, as Eugène Vinaver has recently shown.[7]

The term interlace may be taken in a larger sense; it is an organizing principle closer to the workings of the human imagination proceeding in its atemporal way from one associative idea to the next than to the Aristotelian order of parts belonging to a temporal sequence with a beginning, middle, and end. If internal human experience of the imagination is taken as the basis, the Aristotelian canon of natural order as moving in chronological progression is really *ordo artificialis,* not the other way around as the rhetoricians taught. The human imagination moves in atemporal, associative patterns like the literary interlace. *Don Quixote* presents a useful illustration. The Don, supposedly mad, is brought home in a cage on wheels at the end of Part I. He could be taken as the interlacing fecundity of the associative mind, caught in the skull-cage, reacting with complex atemporal imagination, weaving sensory impressions with literary experience. The Canon of Toledo who rides along outside mouthing Aristotelian criticism of romances is, as his name suggests, an uncomprehending set of external rules, or canons, sent to bedevil and torment the poetic imagination.

There is a substantial amount of literature having interlace structure, if I may extend the term without presenting evidence here. Mediaeval dream poetry, such as *Le Roman de la Rose* and *Piers Plowman*, is largely a mixture of literary and imaginative experience with an atemporal interlace structure as are many complex romances, especially those with allegorical content like the *Faerie Queene*. The allegorical impulse in literature is often presented with an interlace structure because it is imaginative, literary and atemporal. Stream-of-consciousness novels frequently have something like interlace structures as well, for the same reasons.[8]

Like the poem, this lecture will make an end as it began. Scyld's glorious accomplishments and ship funeral at the opening of the poem mark the start of a dynasty and a period of prosperity for the Danes after the leaderless affliction they suffer following the death of Heremod. The funeral in the Finnesburh episode begins the period of affliction of the Half-Danes and presages the destruction of Finn's dynasty. At the end of the poem Beowulf's death begins a period of affliction for the Geats. The poem ends as it began with a funeral, the return of the interlace design to its start. The sudden

6. Ed. F. J. Furnivall (London, 1887). See lines 71–128.
7. "Form and Meaning in Medieval Romance," The Presidential Address of the Modern Humanities Research Association (1966).
8. Interlace structure in later texts will be the subject of a larger work now in preparation. I wish to thank Mrs. Medora Bennett of the University of Toronto for help in the final preparation of this article for press.

reversals inherent in the structure as one theme intersects another without regard to time give to the whole poem a sense of transience about the world and all that is in it as beginnings and endings are juxtaposed; this is the much-remarked elegiac texture of *Beowulf*. Scyld's mysterious arrival as a child is placed beside his mysterious departure in death over the seas. A description of Heorot's construction is followed by an allusion to its destruction. The gift of a golden torque, by its loss. Beowulf's victories over monsters, by his defeat by a monster. With each reversal the elegiac texture is tightened, reminding us of impermanence and change, extending even to the greatest of heroes, Beowulf, a man mourned by those who remain behind as

> manna mildust   ond mon(ðw)ærust,
> leodum liðost   ond lofgeornost. (3181–82)

> the most gentle and kind of men,
> most generous to his people and most anxious for praise.

A bright and golden age of a magnanimous man vanishes, even as it seems hardly to have begun.

> The jawes of darkness do devoure it up:
> So quicke bright things come to confusion.
> (*Mids*. I. i. 148–49)

JANE CHANCE

The Structural Unity of *Beowulf*: The Problem of Grendel's Mother†

The episode in *Beowulf* involving Grendel's Mother has been viewed as largely extraneous, a blot upon the thematic and structural unity of the poem. If the poem is regarded as two-part in structure, balancing contrasts between the hero's youth and old age, his rise as a retainer and his fall as a king, his battles with the Grendel family and his battle with the dragon, then her episode (which includes Hrothgar's sermon and Hygelac's welcoming court celebration with its recapitulation of earlier events) lengthens the first "half" focusing

† From *Texas Studies in Literature and Language* 22, pp. 287–303.

on his youth to two-thirds of the poem (lines 1–2199).[1] If the poem is regarded as three-part in structure, with each part centering on one of the three monsters or the three fights, then the brevity of her episode again mars the structural balance: her section, roughly 500 lines (1251–1784), is not as long as Grendel's, roughly 1100–1200 lines (86–1250), or the dragon's, 1000 lines (2200–3182).[2] Even if her episode is lengthened to a thousand lines (from line 1251 to 2199) so as to include Hrothgar's sermon and Hygelac's court celebration, still Grendel's Mother hardly dominates these events literally or symbolically as Grendel and the dragon dominate the events in their sections.

But her battle with Beowulf (and this middle section of the poem) is more than merely a "transition between two great crises," even though it is "linked with both the Grendel fight and the Dragon fight."[3] The key to her significance[4] may indeed derive from her links

1. This view of the structure as two-part has generally prevailed since its inception in J. R. R. Tolkien's "Beowulf: The Monsters and the Critics," in *Proceedings of the British Academy* 22 (1936): 245–95, rpt. in *An Anthology of Beowulf Criticism*, ed. Lewis E. Nicholson (Notre Dame: University of Notre Dame Press, 1963), pp. 51–104. The edition used throughout is Fr. Klaeber, *Beowulf and the Fight at Finnsburg*, 3rd ed. (Boston: D. C. Heath and Co., 1936, with supplements in 1941 and 1950).
2. This increasingly popular view of the structure as tripartite has been advanced by H. L. Rogers, "Beowulf's Three Great Fights," *Review of English Studies* 6 (1955): 339–55, rpt. in Nicholson, *Anthology*, pp. 233–56; John Gardner, "Fulgentius' *Expositio Vergiliana Continentia* and the Plan of *Beowulf*: Another Approach to the Poem's Style and Structure," *Papers in Language and Literature* 6 (1970): 227–62; and most recently, Kathryn Hume, "The Theme and Structure of *Beowulf*," *Studies in Philology* 72 (1975): 1–27. Hume's fine analysis includes an extensive survey of the various approaches to and interpretations of structural and thematic unity in *Beowulf* (see pp. 2–5). She declares, p. 3, "That critics should disagree over whether the structure has two parts or three is hardly surprising. Those concentrating on the hero tend to see two, those on action usually prefer three. But neither camp has produced a structural analysis which does not, by implication, damn the poet for gross incompetence, or leave the critic with a logically awkward position." For example, William W. Ryding, *Structure in Medieval Narrative* (The Hague: Mouton, 1971), first regards the middle of *Beowulf* as "a point of maximum logical discontinuity," p. 40, and then, contradicting himself, as a more difficult, more intense, more exciting combat than the fight with Grendel, illustrating a "varied repetition" of the same narrative motif, therefore implying logical continuity (p. 88).
3. Adrien Bonjour, "Grendel's Dam and the Composition of *Beowulf*," *English Studies* 30 (1949): 117. Other early *Beowulf* studies similarly ignored Grendel's Mother or treated her as a type of Grendel. See also Tolkien, "Monsters," in which he declares, "I shall confine myself mainly to the monsters—Grendel and the Dragon . . . ," in Nicholson, *Anthology*, p. 52. Similar treatments occur in T. M. Gang, "Approaches to *Beowulf*," *Review of English Studies* 3 (1952): 1–12; Bonjour, "Monsters Crouching and Critics Rampant: or the *Beowulf* Dragon Debated," *Publications of the Modern Language Association* 68 (1953): 304–12; and even more recently, in Margaret Goldsmith, *The Mode and Meaning of Beowulf* (London: Athlone Press, 1970), e.g., p. 144; Alvin A. Lee, *The Guest-Hall of Eden* (New Haven: Yale University Press, 1972), pp. 171–223; and Daniel G. Calder, "Setting and Ethos: The Pattern of Measure and Limit in *Beowulf*," *Studies in Philology* 69 (1972): 21–37.
4. Recently interpretations have stressed her significance in Germanic social terms, but without developing the implications of such insights: a Jungian analysis views her as symbolic of the "evil latent in woman's function, as Grendel symbolizes the destructive element hidden in Beowulf's *maegen*. . . . Grendel's Mother symbolizes the feud aspect of the web of peace. . . ." Further, as a destroyer she signifies "the obverse of the women we meet in the two banqueting scenes which precede Beowulf's descent into Grendelsmere," both of

with the other two monsters in a way Bonjour did not envision when he made these statements.

Grendel and the dragon have been interpreted recently as monstrous projections of flaws in Germanic civilization portrayed by the poet as "Negative Men."[5] Grendel is introduced as a mock "hall-retainer" (*renweard*, 770; *healðegn*, 142) who envies the men of Heorot their joy of community; he subsequently attacks the hall in a raid that is described through the parodic hall ceremonies of feasting, ale-drinking, gift-receiving, and singing.[6] The dragon is introduced as a mock "gold-king" or *hord-weard* (2293, 2303, 2554, 2593) who avariciously guards his barrow or "ring-hall" (*hringsele*, 3053),[7] and attacks Beowulf's kingdom after he discovers the loss of a single cup. The envy of the evil hall-retainer and the avarice of the evil gold-king antithesize the Germanic *comitatus* ideal first enunciated in Tacitus' *Germania* and pervading heroic and elegiac Anglo-Saxon literature: the *comitatus'* well-being depended upon the retainer's valor in battle and loyalty to his lord and the lord's protection and treasure-giving in return.[8]

---

whom combine to form the dual mother image. See Jeffrey Helterman, "*Beowulf*: The Archetype Enters History," *ELH* 35 (1968), 12–13, 14. To other critics she represents vengeance (Nist, Irving, Hume), false loyalty (Gardner), revenge (Leyerle). See John A. Nist, *The Structure and Texture of Beowulf* (Línguia e Literature Inglése, vol. 1; São Paulo: Universidade de São Paulo, Faculdade de Filosofia, Ciências, e Letres, 1959), p. 21; Edward B. Irving, Jr., *A Reading of Beowulf* (New Haven: Yale University Press, 1968), p. 113, and *Introduction to Beowulf* (Englewood Cliffs, N.J.: Prentice-Hall, 1969), p. 57; Kathryn Hume, "The Theme and Structure of *Beowulf*," p. 7; Gardner, "Fulgentius' *Expositio Vergiliana Continentia* and the Plan of *Beowulf*," p. 255; and John Leyerle, "The Interlace Structure of *Beowulf*," *University of Toronto Quarterly* 37 (1967–68): pp. 11–12.

Other recent interpretations have explored not only Jungian but also Scandinavian and Celtic mythic and legendary parallels, sources, or analogues of this figure: for the Scandinavian parallels, see Nora K. Chadwick, "The Monsters and *Beowulf*," in *The Anglo-Saxons: Studies in Some Aspects of their History and Culture Presented to Bruce Dickins*, ed. Peter Clemoes (London: Bowes and Bowes, 1959), pp. 171–203, and Larry D. Benson, "The Originality of *Beowulf*," in *The Interpretation of Narrative: Theory and Practice*, ed. Morton W. Bloomfield (Harvard English Studies, vol. 1; Cambridge, Mass.: Harvard University Press, 1970), pp. 1–43; for the Celtic parallels, see Martin Puhvel, "The Might of Grendel's Mother," *Folklore* 80 (1969): 81–88; and for amalgamated parallels—English, German, Latin, and Scandinavian—viewing Grendel and his mother as incubus and succubus, see Nicolas K. Kiessling, "Grendel: A New Aspect," *Modern Philology* 65 (1968): 191–201.

5. Groundwork for this interpretation of the monsters as enemies of man was first laid by Arthur E. Dubois, "The Unity of *Beowulf*," *Publications of the Modern Language Association* 49 (1934): 391 (Grendel and his mother become "the Danes' liability to punishment" for the secular sins of weakness, pride, and treachery; the dragon, "a variation upon Grendel," is "internal discord"). More recently they have been understood as adversaries of both man and God: see Richard N. Ringler, "*Him Sēo Wēn Gelēah*: The Design for Irony in Grendel's Last Visit to Heorot," *Speculum* 41 (1966): 64, in which Grendel represents *ofermōd* or *fortrūwung*, "held suspect by both Germanic instinct and Christian doctrine." See also Lee, *Guest-Hall*, p. 186.
6. For this interpretation of Grendel, see especially Edward B. Irving, Jr., "*Ealuscerwen:* Wild Party at Heorot," *Tennessee Studies in Literature* 11 (1966): 161–68, and *A Reading*, p. 16; also William A. Chaney, "Grendel and the *Gifstol*: A Legal View of Monsters," *Publications of the Modern Language Association* 77 (1962): 513–20; Joseph L. Baird, "Grendel the Exile," *Neuphilologische Mitteilungen* 67 (1966): 375–81.
7. Irving, *A Reading*, p. 209; Lee, *Guest-Hall*, pp. 215–16.
8. Tacitus, *Germania*, ed. Rodney Potter Robinson (Philological Monographs, vol. 5; Middletown, Conn.: American Philological Association, 1935), p. 291 (cap. 14).

Like these monsters, Grendel's Mother is also described in human and social terms. She is specifically called a *wīf unhȳre* "a monstrous woman" (2120), and an *ides āglǣcwīf* "a lady monster-woman" (1259). *Ides* elsewhere in *Beowulf* denotes "lady" and connotes either a queen or a woman of high social rank; outside *Beowulf*, primarily in Latin and Old English glosses, *ides* pairs with *virgo* to suggest maidenhood, as when *on idesan* equals *in virgunculam.*[9] In addition, as if the poet wished to stress her maternal role, she is characterized usually as Grendel's *mōdor* or kinswoman (*māge*, 1391), the former a word almost exclusively reserved for her, although other mothers appear in the poem.[1] It seems clear from these epithets that Grendel's Mother inverts the Germanic roles of the mother and queen, or lady. She has the form of a woman (*idese onlīcnes*, 1351) and is weaker than a man (1282ff) and more cowardly, for she flees in fear for her life when discovered in Heorot (1292–93). But unlike most mothers and queens, she fights her own battles. *Maxims* I testifies that, "Battle, war, must develop in the man, and the woman must flourish beloved among her people, must be light-hearted."[2]

Because the poet wishes to stress this specific inversion of the Anglo-Saxon ideal of woman as both monstrous and masculine he labels her domain a "battle-hall" (*nīðsele*, 1513; *gūðsele*, 2139).[3] (The dragon's barrow he describes equally appropriately, given the monster's avaricious symbolic nature, as a "ring-hall," as we saw previously.) In addition, he occasionally uses a masculine pronoun in referring to her (*sē þe* instead of *sēo þe* in 1260, 1497; *hē* instead of *hēo* in 1392, 1394). Such a change in pronoun occurs elsewhere in the poem only in reference to abstract feminine nouns used as personifications and to concrete feminine nouns used as synecdoches.[4] Other epithets applied to her are usually applied to male figures: warrior, *sinnige secg*, in 1379; destroyer, *mihtig mānscaða*, in 1339; and [male] guardian, *gryrelīcne grundhyrde*, in 2136. Indeed, in the phrase *ides āglǣcwīf* applied to Grendel's Mother as a "lady monster-

9. In *Beowulf*: in 620, 1168, and 1649 used of Wealhtheow, lady of the Helmings or Scyldings; in 1075 and 1117 of Hildeburh; in 1941 of Queen Thryth. Outside *Beowulf*: see "Kentish Glosses" (ca. ninth century) in Thomas Wright, *Anglo-Saxon and Old English Vocabularies*, ed. Richard Paul Wülcker, 2nd ed. (London: Trübner and Co., 1884), vol. 1, p. 88. For *on idesan* paired with *in virgunculam*, see *in iuuenculam* in the gloss on Aldhelm's *De Laudibus Virginitatis* 29.14, in *Old English Glosses*, ed. Arthur S. Napier (Oxford: Oxford University Press, 1900), p. 57; also for *ides* as *virguncula* see the gloss on Aldhelm's *De Laudibus Virginum* 191.7 and 194.14, pp. 181, 183.

1. Used of Grendel's Mother in 1258, 1276, 1282, 1538, 1683, 2118, and 2139. In 2932 *mōdor* refers to the mother of Onela and Ohthere.

2. George Philip Krapp and Elliott Van Kirk Dobbie, eds., *The Exeter Book*, vol. 3 of *The Anglo-Saxon Poetic Records* (New York: Columbia University Press, 1936), p. 159 (lines 83–85).

3. Bosworth-Toller's *Anglo-Saxon Dictionary* lists *hringsele* and *nīðsele* as compounds singular to *Beowulf*, underscoring the intentionality of the poet's irony.

4. Masculine pronouns refer to the feminine personifications of Old Age (1887) and Change or Death (2421), and to the feminine synecdoche "hand" (1344).

woman" the *āglǣca* not only means "monster," as it does when directed at Grendel (159, 425, 433, 556, 592, 646, 732, 739, 816, 989, 1000, 1269) or the water monsters (1512), but also "fierce combatant" or "strong adversary," as when directed at Sigemund in line 893 and Beowulf and the dragon in line 2592.[5] Such a woman might be wretched or monstrous because she insists on arrogating the masculine role of the warrior or lord.

Her episode is thus appropriately divided like her monstrous but human nature and her female but male behavior into two parts to illustrate the various feminine roles—of the mother or kinswoman (*mōdor*) and queen or lady (*ides āglǣcwīf*)—she inverts. The poet constantly contrasts the unnatural behavior of Grendel's dam with that of the feminine ideal by presenting human examples as foils in each of the two parts. We turn first to an examination of the female ideal in *Beowulf*, then to a detailed analysis of the episode involving Grendel's Mother and its two parts, and finally to some conclusions regarding the structural unity of the entire poem.

I

The role of woman in *Beowulf* primarily depends upon "peace-making," either biologically through her marital ties with foreign kings as a peace-pledge or mother of sons, or socially and psychologically as a cup-passing and peace-weaving queen within a hall. Wealhtheow becomes a peace-pledge or *friðusibb folca* (2017) to unite the Danes and Helmings; Hildeburh similarly unites the Danes and Frisians through her marriage; and Freawaru at least intends to pledge peace between the Danes and Heathobards. Such a role is predicated upon the woman's ability to bear children, to create blood ties, bonds to weave a "peace kinship."

In addition, woman functions domestically within the nation as a cup-passer during hall festivities of peace (*freoþo*) and joy (*drēam*) after battle or contest. The mead-sharing ritual and the cup-passer herself come to symbolize peace-weaving and peace because they strengthen the societal and familial bonds between lord and retainers. First, the literal action of the *freoðuwebbe* "peace-weaver" (1942) as she passes the cup from warrior to warrior weaves an invisible web of peace: the order in which each man is served, according to his social position, reveals each man's dependence upon and responsibility toward another. For example, after Wealhtheow gives the cup

5. *Āglǣca* apparently means "fierce adversary" in *Juliana* 268 and 319 where the Devil in the garb of an angel brings tidings to the maiden; when she asks who sent him, *Hyre se aglǣca ageaf ondsware* 'The fierce adversary answered her' (319) in *The Exeter Book*, p. 122. Because he no longer appears to be a "wretch, monster, miscreant," the term *āglǣca* must denote "foe" in this passage. Indeed, Juliana addresses him in line 317 as *feond moncynnes*, "foe" or "enemy of mankind."

to Hrothgar, she bids him to be joyful at drinking as well as loving to his people (615ff). Then she offers it to the *duguð* "old retainers," then to the *geoguð* "young retainers," and finally to the guest Beowulf. Second, her peace-weaving also takes a verbal form: her speeches accompanying the mead-sharing stress the peace and joy contingent upon the fulfillment of each man's duty to his nation. At the joyous celebration after Grendel's defeat, Wealhtheow concludes her speeches with a tribute to the harmony of the present moment by reminding her tribe of its cause, that is, adherence to the *comitatus* ethic. Each man remains true to the other, each is loyal to the king, the nation is ready and alert, the drinking warriors attend to the ale-dispenser herself (1228–31). Yet minutes before she attempted to forestall future danger to her family and nation by preventive peace-weaving, she advised Hrothgar to leave his kingdom to his sons, and then, as if sensing the future, she reminded Hrothulf, his nephew, of his obligations to those sons (obligations he will later deny). Third, the peace-weaver herself emblematizes peace, for she appears in the poem with her mead-vessel only after a contest has been concluded. Thus Wealhtheow enters the hall only after the contest between Unferth and Beowulf (612); she does not appear again until after Beowulf has overcome Grendel, when the more elaborate feasting invites the peace-making speeches mentioned above. After Grendel's Mother is defeated the poet preserves the integrity of the pattern of feminine cup-passing after masculine contest by describing the homecoming banquet at Hygelac's court, where Hygd conveys the mead-vessel. This structural pattern to which we shall return simultaneously weaves together the Danish part of the poem with its Geatish part.

Most of the other female characters figure as well in this middle section so that the female monster's adventures are framed by descriptions of other women for ironic contrast. The role of mother highlights the first half of the middle section with the scop's mention of Hildeburh (1071ff) and the entrance of Wealhtheow, both of whom preface the first appearance of Grendel's dam (1258) in her role as avenging mother. Then the introduction of Hygd, Thryth, and Freawaru after the female monster's death (1590) stresses the role of queen as peace-weaver and cup-passer to preface Beowulf's final narration of the female monster's downfall (2143). The actual adventures of Grendel's Mother cluster then at the middle of the middle section of the poem.

II

In the first part of the female monster's section, the idea is stressed that a kinswoman or mother must passively accept and not actively avenge the loss of her son. The story of the mother Hildeburh is recited by the scop early on the evening Grendel's Mother will visit Heorot. The lay ends at line 1159; Grendel's Mother enters the poem a mere hundred lines later when she attacks the Danish hall, as the Frisian contingent attacked the hall lodging Hildeburh's Danish brother in the *Finnsburh Fragment*. The *Beowulf* poet alters the focus of the fragment: he stresses the consequences of the surprise attack rather than the attack itself in order to reveal Hildeburh's maternal reactions to them.

Hildeburh is unjustly (*unsynnum*, 1072) deprived of her Danish brother and Frisian son, but all she does, this sad woman (*geōmuru ides*, 1075), is to mourn her loss with dirges and stoically place her son on the pyre. In fact, she can do nothing, caught in the very web she has woven as peace-pledge: her husband's men have killed her brother, her brother's men have killed her son. Later the Danish Hengest will avenge the feud with her husband Finn, whether she approves or not, by overwhelming the Frisians and returning Hildeburh to her original tribe. The point remains: the peace-pledge must accept a passive role precisely because the ties she knots bind *her*—she *is* the knot, the pledge of peace. Her fate interlaces with that of her husband and brothers through her role as a mother bearing a son: thus Hildeburh appropriately mourns the loss of her symbolic tie at the pyre, the failure of herself as peace-pledge, the loss of her identity. Like Hildeburh Grendel's dam will also lose her identity as mother, never having had an identity as peace-pledge to lose.

As if reminded of her own role as mother by hearing of Hildeburh's plight, Wealhtheow demonstrates her maternal concern in an address to Hrothgar immediately after the scop sings this lay. In it she first alludes to Hrothgar's adoption of Beowulf as a son: apparently troubled by this, she insists that Hrothgar leave his kingdom only to his actual kinsmen or descendants when he dies (1178–79). Then she urges her foster "son" Hrothulf (actually a nephew) to remember his obligations to them so that he will "repay our sons with liberality" (1184–85). Finally, she moves to the mead-bench where the adopted Beowulf sits, rather symbolically, next to her sons Hrethric and Hrothmund (1188–91). The *past* helplessness of the first mother, Hildeburh, to requite the death of her son counterpoints the anxiously maternal Wealhtheow's attempts to weave the ties of kinship and obligation, thereby forestalling *future* danger to her sons. Later that night, Grendel's Mother intent on avenging the loss of her son in the *present* attacks Heorot, her masculine aggression contrasting with the feminine passivity of both Hildeburh and Wealhtheow. Indeed, she resembles a grieving human mother: like Hildeburh she is guiltless and *galgmōd* "gloomy-minded" (1277); her journey to Heorot must be sorrowful (1278) for she "remembered her misery" (1259). But a woman's primary loyalty as peace-pledge was reserved for her husband, not her son, according to the Danish history of Saxo Grammaticus.[6] Perhaps for this reason Grendel's Mother is presented as husbandless and son-obsessed—to suggest to an Anglo-Saxon audience the dangers inherent in woman's function as *friðusibb* "pledge of peace".

However, her attempts to avenge her son's death could be justified if she were human and male, for no *wergild* "man price" has been offered to her by the homicide Beowulf.[7] The role of the masculine avenger is emphasized throughout the passage (1255–78) in defining her motivation to attack: she performs the role of avenger (*wrecend*, 1256) "to avenge the death of her son" (1278). Whatever her maternal feelings, she actually fulfills the duty of the kinsman. Unlike Hildeburh, she cannot wait for a Hengest to resolve the feud in some way; unlike Freawaru, she cannot act as a peace-pledge to settle the feud. Tribeless, now kinless, forced to rely on her own might, she seizes and kills Aeschere, Hrothgar's most beloved retainer, in an appropriate retribution for the loss of her own most beloved "retainer" and "lord"—her son.

The monstrosity of her action is at first not evident. Hrothgar suspects she has carried the "feud" too far (1339–40). And from the Danish and human point of view she possesses no legal right to exact compensation for her kinsman's loss because Grendel is himself a homicide. However, Beowulf later implies that the two feuds must remain separate, as she desires her own "revenge for injury" (*gyrnwracu*, 2118). Because she is legally justified in pursuing her own feud given the tribal duty of the retainer to avenge the death of his lord, regardless of the acts he has committed, she behaves monstrously then in only one way. For a mother to "avenge" her son (2121) as if she were a retainer, he were her lord, and avenging more important than peace-making, is monstrous. An analogy conveying her effect on the men in Heorot when she first appears suggests how unusual are her actions in human terms. Her horror "is as much less as is the skill (strength) of maidens, the war-horror of a woman, in comparison to a (weaponed) man, when the bound sword shears the one standing opposite" (*Wæs se gryre lǣssa / efne swā micle, swā bið mægþa cræft, / wīggryre wīfes be wæpnedmen, / þonne heoru*

6. See the stories of the treacherous wife but loyal mother Urse in the twelfth-century *Saxonis Grammatici Gesta Danorum*, ed. Alfred Holder (Strassburg: K. J. Trübner, 1886), pp. 53–55; (*The First Nine Books of the Danish History of Saxo Grammaticus*, tr. Oliver Elton [London: D. Nutt, 1894], pp. 64–65 [II, 53–55]).
7. Dorothy Whitelock, *The Beginnings of English Society* (Baltimore: Penguin Books, 1952), p. 41; on duty to one's kin, see pp. 38–47; on duty to one's lord, see pp. 31ff. Duty to one's lord superseded duty to one's kin (p. 37). See also *Saxonis Grammatici Gesta Danorum*, p. 254 (VII), for the retainer's duty to lord; in cases of blood revenge the son remained most deeply obligated to his father, pp. 75, 96 (III), then to his brother or sister, pp. 53, 280 (II, VIII), finally to his grandfather, p. 301 (IX).

bunden . . . / . . . / . . . *andweard scireð*, 1282–87). In their eyes recognizably female, she threatens them physically less than her son. But because female "peacemakers" do not wage war, the analogy implies, by litotes, that her unnatural behavior seems *more* horrible.

In the second part of her adventure she no longer behaves solely as an avenging monster, antitype of Hildeburh and Wealhtheow, who are both through marriage "visitors" to a hall like Grendel and his dam. Such hall-visitors contrast with the hall-rulers of this second part: the *merewīf* as queen or guardian (*grundhyrde*, 2136) protects her "battle-hall," the cave-like lair, from the visiting hero like the regal dragon guarding his ring-hall, and like King Beowulf his kingdom, in the last section of the poem. Accordingly, the stress on the relationship between mother and son delineated in the first part of her adventure changes to a stress on the relationship between host and guest.

As a tribeless queen or lady (*ides āglǣcwīf*) she rudely receives her "hall-guest" Beowulf (*selegyst*, 1545; *gist*, 1522) by "embracing" him and then "repaying him" for his valor not with treasure but with "grim grips" (*Hēo him eft hraþe andlean forgeald / grimman grāpum*, 1541–42) just as the dragon will "entertain" him in the future.[8] Indeed, the parody of the hall-ceremony of treasure-giving is complete when a "scop" (Beowulf's sword, acting as bard) sings a fierce "war song" off the side of her head (*hire on hafelan hringmǣl āgōl / grǣdig gūðlēoð*, 1521–22). It is interesting to note that this "hall-celebration" of the mock peace-weaver to welcome her valorous guest Beowulf following her attack on Heorot and her curiously listless "contest" with Aeschere duplicates the pattern of mead-sharing ceremonies involving peacemakers which follow masculine contests throughout the poem.

It is also interesting to note that the contest between this apparently lordless "queen" and her "guest" contrasts in its mock-sensual embracing and grasping with the other two major battles of the hero—the briefly described arm-wrestling between Grendel and Beowulf and the conventional sword-wielding of Beowulf against the fire-breathing dragon. Indeed, before Beowulf arrives at the "battle-hall" Hrothgar introduces the possibility of a Grendel's father in addition to the mother, even though they do not know of such a father (1355), and of possible additional progeny of such a father or

8. The poet uses similar wordplay in describing the "reception" of the guest Beowulf in the "hall" of the gold-lord dragon. First, Beowulf does not dare attack (or more figuratively, "approach") the gold-lord dragon in his ring-hall (*hringsele*, 2840, 3053); Wiglaf admits *hē ne grētte goldweard þone* 'he did not approach the guardian of the gold' (3081), literally because of the danger from fire, figuratively because of the dragon's avarice. Instead, *wyrd* 'fate' will dispense or distribute his "soul's hoard" for which Beowulf has paid with his life (*wyrd* will seek his *sāwle hord, sundur gedǣlan / līf wið līce* 'soul's hoard, separate his life from his body', 2422–23a; he "buys" the hoard with his life in 2799–800). After this "treasure-giving," the cup-passer—Wiglaf—pours water from the cup—Beowulf's helmet.

even of Grendel himself (through an incestuous union with his mother?): *hwæþer him ǣnig wæs ǣr ācenned / dyrnra gāsta* (1356–57). His ostensible point is to warn Beowulf of additional monsters lurking nearby, but it serves as well to remind the reader that Grendel's Mother has an animal nature very different from that of a human lady. For during the passage describing their battle the poet exploits the basic resemblance between sexual intercourse and battle to emphasize the inversion of the feminine role of the queen or hall-ruler by Grendel's Mother. This is achieved in three steps: first, the emphasis upon clutching, grasping, and embracing while they fight; second, the contest for a dominant position astride the other; and third, the use of fingers, knife, or sword to penetrate clothing or the body, the latter always accompanied by the implied figurative kinship between the sword and the phallus and between decapitation and castration.

First, she welcomes him to the *mere* with an almost fatal embrace similar to the "embrace" (*fæðm*, 1218) to which Aeschere has succumbed. She "grasped then towards him" (1501), seizing him with "horrible grips" (1502–03) envisioned earlier by the hero as a "battle-grip" (1445) and a "malicious grasp" (1447). Second, inside the "castle" (*hof*, 1507) where she has transported him, both grapple for a superior position over the other. After his sword fails him, for example, he "grasped her by the shoulder," hurling her to the ground. The poet, conscious of the monster's sex and Beowulf's definitely unchivalrous behavior, drily protests that in this case "the lord of the Battle-Geats did not at all lament the hostile act" (1537–38). Then, as "reward" for his valor, this lady "repaid" him with the treasure of her *grimman grāpum* "fierce graspings," forcing him to stumble and fall (1541–44), after which she climbs, rather ludicrously, on top of her "hall-guest" (*selegyst*, 1545), intent on stabbing him and thereby (again) avenging her only offspring (1546–47). Third, the battle culminates in very suggestive swordplay, and wordplay too. Earlier her "hostile fingers" (1505) tried to "penetrate" (*ðurhfōn*, 1504) his locked coat-of-mail; now she tries unsuccessfully to pierce the woven breast-net with her knife. Previously Beowulf discovered his own weapon was impotent against the spell or charm of the "sword-greedy" woman (*heorogīfre*, 1498), who collects the swords of giants. Now the "sword-grim" hero substitutes one of these swords, an appropriate tool to quell such a woman. The "sword entirely penetrated (*ðurhwōd*) the doomed-to-die body" (1567–68). After this final "embrace" of the "grasping" of her neck, the sword *wæs swātig secg weorce gefeh* "was bloody, the warrior rejoiced in the work" (1569). The alliteration links *sweord* with *secg*, to identify the bloody sword with the rejoicing, laboring "man-sword" (*secg*); the "battle" appropriately evokes erotic undertones. The equation of the sword and warrior, with the subsequent sexual connotations, resembles the synedoche controlling Riddle Twenty, "The Sword," in which the sword becomes a retainer who serves his lord through celibacy, forgoing the "joy-game" of marriage and the "treasure" of children, and whose only unpleasant battle occurs with a woman, because he must overcome her desire while she voices her terror, claps her hands, rebukes him with words, and cries out *ungod* "not good."[9] Similarly in *Beowulf* once the sword finally penetrates the body its blade miraculously melts—like ice into water—either from the poison of Grendel's blood or of his mother's, the poem does not specify which (1601). And even the *mere* itself, approached through winding passageways, slopes, and paths, and in whose stirred-up and bloody waters sea monsters lurk and the strange battle-hall remains hidden, almost projects the mystery and danger of female sexuality run rampant.

Such erotic overtones in descriptions of battles between a male and a female adversary are not especially common in Anglo-Saxon literature but can be found in various saints' lives in the Old English *Martyrology* (ca. 850) and in Ælfric's *Lives of the Saints* (ca. 994–early eleventh century), and in another epic poem also contained in the same manuscript as *Beowulf, Judith*. In the saints' lives a large group of thirty-four portrays a physical conflict between a Christian woman and a pagan man wishing to seduce her physically or spiritually. The description of the torture the saint undergoes to preserve her chastity often veils with obvious sexual symbolism the act of intercourse, or else it lovingly lingers over the description of the virgin's rape (see, for example, the life of St. Lucia).[1] The reason for such descriptions should be clear to those acquainted with the *Can-*

9. *The Exeter Book*, pp. 190–91. The sword declares:

Ic wiþ bryde ne mot
hæmed habban, ac me þæs hyhtplegan
geno wyrneð, se mec geara on
bende legde; forþon ic brucan sceal
on hagostealde hæleþa gestreona.
Oft ic wirum dol wife abelge,
wonie hyre willan; heo me wom spreceð,
floceð hyre folmum, firenaþ mec wordum,
ungod gæleð. Ic ne gyme þæs compes.

(I may not have sexual intercourse with a bride, but he who formerly laid bonds on me denies me still the joy-game; therefore I must enjoy the treasures of heroes while living in my lord's house. Often I, foolish in ornaments, anger the woman, diminish her will; she speaks evil to me with words, cries out "not good." I do not care for the contest.)

Similarly erotic riddles include no. 21, "Plow"; no. 44, "Key"; no. 53, "Battering Ram"; no. 62, "Poker" or "Burning Arrow"; and no. 91, "Key."

1. When St. Lucia resists the advances of the pagan Paschasius and he condemns her to be 'defiled' (*bysmrian*) in a whorehouse as punishment, she retorts, 'To me intercourse with thy slave is not more pleasant than if an adder would hurt me' (*nis me þynes weales hæmed næfre þe leofre þe me nædre toslyte*). See *An Old English Martyrology*, ed. George Herzfeld (Early English Text Society, o.s., vol. 116; London: The Early English Text Society, 1900), p. 218.

ticum Canticorum and its celebration of the love of the Sponsa for the Sponsus (of man's soul for God, of the Church for Christ), providing an analogous basis for the holy sacrament of marriage. The woman saint as a type of the soul longs to be joined, as in intercourse, with her spouse Christ; the threat of seduction by a human male must be read as an assault on the soul by the Devil.

In *Judith*, a work like *Beowulf* contained in MS Cotton Vitellius A.xv,[2] the fragmentary epic portrays similar sexual overtones in Judith's "battle" with Holofernes. As in *Beowulf* a warrior battles a monster: the blessed maiden grapples with the "drunken, vicious monster" (*se inwidda* 'the evil one', 28) Holofernes. However, the sexual role behavior of *Beowulf* occurs in reverse in *Judith*: Holofernes parallels Grendel's dam, but whereas the *wīf* is aggressive and sword-greedy, Holofernes seems slightly effete (his bed enclosed by gold curtains, for example) and impotent from mead-drinking: "The lord fell, the powerful one so drunken, in the middle of his bed, as if he knew no reason in his mind" (67–69). These hypermetrical lines heighten the irony of his situation, for the warrior swoons on the very bed upon which he intended to rape the maiden. Having lost his head to drink in a double sense he himself is penetrated by the virgin's sharp sword, "hard in the storm of battle" (79), thereafter literally losing his head. But first Judith draws the sword from its sheath in her right hand, seizes him by the hair in a mock loving gesture (98–99), then "with her hands pulls him toward her *shamefully*" (*teah hyne folmum wið hyre weard / bysmerlice*, 99b–100a). The "b" alliteration in line 100 (*bysmerlice, ond þone bealofullan*) draws attention to *bysmerlice*, which as a verb (*bysmrian*) elsewhere suggests the act of "defiling" (intercourse).[3] In this line what seems shameful is apparently her embrace of the warrior's body while she moves it to a supine position. As in *Beowulf*, the female assumes the superior position; she lays him down so that she may "control" (*gewealdan*, 103) him more easily in cutting off his head. The ironic embrace and mock intercourse of this couple parallels that of Beowulf and the *ides āglǣcwīf*: the aggressive and sword-bearing "virgin" contrasts with the passive and swordless man (Holofernes, Aeschere, and even Beowulf are all momentarily or permanently swordless). The poet's point in each case is that a perversion of the sexual roles signals an equally perverse spiritual state. Holofernes' impotence is as unnatural in the male as the *wīf*'s aggression is unnatural in the female; so the battle with the heroine or hero in each case is

2. Although the poems were written by different poets, *Beowulf* in the late seventh or eighth century and *Judith* in the middle or late tenth century, the second *Beowulf* scribe did transcribe all of the *Judith* fragment, probably in the late tenth century. All references to *Judith* derive from Elliott Van Kirk Dobbie, ed., *Beowulf and Judith*, vol. 4 of *The Anglo-Saxon Poetic Records* (New York: Columbia University Press, 1953).
3. See, for example, the life of St. Lucia in the *Martyrology*, p. 218.

described with erotic overtones to suggest the triumph of a right and natural sexual (and social and spiritual) order over the perverse and unnatural one. In the latter case Grendel's dam and her son pose a heathen threat to Germanic society (the macrocosm) and to the individual (Beowulf the microcosm) as Holofernes and the Assyrians pose a heathen threat to Israelite society (the macrocosm) and to the individual (Judith the microcosm).[4]

In this second part of her adventure, Hygd and Freawaru contrast with the *wīf* as queen or cup-passer as Hildeburh and Wealhtheow contrasted with Grendel's dam as mother in the first. Hygd, the first woman encountered after the defeat of Grendel's Mother, as truly fulfills the feminine ideal of *Maxims* I as does Wealhtheow. Her name, which means "Thought" or "Deliberation," contrasts her nature with that of the bellicose *wīf* and possibly that of the war-like Thryth, whose actions, if not her name, suggest "Strength" (only in the physical sense; the alternate form of her name, "Modthrytho" or "Mind-Force," implies in a more spiritual sense stubbornness or pride).[5] Although Hygd like the *wīf* and Thryth will be lordless after Hygelac's death, she does not desire to usurp the role of king for herself: doubting her son's ability to prevent tribal wars she offers the throne to Beowulf (2369ff). In addition, this gracious queen bestows treasure generously (1929–31), unlike the *wīf* and Thryth, the latter of whom dispense only "grim grips" and sword blows upon their "retainers."

The Thryth digression is inserted after Hygd enters to pass the cup upon Beowulf's return to Hygelac. Its structural position invites a comparison of this stubborn princess and the other two "queens," Hygd and the *wīf*. She appears to combine features of both: she begins as a type of the female monster, but upon marriage to Offa changes her nature and becomes a much-loved queen. According to the poet, Thryth commits a "terrible crime"; she condemns to death any retainer at court caught staring at her regal beauty. That she

4. For a discussion of these planes of correspondence in *Judith*, see James F. Doubleday, "The Principle of Contrast in *Judith*," *Neuphilologische Mitteilungen* 72 (1971): 436–41.

5. See Klaeber's discussion of Thryth's possible prototypes, 1931–62nn. Thryth's name resembles that of Quendrida (Queen Thryth?) and that of the Scottish Queen Hermutrude, whose story is related in Saxo Grammaticus' *Danish History*, p. 124 (*Gesta Danorum*, pp. 101–102 [IV]). Hermutrude, loved by Amleth, remains unmarried because of her cruelty and arrogance, similar to Thryth's. Finally, note the similarity between the following descriptions and those in *Beowulf*: Offa murdered many without distinction, including King Ethelbert, "thereby being guilty of an *atrocious outrage* against the suitor of his daughter," in William of Malmesbury's *Chronicle of the Kings of England: From the Earliest Period to the Reign of King Stephen*, tr. J. A. Giles (London: H. G. Bohn, 1847), p. 238; in Latin "nefarium rem *in procum filiae operatus*," from *Willelmi Malmesbiriensis Monachi De Gestis Regum Anglorum Libri Quinque*; *Historiae Novellae Libri Tres*, ed. William Stubbs, 2 vols. (Rerum Britannicarum Medii Aevii Scriptores, vol. 90; London: Eyre and Spottiswoode, 1887), p. 262 (II, 210). Compare *Beowulf*: *Modþrȳðo wæg fremu folces cwēn, firen' ondrysne* 'Modthrytho, the excellent queen of the people, carried on terrible wickedness' (1931–32). Did the *Beowulf* poet confuse the father of Modthrytho with the daughter herself?

abrogates her responsibilities as a queen and as a woman the poet makes clear: "Such a custom—that the peace-weaver after a pretended injury deprive the dear man of life—is not queenly for a woman to do, although she be beautiful" (*Ne bið swylc cwēnlīc þēaw / idese tō efnanne, þēah ðe hīo ænlicu sȳ, / þætte freoðuwebbe fēores onsǣce / æfter ligetorne lēofne mannan*, 1940b–43). The label "peace-weaver" (*freoðuwebbe*) seems ironic in this context, especially as she does not weave but instead severs the ties of kinship binding her to her people and the bonds of life tying the accused man to this world. That is, for any man caught looking at her "the deadly bonds, hand-woven, were in store; after his arrest it was quickly determined that the sword, the damascened sword, must shear, make known death-bale" (*ac him wælbende weotode tealde / handgewriþene; hraþe seoþðan wæs / æfter mundgripe mēce geþinged, / þæt hit sceādenmǣl scȳran mōste / cwealmbealu cȳðan*, 1936–40a). If she weaves at all then she weaves only "deadly hand-woven bonds" binding him to a grisly end. The "peace-weaver" *cuts* these bonds—imprisoning ropes—with a sword, simultaneously shearing the bonds of life to "make known death-bale." She resembles that other ironic peace-weaver, the *wīf*, who tried to penetrate the braided breast-net of Beowulf with her knife.

Both antitypes of the peace-weaving queen behave like kings, using the sword to rid their halls of intruders or unwanted "hall-guests." Unlike Thryth, the monstrous *wīf* remains husbandless, having lost her son, "wife" only to the *mere* she inhabits both in life and in death. At this moment in the poem, both Thryth and Grendel's Mother belong to the past. If they represent *previous* inversions of the peace-weaver and cup-passer, and Hygd who is now passing the mead-cup to Beowulf's weary men in celebration signifies a *present* cup-passer, so the poet introduces a final queen, this time a cup-passer of the *future*, who will fail in her role as the first woman, Hildeburh, failed in hers.

Freawaru, like Hildeburh, seems innocent of any crime. She is envisioned by Beowulf as a queen married to Ingeld of the Heathobards in a digression (2032–69) immediately preceding his summary of the battles with Grendel and with his mother. She will fail in her role as peace-weaver because of an underlying hostility—an old Heathobard warrior's bitterness over ancient Heathobard treasure acquired through previous wars and worn by a young Danish man accompanying the new queen. The fragility of this role is heightened even further when, in the third section involving the dragon, Beowulf inhabits a queenless kingdom and when Wiglaf must become the cup-passer, pouring water from the "cup" of Beowulf's helmet in a futile attempt to revive his wounded lord.

Indeed, three women characters appear outside this middle section to convey dialectically the idea that woman cannot ensure peace in this world. First, Wealhtheow, unlike other female figures, appears in the first (or Grendel) section of the poem to pour mead after Grendel's challenge has been answered by the hero. This first entrance symbolizes the ideal role of Germanic woman as a personification of peace, as we have seen. In antithesis, Beowulf's account of the fall of the *wīf unhȳre* "monstrous woman" appropriately ends the poem's second (Grendel's Mother) section which has centered on this role: the personification of discord, the antitype of the feminine ideal, has been destroyed. But in the poem's third section a synthesis emerges. The nameless and unidentified Geat woman who appears, like the other female characters, after a battle—this one between Beowulf and the dragon—mourns at the pyre. That is, the efforts of the peacemaker, while valuable in worldly and social terms, ultimately must fail because of the nature of this world. True peace exists not in woman's but in God's 'embrace' (*fæþm*, 188).

III

This idea is implied in Hrothgar's sermon (1700–84); like the court celebration of Hygelac, it is a part of the middle section belonging to Grendel's Mother but apparently unrelated to it. In it Hrothgar describes three Christian vices in distinctly Germanic terms. Impelled by envy like Grendel, Heremod kills his "table-companions" (1713–14). Next, the wealthy hall-ruler in his pride is attacked by the Adversary while his guardian conscience sleeps within the hall of his soul (1740–44). So the monster that specifically epitomizes pride in *Beowulf*, as in Genesis, is female—Grendel's Mother—thematically related to Thryth or Modthrytho, whose name (if it can be said to exist in manuscript in that form) means "pride." Grendel's Mother substitutes war-making for the peace-weaving of the queen out of a kind of selfish pride—if she were capable of recognizing it as such. Finally, this same hall-ruler "covets angry-minded" (*gȳtsað gromhȳdig*, 1749) the ornamented treasures God had previously given him by refusing to dispense any to his warriors. So the mock gold-king dragon avariciously guards his treasure. Although the poet portrays the monsters as antitypes of Germanic ideals, his integument conceals a Christian idea. The city of man, whether located in a Germanic or Christian society, is always threatened by sin and failure.

Such sin alienates Christian man from self, neighbor, and God; it alienates Germanic man primarily from other men. Note that although in *Beowulf* each of the three monsters is described as guarding or possessing a hall, whether Heorot, a watery cavern, or a barrow, each remains isolated from humanity (and from each other—Grendel and his mother live together, but they never appear together in the poem until he is dead). Ideally when the retainer, the queen, and the gold-lord cooperate they constitute a viable nucleus of Germanic society: a retainer must have a gold-lord from whom to receive gold for his loyalty in battle; the peace-weaver must have a "loom"—the band of retainers and their lord, or two nations—upon which to weave peace.

Despite the poet's realization that these roles cannot be fulfilled in this world, this Germanic ideal provides structural and thematic unity for *Beowulf*. Grendel's Mother does occupy a transitional position in the poem: as a "retainer" attacking Heorot she resembles Grendel, but as an "attacked ruler" of her own "hall" she resembles the dragon. As a monstrous mother and queen she perverts a role more important socially and symbolically than that of Grendel, just as the queen as peace-pledge or peace-weaver ultimately becomes more valuable than the retainer but less valuable than the gold-giver himself.

If it seems ironic that a Germanic ideal that cannot exist in this world *can* exist in art, unifying the theme and structure of the poem, then Grendel's Mother, warring antitype of harmony and peace, must seem doubly ironic. The structural position of her episode in the poem, like woman's position as cup-passer among members of a nation, or as a peace-pledge between two nations, is similarly medial and transitional, but successfully so.

ROBERTA FRANK

The *Beowulf* Poet's Sense of History†

> I don't know how humanity stands it
> with a painted paradise at the end of it
> without a painted paradise at the end of it
> —Ezra Pound, *Canto* LXXIV

Awareness of historical change, of the pastness of a past that itself has depth, is not instinctive to man; there is nothing natural about a sense of history. Anthropologists report that the lack of historical perspective is a feature of primitive thought, and historians that its absence characterizes medieval thinking: Herod in the Wakefield

† From *The Wisdom of Poetry: Essays in Early English Literature in Honor of Morton W. Bloomfield*, ed. Larry D. Benson and Siegfried Wenzel (Kalamazoo: Medieval Institute Publications, 1982) 53–65. Reprinted by permission of the publisher.

Cycle swears "by Mahoun in heaven," the medieval Alexander is a knight, and heathen Orléans boasts a university.[1] Morton Bloomfield has shown that a sense of history, even a tentative, underdeveloped one, was a rare thing in fourteenth-century England, and that Chaucer's attention to chronology and his preoccupation with cultural diversity have affinities with aspects of the early Italian Renaissance.[2] But what in the Anglo-Saxon period stimulated a monastic author to stress the differences between ancient days and his own, to paint the past as if it were something other than the present?[3] The *Beowulf* poet's reconstruction of a northern heroic age is chronologically sophisticated, rich in local color and fitting speeches. The poet avoids obvious anachronisms and presents such an internally consistent picture of Scandinavian society around A.D. 500 that his illusion of historical truth has been taken for the reality.[4]

The poet's heroic age is full of men both "emphatically pagan and exceptionally good," men who believe in a God whom they thank at every imaginable opportunity.[5] Yet they perform all the pagan rites known to Tacitus, and are not Christian. The temporal distance between past and present, acknowledged in the opening words of the poem—"in geardagum" ("in days of yore")—is heard again when Beowulf, as yet unnamed, makes his entrance. He is the strongest of men "on þæm dæge þysses lifes" ("on that day of this life" 197, 790).[6] The alliterating demonstratives stress the remoteness of the past, here and later when a hall-servant in Heorot looks after all the visitors' bedtime needs "swylce þy dogore heaþoliðende habban scoldon" ("such as in those days seafarers were wont to have" 1797–98). The descriptive clause distances but also glosses over, shadowing with vagueness an unknown corner of the past. The poet is so

1. Peter Burke, *The Renaissance Sense of the Past* (London, 1969), pp. 1–6; Michael Hunter, "Germanic and Roman Antiquity and the Sense of the Past in Anglo-Saxon England," *Anglo-Saxon England* 3 (1974), 45–48.
2. "Chaucer's Sense of History," *Journal of English and Germanic Philology* 51 (1952), 301–13; rpt. in Morton Bloomfield, *Essays and Explorations: Studies in Ideas, Language, and Literature* (Cambridge, Mass., 1970), pp. 13–26.
3. In assuming that literate composition indicates authorship by a cleric, I am following, among others, C. P. Wormald, "The Uses of Literacy in Anglo-Saxon England and its Neighbours," *Transactions of the Royal Historical Society*. 5th ser., 27 (1977), 95–114.
4. On the use of *Beowulf* as a historical document, see J. R. R. Tolkien, "*Beowulf*: The Monsters and the Critics," *Proceedings of the British Academy* 22 (1936), 245–51; sep. rpt. (London, 1937, 1958, 1960), pp. 1–6; Robert T. Farrell, "*Beowulf*, Swedes and Geats," *Saga-Book* (Viking Society for Northern Research) 18 (1972), 225–86. Kemp Malone found the most remarkable feature of *Beowulf* to be its "high standard of historical accuracy": the anachronisms "that one would expect in a poem of the eighth century" are missing ("Beowulf," *English Studies* 29 [1948], 161–72, esp. 164). But the *Beowulf* poet occasionally nodded; see Walter Goffart, "Hetware and Hugas: Datable Anachronisms in *Beowulf*" in *The Dating of Beowulf*, ed. Colin Chase, Toronto Old English Series, 6 (1981), pp. 83–100.
5. Larry D. Benson, "The Pagan Coloring of *Beowulf*" in *Old English Poetry: Fifteen Essays*, ed. Robert P. Creed (Providence, 1967), p. 194.
6. The same line is used to place Grendel's downfall in the distant past (806). Citations of *Beowulf* refer to Frederick Klaeber, ed., *Beowulf and The Fight at Finnsburg*, 3rd ed. (Boston, 1950).

attracted by the aristocratic rituals of life in the hall, so intent on historical verisimilitude, that he imagines everything, even basic human needs, to have changed over time. His proposition that golden tapestries hanging in the hall were a wondrous sight for the partying sixth-century retainers is quickly modified in the direction of reality: "þara þe on swylc starað" ("for those who look upon such things" 996); even in Heorot not all beefy breakers-of-rings in their cups would have had an eye for interior design. The vividness of the past underlines, paradoxically, its distance.

The *Beowulf* poet has a strong sense of cultural diversity, as strong perhaps as Chaucer's. Three times in the "Knight's Tale" Chaucer explains the behavior of characters with the clause "as was tho the gyse"; in "The Legend of Cleopatra" he has Anthony sent out to win kingdoms and honor "as was usance"; and in "The Legend of Lucrece" he notes approvingly that Roman wives prized a good name "at thilke tyme."[7] The Old English poet maintains a similar perspective. He praises the Geats for their ancient custom of keeping armor and weapons at their sides at all times: "They were always prepared for war, whether at home or in the field, as their lord required" (1246–50). He has Hrothgar admire their steadfastness, the dependability of men who live blameless "ealde wisan" ("in the old fashion" 1865). When the dragon's ravages begin, the poet makes the aged Beowulf fear that he has transgressed "ofer ealde riht" ("against ancient law" 2330): pagans have their own moral code, separating them from the author and us. The poet emphasizes cultural differences not only between present and past but also between coeval peoples. He depicts the Swedes and Geats as more authentically primitive, more pagan in outlook and idiom, than the Danes. When a roughhewn Beowulf arrives at the Danish court he puts himself in the hands of a skilled local who "knew the custom of the retainers" (359). Ongentheow, the grizzled king of the Swedes, threatens to pierce ("getan" 2940) captives on the gallows for the pleasure of carrion birds.[8] The Geats consult auspices (204); Beowulf, like the Scandinavian heroes of old, trusts in his own might (418, 670, 1270, 1533); the messenger imagines a raven boasting to an eagle of carnage-feasts (3024–27); and Hæthcyn's slaying of Herebeald (2435–43) imitates a fratricide in the Norse pantheon: euhemerism becomes, in the poet's hands, an aid to historical research.[9]

7. Morton W. Bloomfield observes that Chaucer employs "as was tho the gyse" to qualify pagan funeral customs (line 993), sacrificial rites (line 2279), and cremations (line 2911) (*Essays and Explorations*, p. 21). Citations from *The Legend of Good Women* are to lines 586 and 1813 in the second edition of F. N. Robinson (Boston, 1957).

8. Hans Kuhn relates Ongentheow's threat (*getan* = **gautian*) to a boast by the pagan tenth-century skald Helgi trausti Ólafsson: "I paid to the gallows-prince [Odin] Gautr's [Odin's] sacrifice" ("Gaut," *Festschrift für Jost Trier zu seinem 60. Geburtstag*, ed. Benno von Wiese and Karl Heinz Borck [Meisenheim, 1954], pp. 417–33).

9. Ursula Dronke points out that *Beowulf* contains human analogues for two additional

The poet's sense of anachronism is revealed in his characters' speeches, utterances that avoid all distinctively Christian names and terms. The actors themselves have a sense of the past and of the future. They are able to look back two generations, tracing the origins of the feud between the Geats and the Swedes (2379–96, 2472–89, 2611–19, 2379–96). They can also forecast the feuds of the next generation. There is a fine display of chronological wit when Beowulf, on the basis of a piece of information picked up at the Danish court, turns the Ingeld legend into a political prophecy, a sequence of events likely to occur in the near future (2024–69). The poet's sense of historic succession is so strong and the internal chronology of the poem so carefully worked out that his audience knows why Hrothulf and Heoroweard have to be kept in the wings a little while longer. After Beowulf's death, it is clear even to the messenger that Eadgils is not likely to sit for long on the Swedish throne without avenging his brother's murder on the new king of the Geats, son of the slayer. The poet does not make earlier Danish and Germanic heroes like Scyld, Heremod, Finn, Offa, Sigemund, Eormenric and Hama contemporaneous with the sixth-century events narrated, but sets them in a distant mirror, conveying the illusion of a many-storied long-ago. Such chronological tidiness is all the more remarkable for its appearance in a poetic vernacular that has no distinctive future tense, and whose chief adverbs of recollection and continuation—"þa" and "siððan" ("thereupon": looking forward; "at that time," "from the time that": looking back)—are almost always ambiguous.[1]

Philosophically, in order to have a sense of history at all, the *Beowulf* poet had to hold certain premises about man and his role on earth. Despite his professional concern with the timeless, he had to be engaged to some extent with the things of this world; he needed a positive attitude toward secular wisdom and some notion of natural law. Above all, he had to believe that pagan Germanic legend had intellectual value and interest for Christians. These concepts were available to twelfth-century humanists. Christian Platonists like William of Conches, Bernard Silvestris, and Alan of Lille shared an unpolemical attitude toward the pagan past and stressed the importance of earthly understanding as the base of all human knowledge.[2]

---

mythological incidents recorded in Norse poetry ("*Beowulf* and Ragnarǫk," *Saga-Book* (Viking Society for Northern Research) 17 [1969], 322–25). On Scandinavian heroes' faith in their own *megin* (OE *mægen*), see Peter Foote and David M. Wilson, *The Viking Achievement* (London, 1970), p. 404. A raven, "oath-brother of the eagle," converses again in a section of the tenth-century pagan Norse *Hrafnsmál* (or *Haraldskvæði*) attributed to the skald Þórbjǫrn Hornklofi.

1. Noted by E. G. Stanley, "The Narrative Art of *Beowulf*," in *Medieval Narrative: A Symposium*, ed. Hans Bekker-Nielsen et al. (Odense, 1979), pp. 59–60.
2. See Ursula and Peter Dronke, "The Prologue of the Prose *Edda*: Explorations of a Latin Background" in *Sjötíu ritgerðir helgaðar Jakobi Benediktssyni* (Reykjavik, 1977), pp. 169–70.

But in the central theological traditions of the early medieval West and, more specifically, in the teachings of Aldhelm, Bede, and Alcuin, there is no trace of this liberal mentality.[3] No contemporary of these three concerned himself with man on earth, looking upon heathen virtues and customs with an indulgent eye, and had his vision survive. The patristic tradition that pagan story is diabolically inspired, that unbaptized pagans lie lamenting in hell, was too strong.

Purely from the perspective of the history of ideas, the *Beowulf* poet's chronological acrobatics and fascination with cultural diversity, his positive view of those who lived "while men loved the lawe of kinde," needs explanation.[4] We cannot, wielding editorial knives, remove these ideas from the text the way other late-seeming growths have been excised solely on the grounds that the poem is early.[5] "It is a dangerous principle to adopt in literary investigation that nothing we do not readily understand can be rationally explained. We must as a working principle assume that everything in a work of art is capable of explanation even at the cost of oversubtlety and even error. . . . We must not assume, unless we are finally forced to it, that the writer or composer did not know what he was doing."[6] Professor Bloomfield offered this guidance in a review of Kenneth Sisam's *The Structure of Beowulf*. Sisam contends that "great difficulties stand in the way of all explanations that make the poet a deep thinker, attempting themes and ways of conveying them that might be tried on a select body of readers in a more advance age."[7] The fact remains, however, that the poem, for an early composition, is full of oddly advanced notions. Twenty years ago Morton Bloomfield observed that "ealde riht" ("old law" 2330) in *Beowulf* referred not to the Mosaic Code, the Old Law, but to natural law, and noted that the moral laws of the Old Testament were often equated with this

3. See H. M. and N. K. Chadwick, *The Growth of Literature* (Cambridge, Eng., 1932–40), 1:556–57; Patrick Wormald, "Bede, *Beowulf*, and the Conversion of the Anglo-Saxon Aristocracy" in *Bede and Anglo-Saxon England*, ed. Robert T. Farrell, British Archaeological Reports, 46 (1978), pp. 42–49.
4. Chaucer, *The Book of the Duchess*, line 56 (*The Works of Geoffrey Chaucer*, ed. F. N. Robinson, 2nd ed. [Boston, 1957]).
5. Kenneth Sisam long ago interpreted the Scyld Scefing preamble to *Beowulf* as a contemporary allusion to the West Saxon dynasty; but since he took *Beowulf* as a whole to be seventh or eighth century, the opening episode had to be a late, post-Alfredian addition: better a composite poem than a Viking one. See Sisam, "Anglo-Saxon Royal Genealogies," *Proceedings of the British Academy* 39 (1953), 287–346, esp. 339. The Offa digression of *Beowulf*—a probable allusion to the great ancestor of the Mercian house—would have flattered not only Offa of Mercia but also the descendants of Alfred who had succeeded to the rule of Mercia and who were themselves descendants of the Mercian royal line. But commentators, reluctant to look outside the age of Bede, either reject the Mercian associations of this digression or declare it, too, a later interpolation. See the important article by Nicolas Jacobs, "Anglo-Danish Relations, Poetic Archaism and the Date of *Beowulf*: A Reconsideration of the Evidence," *Poetica* (Tokyo) 8 (1977) [1978], 23–43. Jacobs demonstrates that no linguistic or historical fact compels us to anchor *Beowulf* before the tenth century.
6. *Speculum* 41 (1966), 368–71.
7. *The Structure of Beowulf* (New York and Oxford, 1965), p. 77.

natural law, "although in general this equation is later than the early Middle Ages."[8] More recently, he has seen behind Beowulf's single combat with Grendel the concept of the *iudicium Dei*, a calling upon God to decide the justice of an action: "Let wise God, the holy Lord, adjudge the glory to whichever side he thinks fit," says Beowulf (685–87); the champion will rely in the coming struggle on the judgment of God (440–41).[9] Something like the judicial duel appears to have been a feature of medieval Scandinavian society. Yet all the early evidence for trial by combat from Tacitus to Pope Nicholas I is Continental; there is no documentation for multilateral ordeal in England before the Norman Conquest. The *Beowulf* poet's use of the form and spirit of the judicial duel, whether he derived the concept from Tacitus, from the Franks, or from the Danelaw, emphasizes—like his auguries, sacrifices, and exotic cremations—the temporal and cultural distance between the pagan Scandinavian past and the England of his own day. His backward glance is both admiring and antiquarian.

Anglo-Saxon scholarship has done its best to read *Beowulf* as the seventh and eighth centuries would have. Because Aldhelm and Bede insisted that the only suitable subject for poetry was a religious one, and because secular epics and long historical poems only started to appear in the later ninth century, Margaret Goldsmith had little choice but to interpret *Beowulf* allegorically.[1] Alcuin's only known comment on heroic literature in ecclesiastical contexts is an orthodox denunciation of it as a heathen distraction.[2] W. F. Bolton's new book on *Alcuin and Beowulf* discovers, predictably, that the great schoolmaster would have found Beowulf guilty, flawed, vengeful, incapable even of protecting his people.[3] Charles Donahue attempts to account for the existence of an eighth-century Old English poem about noble pagans by invoking Irish views of pre-Christian goodness, legends that tell of virtuous pagans and their natural knowledge of God.[4] Yet the stories of Cormac and Morand that he cites are not easy to date (that of Cormac is surely no earlier than the last quarter of the tenth century), and Donahue concedes that they are "later than *Beowulf* and can be viewed only as parallel developments of

8. "Patristics and Old English Literature: Notes on Some Poems," *Comparative Literature* 14 (Winter 1962), 36–43; rpt. twice in its entirety, and partially in *An Anthology of Beowulf Criticism*, ed. Lewis E. Nicholson (Notre Dame, 1963), p. 370.
9. "Beowulf, Byrhtnoth, and the Judgment of God: Trial by Combat in Anglo-Saxon England," *Speculum* 44 (1969), 545–59.
1. *The Mode and Meaning of 'Beowulf'* (London, 1970).
2. *Alcuini Epistolae*, 124, ed. Ernest Dümmler, Monumenta Germaniae Historica, *Epistolae* IV. 2 (Berlin, 1895), p. 183.
3. *Alcuin and Beowulf: An Eighth-Century View* (New Brunswick, N.J., 1978), esp. pp. 152–54, 165–70.
4. "*Beowulf*, Ireland, and the Natural Good," *Traditio* 7 (1949–51), 263–77; "*Beowulf* and Christian Tradition: A Reconsideration from a Celtic Stance," *Traditio* 21 (1965), 55–116.

that early insular Christian humanism. . . ."[5] Patrick Wormald has recently located a social and cultural context for the composition of heroic literature in the aristocratic climate of early English Christianity, in the integration of monastic and royal houses.[6] Yet the aristocratic nature of the early English church is, if anything, more pronounced with the passage of time, reaching a kind of culmination under the successors of Alfred.[7] The "vast zone of silence" Wormald observes existing between Bede and the *Beowulf* poet[8] may be due not only to Bede's fundamentalism but also to the centuries separating the two authors.

When in the Anglo-Saxon period did pagans become palatable? A positive attitude toward the pagans of classical antiquity is visible in translations of the Alfredian period. While the real Orosius, writing in the first decades of the fifth century, was as reluctant as Bede to say anything good about those who lived before the Christian Era, the Old English paraphrase of *Orosius* from around 900 contemplates with pleasure the bravery, honorable behavior, and renown of several early Romans, adds references to Julius Caesar's clemency, generosity, and courage, and even suggests that in some of their customs the Romans of the Christian Era were worse than their pagan ancestors.[9] Unlike his source, the Old English translator does not think in an exclusively religious way: what matters is how rulers of the past served God's purpose, not whether they were Christians or pagans.[1]

Boethius' *Consolation of Philosophy*, translated by King Alfred himself, resorted to pre-Christian human history and to pagan mythology for some fifty illustrations, finding archetypal patterns in the behavior of a Nero or a Hercules just as the *Beowulf* poet locates exemplary models in Heremod and Beowulf. In the late ninth and

5. "*Beowulf*, Ireland, and the Natural Good," p. 277.
6. "Bede, *Beowulf*, and the Conversion of the Anglo-Saxon Aristocracy," esp. pp. 49–58.
7. According to Wormald, "the aristocratic climate of early English Christianity is, if anything, more apparent in the age of Offa than in the age of Bede" ("Bede, *Beowulf*, and the Conversion of the Anglo-Saxon Aristocracy," p. 94). Royal and monastic interests seem even more closely integrated in the age of Athelstan. Accompanying that king on his military expedition to Scotland in 934 were the two archbishops, fourteen bishops, seven ealdormen, six jarls with Norse names, three Welsh kings, and twenty-four others including eleven royal thegns. One of Athelstan's laws commanded that every Friday at every monastery all monks were to sing fifty psalms "for the king and those who want what he wants . . ." See P. H. Sawyer, *From Roman Britain to Norman England* (New York, 1978), pp. 126, 192, 243. For a glimpse of aristocratic climates in tenth-century Saxony, see K. J. Leyser, *Rule and Conflict in an Early Medieval Society: Ottonian Saxony* (London, 1979).
8. "Bede, *Beowulf*, and the Conversion of the Anglo-Saxon Aristocracy," p. 36.
9. See Dorothy Whitelock, "The Prose of Alfred's Reign" in *Continuations and Beginnings: Studies in Old English Literature*, ed. E. G. Stanley (London, 1966), p. 91. For the Old English text, see *The Old English Orosius*, ed. Janet Bately, Early English Text Society, s. s. 6 (Oxford, 1980), p. xcix; for the Latin, *Pauli Orosii Presbyteri Hispani adversum Paganos Historiarum Libri Septem*, ed. Karl Zangemeister, Corpus Scriptorum Ecclesiasticorum Latinorum, 5 (Vienna, 1882).
1. See J. M. Wallace-Hadrill, *Early Germanic Kingship in England and on the Continent* (Oxford, 1971), pp. 145–46.

early tenth centuries, the *Consolation* enjoyed a considerable vogue among Carolingian commentators, at least one of whom, Remigius of Auxerre, Alfred may have used.[2] Alfred thrusts aside much of Remigius' Neoplatonic speculation along with his scientific and theological information, but is quick to insert commentary material having to do with classical myths. He occasionally gives a pagan analogy for a Christian concept, something Alcuin never managed to do.[3] Alfred's story of Orpheus teaches that a man who wishes to see the true light of God must not turn back to his old errors.[4] Boethius' tale of Jupiter overthrowing the giants who warred on heaven is shown by Alfred to reflect—*secundum fidem gentilium*—Nimrod's building of the Tower of Babel and God's subsequent division of tongues.[5] Alfred stresses the underlying truthfulness of Boethius' pagan fables. The details of Hercules' taming the Centaurs, burning the Hydra's poisonous heads, and slaying Cacus are skipped, but the myth itself is universalized into a philosophic reflection on life and on the meaning of victory and defeat: good men fight for honor in this world, to win glory and fame; for their deeds, they dwell beyond the stars in eternal bliss.[6] Circe in Alfred's paraphrase is no longer the wicked enchantress of Boethius, but a vulnerable goddess who falls violently in love with Odysseus at first sight; she turns his men into animals only after they, out of homesickness, plot to abandon their lord.[7] Alfred, like the *Beowulf* poet, looks for the moral and psychological laws of things, tries to understand and learn rather than condemn. Only once in his paraphrase does he abandon the world of classical paganism for a Germanic allusion; it is a small step, but full of significance for the future of Old English poetry. He translates Boethius' "Where now are the bones of faithful Fabricius?"

2. Kurt Otten surveys attempts from Schepss (1881) to Courcelle (1937) to locate the Remigian commentaries available to Alfred (*König Alfreds Boethius*, Studien zur englischen Philologie, N. F. 3 [Tübingen, 1964], pp. 4–9). See also Brian Donaghey, "The Sources of King Alfred's Translation of Boethius' *De Consolatione Philosophiae*," *Anglia* 82 (1964), 23–57. Pierre Courcelle favors a ninth-century commentary by an anonymous monk of St. Gall (*La Consolation de Philosophie dans la tradition littéraire: antécédents et postérité de Boèce* [Paris, 1967]). But even if Alfred (d. 899) did not have access to Remigius' work in its final Parisian form (c. 902–908), he could have followed a version modelled on Remigius' earlier teaching at Auxerre and Rheims. See Diane Bolton, "Remigian Commentaries on the *Consolation of Philosophy* and their Sources," *Traditio* 33 (1977), 381–94, and "The Study of the *Consolation of Philosophy* in Anglo-Saxon England," *Archives d'histoire doctrinale et littéraire du Moyen Âge* 44 (1977), [1978], 33–78.
3. Bolton, *Alcuin and Beowulf*, pp. 139, 177.
4. *Anicii Manlii Severini Boethii Philosophiae Consolatio*, ed. L. Bieler, Corpus Christianorum, 94 (Turnhout, 1957), III, m. 12, lines 52–58; *King Alfred's Old English Version of Boethius' De Consolatione Philosophiae*, ed. W. J. Sedgefield (Oxford, 1900), p. 103, lines 14–16. Otten, *König Alfreds Boethius*, p. 133.
5. *De Consolatione Philosophiae*, III, pr. 12, lines 64–65; *King Alfred's Old English Version*, p. 99, lines 4–20. Otten, *König Alfreds Boethius*, pp. 129–32.
6. *De Consolatione Philosophiae*, IV, m. 7; *King Alfred's Old English Version*, p. 139, lines 5–18. Otten, *König Alfreds Boethius*, p. 38.
7. *King Alfred's Old English Version*, p. 116, lines 2–34.

as "Where now are the bones of the famous and wise goldsmith Weland?"[8]

When in the Anglo-Saxon period could a Christian author exploit pagan Germanic legend for its intellectual and moral values? Seventh- and eighth-century sources furnish evidence that English monks were overfond of harpists, secular tales, eating and drinking; but such worldly tastes provoked the scorn and hostility of their superiors: "What has Ingeld to do with Christ? The House is narrow, it cannot hold both. The King of Heaven wishes to have no fellowship with so-called kings, who are pagan and lost."[9] But by the late ninth century, even an archbishop—Fulk of Rheims, who recruited Remigius of Auxerre, corresponded with King Alfred and sent Grimbald to him—could in one and the same sentence refer to a letter of Gregory the Great on kingship and to "Teutonic books regarding a certain King Hermenric."[1] A century and a half later, puritanical youth can be seen shaking its fist at reckless middle age in a letter that one cleric of Bamberg Cathedral wrote to another complaining of their bishop, Gunther, who spent all his time reading of Attila and Theodoric when not composing epics himself.[2]

The *Beowulf* poet insists on the virtue and paganism of his characters, and is unusually explicit about their heathen rites, describing them lovingly at length.[3] A slender tradition of extolling the good customs of Germanic pagans can be traced in Roman authors, but this tradition does not enjoy a continuous run through the medieval period. The first known use of Tacitus' *Germania* after Cassiodorus occurs in the mid-ninth-century *Translatio Sancti Alexandri* by the monk Rudolf of Fulda.[4] This work, commissioned by the aristocratic abbot of the monastery of Wildeshausen in Saxony, opens with a description of the moral practices and brave deeds of the early pagan ancestors of the Saxons. Bede, monk of Wearmouth-Jarrow and historian of the English church and people (c. 731), is reticent about

8. *De Consolatione Philosophiae*, II, m. 7; *King Alfred's Old English Version*, p. 46, lines 16–17.

9. See n. 2. The Council of Clovesho (746/7) specified that priests were not to chatter in church like secular poets (*Councils and Ecclesiastical Documents Relating to Great Britian and Ireland*, ed. A. W. Haddan and W. Stubbs [Oxford, 1869–78], 3:366); for additional examples, including one from the early eleventh century, see Wormald, "Bede, *Beowulf*, and the Conversion of the Anglo-Saxon Aristocracy," pp. 51–52.

1. The reference is to Eormenric of heroic legend and *Beowulf* (1201). Flodoard, *Historia Remensis Ecclesiae*, IV.5, ed. J. Heller and G. Waitz, Monumenta Germaniae Historica, Scriptores Rerum Germanicarum (in folio), 13 (Hanover, 1881), pp. 564, 574.

2. Carl Erdmann, *Studien zur Briefliteratur Deutschlands im elften Jahrhundert*, Schriften des Reichsinstituts für ältere deutsche Geschichtskunde (=Monumenta Germaniae Historica), 1 (Leipzig, 1938), p. 102; K. Leyser, "The German Aristocracy from the Ninth to the Early Twelfth Centuries: A Social and Cultural Survey," *Past and Present* 41 (1968), 25–53.

3. On the poet's featuring of pagan elements, see Benson, "Pagan Coloring," pp. 193–213.

4. Rudolf of Fulda, *Translatio Sancti Alexandri*, ed. B. Krusch, Nachrichten von der Gesellschaft der Wissenschaften zu Göttingen, Phil.-Hist. Klasse, 1933, pp. 405–36.

the doings of the Anglo-Saxons before their conversion and shows no inclination to celebrate heathens or their habits.[5] Widukind, monk of Corvey and historian of the Continental Saxons (c. 967), does not hesitate to do so. He borrows Rudolf of Fulda's account of pagan institutions and shapes the heathen past of his nation into a carefully contoured whole. He develops a single thread of historical tradition into a complex narrative, incorporating heroic dialogue, vivid details, and dramatic scenes, in much the same way that the *Beowulf* poet seems to have worked.[6] Widukind saw his efforts in recording the deeds of the Saxon leaders (*principum nostrorum res gestae litteris . . . commendare*) as equal in value to the service he earlier performed with his two lives of saints. He wrote his history, he said, partly by virtue of his monastic calling, partly as a member of *gens Saxonum*.[7] One historical sense seems to beget another: Widukind, like the *Beowulf* poet, learned much from classical historians, including the art of depicting people whose behavior made sense within the framework of their age and culture.

The *Beowulf* poet's attribution of monotheism to his good heathens is sometimes taken as revealing his ignorance of Germanic paganism, sometimes as a sign of his inability to see the past as anything other than the present. Like Widukind, he mentions pagan error, briefly and in passing (175–88), before depicting noble pagan monotheists for some three thousand lines. In the Alfredian *Orosius*, as in the fifth-century original, God is shown to have always guided the world, even in pagan times. But the paraphraser adds a few touches of his own: the pagan Leonidas places his trust in God; even Hannibal is heard to lament that God would not allow him domination over Rome.[8] The *Beowulf* poet, too, makes his heroes refer again and again to the power and providence of a single God, and he takes Beowulf's victory as a sign that "God has always ruled mankind, as he still does" (700–02, 1057–58). The Danes' hymn in Heorot to a single Almighty (90–98) expresses a Boethian wonder at seeing an invisible God through his creation. Wiglaf's contention that the fallen Beowulf shall for a long time "abide in the Lord's keeping" (3109) suggests a Boethian philosophy of salvation, of individuals ascending by reason alone to a knowledge of one God. It was

5. See Wormald, "Bede, *Beowulf*, and the Conversion of the Anglo-Saxon Aristocracy," pp. 58–63.
6. Larry D. Benson, "The Originality of *Beowulf*" in *The Interpretation of Narrative: Theory and Practice*, Harvard English Studies, 1 (Cambridge, Mass., 1970), pp. 1–43.
7. *Widukindi Monachi Corbeiensis Rerum Gestarum Saxonicarum Libri Tres*, ed. H.-E. Lohmann and P. Hirsch, 5th ed., Monumenta Germaniae Historica, Scriptores Rerum Germanicarum in usum scholarum (Hanover, 1935), Bk. I, chs. 1–15. On Widukind, see especially Helmut Beumann, *Widukind von Korvei* (Weimar, 1950), and "Historiographische Konzeption und politische Ziele Widukinds von Korvei," *Settimane di studio del Centro Italiano di Studi sull'alto medioevo* 17 (Spoleto, 1970), 857–94.
8. *The Old English Orosius*, 49.1–3; 103.27–29.

probably Remigius of Auxerre who around 900 compiled a short treatise on the gods of classical antiquity, announcing—in the final paragraph of his prologue—that a single divine being lay behind the multiplicity of Greek and Roman names for the gods.[9] Renewed contact with the texts of late antiquity, especially Macrobius, Martianus Capella, and Boethius, ended by making some men at least think in a less narrowly religious way.[1] The *Beowulf* poet allows glimpses of a *paradiso terrestre* in the distant past—brief, transitory but glowing moments whose thrust is to remind his hearers of all the unfulfilled potential of their pre-Christian heritage.

What emerges from a sufficiently intense concern for history in any literary work is a series of projections inevitably focused by the particular anxieties of the writer. Alfred's *Boethius* reveals that king's fascination with the psychology of the tyrant, his concern for the proper uses of power and wealth, and his insistence, against Boethius, that temporal possessions can be put to good ends.[2] The *Beowulf* poet seems especially concerned to distinguish between justifiable and unjustifiable aggression, to place the warlike activities of his pagan hero in an ethical context. Beowulf resorts to arms out of concern for the defenseless and for the common good, not exclusively out of lust for conquest, ambition, or vengefulness. He is heroic and pious, a pagan prince of peace.[3] Christianity in the early barbarian West may have thought it was being assimilated by a warrior aristocracy, but it ended up—even before the Crusades—accommodating itself to the heroic values of the nobility. The blending of the two cultures would have begun at the time of conversion, but it was an extended process. At one stage, revelry in the hall, vowing oaths of fidelity to a lord; ambushes and plundering and slaughter, all the duties and responsibilities of heroic society were seen as demonic and damnable, as in the eighth-century *Life of Guthlac* by Felix of Crowland.[4] In the Old English *Guthlac A*, the poet even sends in devils to remind the royal saint and hermit of his secular

9. *Scriptores Rerum Mythicarum Latini Tres*, ed. G. H. Bode (Cellis, 1834), 1:74. See Ursula and Peter Dronke, "The Prologue of the Prose *Edda*," p. 166.
1. John Scotus Eriugena, whose teaching is reflected in the school of Auxerre, wrote commentaries on all three authors. On his life, see E. Jeauneau, *Jean Scot, Homélie sur le Prologue de Jean*, Sources Chrétiennes, 151 (Paris, 1969), pp. 9–50, and *Jean Scot, Commentaire sur l'Evangile de Jean*, Sources Chrétiennes, 180 (Paris, 1972), pp. 11–21.
2. Otten, *König Alfreds Boethius*, pp. 99–118.
3. See especially Levin L. Schücking, "Das Königsideal im Beowulf" in *Modern Humanities Research Association Bulletin* 3 (1929), 143–54; rpt. *Englische Studien* 67 (1932), 1–14. English trans. as "The Ideal of Kingship in *Beowulf*" in *An Anthology of Beowulf Criticism*, ed. Nicholson, pp. 35–49. Robert E. Kaske, "*Sapientia et Fortitudo* as the Controlling Theme of *Beowulf*," *Studies in Philology* 55 (1958), 423–56; rpt. in *An Anthology of Beowulf Criticism*, pp. 269–310.
4. *Felix's Life of Saint Guthlac*, ed. and trans. Bertram Colgrave (Cambridge, Eng., 1956), pp. 81–83. See E. G. Stanley, "Hæthenra Hyht in *Beowulf*" in *Studies in Old English Literature in Honor of Arthur G. Brodeur*, ed. Stanley B. Greenfield (Eugene, Ore., 1963), pp. 136–51, and Colin Chase, "Saints' Lives, Royal Lives, and the Date of *Beowulf*" in *The Dating of Beowulf*, pp. 161–71.

obligations, to tempt him with the hall-delights long abandoned after a warlike youth (191–99). The heroic life is the opposite of the life that leads to salvation.

The synthesis of religious and heroic idealism present in *Beowulf* was probably not available to monastic authors at an early date. In the 930s, Odo of Cluny wrote his *Life of St. Gerald of Aurillac* in order to demonstrate for his own aristocratic circle how a layman and noble lord, a man out in the world, could lead a holy existence.[5] Odo gives moral and religious dimensions to Gerald's lifelong martial career. The warrior soothes the suspicious, squelches the malicious, and puts down the violent who refuse to come to terms; he does this not for personal gain but in order to achieve peace for his society. So Beowulf restrains, one after the other, coastguard, Unferth, and Grendel, making friends of two potential foes and ridding Denmark of monsters who pay no wergild. Ottonian Saxony as portrayed by Widukind is—in the heroic cast of its values and the ferocity of its feuds—very close to the world of *Beowulf.*[6] Tenth-century monastic narratives seem, like *Beowulf*, able to find a place for heroic values—even fighting and the bonds of kinship—within a Christian framework. In Hrotsvitha's *Gongolfus* the ideals of a warrior's life are fused with the Christian goal of *caritas*, while Ruotger's *Life of Bruno*, archbishop of Cologne and brother of Otto the Great, reports with some understatement that "priestly religion and royal determination united their strength" in him.[7] Like these works, the Old English poems that we can date to the tenth century set up no unresolvable contradictions between piety and the heroic life. *The Battle of Maldon*, composed after 991 and regarded as the finest utterance of the Anglo-Saxon heroic age (and most "Germanic" since Tacitus), contains a prayer by a warlord soon to be venerated by the monks of Ely.[8] *The Battle of Brunanburh*, from around 937, is red with blood, God's rising and setting sun, and a historical perspective reminiscent of manifest destiny. *Judith*, probably from the same century, focuses on a prayerful heroine who chops off heads with only slightly less savoir-faire than Beowulf. Between *Bede's Death Song* and *Maldon* something happened to Old English poetry, whether we call this

5. Odo, *Vita S. Geradli Aureliacensis Comitis*, Patrologiae Cursus Completus, Series Latina 133:639–703. See Carl Erdmann (*Die Entstehung des Kreuzzugsgedankens* [Stuttgart, 1935]), trans. M. W. Baldwin and W. Goffart, *The Origin of the Idea of Crusade* (Princeton, 1977), pp. 87–89. Odo was among Remigius' students at Paris (*Vita Odonis Abbatis Cluniacensis*, ch. 19, in J. Mabillon and L. d'Achery, *Acta Sanctorum Ordinis S. Benedicti* [Paris, 1668–1701], VII.124).
6. Leyser, passim.
7. *Hrotsvithae Opera*, ed. P. Winterfeld, Monumenta Germaniae Historica, Scriptores Rerum Germanicarum in usum scholarum (Berlin, 1902), pp. 35–51; *Ruotgeri Vita Brunonis Archiepiscopi Coloniensis*, ed. Irene Schmale-Ott, Monumenta Germaniae Historica, Scriptores Rerum Germanicarum, n. s. 10 (Weimar, 1951), p. 19.
8. See Rosemary Woolf, "The Ideal of Men Dying with their Lord in the *Germania* and in *The Battle of Maldon*," *Anglo-Saxon England* 5 (1976), 63–81.

something rebarbarization or adapting Christian models for a new and only partly literate secular aristocracy. New syntheses were becoming possible. Unlike Anglian stone crosses of the eighth century, English religious sculpture after the Danish invasions was able to draw, like *Beowulf*, on pagan myth and heroic legend.[9]

In still another area, the vision of the *Beowulf* poet seems to derive from contemporary concerns, from a need to establish in the present an ideological basis for national unity. I suggested in an earlier paper that the *Beowulf* poet's incentive for composing an epic about sixth-century Scyldings may have had something to do with the fact that, by the 890s at least, Heremod, Scyld, Healfdene, and the rest, were taken to be the common ancestors both of the Anglo-Saxon royal family and of the ninth-century Danish immigrants, the *Scaldingi*.[1] The *Beowulf* poet admires kings who, like Hrothgar, have regional overlordship of surrounding tribes and who, like Beowulf, are powerful enough to keep neighbors in check. A key political catchword—"þeodcyning" ("great" or "national king")—is prominently displayed by the poet in his opening sentence. He depicts the Danish nation's former glory in a time when powerful kings had been able to unite the various peoples of the land, something that did not occur with any permanence in Denmark or England until the tenth century.[2] The *Beowulf* poet does his best to attach his pagan champion to as many peoples as possible—Danes, Geats, Swedes, Wulfings, and Wægmundings—as if to make him the more authentically representative of the culture and traditions of central Scandinavia: an archetypal Northman. Epics have their propagandist appeal. There is a relationship, however indirect, between Virgil's account of the majesty of Rome's legendary past, the glory of her ancient traditions, and the Augustan program to bring back a "pristine" patriotism and code of morals. Both the *Aeneid* and *Beowulf* are in some sense historical novels, mythically presented, philosophically committed, and focused on the adventures of a new hero.[3] Both poets project

9. E.g., Wayland in Leeds Parish Church, Thor in Gosforth Church, and Sigemund at Winchester Old Minster. See Richard N. Bailey, *Viking Age Sculpture in Northern England* (London, 1980).

1. "Skaldic Verse and the Date of *Beowulf*" in *The Dating of Beowulf*, pp. 123–39 and Alexander Murray, "*Beowulf*, the Danish Invasions, and Royal Genealogy," pp. 101–11 in the same volume.

2. See discussion in Horst Zettel, *Das Bild der Normannen und der Normanneneinfälle in westfränkischen, ostfränkischen und angelsächsischen Quellen des 8. bis 11. Jahrhunderts* (Munich, 1977), pp. 69–84. On West Saxon hegemonial tendencies during the first half of the tenth century, see E. E. Stengel, "Imperator und Imperium bei den Angelsachsen," *Deutsches Archiv für Erforschung des Mittelalters* 16 (1960), 15–72; J. L. Nelson, "Inauguration Rituals" in *Early Medieval Kingship*, ed. P. H. Sawyer and I. N. Wood (Leeds, 1977), pp. 68–70.

3. See Robert W. Hanning, *The Vision of History in Early Britain* (New York, 1966), p. 19. Tom Burns Haber makes one of several attempts to list verbal echoes and narrative parallels between the two poems (*A Comparative Study of the 'Beowulf' and the 'Aeneid'* [Princeton, 1931]). Recent publications demonstrating Virgilian influence on the narrative structure and perspective of *Beowulf* include Theodore M. Andersson, *Early Epic*

onto the distant past features of the society of their own day, consciously and deliberately, in order to provide a sense of continuity. Virgil's Rome is grounded in an earlier Rome; the *Beowulf* poet anchors the West Saxon *imperium* in a brilliant North Germanic antiquity. By the twelfth century, the Normans were very French; yet the more French they became, the more they stressed their Danish ancestry and the heroic deeds of their founding dynasty.[4] By the first quarter of the tenth century, the Danes in England were working hard to be more Christian and English than the English: at mid-century both archbishops of England, Oda and Oskytel, were of Danish extraction.[5] An Old English poem about northern heathens and northern heroes, opening with the mythical figure of Scyld from whom the ruling houses of both Denmark and England were descended, fits nicely with the efforts of Alfred and his successors to promote an Anglo-Danish brotherhood, to see Dane and Anglo-Saxon as equal partners in a united kingdom.

The sadness, the poignancy, the *lacrimae rerum* we associate with *Beowulf* come from the epic poet's sense of duration, of how "time condemns itself and all human endeavor and hopes."[6] Yet though Heorot is snuffed out by flames and noble pagans and their works perish, the poet does not scorn the heroic fellowship whose passing he has had to tell. There is still something left worth ambition: "The task to be accomplished is not the conservation of the past, but the redemption of the hopes of the past."[7] The last word in the poem is uttered by sixth-century Geats who commend Beowulf as "lofgeornost" ("most intent on glory"). Lady Philosophy assured Boethius (II, pr. 7) that the praise won even by noble souls is of slight value: only a small part of a tiny earth is inhabited, and by nations differing in language, custom, and philosophy; even written eulogies fail because time veils them and their authors in obscurity. King Alfred did not entirely accept her last point. He argued that the fame of a great man can also fade through a kind of *trahison des clercs*—"þurh þa heardsælþa þara writera ðæt hi for heora slæwðe ond for gimeleste

---

Scenery: Homer, Virgil, and the Medieval Legacy (Ithaca, N. Y., 1976), pp. 145–59, and Alistair Campbell, "The Use in *Beowulf* of Earlier Heroic Verse" in *England before the Conquest: Studies in Primary Sources Presented to Dorothy Whitelock*, ed. Peter Clemoes and Kathleen Hughes (Cambridge, Eng., 1971), pp. 283–92.

4. R. H. C. Davis, *The Normans and their Myth* (London, 1976), pp. 27, 54.
5. Oda, bishop of Ramsbury under Athelstan and archbishop of Canterbury from 940–958, was the son of a Dane who came to England with the first settlers. Oskytel, kinsman of Oda, was the archbishop of York. Oda's nephew was St. Oswald, prominent founder and renovator of monasteries. See J. Armitage Robinson, *St. Oswald and the Church of Worcester*, British Academy Supplemental Papers, 5 (London, 1919), pp. 38–51. The Danes appear to have been widely accepted in English society from at least 927 onwards; see Jacobs, p. 40, and R. I. Page, "The Audience of *Beowulf* and the Vikings" in *The Dating of Beowulf*, pp. 113–22.
6. Bloomfield, "Chaucer's Sense of History" in *Essays and Explorations*, p. 25.
7. Max Horkeimer and Theodor Adorno, *Dialectic of Enlightenment*, tr. John Cumming (New York, 1972), p. xv.

ond eac for recceleste forleton unwriten þara monna ðeawas ond hiora dæda, þe on hiora dagum formæroste ond weorðgeornuste wæron"[8] ("through the bad conduct of those writers who—in their sloth and in carelessness and also in negligence—leave unwritten the virtues and deeds of those men who in their day were most renowned and most intent on honor"). The purpose of *Beowulf*, as Morton Bloomfield has often reminded us, is heroic celebration, to present the deeds of a great man in order "to give his audience new strength and a model."[9] Those of us who were privileged to be Professor Bloomfield's students at Harvard know what such a model can be worth.

FRED C. ROBINSON

The Tomb of Beowulf†

The Old English poem to which we have assigned the name *Beowulf* was composed, apparently, by a Christian poet—some say a monk or a priest—who was concerned to extol the virtues of ancient Germanic heroes while acknowledging regretfully (for example, in lines 175–88) that they were deprived of the Christian revelation enjoyed in his own era. This poignant intermingling of veneration and regret, of pride in the Anglo-Saxons' Germanic ancestors shadowed by sadness over the perilous state of their souls, permeates, I believe, the poem's tone and lends it intellectual sophistication and complexity which exceed mere admiration of a heroic past.[1] Young Beowulf's achievements in the first part of the poem—his deliverance of the Danes from the incursions of the Grendelkin, his farsighted diplomacy in committing his nation to an alliance with the Danish royal family, and his discerning report to his own king Hygelac on the state of the nation which he has just visited—are all circumscribed by discreet reminders of the heathen status of the heroic participants; and the displays of wisdom, such as the speeches of Hrothgar, leave us simultaneously impressed by their loftiness of thought and saddened by their always falling short of ultimate truth, which, to a medieval English audience, would have been Christian truth. In the last half of the poem we see the hero devoting his strength, courage, and wisdom to the protection of his nation until, at the end of his

8. *King Alfred's Old English Version of Boethius*, p. 44, lines 1–4. [The abbreviation "⁊" has been expanded to "ond"—*Editor.*]
9. *Speculum* 41 (1966), 369.
† From *"The Tomb of Beowulf" and Other Essays on Old English* by Fred C. Robinson (Oxford: Blackwell Publishers, 1993) 3–19. Reprinted by permission of the publisher.
1. I have discussed this feature of the poem *in extenso* in *Beowulf and the Appositive Style* (Knoxville, TN, 1985).

fifty-year reign as king, he protects them against the attacks of the dragon, which he slays at the cost of his own life. At his death he leaves to his people as a legacy a vast hoard of treasure, which he seems to think might ensure their survival in the militant and hostile world surrounding them:

> Nū ic on māðma hord mīne bebohte
> frōde feorhlege, fremmað gēna
> lēoda þearfe; ne mæg ic hēr leng wesan.[2] (2799–801)

"Now that I have exchanged my old life for this hoard of treasures, they will now meet the needs of the people; I can be here no longer."[3] But, in a gesture which seems to express that sense of despair which darkens all the triumphs and hazards in the poem, the Geatas bury the treasure with the ashes of their king—a pagan ritual following upon the pagan rite of cremation—and the last words of the poem are the warriors' solemn encomia as they pace their horses around his splendid tomb.

The tomb of Beowulf and the rites enacted there make up a scene of strange and somber majesty which readers have often found reverberant with dark implications beyond the merely scenic. The hero's obsequies have also been regarded as problematic by scholars of the poem, who are troubled by the fact that Beowulf's funeral rites are not merely grander than the funerals of other characters described in the poem, but peculiarly complex in a way that makes them unique. The hero's obsequies begin with these verses:

> Him ðā gegiredan Gēata lēode
> ād on eorðan unwāclīcne,
> helm[um] behongen, hildebordum,
> beorhtum byrnum, swā hē bēna wæs;
> ālegdon ðā tōmiddes mǣrne þēoden
> hæleð hīofende, hlāford lēofne. (3137–42)

"The people of the Geatas erected then on the ground a splendid pyre hung about with helmets, with battle-shields, and with shining mail-coats, as he had asked; then the lamenting warriors laid in the midst the renowned king, their beloved lord." The poet then tells us that the roaring flames and dark smoke rise into the sky, intertwined with the lamentations of the mourners. "With grief-stricken hearts they bemoaned their sorrow, the death of their king" (3148–49), he

2. *Beowulf and the Fight at Finnsburg*, ed. Fr. Klaeber, 3rd edn with 1st and 2nd supplements (Boston, 1950). All quotations from the poem are from this edition. Quotations from other Old English poems will be from *The Anglo-Saxon Poetic Records*, ed. G. P. Krapp and E. V. K. Dobbie (New York: Columbia UP, 1931–1953).

3. Charles Donahue, "Potlatch and charity: notes on the heroic in *Beowulf*," in *Anglo-Saxon Poetry: essays in appreciation: for John C. McGalliard*, ed. Lewis E. Nicholson and Dolores Warwick Frese (Notre Dame, 1975), p. 32, reminds us that the plural *fremmað* cannot be an imperative singular addressed to Wiglaf, as some have thought.

says, and following this a mysterious old woman steps forward and prophesies the doom of the nation now that their king and protector has fallen. The scene closes with the evocative detail *Heofon rēce swealg* ("Heaven swallowed up the smoke.")[4]

This impressive tableau with grieving comrades, a lamenting woman, and flames consuming the corpse and battle-gear is much the same as the ritual cremation which followed the fight at Finnsburg earlier in the poem. The peculiarity of Beowulf's last rites is that ten days after the very formal closure of the scene we have just examined, Beowulf's subjects initiate a whole new series of ceremonies. Having erected a magnificent *beorh* or tumulus, which they fill with sumptuous treasure together with their king's ashes, they surround it with a splendid wall devised by *foresnotere men* "exceedingly wise people," and then twelve mounted, chanting warriors circle the wall:

Þā ymbe hlǣw riodan   hildedēore,
æþelinga bearn,   ealra twelf*e*,
woldon (care) cwīðan,   [ond] kyning mǣnan,
wordgyd wrecan,   ond ymb w(er) sprecan;
eahtodan eorlscipe   ond his ellenweorc
duguðum dēmdon,—   swā hit gedē(fe) bið,
þæt mon his winedryhten   wordum herge,
ferhðum frēoge,   þonne hē forð scile
of līchaman   (lǣded) weorðan.
Swā begnornodon   Gēata lēode
hlāfordes (hry)re,   heorðgenēatas;
cwǣdon þæt hē wǣre   wyruldcyning[a]
manna mildust   ond mon(ðw)ǣrust,
lēodum līðost   ond lofgeornost.   (3169–82)

"Then around the barrow rode twelve sons of noblemen, valiant in battle. They wanted to declare their sorrow and speak of their king, to utter a chant and speak of the man. They praised his nobility and his deeds of valor, proclaimed them majestically, as it is fitting that one should do—to extol with words and cherish in the heart one's lord and friend when he must be led forth from his garment of flesh. Thus the people of the Geatas, the companions of his hearth, bewailed the fall of their lord. They said that he was of all the kings

4. The prophesying woman and the rising smoke are among the details that scholars have found suggestive of some special significance. Several people have noted that the smoke from the cremation fire passing directly up to the heavens is a Germanic pagan motif documented in the *Ynglinga saga*; see for example Paul Beekman Taylor, "*Heofon riece swealg*: a sign of Beowulf's state of grace," *Philological Quarterly*, 42 (1963), 257–9. On the funeral in general see both text and bibliographical footnotes in Ute Schwab, *Servire il Signore Morto: Funzione e trasformazione di riti funebri germanici nell'epica medievale inglese e tedesca,* Università Catania: Collana di studi di filologia moderna 5 (Catania, 1990), pp. 22–5, 64–5.

of the world the kindest and most mildhearted of men, the most gracious to his people, and the most eager for praise." The sentiment in this passage is so noble, the style so consciously sublime, that an early translator of *Beowulf* and the only prominent poet ever to edit the poem—N. S. V. Grundtvig—believed that the closing scene is central to the meaning of *Beowulf* and therefore he named the poem *Beowulfes Beorh* "the tomb of Beowulf" (cf. line 2807). Grundtvig even composed a poem of his own in Old English and in Danish in which he justifies this title, suggesting that the *beorh* of Beowulf is analogous to the poem itself, both being monuments which preserve the hero's name and fame in succeeding ages. * * *[5]

But however much we might agree with Grundtvig that the memorable closing of *Beowulf* distills and reifies the sense of the whole narrative, we cannot deny that it is also problematic. "It is the peculiarity of the *Beowulf* account," says Klaeber, "that two distinct and, as it were, parallel funeral ceremonies are related in detail, . . . and that the greater emphasis is placed on the closing stage, which is made the occasion of rehearsing solemn and inspiring songs."[6] The archeologist Knut Stjerna found the two ceremonies such an extraordinary departure from actual practice in pagan days that he concluded the poet must have had two separate sources treating Beowulf's funeral, one in which he was cremated and one in which he was buried with treasure, and that he somewhat ineptly conflated them in his poem; but R. W. Chambers disagrees, saying that the double ceremony simply shows the Christian poet's ignorance of pagan practice.[7] He would agree no doubt with a recent scholar's judgment that "there must be some confusion of tradition."[8] No one has ever doubted, so far as I am aware, that the ceremony around the walled monument is simply a second funeral for Beowulf, a curious redundancy which, however impressive, means nothing more than that the poet was confused about pagan burial customs.[9]

My purpose in this essay is to suggest that the second rite described at the end of *Beowulf* may have had a significance beyond confused redundancy. I shall supply evidence to suggest that at least some in the poet's audience would have seen in the final ceremony of the poem suggestions of an apotheosis. King Beowulf's bereaved

5. See F. C. Robinson, "The Afterlife of Old English: A Brief History of Composition in Old English after the Close of the Anglo-Saxon Period," in *The Tomb of Beowulf*, pp. 275–303 at 299–303 [*Editor*].
6. Klaeber, *Beowulf and the Fight at Finnsburg*, p. 229.
7. Chambers, *Beowulf: an introduction to the study of the poem*, 3rd edn with a supplement by C. L. Wrenn (Cambridge, 1959), p. 124.
8. Paula Loikala, "Funeral rites in *Beowulf*," *Quaderni di Filologia Germanica della Facoltà di Lettere e Filosofia dell'Università di Bologna*, 2 (1982), 287.
9. That the Geatas should erect a monument on the cliff as Beowulf wished (2802–8) is of course to be expected. But the consignment of a vast treasure to the *beorh* and (especially) the ceremony of chants and marching seem to be a puzzling repetition and expansion of what went on at the cremation ten days before.

subjects, I will suggest, are so overawed by their fallen leader's accomplishments and so unwilling to accept the finality of his death that they turn desperately to the pagan resources available to them to accord him ultimate veneration and, perhaps, recruit his protective force beyond the grave. Such an act would be a closing parallel with the act of the Danes at the beginning of the poem in lines 175–88, where in a time of crisis they turn to their heathen gods with propitiatory sacrifices.

My procedure will be to survey the cultural background of the Anglo-Saxons to determine how familiar they would have been with the concept of deifying a deceased hero and to see whether manifestations of apotheosis in their culture bear any resemblance to the events described at the end of *Beowulf*. And finally I shall consider what the attitude of at least a portion of a Christian Anglo-Saxon audience might have been toward a poem that implies that their ancestors may have ascribed divine status to a slain hero.[1]

Herotheism is attested fairly widely in the early stages of the western European culture of which Anglo-Saxon England forms a part. We might begin with a glance at the classical world.[2] Hector, whose funeral ceremony in the *Iliad* has so often been compared with that of Beowulf, was worshipped in the Troad and also at Tanagra, east of Thebes, and later poetry speaks of him as a god. Theseus was worshipped in Athens, and there were cults of Oedipus, while the Argive hero Adrastus of Sicyon was venerated at a *heroön* (a shrine to a hero, which is usually located at or identical with his tomb) in the marketplace of that city, with tragic choruses recounting his sad

1. The verb "implies" is carefully chosen here. I am also careful to say that the implication would have been understood by "at least a portion of" the poet's audience. I am mindful of Bruce Mitchell's well-directed impatience with some scholars' "assumption that the audience of *Beowulf* was homogeneous; that all its members reacted in the same way, had all heard—or not heard—the story before hearing the poem, had all heard—or not heard—the poem before; were all equally intelligent and equally knowledgeable about theology or the Church Fathers or scriptural exegesis or whatever; were all equally sensitive and capable—or insensitive and incapable—of making such connexions." (See "1987: postscript on *Beowulf*," in *On Old English* (Oxford, 1988), pp. 41–2.) On the other hand, I would not think that the point of this essay were worth making if I did not believe that the implication was likely to be a conscious element in the poet's design, available to that part of his audience which was knowledgeable and attentive enough to perceive it. As I have suggested elsewhere (see footnote 1, p. 181, above), a medieval Christian who addresses a Christian audience about their pagan ancestors will necessarily work more by implication than by overt declaration.
2. The ensuing examples (and many others) are cited in *Paulys Realencyclopädie der classischen Altertumswissenschaft*, neue Bearbeitung begonnen von Georg Wissowa, vol. 14 (Stuttgart, 1912), pp. 2814–15, s.v. *Heros*, and vol. 15, pp. 1119–27, s.v. *Heros . . . Der Kultus*; also *The Oxford Classical Dictionary*, ed. N. G. L. Hammond and H. H. Scullard, 2nd edn (Oxford, 1970), p. 491, s.v. *Hector*, and p. 506, s.v. *Hero-cult*. In Greek, it should be mentioned, a hero was less powerful than the primary gods but had divine status, and cult was paid to him, usually at his tomb or *heroön*. Conceived of as mortals who had died and were apotheosized, heroes in this sense were not the same as the heroes of Homer—Ajax, Odysseus, etc.—although some (e.g. Hector) were in both groups. In the case of Hercules the distinction between god and hero was uncertain, as it was in some others.

fate being sung in his honor. Turning to the Romans, an Anglo-Saxon who read Virgil would have seen that in book VI of the *Aeneid* Palinurus is assured that he will be deified and worshipped at his tomb, and Dardanus in book VII is similarly deified and worshipped. In book XII Juno says that Aeneas has his niche as a god in heaven. Pliny discusses the *heroön*, using the Latinized name *heroum*. These instances are all from the realm of classical legend or literature, but, as is well known, the deification of mortals was also a part of ancient history. Alexander the Great, after he was hailed as the son of Amon-Zeus by the oracle of Amon in 332 BC, became increasingly convinced that he was a god and as such began demanding veneration from his subjects. The Spartans' cynical response to this demand ("If Alexander wants to be a god, let him be a god") finds an echo in the Old English *Orosius*, where Alexander's claims to divinity are similarly scorned. But the example of Alexander was not lost on the Roman emperors, who came to make similar pretensions. Later we shall return to these historical examples as they impinged on the Anglo-Saxon consciousness.

In the Germanic world texts both early and late attest to deification of heroes.[3] Jordanes tells us that during the reign of Domitian (one of the self-deified Roman emperors) the Goths so venerated the generals who had led them to victory that they elevated them to the status of demigods. The Latin word Jordanes uses is *semideos*, which he translates for his Gothic audience, "id est *ansis*."[4] *Ansis* is the Gothic word for "gods," cognate with Old Icelandic *Æsir* (and Old English *ōs*, preserved in personal names and the rune-name). The Gothic royal family known as the Amali always claimed to be the descendants of the *ansis*. More deifications of kings occur in Scandinavia. The eleventh-century historian Adam of Bremen reports that the Swedes made gods out of men who had accomplished extraordinary deeds, and he cites the example of a King Eric, who, according to the *Vita Anskarii* of Rimbert, was deified by his people after his death and worshipped by them with prayers and sacrifices at his *heroön*.[5] Another king who was deified and served with sacrifices after his death was King Olaf, brother of Halfdan, who according to the Icelandic *Flateyarbók* is laid in a mound with a certain

3. Among the works of reference I have drawn on are Richard M. Meyer, *Altgermanische Religionsgeschichte* (Leipzig, 1910), esp. pp. 90–2, Wolfgang Golther, *Handbuch der germanischen Mythologie* (Leipzig, 1895), esp. pp. 92–5, and Hilda Roderick Ellis, *The Road to Hel: a study of the conception of the dead in Old Norse literature* (Cambridge, 1943), esp. pp. 99–111.

4. Jordanes, *Getica*, XIII, 78: "iam proceres suos, quorum quasi fortuna vincebant, non puros homines, sed semideos, id est ansis, vocaverunt." Herwig Wolfram, *History of the Goths*, tr. Thomas Dunlap (Berkeley, CA, 1987), p. 324, points out that Theodoric continued to encourage the belief in the divinity of the Amali rulers. See also Walter Goffart's comments on barbarian *memoria* in *Barbarians and Romans: techniques of accommodation* (Princeton, 1980), esp. pp. 21–4.

5. Golther, *Handbuch*, pp. 93–4, supplies full Latin text with translation.

amount of silver coin and venerated there as *geirstaðaálfr* by his subjects.[6] Icelandic sagas tell us that King Guðmundr was proclaimed a god and worshipped after his death, as was another Icelander named Barðr.[7] In the *Skáldskaparmál* Snorri Sturlusson says, "That king who is called Helgi, after whom Halogaland is named, was the father of Þorgerðr Hölgabrúðr; they were both worshipped with sacrifice, and a mound was reared for Helgi, one layer being of gold and silver—that was the sacrificial wealth—and the other of earth and stones."[8]

"Die Apotheose bleibt in der Regel auf Könige beschränkt," observes Richard Meyer, but he notes that others too are deified from time to time.[9] The *Landnámabók* tells of a Norwegian chieftain named Grimr who was so popular among his people that after his death he was worshipped with sacrifices.[1] We have already seen that Þorgerðr Hölgabrúðr was worshipped as a goddess along with her father, King Helgi. Another woman who was regarded by the common people as a kind of goddess is a prophetess mentioned by Gregory of Tours in the *Historia Francorum.*[2]

The Frankish prophetess was apparently venerated during her lifetime, but worship of mortals among the Germanic peoples was normally accorded only to select persons among the dead, a practice which is documented from the early eighth century on, primarily in ecclesiastical prohibitions. In his letter to the people of Hesse and Thuringia Pope Gregory III lists sacrifices to the dead among the pagan Germanic customs which they must reject absolutely, and in his letter to the bishops in Bavaria and Alemania he tells the missionary bishops that they must make the people stop sacrificing to the dead.[3] In his publication of the decrees of the synod of 742, Karlmann, palace mayor of the Eastern Franks, says that every bishop within his own diocese must root out all the filth of the heathen, such as sacrifices to the dead.[4] The *Indiculus superstitionum et Paganiarum* (AD 743) has prohibitions "de sacrilegio ad sepulchra mortuorum" and "de sacrilegio super defunctos, id est, dadsisas"—thus supplying the native Germanic word for veneration of the dead.[5]

6. Golther, *Handbuch*, pp. 94–5, and Ellis, *The Road to Hel*, pp. 100–2, who draws attention also to the sacrifices offered after the death of Halfdan the Black at the burial mounds containing his remains.
7. Ellis, *The Road to Hel*, p. 102.
8. Quoted in Ellis, *The Road to Hel*, p. 105.
9. Meyer, *Altgermanische Religionsgeschichte*, p. 91.
1. Golther, *Handbuch*, p. 94.
2. *Gregoire de Tours: Histoire des Francs*, ed. Henri Omont and Gaston Collon, 2 vols (Paris, 1886–93), VII, 44.
3. *Die Briefe des heiligen Bonifatius und Lullus*, ed. Michael Tangl (Berlin, 1916), XXXIII, 43, and XXXIV, 44.
4. Ibid., XLIV, 56.
5. Quoted from Francis B. Gummere, *Founders of England*, with a supplementary note by Francis B. Magoun, Jr (New York, 1930), p. 349. Gummere's entire chapter on "The worship of the dead," pp. 337–65, supplies a wealth of evidence for Germanic practices.

The phrase *ad sepulchrum* is noteworthy, for it reminds us that worship of the dead was normally conducted at the tomb (or *heroön*) of the apotheosized mortal.[6]

Conforming with the widespread reports of deified kings and heroes in early Germanic times was the euhemeristic explanation of the origin of pagan gods, a theory that became increasingly popular as Christianity took root in Germanic lands. Euhemerus was a Sicilian mythographer who, in the third century BC, advanced the theory that the Greek gods had all been human kings or heroes who were deified after their deaths by the people they had ruled over or benefited. Early Christians seized eagerly on the euhemeristic rationale since it provided a simple explanation for how so many different pagan gods could have come into existence among so many different peoples. The Icelander Snorri Sturlusson provides euhemeristic origins for Odin and Frey, and the manner in which their deification took place has some remarkable similarities to Beowulf's death and funeral.[7] In the *Ynglinga Saga*, chapter 10, we are told that Odin was a king, and when he died after a long and prosperous reign, his subjects prepared a sumptuously provided pyre for him and cremated his remains. After the cremation they believed he was a god in Asgaard and prayed to him. Snorri explains that the smoke of the funeral pyre rising into the air was a sign to the people that Odin was being exalted. In chapters 12 and 13 we learn that Frey became king in later days, and after a successful reign he died and was placed in a great mound with a lavish hoard of gold, silver, and copper. His Swedish subjects proclaimed him a god and made sacrifices to him. Saxo Grammaticus's *Gesta Danorum* explains the origin of Norse gods euhemeristically too, as do the *Historia Norvegiæ*, the *Íslendingabók*, and other Scandinavian writings. Outside of Scandinavia, Gregory's *History of the Franks*, II, 29, tells how Queen Clotild the Christian explains to her husband Clovis that his pagan gods are merely mortal men who came to be worshipped by the Germanic heathens. The euhemeristic explanation was codified in the broadly influential *Etymologiae* of Isidore of Seville and in the "De diis gentium" section of Rabanus Maurus's *De universo*, where he emphasizes that powerful men and founders of cities were especially venerated by pagan communities. The pervasive use by Christians of the euhemeristic account of the origin of pagan gods must have served as a constant reminder to Germanic Christians that their ancestors had been accustomed to deifying kings and heroes.

6. Ellis, *The Road to Hel*, pp. 100–5 provides a detailed survey of the evidence for worship at the grave-mound.
7. For a skillful survey and synopsis of euhemerism in the Germanic lands see Anthony Faulkes, "Descent from the gods," *Mediaeval Scandinavia*, 11 (1978–9), 92–125.

The evidence supplied thus far for Germanic apotheosis comes from a wide range of sources both Latin and vernacular, but we have not yet investigated the most important Germanic culture for our purposes—the Anglo-Saxon—except for our glances at certain passages in the eighth-century correspondence of Boniface. In fact, allusions to deification of heroes, to worship of the dead, and to the Germanic pantheon being mere deified rulers are prominent in Old English and Anglo-Latin writings right up to the end of the Anglo-Saxon period. In his *De falsis Deis*, Wulfstan tells how pagan men were not satisfied with the gods they had but took to worshipping "strenuous worldly men who had become mighty in worldly powers and were awesome when they were alive"—a formulation which would fit Beowulf admirably.[8] In his source-text, Ælfric's *De falsis Diis*, we are told that the pagans took for their gods powerful men and giants.[9] This view of pagan worship would no doubt have seemed to Ælfric and Wulfstan to be confirmed by Romans 1: 18–25. In his *Canons of Edgar* Wulfstan urges the priests to tell their congregations that the worship of human beings (*manweorðunga*) is expressly forbidden.[1] Clerics like Ælfric and Wulfstan become especially anxious about lapses into *manweorðung* when they discuss funerals; they evidently thought that it is when saying farewell to the deceased that an Anglo-Saxon is most likely to begin worshipping a mortal. Ælfric tells priests that if they are invited to ceremonies for the dead they must forbid heathen chants by the layfolk and must not participate in drinking and eating in the presence of the corpse.[2] A letter of Pope Zacharius to the Anglo-Saxon Boniface in the early eighth century shows what lies behind these prohibitions: the pope speaks of sacrilegious priests who lapsed into the heathen practice of eating the offerings to the dead.[3] Wulfstan admonishes that when someone dies the people must avoid any vain practices *æt þam lice*, and confessionals and penitentials both early and late forbid the burning of grain to the dead in order to heal living people who are sick.[4] The Old English translator of the *Dicts of Cato* gives biblical authority to warnings against illicit commerce with the deceased by incorporating in his text the Old Testament prohibition against seeking truth from the dead (Deuteronomy 18: 12).[5] The assumption of preternatural

8. *The Homilies of Wulfstan*, ed. Dorothy Bethurum (Oxford, 1957), p. 222.
9. *Homilies of Ælfric: a supplementary collection*, ed. John C. Pope, Early English Text Society o.s. 260 (London, 1968), pp. 681–2.
1. *Wulfstan's Canons of Edgar*, ed. Roger Fowler, Early English Text Society o.s. 266 (London, 1972), p. 4.
2. *Die Hirtenbriefe Ælfrics*, ed. Bernhard Fehr, reprinted with a supplement to the introduction by Peter Clemoes (Darmstadt, 1966), p. 25.
3. *Die Briefe des heiligen Bonifatius*, LXIV, 80.
4. *Wulfstan's Canons*, p. 17.
5. R. S. Cox, "The Old English Dicts of Cato," *Anglia*, 90 (1972), 16.

powers of healing and omniscience on the part of the dead is like the Scandinavians' belief that their deified kings could provide abundant crops.[6]

As we shall see later on, all these practices and prohibitions which we have been examining could have a bearing on the obsequies of Beowulf. For the moment it may be sufficient to observe that while we have long recognized that the cremation of Beowulf and the burial of him with lavish grave goods were flagrant violations of the church's teachings in the poet's day, it seems possible that the chants and processions of the warriors before the hero's grave-mound would have been seen as no less flagrant an infraction of Christian observance.

Deification of their rulers by the ancients in the classical world was known to the Anglo-Saxons both through King Alfred the Great and through the anonymous translator of the Orosius.[7] In one of his original insertions into the text of his translation of Boethius's *De consolatione philosophiae*, Alfred explains to his subjects that Apollo, Jupiter, and Saturn were simply mortals who were members of the royal family and whose foolish subjects (*dysige folc*) believed them when they claimed to be gods. The Orosius translator mentions both Alexander the Great's pretensions to divinity and the deification of the Roman emperor Domitian, who demanded that his people bow to him as to a god. The Anglo-Saxons' added comments about the arrogance of the rulers and the folly of the people may be the result not only of Christian piety but also of the fact that when their own pagan ancestors practiced deification it was almost always a rite performed after the death of the mortal who was to be deified and not a status rulers would assume during their lifetimes. The later Roman practice of deifying emperors posthumously by senatorial decrees would perhaps have seemed less absurd—though not less wicked—to Alfred and his contemporaries.

Euhemeristic explanations of the pagan gods were widespread among the Christian Anglo-Saxons both early and late. Daniel, bishop of Winchester from 705 to 744, writes a letter to Boniface advising him to inform the heathen Germanic tribes on the continent that their gods were actually mortals, not gods.[8] In their treatises on false gods, which are the fullest euhemeristic analyses in a Germanic language, Ælfric and Wulfstan give detailed accounts of how each pagan god was originally a powerful or distinguished man who was declared a god after his death and venerated. Ælfric treats euhemerism further in *De initio creaturae*[9] and in his *Passion of St Sebas-*

6. Ellis, *The Road to Hel*, pp. 100–1.
7. *King Alfred's Old English Version of Boethius*, ed. Walter John Sedgefield (Oxford, 1899), pp. 115–16, and *The Old English Orosius*, ed. Janet Bately, Early English Text Society s.s. 6 (London, 1980), p. 139.
8. *Die Briefe des heiligen Bonifatius*, XV, 23.
9. *Homilies of the Anglo-Saxon Church*, ed. Benjamin Thorpe, vol. 1 (London, 1843), p. 82.

tian, Martyr.[1] In his life of King Alfred, Asser says that the king's ancestors Ingild and Ine were descendants of Geat, "whom the pagans worshipped for a long time as god."[2] (Nennius says people called Geat the son of a god.)[3] The life of St. Kentigern says, "Woden, whom the Angles worship as chief god, and from whom they derive their origin, was a mortal man, and king of the Saxons, and father of many races."[4]

Anglo-Saxon euhemerism, or, more specifically, the concept of pagan Germanic kings being deified, was woven into the fabric of the culture in yet another important way. The numerous surviving Anglo-Saxon royal genealogies, drawn up to establish the kings' ancestral right to rule, always include among the names of ancestors listed the names of pagan Germanic gods. Thus Woden (or Seaxnet) appears in the genealogies as an ancestor in the royal houses of Kent, Essex, Wessex, Deira, Bernicia, East Anglia, Mercia, and Lindsey.[5] Woden's ancestor Geata is also listed, and an annotation in one manuscript (Textus Roffensis) gives us an idea of how the Anglo-Saxons understood this curious incorporation of pagan gods in the lineage of their Christian kings: *Geata, ðene ða hæþena wurþedon for god* ("Geata, whom the heathens worshipped as a god").[6] Æthelweard too attests to the Christian Anglo-Saxons' assumptions about the Germanic god Woden's appearance in the genealogies: he was actually a king of barbarian hordes whose followers ignorantly deified him.[7] Anthony Faulkes is right, then, when he says that "always when such genealogies are recorded by Christian writers (e.g. Bede, *Historia Ecclesiastica* I 15), the gods that appear in them will have been interpreted euhemeristically, i.e. as great kings or heroes who came to be worshipped as gods after their deaths."[8] And, we might add, the same interpretation would presumably have been made by those

Ælfric's euhemeristic account is widely adopted by later homilists: e.g. a sermon from a twelfth-century manuscript draws heavily on Ælfric's *De falsis diis*: see Rubie D. N. Warner, *Early English Homilies from the Twelfth Century MS. Vesp. D.XIV*, Early English Text Society o.s. 152 (London, 1910), pp. 34–41.

1. *Ælfric's Lives of Saints*, ed. W. W. Skeat, Early English Text Society o.s. 76 (1881), pp. 126–8.
2. This translation is from *Alfred the Great: Asser's Life of King Alfred and other contemporary sources*, tr. with an introduction and notes Simon Keynes and Michael Lapidge (Harmondsworth, Middlesex, 1983), p. 67. For the Latin text see Klaeber, *Beowulf and the Fight at Finnsburg*, p. 254.
3. "Geta, qui fuit, ut aiunt, filius dei:" John Morris, in his edition and translation, *Nennius: British history and the Welsh annals* (London, 1980), p. 26, mistakenly capitalizes *Dei* and *God* and mistranslates the passage: "Geta, who said they were son of God."
4. Gummere, *Founders of England*, p. 421.
5. Kenneth Sisam, "Anglo-Saxon royal genealogies," *Proceedings of the British Academy*, 39 (1953), 32. Cf. J. S. Ryan, "Othin in England," *Folklore*, 74 (1963), 462.
6. Chambers, *Beowulf: an introduction*, p. 202 (with *wuþedon* misprinted for *wurþedon*). The source of the comment in both Textus Roffensis and in Asser is presumably Nennius's *Historia Brittonum*; see Sisam, "Anglo-Saxon royal genealogies," pp. 313–14.
7. Chambers, *Beowulf: an introduction*, p. 320, n. 1.
8. Faulkes, "Descent from the gods," p. 93.

who read or heard the genealogies, including the kings themselves.[9] It seems likely, moreover, that Alistair Campbell was right in assuming that the *Beowulf* poet had first-hand acquaintance with one or more of the many genealogies in circulation, for they also contained the names of several important characters in his poem—Scyld Scefing, Heremod, Beaw, Offa, and perhaps Wermund and Eomær. Campbell argues in particular that the account of Scyld Scefing at the beginning of the poem is based on an annotation to a royal genealogy.[1]

This selective interrogation of the surviving records has yielded more copious evidence than we might have expected that posthumous deification of Germanic heroes in pre-Christian days was a subject familiar to the Anglo-Saxons in later, Christian times. An Anglo-Saxon audience contemplating the final scene of *Beowulf* could possibly have had the euhemeristic accounts of deified heathens preached at them in sermons, explained to them by their scholars, and evoked in the genealogies of their kings. They were probably aware that their missionaries tried to convert Germanic heathens (whether Scandinavians in England or their Germanic cousins on the continent) by explaining to them that their pagan deities were mere mortals whom the misguided ancestors had proclaimed gods at their deaths. The Anglo-Saxon audience had available the word *mannweorðung* "worship of human beings" and knew that this was something condemned in both canon and sermon. The sermons also ring with warnings that funerals are flashpoints for outbreaks of heathen practices among Germanic people, whether Anglo-Saxon, Danish, or others. Is it not likely that an Anglo-Saxon contemplating Beowulf's last rites—the pagan cremation followed by the pagan interment of his ashes with lavish treasures as the warriors circle his *bēcn* chanting of his fame—might be reminded of the men of old deifying their kings? The *praecognita* to an understanding of the closing ritual as a dark Germanic apotheosis were to be found, as we have seen, not only in sermons but also in Asser's biography of Alfred, in Nennius, in saints' lives, and in annotations to royal genealogies.

Let us turn again to the actual words spoken by the twelve noblemen who march their horses around the *bēcn*:

þā ymbe hlǣw riodan hildedēore,
æþelinga bearn, ealra twelfe,

9. For a convenient assemblage of the relevant genealogical texts, see Chambers, *Beowulf: an introduction*, pp. 195, 197–203, 311–12.

1. Alistair Campbell, "The use in *Beowulf* of earlier heroic verse," *England before the Conquest: studies in primary sources presented to Dorothy Whitelock*, ed. Peter Clemoes and Kathleen Hughes (Cambridge, 1971), p. 290.

woldon (care) cwīðan, [ond] kyning mǣnan,
wordgyd wrecan, ond ymb w(er) sprecan; (3169–72)

Their utterance is described as a *wordgyd*. This is a nonce-word which Klaeber says means "elegy" and Clark Hall "dirge," but it means nothing so specific as that.[2] Their chant is as much an encomium as a lament and could just as well refer to *dadsisas*, the heathen litany which the *Indiculus . . . paganiarum* forbids the eighth-century Saxons to say in the presence of the dead. The noblemen's chant continues:

eahtodan eorlscipe ond his ellenweorc
duguðum dēmdon,— swā hit gedē(fe) bið,
þæt mon his winedryhten wordum herge,
ferhðum frēoge, þonne hē forð scile
of līchaman (lǣded) weorðan. (3173–7)

"They praised his nobility and his deeds of valor, praised them fittingly, as it is proper that one should do—to extol with words and cherish in the heart one's friend and lord when he must be led forth from the fleshly garment." Klaeber says of this passage, "The lines setting forth the praise of Beowulf by his faithful thanes sound like an echo of divine service, and closely resemble *Gen*[*esis*] 1ff, 15ff" (p. 230). The verses in *Genesis A* to which he refers are the poem's opening, which is based upon the Common Preface to the Mass—

Us is riht micel ðæt we rodera weard,
wereda wuldorcining, wordum herigen,
modum lufien!

"It is right that we praise the Lord of heaven, the glorious King of hosts, cherish him in our hearts"—and the angels' praise of God:

Þegnas þrymfæste þeoden heredon,
sædon lustum lof, heora liffrean
demdon drihtenes, (15–17)

which one translator has rendered, "Servants in glory worshipped the Prince, gladly uttered praise of their Lord of life, glorified God."[3] If we transfer these lexical renderings of *herian* and *deman* to the *Beowulf* passage, the import of the lines will be unambiguously devotional. In any case, the similarities are striking. The prayer-like quality of the *Beowulf* passage is also suggested by Klaeber's further observation that the phrase *manna mildust* in 3181 occurs in the Old

2. Klaeber, *Beowulf and the Fight at Finnsburg*, p. 428; John R. Clark Hall, *A Concise Anglo-Saxon Dictionary*, 4th edn with a supplement by Herbert D. Meritt (Cambridge, 1960), s.v. *wordgydd*.
3. R. K. Gordon, *Anglo-Saxon Poetry Selected and Translated* (London, 1926), pp. 95–6. Gordon's punctuation is used in both translation and original.

High German *Wessobrun Prayer* with reference to God: *almahtico Cot, /manno miltisto*. Klaeber offers no surmise as to why the poet has the warriors' chant echo these prayers, but some modern scholars have suggested that these phrases impart a Christian tone to the passage and imply a Christian Beowulf. It is difficult to see what sense can be made of supposed Christian allusions in a speech made about a pagan hero by his pagan comrades at his emphatically pagan obsequies. But in making the chant prayer-like, the poet is not necessarily making it Christian. (The supplication *kyrie, eleison* was addressed by pagan Greeks to their pagan rulers long before it was transformed into a prayer to Christ, and it implies reverent entreaty in either context.) The chant is not Christian, but it does have a worshipful quality, and perhaps this is what has led more than one modern scholar to see godlike qualities in the hero.[4] And as for the phrase *manna mildust,* its closest analogue in Old English writings is a comment inserted by the Anglo-Saxon translator of *Orosius* into his text: *He wæs eallra monna mildheortast on þæm dagum* "He was the most mild-hearted of all men in those days"—a comment referring to a heathen ruler who was deified.[5]

Lines 3174–7, as they are usually read, are puzzling:

swā hit gedē(fe) bið,
þæt mon his winedryhten wordum herge,
ferhðum frēoge, þonne hē forð scile
of līchaman (lǣded) weorðan.

They seem to imply that ten days after his cremation Beowulf's soul is still in his body, and only now, as the warriors chant Beowulf's praises, is his spirit departing. But a closer look at the text makes clear that this clause does not say "when his soul leaves his body" but rather "when *he* is transported from his physical covering."[6] Per-

4. Robert P. Creed observes, "The *Beowulf*-poet even seems to have sensed, with disapproval, that Beowulf had been regarded as some sort of god. Now the Christian poet was not about to violate the First Commandment. If earlier people had regarded Beowulf as a god, they had simply been mistaken. . . . Beowulf the god seems always to have come from afar, probably at the request of suppliants": "The remaking of *Beowulf,*" in *Oral Tradition in Literature: interpretation in context,* ed. John Miles Foley (Columbia, MO, 1986), pp. 144–5. Earlier, Edward B. Irving suggested much more tentatively that "a mysterious and half-mythic atmosphere surrounds the funeral rites [for Beowulf], perhaps largely because we half recognize the striking of those same notes of feeling we heard in the description of Scyld's funeral. . . . The similarity does not imply that Beowulf is a god, but it lays stress on the hero's role as a rescuer, protector, shield of his people, . . . and hints at some possible unknown order beyond the known seas of men": *Introduction to Beowulf* (Englewood Cliffs, NJ, 1969), p. 99. As for Scyld's funeral, Adrien Bonjour, *The Digressions in Beowulf* (Oxford, 1950), p. 9, says it "is almost an apotheosis."

5. *The Old English Orosius,* p. 128. The reference is to Julius Caesar.

6. *Beowulf,* 3176–7, is frequently compared with *Soul and Body II,* 20–1, *"to won þinre sawle sið siþþan wurde, / siþþan heo of lichoman læded wære,"* which is, in fact, the basis for editors' supplying *læded* for the manuscript lacuna in *Beowulf,* 3177. Kemp Malone, "Some *Beowulf* readings," *Franciplegius: medieval and linguistic studies in honor of Francis Peabody Magoun, Jr.,* ed. Jess B. Bessinger Jr, and Robert P. Creed (New York, 1965), pp. 122–3, rejects the reconstruction *læded* because, he says, the word is too long for the

haps this vaguer statement—"when *he* must go on to another state"—gives latitude for a broader range of meanings so that we are not obliged to assume that the poet has carelessly forgotten that Beowulf's soul parted from his body more than ten days before; he could be referring, rather, to the hero's translation to a higher state.

Finally, let us turn to the actual tomb of Beowulf, the *beorh* on Hronesnæs. When Beowulf conceives of a monument for himself in lines 2802–8—

> Hātað heaðomǣre   hlǣw gewyrcean
> beorhtne æfter bǣle   æt brimes nosan;
> sē scel tō gemyndum   mīnum lēodum
> hēah hlīfian   on Hronesnæsse,
> þæt hit sǣlīðend   syððan hātan
> Bīowulfes biorh,   ðā ðe brentingas
> ofer flōda genipu   feorran drīfað,

his concern is that he be remembered after his death. He wants a monument *to gemyndum minum leodum* "as a remembrance among my people," and he wishes to have it located so that seafarers will see it and, hearing that it is *Beowulfes beorh*, will carry his name to distant lands. This desire that a physical memorial keep his name alive in people's memory after his death is typical of early Germanic folk throughout their era. The great Rök column in Sweden, the Istaby memorial stone in Blekinge, Denmark, the Norse *bautasteinar* in general, and the many Anglo-Saxon memorial stones such as those at Hackness, Thorhill, Great Urswick, Yarm, and Overchurch bear witness to this concern. But the monument and ceremony that Beowulf's survivors provide go far beyond anything he requests in his dying speech. He says nothing about having a splendid wall built around his *becn* and enshrining his ashes within it; he says nothing about filling the structure with treasure and certainly nothing about ritual chants and processions. These elements arc all conceived by his bereaved subjects, and it is these elements that make the structure seem like something more than a monument and the occasion something more than a second funeral.

The words *hlǣw* and *beorh* used to designate the monument are quite general. By far the largest number of their documented occurrences are in charters or placenames, where they seem to mean "mountain, hill, mound" and refer to landmarks. They can also mean a hollow mound such as a dragon might occupy or such as men might

space available in the manuscript. But if this is so, we can simply assume that the scribe (who is everywhere economizing on space as he brings the poem to a close) used the reduced form (by syncopation and simplification of final double consonants) *læd*. In any case, it is significant that while the two passages are otherwise parallel, *heo* (the soul) is the subject of the subordinate clause in *Soul and Body II* while *he* (Beowulf) is the subject in *Beowulf*.

use for a tomb. Placenames like *Wodnes beorh* "Woden's borrow," which occurs in the *Chronicle* (for 592 and 715) and in charters, and *Þunores hlæw* "Thor's barrow," which occurs in the life of St Mildred, suggest that these nouns could also refer to a place for worshipping pagan gods—a shrine or *heroön*.[7] The noun *bēcn* used of the monument in line 3160 lends it a numinous quality, since *bēcn* means "sign, portent, idol," and it is used in Christian times to refer to the Cross and to Christ's miracles.[8] It can designate memorial stones (especially in the inscriptions written on such stones) but never refers to a tomb in Old English. The *beorh* which the Geatas prepared for Beowulf is twice described as *heah* "high" (2805 and 3157), and of course it was, both because it stood on a lofty promontory and because the structure itself was built *hēah ond brād* (3157). High *beorgas* are mentioned also in Ælfric's *De falsis diis,* where it says of Woden, *þone macodan ða hæðenan him to mæran gode, . . . and to heagum beorgum him brohtan onsæg[ed]nysse* "the heathens made that one [that is, Woden] their famous god . . . and brought sacrifices to him on high *beorgas*."[9] Wulfstan's account of the deification of Woden is much the same, noting that the heathens *to heagum beorgum him brohton oft mistlice loflac* "often brought manifold offerings to him on high *beorgas*."[1] Pope and Bethurum offer abundant evidence from other sources confirming that cult was paid to pagan Germanic gods at high mounds,[2] and the placename *Wodnes beorh* itself would seem to offer some corroboration. These data in aggregate suggest, I believe, that the monument that the Geatas prepare for Beowulf is patient of an interpretation which would view it as a shrine or *heroön.*

This essay proposes, then, a possible rationale for the funeral rites' "mysterious and half-mythic atmosphere" which "hints at some pos-

7. "Association with a mound or tumulus occurs three times in the case of Woden, twice in the case of Thunor," according to Margaret Gelling. "Place-names and Anglo-Saxon paganism," *University of Birmingham Historical Journal,* 3 (1961), 15. Conjuncture of tomb and temple is not unusual. Clement of Alexandria in his *Exhortation to the Heathen,* chapter 3, states contemptuously that pagan temples are simply tombs at which the heathen began worshipping, and he provides a catalogue of people who had died and whose tombs became places of worship. (In chapter 2 he says that the native countries, the biographies, and especially the sepulchers of the heathen gods prove that they were nothing but human beings.) We have seen earlier that Snorri Sturlusson describes Germanic people worshipping at the tombs of their gods. Even in Christian times the tomb can serve as a shrine. In Spain there is a tradition that a tomb cult developed at the grave of the Cid; see W. J. Entwistle, "La Estoria del noble varón el Cid Ruiz Díaz," *Hispanic Review,* 15 (1947), 206–11, and P. E. Russell, "San Pedro de Cardeña and the heroic history of the Cid," *Medium Ævum,* 27 (1958), 57–79.
8. See *Dictionary of Old English: B,* ed. Antonette diPaolo Healey (Toronto, 1991), s.v. *bēacen.* See also Elisabeth Okasha, " 'Beacen' in Old English poetry," *Notes and Queries,* 221 (1976), 200–8. Among the senses established by Okasha are "idolatrous monument" (p. 205).
9. *Homilies of Ælfric: a supplementary collection,* p. 684.
1. *The Homilies of Wulfstan,* p. 223.
2. See the notes to these passages in the editions of Pope and Bethurum; cf. Ursula Dronke's note to *at Sigtýs bergi* on p. 64 of *The Poetic Edda,* vol. 1: *Heroic Poems* (Oxford, 1969).

sible unknown order beyond the known seas of men."[3] It suggests that some in the poet's audience might have sensed a darker purpose in the Geatas' ceremonies than that of having a redundant second funeral, a purpose which the poet intimates through muted hints, as is his wont in alluding to his characters' paganism. An overt statement that the Geatas proclaimed dead Beowulf a god would have alienated a Christian Anglo-Saxon audience,[4] but by appealing subtly to the knowledge he knew they shared about Germanic apotheosis, he could arouse suspicions that the somber majesty of the ceremonies was an expression of something more precise than the "mysterious and half-mythic," of something more disquieting than mere grief. For those in the audience who thought of pagan deification, the closing rites would have been a powerful culmination of the pervasive tension throughout the poem between inspiring heroism and the sad shame of heathenism. The poet reveres the exemplary conduct of Beowulf and his people while deploring the pagan darkness which leaves that whole world in danger of perdition. His moving depiction of the solemn ritual around Beowulf's *beorh* is his last, melancholy, admiring gaze back on a man so great that people would think him a god; on a people so benighted that they thought a man might become a god.[5]

THOMAS D. HILL

The Christian Language and Theme of *Beowulf*†

One of the traditional topics of medieval English literary criticism is the question of "paganism and Christianity" in *Beowulf*. There have been a number of articles and even books concerned with the problem; recently E. B. Irving and Fred C. Robinson have devoted respectively a major article (Irving, 1984) and a significant portion of a book (Robinson, 1985) to re-examining it. If after over a century of learned discussion and commentary on *Beowulf*, it continues to be necessary to discuss an issue, there must be something rather problematic about it. And there is—most comparable early medieval epic texts are either emphatically and militantly Christian (like the *Chan-*

3. See above, n. 3, p. 194.
4. Howell D. Chickering, Jr, *Beowulf Translated with an Introduction and Commentary* (Garden City, NY, 1977), p. 377, rightly observes that the pagan element "is strong without being explicitly cultic." Allusions to heathenism are common in the poem, but they are always restrained.
5. I wish to thank Robert E. Bjork of Arizona State University for some helpful suggestions he made after hearing this essay read as a lecture.

† From *Companion to Old English Poetry*, ed. Henk Aertsen and Rolf H. Bremmer, Jr. (Amsterdam: VU University Press, 1994) 63–77. Reprinted by permission of the publisher.

son de Roland) or unapologetically pagan or secular in their viewpoint (like the *Táin Bó Cúailnge* or *Egils saga*). *Beowulf* is neither. Klaeber has spoken of "the problem of finding a formula which satisfactorily explains the peculiar spiritual atmosphere of the poem," (1953:cxxi, n.2) and this question remains an important issue in modern *Beowulf* criticism.

Obviously any issue which has received as much attention as this one is difficult and the "solution" or, to be more precise, the way of understanding this issue which I am proposing will inevitably be somewhat controversial. To put the matter succinctly, I think the *Beowulf*-poet is presenting a radical synthesis of pagan and Christian history—which is without parallel in Anglo-Saxon or Anglo-Latin literature (so far as I am aware). There are, however, parallels in Old Irish and Old Norse-Icelandic literature; it is a fascinating although perhaps unresolvable question whether there was any direct intellectual or literary influence between these literatures in the early Middle Ages.

It is necessary first to define the ideological problem which the *Beowulf*-poet (and reflective Anglo-Saxons throughout the era) faced. To begin with, the Anglo-Saxons (like most archaic peoples) were deeply conservative and venerated antiquity. The evidence for this proclivity is massive and pervasive. Good swords in *Beowulf*, for example, are inevitably "old"—ideally a sword is "the work of Weland" the archetypal, oldest and thus the best smith. Anglo-Saxon ideas about—their legal definition of—aristocracy and kingship are obscure to some degree, but it is clear that Anglo-Saxons venerated "old" families and that the ideal of an ancient royal line extending far back into the past was an important ideological concern shared even by a Churchman as hostile towards Germanic antiquity as Alcuin.[1] As far as Anglo-Saxon secular literature is concerned, there is ample evidence of its deliberately archaic and archaizing character. Leaving aside *Beowulf* itself, *Widsith* and *Deor* reflect remarkable and extensive knowledge of the Germanic past.[2] There is also evidence within and without *Beowulf* that Anglo-Saxon poets knew and recited poems now lost about the heroes of the major cycles of Germanic heroic legend as they are known to us from the extant heroic literature preserved in Middle High German and Old Norse-Icelandic.

Anglo-Saxon Christians, however, had to deal with a problem which all European Christians of the first millennium faced, the

1. On the Anglo-Saxon genealogies see Sisam (1953), and Hill (1988). For an interesting comment by Alcuin reflecting his belief in the *gæfa* (victory bringing luck) of a Woden descended king, see Epistola 129 (Duemmler, 1895:129).
2. The editions of those poems by Kemp Malone (1962/1966) provide a useful and illuminating compendium of information which graphically illustrates the extent of the Germanic learning of these poets.

simple and unarguable historical fact that Christianity itself, and in particular their Christianity, was not particularly old. The date of *Beowulf* is much controverted, but there are no conclusive arguments against dating the poem to the age of Bede, a date which was favoured by a majority of *Beowulf* scholars of the last generation, and which is still perfectly possible and plausible. Indeed the arguments for a late dating of the poem are motivated in part by a quite understandable scholarly concern that the reasonable guess—that *Beowulf*, is relatively early rather than relatively late—should solidify into a secure "fact" by dint of much repetition.[3] I should perhaps add that while I myself am agnostic about the dating of *Beowulf*, I find the arguments for an early dating suasive and the possibility congenial.

At any rate whether we accept the early or the late dating of *Beowulf*, it is clear that a reflective Anglo-Saxon must have been aware that the roots of his nation and culture were pagan and Germanic and that Christianity was a relatively recent innovation among a people to whom antiquity was precious and innovation suspect.

One of the ways in which medieval authors dealt with the problem of paganism and its consequences was to pretend that the history of their nation began with the conversion to Christianity and that nothing of real consequence happened before that momentous date. Bede is a conspicuous exemplar of this tradition of historiography—the pagan Anglo-Saxons receive very muted treatment in the *Historia Ecclesiastica*. The sins of the Christian Britons receive much more emphasis than the heroic accomplishments of the pagan Anglo-Saxons and Jutes. But a secular Anglo-Saxon aristocrat, whose claims to prestige and authority depended in part on an ancient and therefore necessarily pagan lineage, would be much less inclined to ignore the achievements of his pagan ancestors than a monk cut off from his own family and culture.

Some literary histories address the "pagan" heritage of the Anglo-Saxons as if that heritage was limited to the few references to Woden in the poetic corpus and the Anglo-Saxon charms—which are almost always treated as if magic was as marginal and "low" in Anglo-Saxon society as it is in ours. If we had a fuller corpus of Anglo-Saxon secular poetry we might well have more material about the Anglo-Saxon pagan pantheon rather than having to depend so heavily on Old Norse-Icelandic texts for information about Germanic paganism in England. Certainly we would know more about "pagan" heroic legend since there is ample evidence in the surviving literature that the Anglo-Saxons were deeply and abidingly interested in Germanic heroic legend—legends whose heroes were after all pagan. But leav-

3. On this problem see the essays collected in Chase (1981).

ing aside the literary evidence of interest in the pagan past in Anglo-Saxon England, this heritage was of interest to Anglo-Saxons in ways much more immediate than in their choice of songs and stories to listen to. The Anglo-Saxon state—the kingdom itself (or for most of this period the various Anglo-Saxon kingdoms)—was founded by pagans. The kings ruled by virtue of a claimed descent from Woden. And if royal descent and royal genealogies were presumably rather remote from the daily experience of most Anglo-Saxons, the genealogies of the lords of the shires were of more immediate concern. Every Anglo-Saxon freeman was expected to have a lord whose claim to aristocratic status was based on aristocratic descent extending into the far past. And in the age of Bede (a perfectly possible milieu for the composition of *Beowulf*) no Anglo-Saxon could claim more than three or four Christian ancestors. Modern historians would of course insist that most if not all of these claims to genealogical antiquity were fraudulent or exaggerated and that powerful men simply adorned their present power with fantastic claims that their ancestors had been similarly powerful in the remote past. For the purposes of the literary historian, however, it is not the truth or falsehood of these claims which is at issue, but rather the ideology implicit in such claims and the fact that royal and aristocratic authority—no matter how devout a Christian a given Anglo-Saxon might be—had to have pagan roots. Anglo-Saxon law was similarly Germanic and pagan in origin, and in so far as it was law based on the idea of personal vengeance, could be reconciled with Christian ideals of forgiveness and universal justice with difficulty.

I would submit that a young Anglo-Saxon warrior who was schooled in Germanic heroic legend, whose claim to aristocratic status extended far into the pagan past, whose law was the old law confirmed by his people since time immemorial, whose homeland had been won by pagan warriors, who bore on his person ancient pagan ornaments, who defended himself with an old sword purportedly made by Weland and certainly made by pagan craftsmen, and whose landscape was dominated by magnificent burial mounds in which the great men (and women) of his race were buried in pagan splendour, had much reason to respect the pagan heritage of his people no matter how pious he was and no matter how deeply he venerated the Church and the priests, the monks, and the nuns who served it. Such a young (or old) aristocrat faced a deep cultural conflict since the dominant authorities in the Church in this period would not, or to put the case more accurately, could not accept the claim that the paganism was a legitimate mode of religious and cultural self understanding. If paganism was legitimate, if pagans too could be saved, what was the point of Christian faith and Christian ascesis?

This cultural problem of how to reconcile Christian faith with an appreciation for the cultural achievements of the pagan past is an issue which recurs throughout the history of Western European thought—this was after all a central concern of that complex intellectual movement we call Renaissance humanism. And there have been different responses to this problem at different places and times in the history of Christian thought. The spectrum of these responses varies from Augustine's statement that the virtues of the ancient Romans were splendid vices, to Erasmus's invocation of Socrates as a saint. Roughly speaking, we may say that Christian thinkers who felt relatively secure about their own culture and faith have tended to be receptive to the merits of pagan past whether it be classical Latin and Greek or Celtic or Germanic paganism, and those who felt themselves threatened by it have harshly rejected "paganism" and pagan culture. Certainly in the history of Western European Christianity the humanists won their case and the classical pagan authors became central in the tradition of Christian European education. The beautiful quotation from Leo XIII with which E. K. Rand concludes his magisterial review of this problem is the utterance of a man supremely confident in his own faith and Christian culture:

> Quarum rerum utilitate perspecta Ecclesia Catholica quemadmodum cetera quae honesta sunt, quae pulchra, quae laudabilia ita enim humanarum litterarum studia tanti semper facere consuevit quanti debuere in eisque provehendis curarum suarum partem non mediocrem perpetuo collocavit.

> Perceiving, then, the usefulness [of the literatures of Greece and Rome,] the Catholic Church, which always has fostered whatsoever things are honest, whatsoever things are lovely, whatsoever things are of good report, has always given to the study of the humanities the favor that it deserves, and in promoting it, has expended no slight portion of its best endeavor.[4]

The point is that while there is a tradition of Christian hostility and suspicion towards the pagan past, there has also been a more positive and receptive attitude which is clearly recognisable in the high Middle Ages and later and which seems to be reflected in *Beowulf*. Hostility towards pagan culture was based in part on the historical situation of any given Christian author, but it was also based in part on individual temperament. The teaching of the Catholic Church is not univalent and unequivocal concerning this problem. It is perfectly true that a famous clause from the Athanasian creed states that "extra ecclesia nullus salvus est", but even for the rigorous theologians who constructed this creed, the term "ecclesia" must

4. Quoted from Rand (1928:68, 299).

include the patriarchs and such righteous gentiles as Melchisedech and Job. Dante's equivocation suggests something of the complexity of the problem. In accordance with the austere tradition of Catholic rigorism, he situates such pagans as Virgil and Aristotle in a pleasant but sad limbo situated before Hell, but Cato who is as much a pagan as any other is a guardian of Purgatory, and a certain Rifeo—known only from two lines in the *Aeneid* as the "iustissimus unus / qui fuit in Teucris et servantissimus aequi" (II. 426–27) is, according to Dante, in heaven. Dante, like the *Beowulf*-poet seems to have thought that some gentile "pagan" heroes could be saved, but unlike the *Beowulf*-poet, he is very cautious and hesitant about this possibility.

There are of course various solutions to the problem of the "peculiar spiritual atmosphere" of *Beowulf* and indeed it is possible to ignore the problem altogether, but it seems to me that the most consistent way to read the poem as we have it is to assume that the *Beowulf*-poet had thought long and hard about the problem and had arrived at (or had been taught) an essentially "humanistic" reading of his forefathers' paganism. He seems to have believed that the best and greatest of these men knew about God, creation, and natural moral law, and that when they died their souls went to heaven.[5] All of these beliefs can be explicitly supported from the text, but there are two problems which must be faced before we can simply define the *Beowulf*-poet as a Germanic humanist and turn to other problems. One is internal—the other and more serious one—external.

From the point of view of the literary historian concerned with "the peculiar spiritual atmosphere of the poem," *Beowulf* is a remarkably consistent text in that the religious language of the poem reflects the religious knowledge of those patriarchs who lived before the covenants and the creation of Israel. It is useful to have a term to define the religion of Beowulf, Hrothgar, and the good Germanic heroes in the poem and I would suggest that we define them as Noachites, that is, as gentiles who share the religious heritage and knowledge of Noah and his sons without having access to the revealed knowledge of God which was granted to Abraham, Isaac, and Jacob, a tradition culminated by the revelation of the Law to Moses and continued by the charismatic tradition of prophecy in Israel. Every reference in the poem which touches on religion can be understood in these terms except for one—lines 179–83 in which the poet apparently condemns Hrothgar and the Danes for idol worship.

There can be no question that this passage presents a major difficulty for those of us who would argue that the *Beowulf*-poet is

5. For a magisterial study of Christian ideas and Christian language in *Beowulf*, see Klaeber, 1911–12. For a recent discussion of the salvation of the heathen in *Beowulf*, see Hill (1988).

consistent and careful in depicting the good pre-Christian heroic figures in the poem as monotheistic Noachites. One simple solution to this difficulty is to assume that these lines are an interpolation by a scribe who was offended by the "humanistic" depiction of pre-Christian heroes and heroines in the poem. This solution was favoured (with some reservations) by Tolkien (1936:294, n.34) and Whitelock (1951:78). We have only one manuscript of the poem and there are a number of junctures in the poem in which lines or entire passages have been lost. Interpolations are easily understandable from a paleographical and codicological point of view; and the motivation for an interpolation at this point is also readily understandable. The usual criterion for determining whether a given passage is integral or an interpolation in a given text is whether the suspect passage differs either stylistically or conceptually from the text in which it occurs as a whole. If it is in some way markedly different from its immediate context, then one can reasonably argue that it was not part of the original text.

In this instance there is an immediate discrepancy between this condemnation of paganism in *Beowulf* and the remainder of the poem. The poet who is responsible for this passage states unequivocally that pagans such as the Danes do not "know" the identity of the true God, "*metod hie ne cuþon, / dæda demend, ne wiston hie drihten god / ne hie herian ne cuþon, / wuldres waldend.*" (ll.180–83: 'They did not know the Lord, the Judge of deeds nor did they know of the Lord God, nor did they know how to praise the Ruler of Glory.) This claim is of course generally true of "real" "historical" Germanic paganism. Germanic pagans, like the Romans and the Greeks, worshipped a variety of gods and did not know either the appropriate names for God or the formulas of worship which were current in Christian Latin tradition. In *Beowulf*, however, such historically pagan figures as Beowulf and Hrothgar know, worship and thank the one God of Judeo-Christian faith for the blessings of their lives, know that God judges deeds, and if we accept the straightforward literal significance of the formulas which characterise their deaths, ascend to heaven after their deaths. Indeed, forty-five lines or so after the flat assertion that the pagan Danes do not know how to worship the Lord, the *Beowulf*-poet speaks of how the equally pagan Geats gave thanks to God after their successful sea voyage: "*gode þancodon / þæs þe him yðlade eaðe wurdon.*" (II.227–8; 'They gave thanks to God since the sea passage had been easy for them.') Beowulf and his men cannot be Christian, but their prayer is characterised by a Christian formula and they are praying at an appropriate time and in an appropriate manner from a Christian perspective. And there are numerous other passages in the poem in which characters who would have been "historically" pagan, speak about God and religious issues from a "Noachite" perspective. The discrepancy between the poem as a whole and the condemnation of the Danes' idol worship is absolute; either the *Beowulf*-poet forgot for a moment to maintain the careful balance which he maintains elsewhere in the poem—in which the admirable heroic figures in the poem speak about religious matters from a monotheistic perspective, but know nothing of revealed religion—or someone else added that passage to the poem.

This condemnation of the idol worship of the Danes is in itself a problem for this argument, but one which can be dealt with by the simple assumption that the text of *Beowulf* is corrupt at this point. A larger problem, however, which bears on this argument, and which has led a great many distinguished scholars to be very hesitant about accepting what the simplest and most direct understanding of what the language of the poem would seem to imply, is that no other Anglo-Saxon or Anglo-Latin authors who deal with the pagan past of the Germanic peoples seem to have been at all sympathetic to paganism or to any other aspect of the culture of the ancient Germanic peoples. At various times in the history of Christian thought, Christian authors have been more or less sympathetic towards the excusable ignorance of those who lived before the advent of Christianity, but in the Latin west in the early Middle Ages Christian Latin authors were univocal in their condemnation of the pagan past. Alcuin's famous remarks about the monks at Lindisfarne who listened to heroic poetry are so frequently quoted that Anglo-Saxonists are weary of them and yet the passage is worth citing because of the clarity, force, and directness of Alcuin's language:

> Verba Dei legantur in sacerdotali convivio. Ibi decet lectorem audiri, non citharistam; sermones patrum, non carmina gentilium. Quid Hinieldus cum Christo? Angusta est domus: utrosque tenere non potuit. Non vult rex çelistis cum paganis et perditis nominetenus regibus communionem habere; quia rex ille aeternus regnat in caelis, ille paganus perditus plangat in inferno.
>
> Let the words of God be read at the meal of the clergy. There it is proper to listen to the lector, not a harp-player; the sermons of the Fathers not the songs of the people. For what has Ingeld to do with Christ? Narrow is the house; it cannot hold both. The King of Heaven wants nothing to do with so-called kings who are pagan and damned. For the eternal King reigns in heaven; the damned pagan laments in hell.[6]

The *Beowulf*-poet is even more anomalous in the context of early medieval Christian thought in that the admirable characters in *Beo-*

6. Alcuin, "Epistola 124" (Duemmler, 1895:183).

wulf are not strictly speaking pagans, but rather monotheists, Noachites, as I have chosen to call them. In this respect we may begin by observing that the *Beowulf*-poet is (as far as we know) historically wrong since the pre-Christian Germanic peoples were in fact pagans who worshipped a number of different gods and there is no historical evidence that any of these peoples anticipated the distinctive Judeo-Christian claim that there is one God, who created the heavens and the earth (*Beowulf* lines 90–98) and who governs the course of history (*Beowulf* lines 696–702). In a strict sense the *Beowulf*-poet is not being particularly sympathetic to pagans—with the problematic exception of lines 175–88 he does not even mention pagans or pagan worship. (He does mention pagan burial practices, but that is another and a special topic.)

In this respect the *Beowulf*-poet seems wholly *sui generis*; no other Anglo-Saxon author seems to have made such claims and since most medievalists are very reluctant, and generally rightly so, to accept any feature of a medieval poem as essentially original, many *Beowulf* scholars are not inclined to accept the implications of the Christian language of the poem at face value. Thus when Beowulf says of his grandfather Hrethel that when he died "*godes leoht geceas*" (line 2469) 'he chose God's light'—language which in a Christian context would clearly imply that the person who died went to heaven—many scholars implicitly assume that the poet is more or less thoughtlessly using Christian formulas without careful attention to their implications. If there were only a few instances of this kind of usage, or if there was more in the poem which reflected conventional Christian hostility to the pre-Christian past than one suspect passage, then one would, in my judgment, be justified in assuming that the *Beowulf*-poet was conventional or muddled in his thinking about these problems. The poet is, however, quite careful and consistent in his treatment of religious issues and his use of religious language, and I would argue that it is necessary to view this aspect of the poem from a somewhat broader perspective than Anglo-Saxonists generally do and to consider the poet's depiction of the religion of such figures as Beowulf and Hrothgar in the context of Celtic (particularly Old Irish) and Old Norse-Icelandic literary history as well. In so doing I am following the suggestions of J. R. R. Tolkien and in particular the arguments of Charles Donahue (Donahue, 1949–51).

We may begin by observing that Anglo-Saxon literature is preserved in fragmentary form in that we only have a small portion of what was once a very extensive corpus. Almost every Anglo-Saxon poem, for example, is preserved in a single manuscript copy. Even the much more extensive corpus of Anglo-Latin literature is only a portion of what once existed. Did the abbot or monks at Lindisfarne, for example, defend themselves against Alcuin's attack? This raises another problem which needs at least to be noted. Alcuin's works were preserved because he was an eminent and orthodox Catholic authority. The protest of a secularized abbot would have received much less respectful attention. This is not to raise again the fantasy of narrow minded monks erasing the remembrance of a religiously "incorrect" past, but simply to observe that the preservation of the texts which we have occurred in a particular religious and social milieu, and that the character of that milieu affected what was preserved. For better or worse, *Beowulf* is the only lengthy secular poem preserved in Old English and it is preserved in one manuscript which was nearly lost. By contrast there are over thirty manuscripts of Aelfric's second series of *Catholic Homilies*. It is hardly a novel observation that secular texts, even secular texts written by Christian authors, reflect a significantly different perspective than specifically Christian literary texts, particularly so if the latter are written by clerics or monks. If we had more Anglo-Saxon secular literature, *Beowulf* might seem much less anomalous than it does when compared with the rest of the Old English poetic corpus, which is almost all specifically religious.

Again it is important to remember that much of the Christian Latin literature which deals with the conversion of the Germanic pagans was written generations after the actual conversion process and the authors of these texts had an obvious interest in depicting the conversion as a straightforward and relatively quick one in which the missionaries had no occasion to make compromises and in which their new converts understood and accepted their new faith without hesitations or doubt. The actual process of conversion must inevitably have involved many ambiguities and complexities, and even willing converts could only have acquired a relatively sophisticated understanding of their new faith after years of instruction and worship. In fact, on the level of popular Christianity there is ample evidence for the existence of semi-Christian magic and folk-belief as exemplified most clearly in the Anglo-Saxon charms which were current for generations after the conversion. Thus if the *Beowulf*-poet seems to exhibit anomalous views about such topics as the salvation of unbaptised Germanic kings and heroes, we must remember that there is a great deal of evidence for other "unorthodox" religious ideas being current in Anglo-Saxon literary culture, even if this particular unorthodox idea seems unique to *Beowulf*.

If the *Beowulf*-poet's ideas about the existence and salvation of Germanic Noachites cannot be paralleled in Old English or Anglo-Latin literature as such, these ideas can be paralleled readily enough in the two vernacular literatures which are geographically and culturally closest to Old English literature. Both Old Irish and Old

Norse-Icelandic literature are "insular" literatures in that both languages were spoken as native languages in England and Scotland during the Anglo-Saxon period. Again, both Old Irish and Old Norse-Icelandic literature possessed a rich literary tradition which was originally pagan. One of the immediate contrasts between Old French epic tradition and the heroic literature of the Anglo-Saxons, the Norse and the Irish is that the heroic literature of these insular peoples is much more archaic and looks back to the pagan roots of these nations. For linguistic and historical reasons the historical memory of the romance speaking peoples of Europe simply did not extend before the advent of Christianity; their "pagan" epics were the classical Latin epics.

In Old and (early Middle) Irish secular literature the *ollaimh, ollaves* and the bards faced an ideological problem quite similar to that which the *Beowulf*-poet faced in that the traditional heroic literature of the Irish peoples concerned heroes born long before the advent of Christianity. It seems clear, however, that the learned secular authors of Ireland were willing to argue that their great heroes were saved and are now in heaven although the ways which the authors of these texts devised to achieve this happy result reflect a bold and imaginative effort on their part. Thus in the death tale of Conchobor, Conchobar is wounded (the solidified brain of a slain enemy is embedded in his skull) and only partially healed—any excitement will kill him. He remains seven years in this parlous state until he is told of the passion of Jesus, leaps up to lead an onslaught of the Ulstermen to avenge this crime, and dies as an Irish martyr to the faith (Cross and Slover,[7] 1969:346). According to "The Phantom Chariot of Cu Chulainn" Cu Chulainn was summoned out of hell by Saint Patrick in order to convince the high king of Ireland of the merits of Christianity, and Cu Chulainn persuaded Patrick to arrange for his salvation during this process (Cross and Slover, 1969: 354). The death tale of Cu Chulainn concludes with Christian prophecy by the spirit of Cu Chulainn and in "The Colloquy of the Old Men" Patrick's guardian angels specifically assure him that it is appropriate for him to listen and to record the stories of the *fian* and so Patrick himself and his clerics record the stories from the lips of Ossin (Cross and Slover, 1969:464). It is difficult for someone who is not a specialist in the field to evaluate and interpret the complex narrative strategies by which the authors of these texts reconcile—at least on a formal level—the conflicting world views of Old Irish heroic legend and Christianity. A broad generalisation does seem

7. The 1969 reprint of this anthology contains a bibliographical supplement which directs the reader to the Irish editions of these texts.

appropriate however—the Irish bards and *ollaves* were sure enough of themselves and their literary and cultural traditions to claim that their great "pagan" heroes and kings were saved and rejoicing in the Christian heaven—heaven itself would be a poorer place without them.

In some ways Old Norse-Icelandic literary tradition is more directly relevant to *Beowulf* than Old Irish secular heroic prose. Old English and Old Norse-Icelandic are cognate languages and can be defined as cognate literatures. There are many striking parallels between the two literary traditions and there was much contact and mutual influence between the two. Hence the treatment of "paganism" or to be more precise, pre-Christian religious ideas in the family sagas is important for students of *Beowulf* in that Icelandic secular literature provides the closest approximation of the lost secular literature of Anglo-Saxon England which still exists. Obviously we cannot treat Icelandic texts of the high middle ages as if they could provide direct evidence of what we have lost, but Icelandic literature is an important resource for the Anglo-Saxonist and indeed has long been recongnised as such.

For the purposes of the present discussion, one immediate problem with the issue of the presentation of the conversion from Germanic paganism to Christianity in Old Norse-Icelandic literature is that this literature is so rich that one could write extensively about the problem without even beginning to treat it adequately. For two relatively recent discussions see Lönnroth (1969) and Harris and Hill (1989). In the context of this paper I wish to concentrate on one particular literary text which is strikingly similar to *Beowulf* in its treatment of "pagan" heroes who are nonetheless committed monotheists set apart from their pagan surroundings. *Vatnsdœla Saga* is an interesting text of considerable literary merit, but no one would claim that it is one of the great literary monuments of the period. The saga is a family saga concerned with the history of a given family over generations and the author of the saga makes several quite distinctive claims about the early history of this family. One is that unlike the other great founding families of Iceland who were at odds with Harald the Fairhaired, the leading men of this family were actually on good terms with him and emigrated to Iceland because of the power of fate as articulated by the disappearance of a magic amulet and its reappearance in Iceland. Again the family had their own distinctive form of religious commitment. When the first bishop arrives to convert the Icelanders Thorkel krafla demurs:

> Þorkell kvazk eigi vilja aðra trú hafa—"en þeir Þorsteinn Ingimundarson hǫfðu ok Þórir fóstri minn; þeir trúðu á þann, er sólina hefir skapat ok ǫllum hlutum ræðr."
>
> (*Vatnsdœla saga*, kap. 46 [Sveinsson, 1939: 125])

> (But Thorkell said he did not want a faith different from that Thorsteinn Ingimundarson and the rest of them had held—and Thorir my foster father. They believed in Him who made the sun and ruled all things.)

The bishop, of course, quickly explains that this faith is perfectly compatible with Christianity and Thorkel and his family, after some hesitation, are converted. The monotheistic and ethical principles of the pre-Christian Vatnsdœla dwellers are mentioned repeatedly throughout the saga. These men not only knew that one God had created the sun and ruled all things but that aggressive behavior was morally wrong (cap. 11) and that God would punish or reward men according to their deeds (cap. 23) and the theme of the one god who made the sun recurs repeatedly. In terms of historical plausibility the edifying moral monotheism of the Vatnsdœla family before the conversion is historically unlikely and since there is much magic and fantasy woven into the saga, one might be tempted to dismiss this aspect of the saga as simply late pious fantasy projected into the far past. It is important, however, to distinguish between *Vatnsdœla saga* as an aesthetic success or failure and its literary historical interest as an attempt to bridge the gulf between the pagan Germanic past and the Christian present. The author of *Vatnsdœla saga* like the *Beowulf*-poet was attempting to reconcile pious antiquarian sympathy for the Germanic past and the claims of Christian truth. The kind of dogmatic hostility to the Germanic past reflected in Alcuin's letter about the monks of Lindisfarne was as current in thirteenth century Europe and Iceland as it was in Anglo-Saxon England, but it did not prevent the author of *Vatnsdœla saga* from depicting noble monotheistic pre-Christian Germanic heroes just as the *Beowulf*-poet had done before him. To summarize then, the peculiar spiritual atmosphere of *Beowulf* looks a good deal less peculiar and unique if one compares the poem to the other heroic literatures of Northern Europe whose poets and learned men faced the kind of ideological problem which the *Beowulf*-poet faced. There are other similar depictions of the pagan past current in Old Irish and Old Norse-Icelandic literature and a simple solution to the problem of Christianity in *Beowulf* is to assume that the *Beowulf*-poet approximated the solution that these other authors arrived at either independently or as the result of the influence of poems and histories now lost.

This discussion of the Christian context of *Beowulf* is necessarily controversial and partial; there are a number of smaller problems which could receive fairly extended discussion in their own right. Thus, for example, the poet alludes to the practice of sortilege in lines 202–04; this is a "pagan" practice but one sanctioned by the precedent of Old and New Testament practice. Again, there is the problem of lines 589–90 in which Beowulf apparently threatens

Unferth with hell-torment, an anomaly convincingly explained by Fred C. Robinson (1974:129–30). These smaller problems lead us to a larger issue, however, which is that there is no received answer to the question of the "peculiar spiritual atmosphere of *Beowulf*" and eminent and well respected Anglo-Saxonists have offered quite divergent interpretations of this problem in the poem. Of the most recent discussions of the issue I particularly recommend that by Fred C. Robinson in *Beowulf and the Appositive Style*; Robinson's conclusions are quite different than mine, but they merit careful attention. Again, E. B. Irving has reargued the more traditional view that the *Beowulf*-poet was bound by and committed to the traditions of Germanic poetry and simply was not concerned with theological consistency. In a sense both these scholars are arguing for a more traditional and "orthodox" view of the Christianity of the *Beowulf*-poet than my argument would imply. Robinson is arguing that the *Beowulf*-poet was deeply concerned about the paganism of his characters, but had to accept the harsh traditional views of churchmen such as Alcuin, whereas Irving simply thinks that the poet was unconcerned with theological issues. In contrast, I am arguing that on this crucial ideological issue the *Beowulf*-poet was willing to question the authority of what must have been the majority opinion of the church of his time. The language of the poem can be most readily understood in these terms, but many scholars are reluctant to grant that an Anglo-Saxon poet could have challenged the authority of the church so directly. There are other Old English and Anglo-Latin texts which reflect the tension between a natural respect for traditional Germanic culture and the radical and exclusive claims of Christian faith; but there are none which so clearly affirm the positive, admirable, spiritual dimension of Old Germanic culture as the *Beowulf*-poet does. (It may also be added that the *Beowulf*-poet was keenly aware of the problematic features of the Germanic heroic ethic, but that would have to be the occasion for another paper or monograph.) When one considers the problem in a somewhat broader perspective, however, both the achievement and the ideological perspective of the *Beowulf*-poet come into sharper focus. We can see more clearly if we broaden our perspective.

I would be surprised if the problem of the "peculiar spiritual atmosphere" of *Beowulf* did not continue to be the occasion of scholarly controversy, but I do think it is important that the "humanistic" sympathy which the *Beowulf*-poet exhibits towards the best of the pagan past is not "heretical" even if it was (apparently) a minority view in the Anglo-Saxon church. As time passed and the western church emerged from the trauma of the destruction of the Roman empire, "high" medieval and renaissance philosophers and theologians began to reconsider the ramifications of the contempt for the pagan past implicit in such texts as Alcuin's letter to the monks at Lindisfarne, and a much more nuanced and appreciative view of the achievements of the pagan past became possible. The question of the salvation of the heathen became an important issue for poets such as Langland and Dante and the philosophy of Thomas Aquinas is based upon the recovery and assimilation of Aristotle's thought. Great poets often see more deeply than their contemporaries; and if the *Beowulf*-poet seems to have anticipated by generations the humanism and tolerance of thinkers like Erasmus, we need not be surprised. Irish *ollaves* and Icelandic saga-men and women learned to recognise the spiritual validity of their own heritage and its essential compatibility with Christianity. This tradition of tolerance and respect for the past is as much part of the heritage of early medieval Europe as the rigid and bigoted contempt for the pagan past which we commemorate in school handbooks. We could even argue that this was the better way, and we may hope that it will be the more enduring part of that heritage.

REFERENCES

Chase, Colin (1981). *The Dating of Beowulf.* Toronto: University of Toronto Press.

Cross, Tom Peete, and Clark Harris Slover (1969). *Ancient Irish Tales*. Rev. bibliography by Charles W. Dunn. New York: Barnes and Noble.

Donahue, Charles (1949–51). "Beowulf, Ireland and the Natural Good." *Traditio* 7.263–77.

Duemmler, Ernestus (ed.) (1895). *Alcuin: Epistolae Karolini Aevi II.* Monumenta Germaniae Historica. Berlin: Weidmann.

Harris, Joseph and Thomas D. Hill (1989). "Gestr's 'Prime Sign': Source and Signification in *Norna-Gests Þáttr,*" *Arkiv för Nordisk Filologi* 104. 103–22.

Hill, Thomas D. (1988a). "The 'Variegated Obit' as an Historiographic Motif in Old English Poetry and Anglo-Latin Historical Literature." *Traditio* 44. 101–24.

———. (1988b). "Woden as 'Ninth-Father': Numerical Patterning in Some Old English Royal Genealogies." In: *Germania: Comparative Studies in Old Germanic Languages and Literatures.* Ed. Daniel G. Calder and T. Craig Christy. Exeter: D. S. Brewer. 161–74.

Irving, Edward B. Jr. (1984). "The Nature of Christianity in Beowulf." *Anglo-Saxon England* 13. 7 21.

Klaeber, Fr. (1911–12, 1912). "Die christlichen Elemente im *Beowulf.*" *Anglia* 35. 111–36, 249–70, 453–82; 36. 169–99.

———. (ed.) (1953). *Beowulf and the Fight at Finnsburg*. 3rd ed. Boston: D. C. Heath.

Lönnroth, Lars (1969). "The Noble Heathen: A Theme in the Sagas." *Scandinavian Studies* 41. 1–29.

Malone, Kemp (ed.) (1962). *Widsith*. Anglistica 13. Copenhagen: Rosenkilde and Bagger.

———. (ed.) (1966). *Deor*. 2nd ed. New York: Appleton-Century-Crofts.

Rand, E. K. (1928). *Founders of the Middle Ages*. Cambridge, MA: Harvard University Press.

Robinson, Fred C. (1974). "Elements of the Marvellous in the Characterisation of Beowulf: A Reconsideration of the Textual Evidence." In: *Old English Studies in Honour of John C. Pope*. Toronto: University of Toronto Press. 119–37.

———. (1985). *Beowulf and the Appositive Style*. Knoxville, TN: The University of Tennessee Press.

Sisam, Kenneth (1953). "Anglo-Saxon Royal Genealogies." *Publications of the British Academy* 39. 287–348.

Sveinsson, Einar Ol. (ed.) (1939). *Vatnsdœla saga.* Íslenzk Fornrit VIII. Reykjavík: Hið Íslenzka Fornritafélag.

Tolkien, J. R. R. (1936). "*Beowulf*: The Monsters and the Critics." *Publications of the British Academy* 22. 245–95.

Whitelock, Dorothy (1951). *The Audience of Beowulf.* Oxford: Clarendon Press.

LESLIE WEBSTER

Archaeology and *Beowulf*†

Introduction

§1 In his introduction to the 1925 Wyatt and Chambers edition of *Beowulf*, Chambers wrote eloquently of the subtle pitfalls of translating Old English, especially of being led astray by our knowledge of the modern language.[1] Any study of the archaeological background to *Beowulf* must be aware that this is even more true of attempts to relate academic knowledge of the archaeology of early medieval north-western Europe to the poem. Marrying the specialized intentions of poetic description and the complex history of the text with the archaeological record as it survives, with the intentions of those who created it, and with our own contemporary perceptions, presents multiple opportunities for misunderstanding.[2] To take burials, for example: the poetic description of Beowulf's burial and the great Sutton Hoo ship burial are both carefully constructed messages for their respective contemporary audiences, in which conceptions of the past play a significant part; but they may not necessarily have had identical aims in view.[3] Moreover, archaeology is a fragile and incomplete witness; what survives in a burial is only a small part of what was involved in the process, including rituals and organic offerings which we can only guess at. In making sense of that partial evidence, we bring our own contemporary preconceptions, just as nineteenth-century archaeologists and editors interpreted the

† From *Beowulf: An Edition*, by Bruce Mitchell and Fred C. Robinson (Oxford: Blackwell, 1998) 183–94. Reprinted by permission of the publisher.

1. A. J. Wyatt, ed., rev. R. W. Chambers, *Beowulf and the Finnsburg Fragment* (Cambridge, 1925), p. xxiv.
2. The most useful and comprehensive archaeological studies of *Beowulf* are K. Stjerna, *Essays on Questions Connected with the Old English Poem of Beowulf*, Viking Society Extra Series 3 (Coventry, 1912); R. J. Cramp, 'Beowulf and Archaeology', *Medieval Archaeology*, 1 (1957), 57–77; Rosemary Cramp, 'The Hall in *Beowulf* and in Archaeology', in *Heroic Poetry in the Anglo-Saxon Period: Studies in Honor of Jess B. Bessinger. Jr.*, eds Helen Damico and John Leyerle (*Studies in Medieval Culture* XXXII; Medieval Institute, Kalamazoo, 1993), 331–46; and C. M. Hills, 'Beowulf and Archaeology', in *A Beowulf Handbook*, eds R. E. Bjork and J. D. Niles (Lincoln, 1997), pp. 291–310. The first, though now very outdated in both contents and its use of evidence, remains a remarkable survey. Cramp's excellent 1957 study, though again to some extent overtaken by new discoveries and research, is still essential reading, as is her more recent discussion of halls (1993). Hills' survey article gives a thoroughgoing review of past and current archaeological approaches to the poem.
3. Indeed M. O. H. Carver, 'Ideology and Allegiance in East Anglia', in *Sutton Hoo: Fifty Years After*, ed R. Farrell and C. Neuman de Vegvar (Oxford, Ohio, 1992), pp. 173–82, esp. 181, has argued that, in a sense, the Sutton Hoo Mound 1 burial is itself a form of poem. See also L. Webster, 'Death's Diplomacy: Sutton Hoo in the Light of Other Male Princely Burials', in Farrell and Neuman de Vegvar, *Sutton Hoo*, pp. 75–82, esp. 75–81; and L. Webster and M. P. Brown, eds, *The Transformation of the Roman World AD 400–900* (London and Los Angeles, 1997), pp. 222–3.

sources very differently from their twentieth-century successors. How we relate these differing forms of evidence therefore needs delicacy and care. What follows aims to avoid too literal and dogmatic an approach, in the hope of respecting the subtleties of both the poem and archaeology.

How the past was looked at is an important factor in this. Its own past was certainly important to the audience of *Beowulf*. The poem is, of course, set in the past; it reverberates not only with ancestral legend, but also with repeated reference to heirlooms, to the mighty works of forebears, long-dead smiths and giants, and to ancient treasure, *ealde lāfe* (ll. 795, 1488, 1688) of all kinds; indeed, mention of *gēardagum* (l.I) sets the scene in the opening line. Significantly, however, descriptions of past treasures—the dragon's hoard, for example—though sometimes characterized as decayed (ll. 2255–62, ll. 2756–64), differ little from those of the possessions of Beowulf and his contemporaries in the surviving text, which would themselves have been archaic in the late tenth century when it was written down. So for Anglo-Saxons, the past was, in a sense, the present, and this too colours the way in which things are represented in the poem, and hence the way in which we need to look at them—there is little point, for example, in using archaeological evidence for attempting any sophisticated chronological analysis of the text,[4] or in speculating why relevant practices known from the archaeological record—votive offerings of weapons and gold, for example—find no reference in *Beowulf*. It is a poem, not an archaeological textbook.

Warrior Culture

§2 Before going on to examine specific topics in a little more detail, a general word on the archaeology of aristocratic warrior culture and its place in the understanding of *Beowulf* is appropriate. Much stress is laid in the poem on the integrity and loyalty of the fighting troop, the virtues of the warrior hero on whom they depend, and the almost chivalric bonds between the two. Wiglaf's rallying speech to Beowulf's *comitatus* (warrior band, ll. 2633–60) is one of several such statements of *duguðe þēaw* (l. 359) in the poem. We know from many documentary sources of the importance of warrior culture in the Germanic world; and how the opportunistic getting and ritual dispensing of treasure, made easier in the fluid circumstances of post-Roman Europe, underpinned and sustained this power-base.[5] Archaeology also reflects this, not only in the migration-period trea-

4. Though it seems that the most detailed and concrete descriptions—those of swords and helmets especially—probably reached their present form no later than the eighth century.
5. For a general survey of the historical context, see Webster and Brown, *Transformation of the Roman World, passim*.

sure-hoards of gold coins and neck-rings from Scandinavia and the Netherlands (Figure 31),[6] but also nearer home, in the great seventh-century burials at Sutton Hoo and Taplow.[7] In both, the dead man was accompanied by a symbolic array of vessels for the provisioning of a troop, buckets, hanging cauldrons, and great tubs for the feasts in hall, as well as many drinking vessels of every kind—from elaborately mounted aurochs horns to tiny burr-wood cups for stronger stuff than ale (Figure 17).[8] Horns, like the equally unstable glass claw beakers from Taplow, were designed to be passed from hand to hand, perhaps by women, in formal drinking ceremonies of the kind described at Heorot and in Hygelac's hall, where Wealhtheow and Hygd served the warriors in courtly ritual. Other symbols of the joys and ceremonies of life in hall are to be seen in the lyres which occur in both burials; this instrument is the *glēobēam* (l. 2263), *hearpe* (l. 89), *gomenwudu* (l. 1065) of the poem, the essential accompaniment to the deeds of heroes sung in hall. Multiple weapon sets too are a feature of both burials, symbolizing the arming of the warrior band; and so too, is treasure *nēan ond feorran* (l. 1174). At Sutton Hoo, for instance, treasure took the shape of Frankish gold, Byzantine silver, Swedish armour, and Celtic precious vessels. It is in this context that we can see something of the leader of the war-band as gainer and giver of gold, provider of battle-gear, and of the joys of life in hall. It is time to turn to that centre of lordly activity, the hall itself.

Halls

§3 The idea of the hall—as a place of joy and security until threatened by external forces of evil—plays a major part in the poem. Heorot, above all, symbolizes this; and recent work has now shown that its lofty splendor can be paralleled by archaeological examples. Edwin's Northumbrian seventh-century royal palace at Yeavering provided an excavated Anglo-Saxon example of the kind of massive wooden hall described in the poem, while even grander halls are known from Danish and other Germanic early medieval contexts (Figure 14).[9] The recent discovery of an Anglo-Saxon high-status hall

6. M. Alkemade and A. Pol, 'Elite Lifestyle and the Transformation of the Roman World in Northern Gaul' and 'The Lifestyle of the Elite', in Webster and Brown, *Transformation of the Roman World*, pp. 180–4, 185–93, esp. pls 50–1; J. P. Lamm, 'The Great Ring-Gold Hoards' and 'The Gold Collars', in *The Magic of Gold in Life and Legend*, ed. A. Knape (Stockholm, 1994), pp. 33–51, esp. 37–51.
7. A. C. Evans, *The Sutton Hoo Ship Burial* (London, 1986); R. A. Smith, 'Anglo-Saxon Remains', *Victoria County History of Buckinghamshire*, 1 (1905), pp. 199–204; L. Webster, 'The Taplow Barrow', in *The Blackwell Encyclopedia of Anglo-Saxon England*, eds M. Lapidge with J. Blair, S. Keynes and D. Scragg (Oxford: Blackwell, 1999); K. East and L. E. Webster, *The Anglo-Saxon High-Status Burials at Taplow (Bucks.), Broomfield (Essex) and Caenby (Lincs.)* (London, forthcoming).
8. C. Fell, 'Old English *beor*', *Leeds Studies in English*, n.s. 8 (1975), 76–95.
9. Cramp, 'Beowulf and Archaeology', pp. 68–77; B. Hope-Taylor, *Yeavering: An Anglo-*

complex at Cowdery's Down, Hampshire, has given a much more concrete idea of how Heorot might have looked, in the form of building C12, which is dated to the seventh to eighth century.[1] The excavators have suggested various superstructures which could have fitted on the excavated ground-plan (Figure 15). But common to all is the evidence for a raised wooden floor, which would have echoed to any step—*healwudu dynede* (l. 1317)—and an elaborate scheme of external supporting timber braces. Could this latter be what is implied by the well-known crux of *stapol* (l. 926), elsewhere in the poem unambiguously a pillar or support (l. 2718)? In this interpretation, Hrothgar would have had to stand at, not on, the *stapol* to look up at Grendel's hand hanging from the gable. This may stretch the grammar too far. Fortunately, the Cowdery's Down building also provides support for the usual explanation of *stapol* as a step of some kind. The archaeological evidence confirms that the raised floor of that elaborate structure had timber supports for steps to the entrance as its gable end. The excavators have also deduced from the complex and massive ground-plan that the building must have a steeply pitched roof of gabled construction. Heorot's *stēapne hrōf* (l. 926) certainly finds a parallel here. The descriptions of Heorot as *horngēap* (l. 82) and *hornreced* (l. 704) have also more usually been interpreted as references to gables, rather than to decoration with antlers or horns. From another perspective, however, *horn* could imply an architectural element invisible in excavation, but well known from manuscripts, and from the evidence of certain house-shaped shrines and oratories. Some manuscript depictions of Insular gabled wooden structures—and their occasional stone and metal imitations—have projecting cross members at the peak of the gable, rather like a pair of horns (Figure 16).[2] Could this be an explanation both of *horngēap* and even of that term opaque to archaeological scrutiny, *bānfāg* (l. 780)? This is probably to stray too far into unsubstantiated speculation; but there are possible explanations for other descriptions of Heorot's external appearance, notably terms such as *goldfāh* (l. 308) and *fǣttum fāhne* (l. 716). There is no archaeological evidence for the embellishment of Anglo-Saxon or any other Germanic halls with gold; but if the description is not simply pure hyper-

British Centre of Early Northumbria, Department of the Environment Archaeological Report 7 (London, 1977), p. 315; Cramp, 'The Hall in *Beowulf* and in Archaeology'; Hills, 'Beowulf and Archaeology', pp. 302–3.

1. M. Millett and S. James, 'Excavations at Cowdery's Down, Basingstoke, Hampshire, 1978–81', *Archaeological Journal*, 140 (1983), 151–279, esp. 215–17, 233–46.
2. P. Harbison, 'How Old is Gallarus Oratory?', *Medieval Archaeology*, 14 (1970), 34–59. esp. 54–5; F. Henry, *The Book of Kells: Representations from the Manuscript in Trinity College Dublin* (London, 1974), pl. 68; J. D. Alexander, *A Survey of Manuscripts Illuminated in the British Isles, vol. 1: Insular Manuscripts, Sixth-Century to Ninth-Century* (London, 1978) fig. 255; L. Webster and J. Backhouse, eds, *The Making of England: Anglo-Saxon Art and Culture* AD *600–900* (London, 1991), p. 176.

bole, it would not seem unreasonable to read in the description of the golden, shining-plated exterior a poetic image of thatch or of gleaming shingles, both attested in the archaeological record.

Among other constructional details, the references to iron fittings and door-hinges (ll. 998–9) can now find clear archaeological parallels; the *īrenbendum searoþoncum besmiþod* which secured the hall *innan and ūtan* (ll. 774–5) are well represented in the numerous clench-bolts from sites such as York and Flixborough, where they were clearly used in the construction of planked timber buildings.[3]

Inside the hall, the evidence for hangings and fittings is inevitably less good. Benches are known from excavated Scandinavian and continental timber buildings;[4] more ephemeral details such as wall-hangings (ll. 994–5) hardly at all, though the presence of what seem to have been coloured hangings in the burial chamber at Sutton Hoo Mound I clearly hints at the splendours of earthly halls.[5]

Arms and Armour

§4 Essential to the conduct of warrior culture was the weapon set, more rarely accompanied in the archaeological record by armour (Figures 18–20). In the poem, it too is presented as a kit (e.g. ll. 1242–50), though the elements are different: the possession of swords, not uncommon in archaeological contexts, seems confined to those of the highest status in the poem, while helmets and chain mail, still exceptionally rare survivals, are depicted in the poem as the regular equipment of the warrior troop. It is impossible to say whether this apparent discrepancy arises from an artificial poetic convention, or from the practice of handing on such expensive prestige items, rather than discarding them in graves. However recent discoveries of complete Anglo-Saxon helmets (see below) and the identification of fragments from others suggest that these were in more widespread use than was formerly apparent; the poem may indeed reflect the realities of *comitatus* equipment more accurately than had been imagined.

Helmets

§5 The image *par excellence* of the Germanic warrior, the helmet is one of the dominant images of the poem. Like a number of late sixth-

3. P. Ottaway, *Anglo-Scandinavian Ironwork from 16–22 Coppergate, The Archaeology of York: The Small Finds*, 17/8 (London, 1992), pp. 615–18.
4. E. Roesdahl, *The Vikings* (Harmondsworth, 1987), p. 45.
5. R. L. S. Bruce-Mitford, *The Sutton Hoo Ship Burial, vol. 1: Excavations. Background, the Ship, Dating and Inventory* (London, 1975), p. 480; Roesdahl, *Vikings*, pp. 44–5.

to seventh-century Scandinavian helmets,[6] it is explicitly a crested or combed helmet of the kind known from the seventh- and eighth-century Anglo-Saxon examples at Sutton Hoo, Wollaston, and York:[7]

> Ymb þæs helmes hrōf   hēafodbeorge
> wīrum bewunden   wala ūtan hēold. (ll. 1030–1)

These three complete helmets have particularly prominent crests or combs (the *wala*) which pass across the crown to reinforce the iron cap, in the case of the York (Figure 35) and Wollaston (Figure 24) examples, two such crests pass over the crown crosswise. The Sutton Hoo single iron comb (Figure 25) is inlaid with twisted wires, *wīrum bewunden* (l. 1031), while the York helmet, like some of the Swedish examples (Figure 23) copies twisted wire in bronze. Another passage (l. 1451) describes Beowulf's helmet as *befongen frēawrāsnum*, set about with chains; Professor Cramp's perceptive identification of this as a description of a mail curtain is now reinforced by the York helmet, with its neck-guard of mail. These three Anglo-Saxon helmets, and their Swedish counterparts, all have face masks (*heregrīman* l. 396, *grīmhelm* l. 334), cheek-guards (*hlēorbergan* l. 304), and neck protection, which also derive from late antique parade models.[8] The descent from this particular helmet type is also significant, in that the archaeological evidence suggests that its use is confined to the peripheral areas of north-western Europe—Anglo-Saxon England and Scandinavia. In the Frankish territories and beyond, a different kind of helmet was current. The archaeological evidence here thus corresponds directly to the cultural milieu of the poem. These late antique prototypes were often gilded, and the Sutton Hoo and York helmets emulate this in being decorated with bronze, silvered or gilded elements—*brūnfāgne* (l. 2615), *hwīta* (l. 1448), and *goldfāhne* (l. 2811). *Beowulf* interestingly refers to the stripping of precious fittings from helmets (ll. 2255–6), a practice now visible in a number of bronze fittings from helmets which have been recognized in recent years.[9] The new helmet find from a seventh-century warrior grave at Wollaston, Northamptonshire, at first appeared as if it might have been stripped of precious metal fittings, but close examination now suggests that it is simply a very sturdy all-iron construction—not a ceremonial item, but a highly functional piece of regular fighting equipment.

6. D. Tweddle, *The Anglian Helmet from 16–22 Coppergate, The Archaeology of York: The Small Finds*, 17/8 (London, 1992), pp. 1104–25.
7. Cramp, 'Beowulf and Archaeology', pp. 60–3; Evans, *Sutton Hoo Ship Burial*, pp. 46–9; I. Meadows, 'The Pioneer Helmet', *Current Archaeology*, 154 (1997), 391–5; Tweddle, *Anglian Helmet*.
8. Tweddle, *Anglian Helmet*, pp. 1087–90; Webster and Brown, *Transformation of the Roman World*, p. 222.
9. E.g. Tweddle, *Anglian Helmet*, p. 1083.

The most spectacular aspect of this helmet is, however, the presence of a three-dimensional boar figure on its crown (Figure 24). Such images resonate throughout the poem—the *swȳn ealgylden eofer īrenheard* of Hnæf's funeral pyre (ll. 1111–12), the *swīn ofer helme* (l. 1286)—to the extent that the boar image even comes to represent the warriors themselves (l. 1328). The Wollaston helmet is, moreover, not the only surviving example of this potent tradition: the Benty Grange, Derbyshire, helmet also bears a fine boar figure on its crown (Figure 36),[1] and an unmounted boar helmet crest comes from an old grave find at Guilden Morden in Cambridgeshire.[2] Depictions of warriors wearing helmets of this kind are also known from Swedish contexts (Figure 22); one of the best known occurs on a die for making repoussé panels from a seventh-century site at Torslunda, Gotland (Figure 21). A very late representation of a boar or similar animal on a helmet crest can be seen in an eighth-century Anglo-Saxon manuscript now in St Petersburg, where it adorns the defeated Goliath's helmet.[3] Perhaps in such a context, and by this time, it was only possible to depict such a pagan image of courage and strength on the headgear of the unrighteous. In the poem the motif is certainly one of strength and protection; it also appears (ll. 303–6, 1451–4) in contexts where it seems to be not a crest but an image on a helmet, protecting the wearer in a manner similar to the amuletic boar and beast heads which shield the brows of the Sutton Hoo and York helmets. A more ambiguous image is presented by the *eafor hēafodsegn* (l. 2152) on the list of Beowulf's gifts to Hygelac (ll. 2152–4a), which match those given by Hrothgar to Beowulf (ll. 1020–4a). If the reading of this as a boar ensign, a standard with a boar image, is correct, it serves to remind us that archaeological evidence has its own limitations.

Mail-Coats

§6 Like the helmet, the mail-coat is a rarity in archaeological contexts though, as we have already seen, this probably reflects burial practice rather than actual usage. The latter wills and the evidence of the Bayeux Tapestry suggest that mail-coats were in widespread military use by the later tenth century.[4] The mail-coat from the Sutton Hoo ship burial is an elaborate construction consisting of rows

1. R. L. S. Bruce-Mitford and M. R. Luscombe, 'The Benty Grange Helmet and Some Other Supposed Anglo-Saxon Helmets', in *Aspects of Anglo-Saxon Archaeology*, R. L. S. Bruce-Mitford (London, 1974), pp. 223–52.
2. J. Foster, 'A Boar Figurine from Guilden Morden, Cambs.', *Medieval Archaeology*, 21 (1977), 166–7.
3. M. J. Swanton, 'The Manuscript Illustration of a Helmet of Benty Grange Type', *Journal of the Arms and Armour Society*, 10 (1980), 1–5; Tweddle, *Anglian Helmet*, fig. 534.
4. S. A. O'Connor, 'Technology and Dating of the Mail', in Tweddle, *Anglian Helmet*, pp. 1052–87, esp. 1052–9.

of riveted rings apparently alternating with rows of butt-welded ones;[5] a similar technique is seen in the chain-mail neck-guard on the York helmet in the later eighth century, where lapped and riveted rings are combined in alternate rows with welded ones. The poetic accounts of these garments accord very precisely with the archaeological evidence. They are of grey steel (l. 334), skilfully formed of rings in an intricate mesh (ll. 321–3, 406, 550–3), and they clink and jingle on the move (l. 226).

Shields

§7 Shields are a much more standard item of warrior equipment as represented in Anglo-Saxon and other Germanic burials; they form, with the spear, the basic fighting kit of the member of a war-band.[6] The poetic vocabulary highlights elements of the shield which have a certain archaeological reality (Figures 19 and 20). They are characteristically described as broad, probably with a rim of some kind, e.g. *rondas regnhearde* (l. 326), *sīdrand* (l. 1289), *bordrand* (l. 2559), and they may possess a tall central boss (*stēapne rond* l. 2566). Each of these elements can be matched in archaeological material from the early Anglo-Saxon period, though metal edge bindings are rare; Sutton Hoo again provides the best surviving example of this, and interestingly, a rare instance of the use of lime-wood in a shield.[7] The regular use of *lind* and its compounds to denote shields or warriors in *Beowulf* may therefore depend upon a notion of high-class rather than everyday shields, but it would be unwise to press the meaning of this trope too far.

Swords and Seaxes

§8 The defining heroic weapon, swords (Figures 27–29) play a large part in the poem, and are described in considerable detail. They are archetypally the *ealde lāfe* (§1), powerful heirlooms to be prized for their power and might; some are the work of marvellous smiths (l. 1681), or *eotenisc* (l. 1558), the work of giants long ago; they may have names, or carry owner inscriptions and images which tell of the mythic past (ll. 1688–98). They have richly decorated hilts (l. 1698) and bear twisting and branching patterns (*wyrmfāh* l. 1698, *ātertānum fāh* l. 1459); their iron blades are fearsome double-edged weapons, which need two hands to swing them (l. 1461). Supporting archaeological evidence for much of this has long been recognized.[8]

5. Evans, *Sutton Hoo Ship Burial*, p. 41.
6. T. M. Dickinson and H. Härke, *Early Anglo-Saxon Shields, Archaeologia*, 110 (1992).
7. Ibid., p. 48.
8. H. R. Ellis Davidson, *The Sword in Anglo-Saxon England: Its Archaeology and Literature* (Oxford, 1962), *passim*.

The descriptions of snaking (l. 1698) and poisonous branching patterns (l. 1459) suggest the intricate twisted patterns produced by the pattern welding technique used to make the best and strongest of blades in the pre-Viking period[9] (Figure 27). The word *hringmæl*, which occurs more than once as a description of swords (ll. 1521, 1564, 2037), may also refer to the twisted coiling patterns sometimes seen in pattern-welded blades (Figure 27). An alternative explanation has been that this signifies the attached rings seen on certain Anglo-Saxon and other Germanic swords (Figure 21 and 29b), which possibly denote a bond between lord and retainer.[1] The reference to *fetelhilt* (l. 1563) has also sometimes been taken to refer to this phenomenon, but the more probable and simpler explanation is that this term, 'belted hilt,' denotes a sword harness such as one sees in very grand form in the Sutton Hoo burial, as well as in more modest Anglo-Saxon and other Germanic examples (Figure 29c).

A number of sixth-century sword-hilts from Anglo-Saxon graves carry runic inscriptions which seem to include personal names,[2] like the hilt of the mighty sword which despatched Grendel's mother (ll. 1694–8); and while no surviving sword carries anything resembling the story of the downfall of the giants (ll. 1687–93), there are a number of elaborately decorated hilts dating from the sixth to the eighth century in both England and Scandinavia where the complex motifs may carry special meaning. Professor Cramp has drawn attention to the images on the gold-sheeted hilt of the early sixth-century sword from Snartemo, Norway,[3] while from Anglo-Saxon contexts, the eloquent and complex animal decorations on the eighth-century Fetter Lane hilt and the Beckley pommel present other examples of swords which may carry a visual message[4] (Figures 29d and 29a). There is even a certain amount of archaeological as well as documentary evidence for swords as heirlooms: some from graves show extreme wear, or have had their fittings removed, sometimes only the pommel is buried, the sword apparently kept for another generation.[5] These potent weapons were as significant in real life as in poetry.

9. Cramp, 'Beowulf and Archaeology', p. 65; J. Lang and B. Ager, 'Swords of the Anglo-Saxon and Viking Periods in the British Museum: A Radiographic Study', in *Weapons and Warfare in Anglo-Saxon England*, ed. S. C. Hawkes, Oxford University Committee for Archaeology Monograph 21, pp. 85–122; R. Engstrom, S. M. Lankton and A. Lesher Engstrom, *A Modern Replication Based on the Pattern-Welded Sword of Sutton Hoo*, Medieval Institute Publications (Kalamazoo, 1989).
1. Cramp, 'Beowulf and Archaeology', p. 64; V. I. Evison, 'The Dover Ring-Sword and Other Sword-Rings and Beads', *Archaeologia*, 101 (1967), 63–118.
2. S. C. Hawkes and R. I. Page, 'Swords and Runes in South-East England', *Antiquaries Journal* 47 (1967), 11–18.
3. Cramp, 'Beowulf and Archaeology', pl. Xlb.
4. Webster and Brown, *Transformation of the Roman World*, pp. 211, 236–7.
5. Ellis Davidson, *Sword in Anglo-Saxon England*, p. 13; and e.g. the Sarre Anglo-Saxon cemetery contained at least two graves where pommels only seem to have been buried with the dead (J. Brent, 'Account of the Society's Researches in the Anglo-Saxon Cemetery at Sarre', *Archaeologia Cantiana*, 6 [1866], 157–85, esp. 173).

The sword was a double-edged, two-handed weapon; but the seax (Figure 28), its single-edged counterpart, though a slighter weapon, was just as effective. The broad and bright-edged knife that Grendel's mother draws on Beowulf (l. 1545) and the *wællseax* with which Beowulf despatched the dragon (l. 2703) were as deadly as swords. Seaxes grew in popularity throughout the Anglo-Saxon period; a fine example, seemingly drawn, like Beowulf's from the mail-coat, is shown on one of the Torslunda plates (Figure 26), and by the eighth century, they appear on Insular figural sculpture as equipment proper to the highest rank; the Repton warrior king bears one alongside his sword, and so does the mighty figure of King David on the great Pictish St Andrews Sarcophagus.[6]

Ships and Other Transport

§9 The ship (Figure 13) plays a prominent part in the poem, in the rituals of death, which we shall turn to shortly, as well as in the life of these North Sea fighting bands. It is of tarred clinker-built construction (l. 295), like the Sutton Hoo Mound I ship and other migration-period boats, broad-beamed to accommodate the warriors and their fighting gear. Unlike the Sutton Hoo ship, however, it goes under sail (ll. 217–24 and 1905–10), rather than propelled by oarsmen; Viking ships certainly used sail, and it was certainly in use during the later Saxon period, as the evidence of the tenth-century Graveney boat shows.[7] The ship is variously described as *hringedstefna* (l. 32), *hringnaca* (1. 1862), *bundenstefna* (l. 1910), and *wundenstefna* (l. 220), all of them terms which have given rise to suggestions that it had ring-decorated or twisted prows. More prosaically, these terms may rather describe a prow like the ship's stem post dredged from the River Scheldt at Moerzeke-Mariekerke,[8] which is radio-carbon-dated to the mid-fourth century ± 70 years. The curving neck of this open-jawed creature is encircled by a series of carved collars, a feature which can also be seen on some of the English ships' prows on the Bayeux Tapestry.

Land-based transport, when not on foot, was by horse; and though the references in the poem are few, it is worth noting in passing that the equipment of these splendid creatures finds echoes in the archaeological record. The *fǣtedhlēore* (l. 1036), decorated bridle plates, now have a close parallel in the gilded bridle and other horse trappings from the new prince's burial at Sutton Hoo Mound 17

6. Webster and Brown, *Transformation of the Roman World*, p. 227, fig. 100.
7. V. H. Fenwick, ed., The Graveney Boat: A Tenth-Century Find from Kent, National Maritime Museum Archaeological Series 3, British Archaeological Reports, British Series 53 (Oxford, 1978).
8. R. L. S. Bruce-Mitford, 'A New Ship's Figure-Head Found in the Scheldt, Moerzeke-Mariekerke', *Acta Archaeologica*, 38 (1967), 199–209.

(Figure 30).[9] The horses are also equipped with gleaming saddles, described as *searwum fāh since gewurþad* (l. 1038.) These recall the sixth-century Germanic saddle fittings from burials at Krefeld Gellep in the Rhineland and from Ravenna, which are lavishly decorated with gold and garnet inlays.[1] Richly adorned saddles must also have existed in Anglo-Saxon England, as the Anglo-Saxon ninth-century saddle fragment from York suggests; it is worthily embellished with animal ornament and silver studs.[2]

Death and Burial

§10 This is a powerful theme in the poem; *Beowulf* begins and ends with a hero's funeral, and other burials—Hnæf's cremation, and the ancient barrow burial guarded by the dragon—play a significant part in the narrative. Each of these contexts recalls elements which can be matched with archaeological evidence, but in doing so, we should be aware that each is a literary construction, with its own purpose within the text, rather than any kind of documentary account. The burial of Scyld Scefing, with which the poem opens, has often attracted comparison with the great Sutton Hoo ship-burial, and other boat-burials from East Anglian and Swedish contexts;[3] here too, the dead man is buried amidships surrounded by treasures and battle-gear of all kinds. But Scyld's boat is consigned to the sea, not buried under a mound like the others. We cannot know whether this is a genuine or garbled tradition of the past, or a literary invention. It is striking, however, that each of the burials in the poem exemplifies a different theme, which suggests a conscious literary intention. Beowulf's own burial, with which the poem ends, is by contrast a barrow on the headland, visible for miles:

> hlǣw on hlīðe   se wæs hēah ond brād
> wēglīðendum   wīde gesȳne; (ll. 3157–8)

exactly the kind of sentinel burial we see in the Taplow barrow (Figure 34), and again at Sutton Hoo;[4] this is an expression of fame and a territorial claim that is equally familiar from the archaeological evidence. But first, Beowulf is cremated, like Hnæf (ll. 1107–24), with full battle equipment. This recalls the unusual case of the

9. A. C. Evans, 'The Pony-Bridle in Mound 17: Problems and Challenges', *Saxon*, 25 (1997), 1–3; and see, for a fine Frankish example, R. Pirling, 'Ein Frankisches Fürstengrab aus Krefeld Gellep', *Germania*, 42 (1964), 188–216, esp. pls 47 and 52.
1. Pirling, 'Ein Frankisches Fürstengrab', pl 46, 2.
2. Webster and Backhouse, *Making of England*, pp. 278–9.
3. R. L. S. Bruce-Mitford, *The Sutton Hoo Ship Burial: A Handbook*, 3rd edn (London, 1979), pp. 81–3.
4. E. O'Brien, 'Post-Roman Britain to Anglo-Saxon England: The Burial Evidence Reviewed', vol. 1, unpublished D. Phil. thesis, Oxford, 1996.

Asthall barrow, where a rich cremation was buried in the mound,[5] but the placing of the unburnt treasure with the cremated remains in Beowulf's barrow finds no real archaeological parallel, and suggests that the narrative is led by the need to consign the ill-gotten treasure back to the earth.

The account of the fated ancient barrow which became the dragon's lair is a particularly fascinating blend of archaeological verisimilitude and moral fable. The Anglo-Saxons certainly were not averse to robbing the graves of their own contemporaries;[6] they were equally aware of the ancient past about them, often choosing prehistoric burial sites for their own cemeteries in the pagan period. So the description of the stone barrow, *stānbeorh stēapne* (l. 2213), with its chambers and elaborate masonry (ll. 2542–5, 2717–19) could certainly represent a contemporary awareness of the inside of a neolithic tomb, such as Weland's Smithy. The treasure it contains, with its goblets, helmets, swords, and mail-coats, its jewelled gold artefacts and golden standard, is, however, an image of Anglo-Saxon not prehistoric riches (e.g. ll. 2756–71, 3047–50; Figures 32–33); these are earthly treasures intended to be recognizable to the audience, gold which, in the end, brought grief.

As this final example shows, the poem's adaptation here of archaeological evidence demonstrates that subtlety and invention in marrying past to present which makes this such a remarkable and densely textured poetic achievement.

5. T. M. Dickinson and G. Speake, 'The Seventh-Century Cremation Burial in Asthall Barrow, Oxfordshire: A Reassessment', in *The Age of Sutton Hoo*, ed. M. O. H. Carver (Woodbridge, 1992), pp. 95–130, esp. 95–127.
6. Unequivocal instances of persistent contemporary grave-robbing were observed at the St Peter's Tip cemetery, Broadstairs, Kent (C. Hogarth, pers. comm.; C. Haith, *The Anglo-Saxon Cemetery at St Peter's Tip, Broadstairs, Kent* (London, forthcoming).

Figure 13. Viking ships at sea.

Figure 14. Reconstruction of a hall from the late-tenth-century Viking fortress at Trelleborg, Denmark. Photograph: Sonia Hawkes.

Figure 15. Reconstruction of an eighth-century Anglo-Saxon hall from Cowdery's Down, Hampshire. Reproduced with the permission of the Royal Archaeological Institute, London.

Figure 16. The Temple of Jerusalem from the Book of Kells (fol. 202v), showing horned gables. Insular, *c*.800. Courtesy of The Board of Trinity College, Dublin.

Figure 17. Anglo-Saxon drinking-horns and glassware.

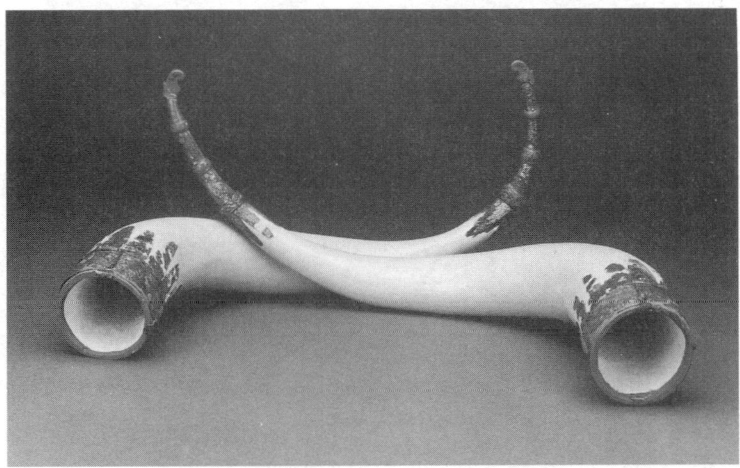

(a) The Sutton Hoo drinking-horns. Courtesy of the Trustees of The British Museum.

(b) The Taplow claw beakers. Courtesy of the Trustees of The British Museum.

Figure 18. Goliath depicted as an Anglo-Saxon warrior from the Tiberius Psalter (f. 9). Anglo-Saxon, c.1050. Courtesy of Eva Wilson.

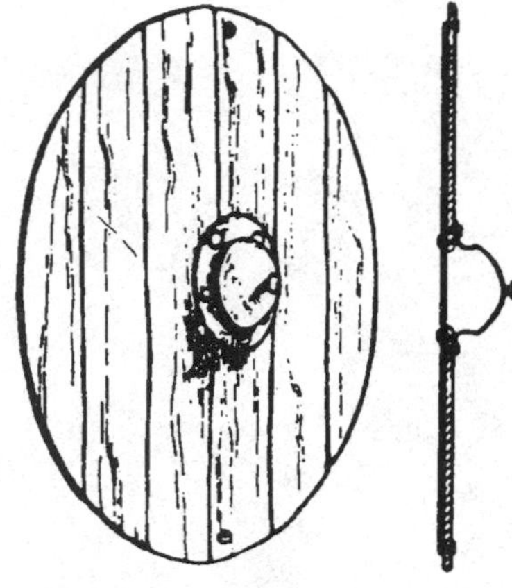

Figure 19. Reconstruction of a sixth-century Anglo-Saxon shield. Courtesy of Eva Wilson.

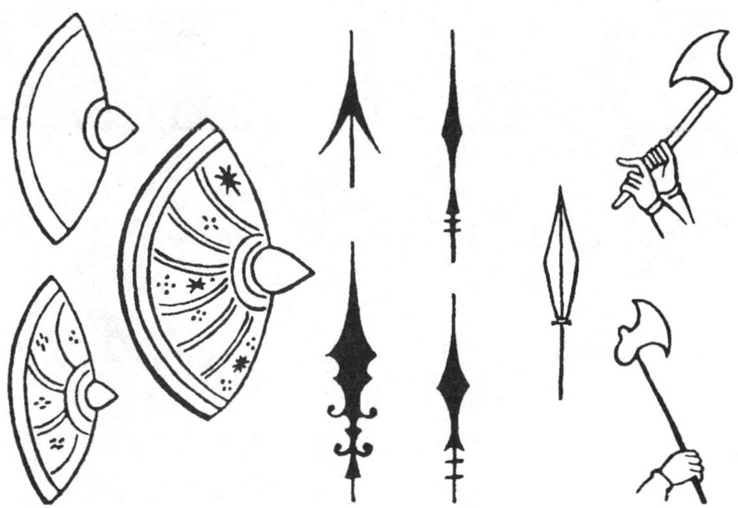

Figure 20. Shields, spears, and battleaxes, depicted in late Anglo-Saxon manuscripts. Courtesy of Eva Wilson.

Figure 21. Bronze die with warriors, from Torslunda, Öland, Sweden, late sixth or seventh century. Courtesy of Antikvarisk-topografiska arkivet, the National Heritage Board, Stockholm.

Figure 23. Iron helmet with ribbed crest from grave 5, Valsgärde, Uppland, Sweden, mid-seventh century. Photo: Dominic Tweddle/ York Archaeological Trust.

Figure 22. An engraving showing a warrior (perhaps Oden/Woden) wearing a helmet with a boar crest, copied from a panel on a helmet in grave 1, Vendel, Sweden, 675–700 C.E. This image replaces, with permission of the editors and author, figure 10 of Leslie Webster's original article in B. Mitchell and F. C. Robinson's *Beowulf: An Edition.* The engraving is from *Graffåltet vid Vendel*, ed. Hjalmar Stolpe and T. J. Arne (Stockholm: K. L. Beckmans Boktryckeri, 1912).

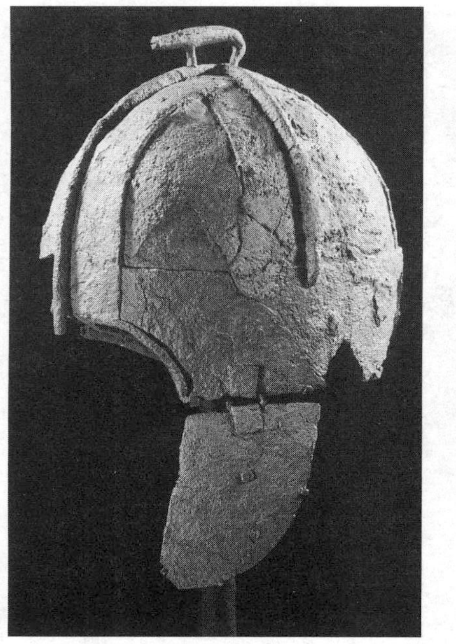

Figure 24. Boar-crested iron helmet from an Anglo-Saxon warrior grave, Wollaston, Northants., seventh century. Courtesy of Hansom Aggregates.

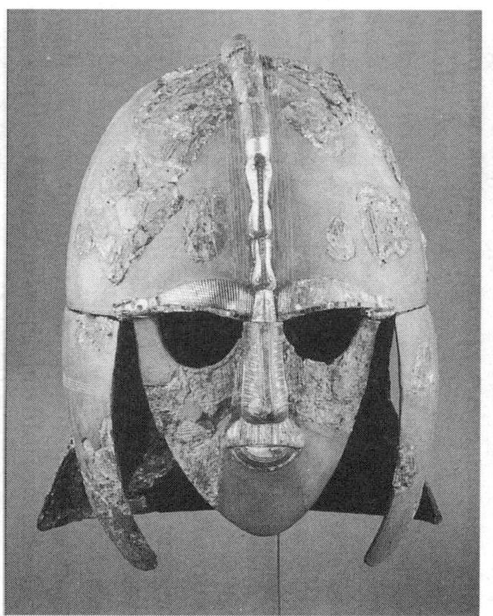

Figure 25. The helmet from the Anglo-Saxon royal ship burial at Sutton Hoo, Suffolk, late sixth or early seventh century. Courtesy of the Trustees of The British Museum.

Figure 26. Bronze die from Torslunda, Öland, Sweden, showing warrior with a seax, late sixth or seventh century. Courtesy of Antikvarisk-topografiska arkivet, the National Heritage Board, Stockholm.

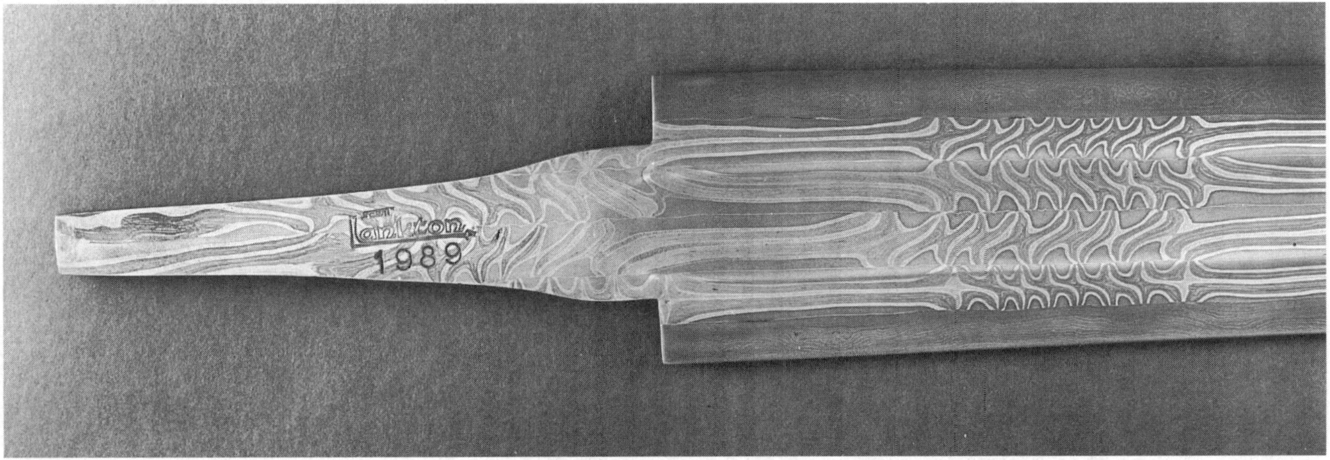

Figure 27. Copy (made by Scott Lankton and Robert Engström) of the sword blade from the Sutton Hoo ship burial, showing the pattern-welded effect. Courtesy of the Trustees of The British Museum.

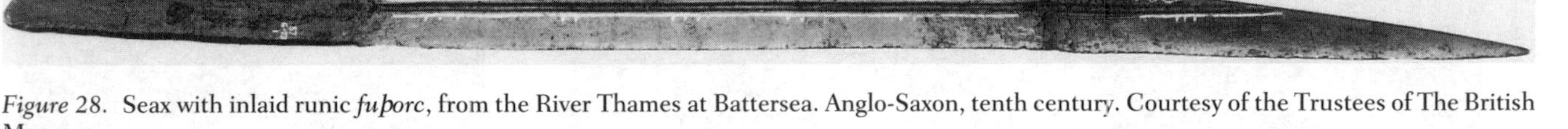

Figure 28. Seax with inlaid runic *fuþorc*, from the River Thames at Battersea. Anglo-Saxon, tenth century. Courtesy of the Trustees of The British Museum.

(a)

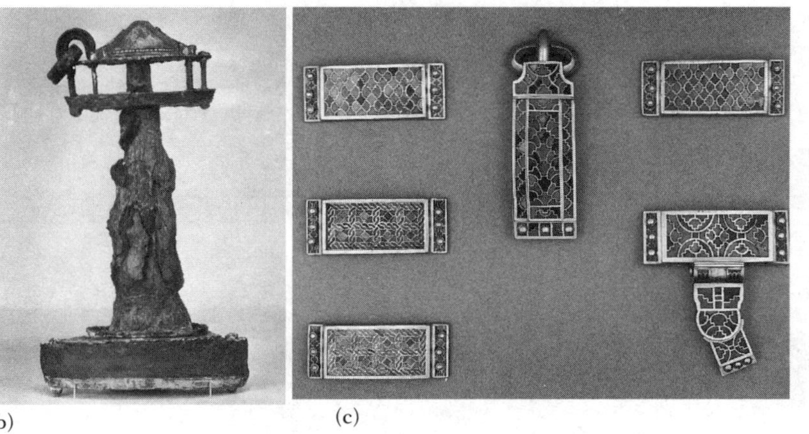

(b) (c)

(d)

Figure 29. Anglo-Saxon sword fittings:
(a) silver-gilt pommel with interlacing animal decoration, Beckley, Oxon, eighth century; (b) ring-hilt with silver mounts, from Gilton, Kent, sixth century; (c) gold and garnet-inlaid mounts from the Sutton Hoo sword and its harness, early-seventh century; (d) silver-gilt sword hilt from Fetter Lane, London, eighth century. Courtesy of the Trustees of The British Museum.

Figure 30. Trappings from a bridle and other horse equipment from the Anglo-Saxon prince's grave (mound 17), Sutton Hoo, Suffolk, early seventh century. Courtesy of the Trustees of The British Museum.

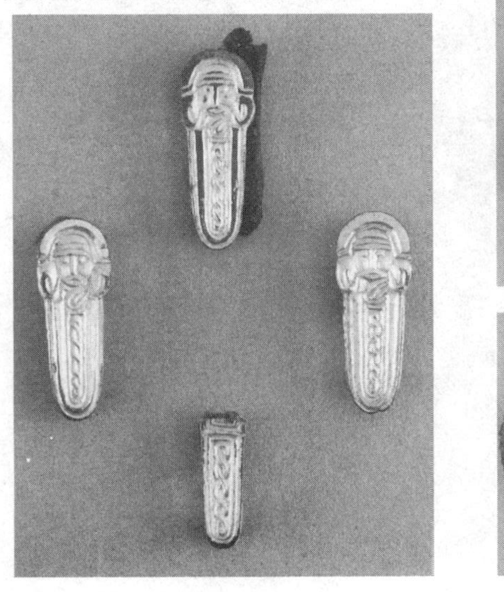

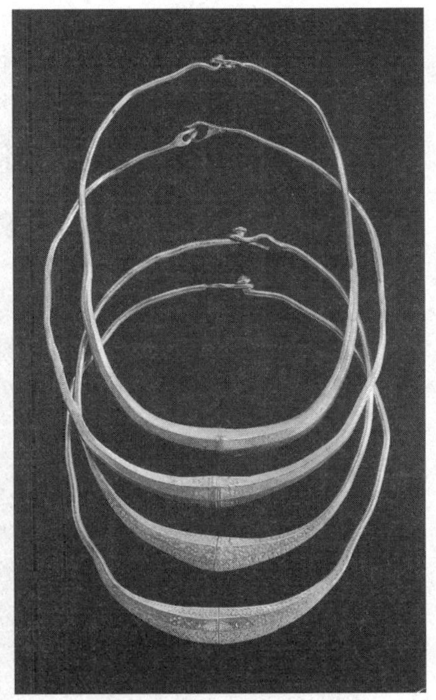

Figure 31. Gold neck-rings from Olst, Netherlands, *c*.400. Courtesy of Rijksmuseum van Oudheden.

Figure 32. Brooches, belt fittings, arm- and finger-rings, from Anglo-Saxon England, fifth to tenth century. Courtesy of the Trustees of The British Museum.

Figure 33. Anglo-Saxon gold and garnet brooch from grave 205. Kingston, Kent, early seventh century. Courtesy of National Museums and Galleries on Merseyside.

Figure 34. The Princely barrow at Taplow, Bucks., looking westward, early seventh century. Photo: R. M. Williams. Courtesy of the Trustees of The British Museum.

Figure 35. York helmet, Anglo-Saxon, eighth century. © Copyright York Castle Museum.

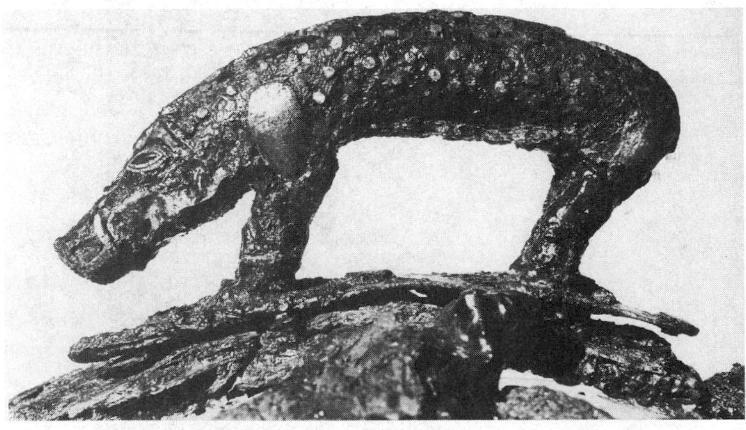

Figure 36. Boar image on the crest of the Benty Grange helmet, Derbyshire. Courtesy of Sheffield Galleries & Museums Trust.

DANIEL DONOGHUE

The Philologer Poet: Seamus Heaney and the Translation of *Beowulf*†

That every translation is also an act of interpretation has been a commonplace at least since Cicero, Horace, and Augustine of Hippo. It arises in response to the notion that the word-for-word and sense-for-sense task that aims for "faithfulness" provides at best only a partial description of all that a good translation entails. Even the most literal effort, according to this commonplace, sets up a tension between the mechanical and the creative as when, for example, one metaphor substitutes for another. Such moments can become the despair of the philologist who detects a net loss when the changes are extensive, especially if the original is a literary masterpiece. In most cases the readers remain unaware of the specific changes. Presumably, they turn to the translation in the first place because they do not know the original language, and they trust that the rhetorical embellishments will not obscure the essential continuity with the source text. When a poet like Seamus Heaney turns his attention to translating *Beowulf*, however, readers pay special attention to the signs of his interpretive touches. What is presumed to be "literal" is taken in stride, perhaps necessary to understanding the narrative but inherently less interesting.

Some strands of literary criticism respond with another commonplace, which rejects the logic behind the mechanical/creative dualism. It questions whether literal accuracy is possible at all. The Old English *cyning*, for example, becomes *king* in Modern English and is always translated so, but what a male monarch meant to the Anglo-Saxons is necessarily different from our notions, which have been colored by later developments such as primogeniture, the divine right of succession, charismatic kingship, constitutional monarchies, and the like. In this case the superficial resemblance between *cyning* and *king* masks a semantic change over the centuries. Such subtle, perhaps imperceptible differences add up in a work of any length. This critical commonplace thus spreads the act of interpretation from a local effect to a universal condition, even in those places where translation seems most mechanical, because the literal meaning is always chimerical.

Without taking up the merits of the critical commonplace, this

† Reprinted with revisions by permission of the author; published in *Harvard Review*. Line and page references have been adjusted to refer to this Norton Critical Edition.

essay questions the mechanical/creative dualism from an opposite direction. Instead of dissolving the philological pole, it provisionally accepts the possibility of literal accuracy and asks whether "faithfulness" can be as innovative as the most radical reinterpretation. Heaney circles around the same idea in a poem from his 1975 collection *North*, in which he teases out traditional connotations of an Old English kenning for the human body, a compound literally meaning "bone-house":

> In the coffered
> riches of grammar
> and declensions
> I found *bān-hūs*,
>
> its fire, benches,
> wattle and rafters,
> where the soul
> fluttered a while
> in the roofspace. ("Bone Dreams")

The word's meaning is something to be "found" in philology, and while the sense of distance between then and now prompts the search, it does not open a gap of despair. The search extends beyond the coffers of grammars and glossaries to the airier halls of culture if one follows the allusion of the fluttering soul to its source, the Anglo-Saxon historian Bede (d. 735). The second book of his *History of the English Church and People* tells how Edwin, king of Northumbria about a century before Bede, was deliberating whether to accept Christianity. He turns to his advisors for their opinion. One of them compares human life to "the swift flight of a single sparrow through the banquetting-hall where you are sitting at dinner on a winter's day with your thanes and counsellors. In the midst there is a comforting fire to warm the hall; outside, the storms of winter rain or snow are raging. This sparrow flies swiftly in through one door of the hall, and out through another."[1] He goes on to compare the bird's brief interval inside the hall to their old religion's conception of human existence: Christianity promises something better than a winter storm when the bird flies out.

Heaney turns the moral of Bede's metaphor from religion to language. The "soul" of a living culture animates *bān-hūs* with meaning for only a short interval before it passes into the oblivion of time. Death hovers in the not-too-distant background: the coffer could turn at any moment from a treasure chest into a coffin holding the lifeless "bone-house," and winter's darkness threatens just outside

1. *A History of the English Church and People*, trans. Leo Sherley-Price, rev. R. E. Latham (Harmondsworth: Penguin, 1968) 127.

the wattle walls. Yet to make poetry about the word's transience is in a way to reverse the process, to breathe life back into the body of language. Heaney's lines gesture toward a model of translation that is optimistic even if it is precarious. It says that literal accuracy does not arrive by a mechanical process but through the translator's imaginative engagement with tradition. "Faithfulness" is capacious enough to include the interpretive moments that every translation demands. Philology and poetry in this case inform one another.

What applies in a local way for *bān-hūs* applies *in extenso* for Heaney's translation of *Beowulf*, where the length and complexity of the poem help generate its own cultural context. His "Introduction" speaks of the poem's "mythic potency" in terms of a movement similar to Bede's sparrow. "Like Shield Sheafson," the eponymous founder of a line of kings who arrived as a foundling washed up on Denmark's shores aboard an abandoned ship, *Beowulf* "arrives from somewhere beyond the known bourne of our experience, and having fulfilled its purpose (again like Shield), it passes once more into the beyond."[2] Two funeral scenes frame the plot of the poem; it ends with Beowulf's, of course, but Shield's magnificent burial dominates the first fifty lines. After his death the Danes pile treasures onto his funeral ship and push him back into the sea:

> They decked his body no less bountifully
> with offerings than those first ones did
> who cast him away when he was a child
> and launched him alone out over the waves. (lines 43–46)

Shield earns such a lavish send-off because of his spectacular success as king, but the "life cycle" of his mysterious arrival, later triumphs, and mysterious departure sets a model for the poem itself. *Beowulf* comes to us from an unknown author, written in an unfamiliar language from an uncertain date. Like Shield's career or the sparrow's flight through the hall, the poem makes its mark on the reader in the interval between its mysterious arrival and departure.

Heaney makes an oblique allusion to Shield's funeral ship in "The Settle Bed," from his 1991 collection *Seeing Things*. It would call to mind an Anglo-Saxon clinker-built ship even if Heaney did not tip us off by including lines from it as an epigraph to his introduction to *Beowulf*:

> And now this is "an inheritance"—
> Upright, rudimentary, unshiftably planked
> In the long ago, yet willable forward
>
> Again and again and again.[3]

2. "Translator's Introduction," p. xxv, above.
3. *Seeing Things* (New York: Farrar, Straus and Giroux, 1991) 50–51; reprinted with small changes in *Opened Ground* (New York: Farrar, Straus and Giroux, 1998) 321.

The settle bed arrives as an unlooked for bequest: clumsy and heavy and bearing a history that can be heard in the "old sombre tide awash in the headboard." It is handed over to a new owner, becomes " 'an inheritance,' " and finally is willed away in a cycle that repeats itself "again and again and again." But what matters more than its four-square presence is the lesson that "whatever is given / Can always be reimagined." It is reimagined not "cargoed with / its own dumb, tongue-and-groove worthiness / And un-get-roundable weight," but as "unkindled boards of a funeral ship" carrying Shield Sheafson piled over with gold. Or the bed/ship can be reimagined as a metaphor for the poem *Beowulf*, as Heaney's epigraph suggests, or more generally as any vehicle for the poet embarking on another exercise of *translatio*.

The vocabulary of "The Settle Bed" gives another hint that *Beowulf*'s Old English is part of the imaginative structure of the poem. The first tercet alone has five compound words, four of which are invented for the occasion: "Trunk-hasped," "cart-heavy," "pew-strait," and "bin-deep." They are hammer-blows of metaphors, announcing the categories "domestic," "rural," "religious," and "mercantile" almost with the force of allegorical figures assigned to the bed's four corners. The English language has always augmented its lexicon by generating compounds, although the preferred way to do so since the later Middle Ages has been through borrowing. But in lines such as these, Heaney's inventiveness rivals that of Gerard Manley Hopkins and the *Beowulf* poet, the most prolific compounder of all. Responding to the interpretive engagement that compounds demand, readers expand elements like "bin" and "deep" into an image of, say, an ample bin holding flour or nuts or nails in a shop. "Pew-strait," for example, calls to mind the upright wooden back of the pew (where "strait" meets "straight") as well as the narrowness of religious doctrine, so its meaning hovers between carpentry and catechism even though it appears within a catalogue of physical features. The inferred meaning of such compounds can be slippery because the relation between the elements is not always self-evident. From their constituent parts "firewall" and "fireplace" might seem to be similar in meaning, yet one stops a fire and the other allows it to burn. When explaining a compound we instinctively expand it into a phrase or a clause ("a wall designed to stop the spread of fire in a building"), but "pew-strait" is not so easy. Does it mean that the settle bed's headboard is "straight and confining like a pew" and therefore physically uncomfortable when one sits against it? Or is "pew" a metonym for "religion" so that the compound means "doctrinally narrow," thus more a commentary on the previous owners than the physical features? Few readers of "The Settle Bed" are likely to tease out the various possibilities for "pew-strait" because we are used to the interplay within compounds, and the context does not force a choice between the physical and the doctrinal. "Pew-strait" is in some essential way both.

"The Settle Bed" is by no means Heaney's only effort to exploit the vivid parallels, syntactic openness, and strong rhythm of compounds. He uses them in many other poems, even those inspired by Greek hexameters, for example: "That killing-fest, the life-warp and world-wrong / It brought to pass."[4] He admires their use by poets like Hopkins, Shakespeare, and Philip Larkin.[5] So when he turns to *Beowulf*, part of the translator's philological "faithfulness" shows itself through an inventiveness. Some passages restrict themselves to compounds already found in the English lexicon, as for example in the scene when Grendel attacks Beowulf in the hall:

he was bearing in
with open claw when the alert hero's
comeback and armlock forestalled him utterly. (lines 746–48)

Some, like "hall-thane" and "neck-torque," are calques from Old English compounds. Just as often, though, newly minted creations glint here and there in the lines. An aging Swedish king dies when his "feud-calloused hand / could not stave off the fatal stroke." An arrow is "feather-fledged." Grendel is a "guilt-steeped, God-cursed fiend." The dragon coils its "snake-folds." Other compounds that may seem to be nonce inventions in *Beowulf* have been used by Heaney in earlier poems. Beowulf comes "first-footing" early in the morning, but so does "Servant Boy" in *Wintering Out* (1972). The dragon emerges from his home "underearth," but "the shut-eyed blank of underearth" also threatens St. Kevin in *The Spirit Level* (1996).[6]

Just as he reimagines the settle bed as a funeral ship, Heaney reanimates the *Beowulf*-poet's skillful use of compounds. Their potential as poetic devices has always been present in English literature, although the *Beowulf* poet had at his command a wealth of traditional poetic elements to combine. The example of *bān-hūs* is illustrative again. One of the two times it appears in *Beowulf* is near the end of the poem, when the Geats have lit Beowulf's funeral pyre. The fire swells, hot to its core, *oð þæt hē ðā bān-hūs gebrocen hæfde.*[7] Heaney translates, "and flames wrought havoc in the hot bone-house." To liken Beowulf's body to a house consumed by

4. "The Watchman's War" from "Mycenae Lookout," quoted from *Opened Ground*, p. 387.
5. See, for example, "Englands of the Mind," in *Preoccupations: Selected Prose 1968–1978* (New York: Farrar, Straus and Giroux, 1980) 166.
6. "Servant Boy," *Opened Ground*, p. 48, and "St. Kevin and the Blackbird," *The Spirit Level* (London: Faber and Faber, 1996) 20–21.
7. Bruce Mitchell and Fred C. Robinson, ed., *Beowulf: An Edition with Relevant Shorter Texts* (Oxford: Blackwell, 1998), line 3147. All Old English quotations come from this edition.

flames is more than a passing metaphoric touch. Earlier the poem alludes to the fate of the Dane's great hall Heorot, which was destined to burn to the ground as a result of the treachery of King Hrothgar's nephew. Just as Heaney reimagines the wooden "benches / wattle and rafters" of *bān-hūs*, the metaphor of a house consumed by fire links the disastrous events suffered by the Danes and the Geats: both the burning of Heorot and the death of Beowulf contribute to a deeper theme concerning the limits of heroic action which dominates the end of the poem. However formidable the hero, however magnificent the hall, the depredations of time and human weakness will bring them down. To aspire to the *Beowulf*-poet's allusiveness in compounding becomes another measure of the translator's philological faithfulness, whether in preserving the elements *bān-hūs* or in forging analogous compounds.

The simple placement of elements side by side in compounds like *bān-hūs* is mirrored in larger syntactic structures using parallel phrases and clauses. The half-line structure of the verse seems to have encouraged a mode of expression where ideas are repeated incrementally. Sometimes the effect is simply cumulative; at other times the repetition allows shifting perspectives to examine the same idea. For example, at the crucial moment in Beowulf's fight with Grendel's mother, when his sword has failed him and he despairs for his life, he spots a weapon that may help him:

Geseah ðā on searwum sigeēadig bil
ealdsweord eotenisc ecgum þȳhtig
wigena weorðmynd. (lines 1557–59)

A literal translation: "Then he saw among the war-gear a victory-blessed sword, an ancient sword made by giants, strong in its edges, of warriors the glory." The three phrases for "sword" do not exactly repeat one another: one hints that it will bring Beowulf success, the second is more than a comment on its enormous size because giants were thought to have superior metalworking skills, and the third draws a correlation between splendid arms and the worthiness of the warrior. The most searching discussion of such constructions is Fred C. Robinson's *Beowulf and the Appositive Style*, which demonstrates how apposition informs much of the poem's theme and structure. Despite the apparent simplicity of the "proximate and parallel status" of the elements in apposition, the rhetorical effect can become complex.[8] The three epithets for sword, for example, have the same referent within a sentence and are not linked syntactically by a function word such as a conjunction. Such appositive constructions are not only ubiquitous in Old English poetry, they are its defining rhetorical

8. Fred C. Robinson, *Beowulf and the Appositive Style* (Knoxville: U of Tennessee P, 1985) 3.

trope, much like the long-tailed simile in classical epic. But more to the point they demand inferential judgment on the part of the reader to make connections, and at times those connections are more various than conjunctions alone can indicate.

Translating appositive constructions can be especially challenging, because Modern English prefers the disambiguating touches of grammatical function words and punctuation. A passage like that describing the gigantic sword, for example, might make use of separate clauses in Modern English; e.g., ". . . the victory blessed sword, which was the ancient work of giants . . ." Adding to the difficulty of translation is the common practice of scattering the opposed elements about the sentence rather than lining them up one after the other as in the "sword" passage. The sentence just before it (lines 1550–56) has five separate elements of apposition, including a triplet for God (as a nod to the doctrine of the Trinity). Such constructions are no longer idiomatic in Modern English. The closest parallels are simple catalogs, as (famously) in Shakespeare's sonnet,

> Th' expense of spirit in a waste of shame
> Is lust in action; and till action, lust
> Is perjured, murd'rous, bloody, full of blame,
> Savage, extreme, rude, cruel, not to trust . . .

And so on.[9] The catalog is also a favorite device of Heaney, and it shares some of the "parallel and proximate" qualities of *Beowulfian* apposition. In "The Pitchfork," for example, an entire stanza sacrifices syntax for a list:

> Riveted steel, turned timber, burnish, grain,
> Smoothness, straightness, roundness, length and sheen.
> Sweat-cured, sharpened, balanced, tested, fitted.
> The springiness, the clip and dart of it.[1]

What could give a better description than the accumulation of modifiers flowing together without the help of syntax? In other instances the bare juxtaposition of words can deliver a sudden shock. In "The Strand at Lough Beg," some spent shotgun shells discovered on the ground are "Acrid, brassy, genital, ejected." The cumulative effect has less to do with description than evoking the feeling of revulsion at the moment of discovery—almost a sense of violation. The effect of apposition is completely different a few lines later in "The Strand at Lough Beg," in a passage introducing some of Heaney's relatives on his father's side, who (he reveals in his "Introduction") supplied him with the imaginative voice for his translation of *Beowulf*:

9. Sonnet 129; quoted from Helen Vendler, *The Art of Shakespeare's Sonnets* (Cambridge, Mass: Harvard UP, 1997) 549.
1. *Opened Ground*, p. 320.

Big-voiced scullions, herders, feelers round
Haycocks and hindquarters, talkers in byres,
Slow arbitrators of the burial ground.[2]

In their formal and slightly old-fashioned way, these epithets come closest to *Beowulfian* apposition. It is intriguing to think that *Beowulf* may have supplied the appositive syntax of these lines years before Heaney returned to the Scullions to find a language for his translation which could be "speakable by one of those relatives." In any case Heaney's parallel phrases in these lines finds a point of congruence with Old English syntax.

When translators of *Beowulf* do not retain appositive constructions, they usually smooth out the idiom by incorporating them into separate clauses or merging some together. Grendel, for example, is introduced into the narrative with the apposed epithets *grimma gǣst* (grim creature) and *mǣre mearcstapa* (notorious border-prowler), who held *mōras . . . fen ond fæsten* (the moors, fen and fastness). Heaney's translation removes the apposition by means of a participial phrase and a conjunction:

Grendel was the name of this grim demon
haunting the marches, marauding round the heath
and the desolate fens; . . . (lines 102–104)

In at least one case, however, Heaney makes a passage more appositive than the Old English:

Afterwards a boy-child was born to Shield,
a cub in the yard, a comfort sent
by God to that nation. (lines 12–14)

Here "boy-child," "cub," and "comfort" are parallel nominals, where in the Old English they are part of different constructions:

Ðǣm eafera wæs æfter cenned
geong in geardum þone god sende
folce tō frōfre. (lines 12–14)

The Old English *geong* ("young") can be taken as a modifier for *eafera* ("son") rather than as a substantive like "cub." A literal translation preserving the word order of Old English would be: "To that one [Shield] a son was later born young in the yards whom God sent to the people as a comfort." The strong impression throughout the poem, however, is that Heaney preserves the rich layering of apposition in the poem without doing violence to his idiom. And as Robinson convincingly points out, apposition extends beyond the sentence boundary to characterization, episodes, and even theology.

2. From *Field Work* (1979); quoted from *Opened Ground*, p. 145; "Introduction," p. xxxvi, above.

For example, just after introducing Hygd, the queen of the Geats, the poem plunges into the story of Thryth, a queen who was famous for her vicious retribution. The implicit lesson is that Hygd is unlike Thryth, although there is no narrative instruction to that effect.

Even images can be apposed. Near the end of the poem, for example, after Beowulf has ruled the Geats for fifty years, he decides to seek out the dragon that has decimated his land. With the help of the warrior Wiglaf, he manages to kill the dragon, but not before it sinks its poisonous fangs into his neck. As Beowulf lies with his life ebbing away, he asks to examine some of the treasure from the dragon's hoard, which he receives with a prayer of thanks. Witnessing the moment of death a short while later brings unbearable anguish for Wiglaf:

> It was hard then on the young hero,
> having to watch the one he held so dear
> there on the ground, going through
> his death agony. The dragon from underearth,
> his nightmarish destroyer, lay destroyed as well,
> utterly without life. No longer would his snakefolds
> ply themselves to guard gold in the hoard:
> Hard-edged blades hammered out
> and keenly filed, had finished him
> so that the sky-roamer lay there rigid,
> brought low beside the treasure-lodge. (lines 2821–31)

The dramatic intensity of the passage gains from its narrative restraint. It dwells less on Beowulf than on Wiglaf and the dragon. There is no maudlin wailing, no memorable expostulation from Wiglaf: just a king quietly dying beside his distraught follower. A narrative technique that the poet employs to great effect here and throughout *Beowulf* is to reveal a character's emotional response before describing the event that provokes it. Learning of Wiglaf's anguish creates a moment of suspense that makes the revelation of its cause—Beowulf's death agonies—all the more poignant.

In the fourth line a sentence break shifts the focus from Beowulf's "death agony" to the "dragon," where alliteration on the *d*-sound and the repeated syllables of *agon* link the two adversaries across a sentence boundary: on one side a virtuous king who defends his people; on the other, a monstrous creature determined to destroy them. The aural link goes even deeper because the repeating syllables *agon* call to mind Heaney's observation that the plot of *Beowulf* is structured around the three great agons in the hero's life.[3]

Even though the juxtaposition of the hero and dragon in death seems straightforward, what it signifies raises questions: is good fated

3. "Introduction," pp. xxv, xxvii, above.

to succumb to evil in the end? Is the dragon morally equivalent to the hero? Is Beowulf's life too high a price for the Geats to pay? Which is more ruinous: the monster alive or the hero dead? It is not just the posture of death that unites them, but the treasure as well. Here again there is no definitive guidance from the poem: is the treasure a good thing or not? To whom does it belong? We learn later that the treasure will be buried with Beowulf "as useless to men now as it ever was" (line 3168). Yet earlier the sight of it cheers the dying Beowulf because he sees it buying security for the Geats when he is no longer there to protect them (lines 2794–98).

The technique of juxtaposing references to the dragon and hero without giving interpretive clues is part of a pervasive narrative technique in *Beowulf*. In this case the syntax drives the visual impact of the scene: Beowulf and the dragon side by side in death. Interpretive judgments are not entirely absent—Beowulf is "dear" and the dragon is a "nightmarish destroyer"—but another writer in another century might offer a more specific evaluation about their relative worth. Heaney finds an affinity in the deftness of *Beowulf*'s appositive style, which opens up rich possibilities by leaving a great deal of the interpretive work up to the reader.

But in a way Heaney's instinct for apposition is hardly surprising. It is as much Heaney's "voice-right" as Hibernicisms like "kesh" and English archaisms like "thole."[4] It is as familiar as the alliteration, stressed lines, and compounding in his verse, because it is as familiar as T. S. Eliot's *Wasteland*, Yeats's hollow moon in "Adam's Curse," and Wallace Stevens's jar in Tennessee. Apposition is as much a master trope of twentieth-century poetry as it is of Old English. Heaney's "Flight Path" from *The Spirit Level* (1996), for example, combines chronology and travel as its organizing principle, but its immediate structure consists of six numbered segments with no overt indication about their relation to one another. Among other things, the use of apposition allows the poem to explore the volatile subject of Heaney's political affiliations in Northern Ireland. The fourth part begins with language that withholds personal judgment in the most familiar official jargon:

> The following for the record, in the light
> Of everything before and since:
> One bright May morning . . .

From this apparently neutral beginning, it slips into the language of the innocence and exhilaration of home-coming. But it is shattered by a blunt-spoken sectarian who finds him on the train back to Belfast:

4. "Introduction," pp. xxxiii–xxxv, above.

So he enters and sits down
Opposite and goes for me head on.
"When, for fuck's sake, are you going to write
Something for us?"

The poem's immediate answer is equivocal; the deeper response waits for the next stanza, which apposes a haunting reference to the protest in Long Kesh and a quotation from Heaney's "Ugolino." Dante's journey through Inferno thus comments on Heaney's journey, but just how the apposed segments comment on one another is left up to the reader. Every part of "The Flight Path," not just the segments outlined here, requires the reader to make the kind of inferential judgments that *Beowulf* does.

There are even more such correspondences. "The Settle Bed," for example, has a series of modifiers—"unkindled," "unwilling," "unbeaten," "unshiftably," "un-get-roundable"—which work by negating an attribute so that the resulting image calls to mind the absence of something that might otherwise be present. It is hard to say what "unkindled" means except as something that is not ignited, but it cannot do so without suggesting fire in the first place. Such negative modifiers are, again, a favorite device of the *Beowulf* poet. When Grendel attacks Heorot at night, *lēoht unfǣger* or "unbeautiful light" shines from his eyes. Because a person's eyes and light itself are strongly associated with beauty, to deny it categorically makes the light from Grendel's eyes worse than ugly. When Wiglaf gazes on his dying king he is described as *unfrōd*—meaning both "un-aged" and "un-wise"—which makes a brief but telling comparison with Beowulf, who after fifty years as king has become *frōd*. It is probably pointless to ask whether the many levels of affinity between Heaney's poetic voice and *Beowulf* is the result of his study of Old English, or somehow gathered indirectly through other poets like Hopkins and W. H. Auden, or by a more anonymous transmission of prosodic devices that have survived the centuries. Most of what has been written about Heaney's translation of *Beowulf*, including his own essays, dwell on the foreignness of Old English, the labor of translation, the difficulty of finding the right voice or the right turn of phrase. But there is another dynamic at work. The many affinities already existing between his poetry and *Beowulf* enables Heaney to enter the old clinker-built ship as familiarly as an inherited settle bed, so that his interpretation is measured not merely by the changes imposed from the outside but also by shaping and reshaping the tradition from within.

Glossary of Personal Names

Many Old English names are compounds in which the meaning of each element would be obvious to native speakers. In the case of "Dæg-hrefn," for example, Heaney translates each part into "Day-raven," which gives an idea how the Anglo-Saxons would understand it. But the regular practice in this translation is to leave the Old English names in much the same form as they are in the original poem. The glossary given here does not translate the names either, but it divides the compounds into their component parts. For Beowulf's name, see pp. 98–100.

Hints for pronunciation: the letter combinations <ae> and <sc> are both illustrated in the name Aesc-here, pronounced "ASH-hair-eh." The pronunciation of <cg> as found in Ecg-laf is "EDGE-lahf." Initial <h> as in Hreth-ric is always pronounced, and final <c> has the value illustrated in "HRETH-rich." For every name the strongest accent falls on the first syllable, and final-*e* is never silent. For the finer points of pronunciation, consult any Old English grammar.

For names of the tribes and geographical regions, consult pp. 96–97.

Abel brother of Cain; for the story see Genesis 4.1–16 (pp. 84–85)
Aelf-here kinsman of Wiglaf
Aesc-here beloved advisor to Hrothgar
Beow an early Danish king, son of Shield
Beowulf son of Ecgtheow, later king of the Geats (see pp. 98–100)
Breca Bronding leader, competed with Beowulf in a swimming match
Cain brother of Abel, progenitor of Grendel and his mother
Day-raven a warrior killed by Beowulf in Hygelac's raid into Frisia
Ead-gils a Swedish prince, son of Ohthere, befriended by Beowulf
Ean-mund another son of Ohthere, killed by Weohstan
Ecg-laf a Dane, father of Unferth
Ecg-theow father of Beowulf
Ecg-wela an early, unknown Danish king
Eofor a Geat who killed the Swedish king Ongentheow
Eo-mer a son of Offa, king of the Angles
Eormen-ric king of the East Goths
Finn king of the Frisians, married to Hnaef's sister Hildeburh
Fitela nephew *and* son of Sigemund

Folc-wald father of Finn
Frea-waru daughter of Hrothgar
Gar-mund father of Offa
Grendel monstrous cannibal killed by Beowulf
Guth-laf a Danish warrior
Haereth father of Hygd
Haeth-cyn second son of the Geatish king Hrethel
Halga younger brother of the Danish king Hrothgar
Half-dane father of the Danish king Hrothgar
Heard-red son of King Hygelac, later king of the Geats
Heatho-laf a warrior of the Wulfing tribe
Hemming a relative of Offa and Eomer
Hengest the leader of the Danish party after Hnaef is killed by Finn's men
Heoro-gar older brother of Hrothgar, a Danish king
Heoro-weard son of Heorogar
Here-beald oldest son of the Geatish king Hrethel
Here-mod a king of the Danes
Hilde-burh wife of the Frisian king Finn, sister of the Dane Hnaef
Hnaef leader of the Danes visiting Finn, brother of Hildeburh
Hoc father of Hildeburh and Hnaef
Hond-scio one of Beowulf's companions, killed by Grendel
Hrethel king of the Geats, Hygelac's father, grandfather of Beowulf
Hreth-ric son of Hrothgar
Hroth-gar king of the Danes, husband of Wealhtheow
Hroth-mund son of Hrothgar
Hroth-ulf son of Halga, nephew of Hrothgar
Hrunting Unferth's sword
Hun-lafing a Danish warrior in Hengest's party
Hygd wife of Hygelac, daughter of Haereth
Hyge-lac king of the Geats, husband of Hygd, uncle of Beowulf
Ing a mythical ancestor of the Danes
In-geld a prince of the Heatho-Bards
Mod-thryth queen of the Angles, wife of Offa
Naegling Beowulf's sword
Offa king of the Angles, husband of Modthryth
Oht-here son of the Swedish king Ongentheow
Onela king of the Swedes, son of Ongentheow
Ongen-theow king of the Swedes
Os-laf a Danish warrior
Shield a legendary king, founder of the Danish royal family
Sige-mund a legendary Germanic hero
Swerting grandfather of Hygelac
Un-ferth a member of Hrothgar's court
Wael father of Sigemund
Wealh-theow queen of the Danes, wife of Hrothgar
Weland a mythical Germanic smith, famous for weapons
Weoh-stan father of Wiglaf, killer of Eanmund
Wig-laf a relative and follower of Beowulf

Wither-geld a Heatho-Bard warrior
Won-red a Geat, father of Wulf and Eofor
Wulf a Geatish warrior
Wulf-gar a Wendel chief attached to Hrothgar's court
Yrmen-laf a Dane, brother of Aeschere

Selected Bibliography

The items have been chosen primarily for students approaching *Beowulf* for the first time using Heaney's translation. The number of books and articles published on *Beowulf* is vast and growing, most of it presupposing a detailed knowledge of the Old English language, but the selection here privileges those studies that can be profitably used by non-specialists, and it includes reference works and general histories of pre-Conquest England. The bibliographies given below offer a comprehensive listing for those who wish to pursue further study. The last decade has seen the publication of a number of new editions of *Beowulf*, but because Old English must be learned as a foreign language, the best way to begin studying the poem in the original language is to enroll in an Old English course. A selection of writings by Seamus Heaney helps put his translation of *Beowulf* in the context of his career as a poet. For a recording of Heaney reading portions of his translation, go to www.wwnorton.com/college/titles/english/nce/beov

EDITIONS AND TRANSLATIONS

Alexander, Michael, ed. *Beowulf*. London: Penguin, 1995.

Chickering, Howell D., trans. and ed. *Beowulf: A Dual-Language Edition*. Garden City, N.Y.: Anchor Books, 1977.

Donaldson, E. Talbot, trans. *Beowulf*. Norton Critical Edition. Ed. Nicholas Howe. New York: Norton, 2001. [Donaldson/Howe]

Fry, Donald K., ed. *Finnesburg Fragment and Episode*. London: Methuen, 1974

Hall, John R. Clark, trans. *Beowulf and the Finnesburg Fragment: A Translation into Modern English Prose*. Ed. C. L. Wrenn. Rev. ed. London: Allen and Unwin: 1950.

Jack, George, ed. *Beowulf: A Student Edition*. Oxford: Oxford UP, 1994.

Kiernan, Kevin. *The Electronic Beowulf*. London: British Library, 1999.

Klaeber, Fr., ed. *Beowulf and the Fight at Finnsburg*. 3rd ed. Boston: Heath, 1950.

Liuzza, Roy Michael, trans. *Beowulf: A New Verse Translation*. Peterborough, Ont.: Broadview, 2000.

Mitchell, Bruce, and Fred C. Robinson, eds. *Beowulf: An Edition*. Oxford : Blackwell, 1998.

Tolkien, J. R. R., and Alan J. Bliss, eds. *Finn and Hengest: The Fragment and the Episode*. London: G. Allen & Unwin, 1982.

Wrenn, C. L., ed. *Beowulf with the Finnesburg Fragment*. 3rd ed. London: Harrap, 1973.

BIBLIOGRAPHIES

Annual bibliographies are compiled by two journals: *Anglo-Saxon England* and *The Old English Newsletter*.

Greenfield, Stanley B., and Fred C. Robinson. *A Bibliography of Publications on Old English Literature to the End of 1972*. Toronto: U of Toronto P, 1980.

Hasenfratz, Robert J. *Beowulf Scholarship: An Annotated Bibliography, 1979–1990*. New York: Garland, 1993. (Supplements Short's bibliography)

Short, Douglas D. *Beowulf Scholarship: An Annotated Bibliography*. New York: Garland, 1980. (Supplemented by Hasenfratz up to 1990)

REFERENCE WORKS, GRAMMARS

Cassidy, Frederic G., and Richard N. Ringler. *Bright's Old English Grammar and Reader*. 3rd ed. Forth Worth, TX: Harcourt Brace Jovanovich, 1971.

Dolan, Terence Patrick. *A Dictionary of Hiberno-English*. Dublin: Gill & Macmillan, 1998.

Garmonsway, G. N., Jacqueline Simpson, and H. E. Davidson, eds. *Beowulf and Its Analogues*. London: Dent, 1980.

Hall, J. R. Clark, and Herbert Dean Meritt. *A Concise Anglo-Saxon Dictionary*. 4th ed. Toronto: U of Toronto P in association with the Medieval Academy of America, 1984.

Hill, David. *An Atlas of Anglo-Saxon England*. Toronto: U of Toronto P, 1981.

Lapidge, Michael; with John Blair, Simon Keynes, and Donald Scragg. *The Blackwell Encyclopedia of Anglo-Saxon England*. Oxford: Blackwell, 1999.

Mitchell, Bruce. *An Invitation to Old English and Anglo-Saxon England*. Oxford: Blackwell, 1995.

Mitchell, Bruce, and Fred C. Robinson. *A Guide to Old English*. 5th ed. Oxford: Blackwell, 1982.

Quirk, Randolph, C. L. Wrenn, and Susan E. Deskis. *An Old English Grammar*. DeKalb: Northern Illinois UP, 1994.

Strayer, Joseph R., et al. *Dictionary of the Middle Ages*. New York: Scribner, 1982.

Szarmach, Paul E., M. Teresa Tavormina, and Joel Thomas Rosenthal, eds. *Medieval England: An Encyclopedia*. Garland Reference Library of the Humanities. New York: Garland, 1998.

Whitelock, Dorothy, ed. *English Historical Documents. Vol 1. C.500–1042*. 2nd ed. London: Routledge, 1979.

COLLECTIONS OF CRITICAL ESSAYS

Baker, Peter S., ed. *Beowulf: Basic Readings*. New York: Garland, 1995. [Baker, *Basic Readings*]

Benson, Larry Dean, Theodore M. Andersson, and Stephen A. Barney. *Contradictions: from Beowulf to Chaucer: Selected Studies of Larry D. Benson*. Aldershot, Hants., England: Scolar Press, 1995. [Benson, *Contradictions*]

Bessinger, Jess B., and Robert F. Yeager. *Approaches to Teaching Beowulf*. Approaches to Teaching Masterpieces of World Literature. New York: Modern Language Association of America, 1984.

Bjork, Robert E., and John D. Niles, eds. *A Beowulf Handbook*. Lincoln: U of Nebraska P, 1997.

Bloom, Harold, ed. *Beowulf*. Modern Critical Interpretations. New York: Chelsea House, 1987. [Bloom]

Chase, Colin, ed. *The Dating of Beowulf*. Repr. with a new Afterword. Toronto: U of Toronto P, 1997. [Chase, *Dating*]

Creed, Robert Payson, ed. *Old English Poetry: Fifteen Essays*. Providence: Brown UP, 1967. [Creed, *Fifteen Essays*]

Damico, Helen, and Alexandra Hennessey Olsen, eds. *New Readings on Women in Old English Literature*. Bloomington: Indiana UP, 1990. [Damico/Olsen]

Damico, Helen, and John Leyerle, eds. *Heroic Poetry in the Anglo-Saxon Period. Studies in Honor of Jess B. Bessinger, Jr.* Kalamazoo: Medieval Institute Publications, 1993. [Damico/Leyerle]

Fry, Donald K., ed. *The Beowulf Poet: A Collection of Critical Essays*. Twentieth Century Views. Englewood Cliffs, NJ: Prentice-Hall, 1968. [Fry, *Collection*]

Fulk, R. D., ed. *Interpretations of Beowulf: A Critical Anthology*. Bloomington: Indiana UP, 1991. [Fulk, *Interpretations*]

Godden, Malcolm, and Michael Lapidge, eds. *The Cambridge Companion to Old English Literature*. Cambridge: Cambridge UP, 1991. [Godden, *Companion*]

Nicholson, Lewis E., ed. *An Anthology of Beowulf Criticism*. Notre Dame: U of Notre Dame P, 1963. [Nicholson, *Anthology*]

Robinson, Fred C. *The Tomb of Beowulf and Other Essays on Old English*. Oxford: Blackwell, 1993. [Robinson, *Tomb*]

Shippey, T. A., and Andreas Haarder, eds. *Beowulf: The Critical Heritage*. London: Routledge, 1998. (A collection of early studies, many translated into English from the original language of publication)

Thompson, Stephen P., ed. *Readings on Beowulf*. San Diego: Greenhaven Press, 1998.

CRITICAL STUDIES

Studies reprinted in one of the collections listed above are cross-referenced, with the exception of those appearing in this volume.
• indicates works included or excerpted in this volume.

Andersson, Theodore M. "Tradition and Design in *Beowulf.*" *Old English Literature in Context: Ten Essays*. Ed. John. D. Niles. Cambridge: Brewer, 1980. 90–106. Rep. in Fulk, *Interpretations*.

Bartlett, Adeline Courtney. *The Larger Rhetorical Patterns in Anglo-Saxon Poetry*. New York: Columbia UP, 1935.

Bennett, Helen. "The Female Mourner at Beowulf's Funeral: Filling in the Blanks/Hearing the Spaces." *Exemplaria: A Journal of Theory in Medieval and Renaissance Studies* 4 (1992): 35–50. Rep. in Donaldson/Howe.

Benson, Larry D. "The Literary Character of Anglo-Saxon Formulaic Poetry." *PMLA* 81 (1966): 334–41. Rep. in Benson, *Contradictions*.

———. "The Pagan Coloring of *Beowulf.*" *Old English Poetry: Fifteen Essays*. Ed. Robert P. Creed. Providence: Brown UP, 1967. 193–213. Rep. in Baker, *Basic Readings*; Benson, *Contradictions*.

———. "The Originality of *Beowulf.*" *The Interpretation of Narrative: Theory and Practice*. Ed. Morton W. Bloomfield. Cambridge, MA: Harvard UP, 1970. 1–43. Rep. in Benson, *Contradictions*.

Bjork, Robert E. "Speech as Gift in *Beowulf.*" *Speculum* 69 (1994): 993–1022.

Bliss, A. J. "The Appreciation of Old English Metre." *English and Medieval Studies Presented to J. R. R. Tolkien*. Ed. Norman Davis and C. L. Wrenn. London: Allen & Unwin, 1962. 27–40.

Bonjour, Adrien. *The Digressions in Beowulf*. Oxford: Blackwell, 1950.

Brodeur, Arthur Gilchrist. *The Art of Beowulf*. Berkeley: U of California P, 1959. Ch. 2 rep. in Fulk, *Interpretations*.

Bullough, Donald A. " 'What Has Ingeld To Do with Lindisfarne?' " *Anglo-Saxon England* 22 (1993): 93–125.

Cable, Thomas. *The English Alliterative Tradition*. Middle Ages Series. Philadelphia: U of Pennsylvania P, 1991.

Campbell, Alistair. "The Old English Epic Style." *English and Medieval Studies Presented to J. R. R. Tolkien*. Ed. Norman Davis and C. L. Wrenn. London: Allen & Unwin, 1962. 13–26.

Campbell, James, gen. ed. *The Anglo-Saxons*. London: Penguin, 1991. (General history)

Carver, M. O. H. "Ideology and Allegiance in East Anglia." *Sutton Hoo: Fifty Years After*. Ed. Robert T. Farrell and Carol Neumann de Vegvar. Kalamazoo: Medieval Institute Publications, 1992. 173–82.

Chambers, R. W. *Beowulf: An Introduction to the Study of the Poem with a Discussion of the Stories of Offa and Finn*. 3rd ed. Cambridge: Cambridge UP, 1959.

Chance, Jane. *Woman as Hero in Old English Literature*. Syracuse: Syracuse UP, 1986. Ch. 7 rep. in Fulk, *Interpretations*.

• ———. "The Structural Unity of *Beowulf*: The Problem of Grendel's Mother." *Texas Studies in Literature and Language* 22 (1980): 287–303.

Clark, George. *Beowulf*. Twayne's English Authors Series. Boston: Twayne, 1990.

Clover, Carol J. "The Germanic Context of the Unferth Episode." *Speculum* 55 (1980): 444–68. Rep. in Baker, *Basic Readings*.

———. "Regardless of Sex: Men, Women, and Power in Early Northern Europe." *Speculum* 68 (1993): 363–87.

Cramp, Rosemary J. "*Beowulf* and Archaeology." *Medieval Archaeology* 1 (1957): 57–77. Rep. in Fry, *Collection*.

———. "The Hall in *Beowulf* and in Archaeology." Damico/Leyerle. 331–46.

Damico, Helen. *Beowulf's Wealhtheow and the Valkyrie Tradition*. Madison: U of Wisconsin P, 1984.

Davis, Craig R. "Cultural Assimilation in the Anglo-Saxon Royal Genealogies." *Anglo-Saxon England* 21 (1992): 23–39.

———. *Beowulf and the Demise of Germanic Legend in England*. New York: Garland, 1996.

Deskis, Susan E. *Beowulf and the Medieval Proverb Tradition*. Tempe: Arizona State University, 1996.

Dockray-Miller, Mary. *Motherhood and Mothering in Anglo-Saxon England*. New York: St. Martin's, 2000.

Donahue, Charles. "*Beowulf*, Ireland and the Natural Good." *Traditio* 7 (1949–51): 263–77.

———. "Grendel and the Clanna Cain." *Journal of Celtic Studies* 1 (1950): 167–75.

———. "*Beowulf* and Christian Tradition: A Reconsideration from a Celtic Stance." *Traditio* 21 (1965): 55–116.

• Donoghue, Daniel. "The Philologer Poet: Seamus Heaney and the Translation of *Beowulf*." *Harvard Review* 19 (2000): 12–21.

Dumville, David N. "Kingship, Genealogies and Regnal Lists." *Early Medieval Kingship*. Ed. P. H. Sawyer and I. N. Wood. Leeds: Leeds UP, 1977. 72–104.

Earl, James Whitby. *Thinking about Beowulf*. Stanford: Stanford UP, 1994.

Eliason, Norman E. "The Burning of Heorot." *Speculum* 55 (1980): 75–83.

Fell, Christine. *Women in Anglo-Saxon England*. Oxford: Blackwell, 1984.

Foley, John Miles. *Traditional Oral Epic: The Odyssey, Beowulf, and the Serbo-Croatian Return Song*. Berkeley: U of California P, 1990.

Frank, Roberta. "Skaldic Verse and the Date of *Beowulf*." Chase, *Dating*. 123–39. Rep. in Baker, *Basic Readings*.

• ———. "The *Beowulf* Poet's Sense of History." *The Wisdom of Poetry: Essays in Early English Literature in Honor of Morton W. Bloomfield*. Ed. Larry Dean Benson and Siegfried Wenzel. Kalamazoo: Medieval Institute Publications, 1982. 53–65. Rep. in Bloom, Donaldson/Howe.

———. "*Beowulf* and Sutton Hoo: The Odd Couple." *Voyage to the Other World: The Legacy of Sutton Hoo*. Ed. Calvin B. Kendall and Peter S. Wells. Minneapolis: U of Minnesota P, 1992. 47–64.

Frantzen, Allen J. *Desire for Origins: New Language, Old English, and Teaching the Tradition*. New Brunswick: Rutgers UP, 1990.

Fulk, R. D. "Unferth and His Name." *Modern Philology* 85 (1987): 113–27.

———. *A History of Old English Meter*. Middle Ages Series. Philadelphia: U of Pennsylvania P, 1992.

Gahrn, Lars. "The Geatas of *Beowulf*." *Scandinavian Journal of History* 11 (1986): 95–113.

Galloway, Andrew. "*Beowulf* and the Varieties of Choice." *PMLA* 105 (1990): 197–208.

Georgianna, Linda. "King Hrethel's Sorrow and the Limits of Heroic Action in *Beowulf*." *Speculum* 62 (1987): 829–50.

Goldsmith, Margaret E. "The Christian Perspective in *Beowulf*." *Comparative Literature* 14 (1962): 71–90. Rep. in Fulk, *Interpretations*; Nicholson, *Anthology*.

Greenfield, Stanley B. "The Authenticating Voice in *Beowulf*." *Anglo Saxon England* 5 (1976): 51–62. Rep. in *Basic Readings*.

———. "Beowulf and the Judgement of the Righteous." *Learning and Literature in Anglo-Saxon England: Studies Presented to Peter Clemoes on the Occasion of His Sixty-Fifth Birthday*. Ed. Michael Lapidge and Helmut Gneuss. Cambridge: Cambridge UP, 1985. Rep. in *Hero and Exile: The Art of Old English Poetry*. Ed. George H. Brown. London: Hambledon, 1989.

———. "Grendel's Approach to Heorot: Syntax and Poetry." Creed, *Fifteen Essays*. 275–84.

———, Daniel G. Calder, and Michael Lapidge. *A New Critical History of Old English Literature*. New York: New York UP, 1986.

Grimm, Jacob. *Deutsche Mythologie*. 3 vols. 4th ed. Rep. Frankfurt/Main: Keip, 1985. (1st ed. 1835)

Harris, Joseph. "*Beowulf* in Literary History." *Pacific Coast Philology* 17 (1982): 16–23. Rep. in Fulk, *Interpretations*.

———. "Beowulf's Last Words." *Speculum* 67 (1992): 1–32.

———. "A Nativist Approach to *Beowulf*: The Case of Germanic Elegy." *Companion to Old English Poetry*. Ed. Henk Aertsen and Rolf H. Bremmer Jr. Amsterdam: VU UP, 1994. 45–62.

Hill, Joyce M. " 'Þæt Wæs Geomuru Ides!': A Female Stereotype Examined." Damico/Olsen. 235–47. Rep. in Donaldson/Howe.

Hill, John M. *The Cultural World in Beowulf*. Anthropological Horizons. Toronto: U of Toronto P, 1995.

• Hill, Thomas D. "The Christian Language and Theme of *Beowulf*." *Companion to Old English Poetry*. Ed. Henk Aertsen and Rolf H. Bremmer, Jr. Amsterdam: VU UP, 1994. 63–77.

Howe, Nicholas. "The Afterlife of Anglo-Saxon Poetry: Auden, Hill and Gunn." *Words and Works: Studies in Medieval English Language and Literature in Honour of Fred C. Robinson*. Ed. Nicholas Howe and Peter S. Baker. Toronto: U of Toronto P, 1997.

———. "The Uses of Uncertainty: On the Dating of *Beowulf*." Chase, *Dating*. 213–20. (An Afterword to the 1997 rep. vol.) Rep. in Donaldson/Howe.

Irving, Edward B., Jr. *A Reading of Beowulf*. New Haven: Yale UP, 1968. Ch. 1 rep. in Fulk, *Interpretations*.

———. *Rereading Beowulf*. Middle Ages Series. Philadelphia: U of Pennsylvania P, 1989.

Jager, Eric. "Speech and the Chest in Old English Poetry: Orality or Pectorality?" *Speculum* 65 (1990): 845–59.

Kaske, Robert E. "*Sapientia et Fortitudo* as the Controlling Theme of *Beowulf*." *Studies in Philology* 55 (1958): 423–56. Rep. in Nicholson, *Anthology*.

Kendall, Calvin B., and Peter S. Wells. *Voyage to the Other World: The Legacy of Sutton Hoo*. Medieval Studies at Minnesota. Minneapolis: U of Minnesota P, 1992.

Ker, W. P. *Epic and Romance: Essays on Medieval Literature*. New York: Dover, 1897.

Kiernan, Kevin S. *Beowulf and the Beowulf Manuscript*. New Brunswick: Rutgers UP, 1981.

Lapidge, Michael. "*Beowulf* and the Psychology of Terror." In Damico/Leyerle. 373–402. Rep. in Donaldson/Howe.

Lee, Alvin A. *The Guest-Hall of Eden: Four Essays on the Design of Old English Poetry*. New Haven: Yale UP, 1972.

Lerer, Seth. "Grendel's Glove." *ELH* 61 (1994): 721–51.

———. *Literacy and Power in Anglo-Saxon Literature*. Lincoln: U of Nebraska P, 1991.

• Leyerle, John. "The Interlace Structure of *Beowulf*." *University of Toronto Quarterly* 37 (1967): 1–17.

Lionarons, Joyce Tally. "*Beowulf*: Myth and Monsters." *English Studies* 77 (1996): 1–14.

Liuzza, Roy Michael. "On the Dating of *Beowulf*." *Basic Readings*. 281–302.

de Looze, Laurence N. "Frame Narratives and Fictionalization: Beowulf as Narrator." *Texas Studies in Literature and Language* 26 (1984): 145–56. Rep. in Fulk, *Interpretations*.

Lord, Albert Bates. "*Beowulf* and Oral Epic Tradition." *The Singer Resumes the Tale*. Ed. Mary Louise Lord. Ithaca: Cornell UP, 1995. 96–116.

Magoun, Francis P., Jr. "The Oral-Formulaic Character of Anglo-Saxon Narrative Poetry." *Speculum* 28 (1953): 446–67. Rep. in Fry, *Collection*; Fulk, *Interpretations*; Nicholson, *Anthology*.

Mitchell, Bruce. "1987: Postscript on *Beowulf*." *On Old English: Selected Papers*. Oxford: Blackwell, 1988.

Newton, Sam. *The Origins of Beowulf and the Pre-Viking Kingdom of East Anglia*. Cambridge: Brewer, 1993.

Niles, John D. "*Beowulf*: Poetry as Social Praxis." *College English* 61 (1998): 143–66. Rep. in Donaldson/Howe.

———. *Beowulf: The Poem and Its Tradition*. Cambridge, MA: Harvard UP, 1983.

———. "Rewriting *Beowulf*: The Task of Translation." *College English* 55 (1993): 858–78.

O'Keeffe, Katherine O'Brien. *Visible Song: Transitional Literacy in Old English Verse*. Cambridge Studies in Anglo-Saxon England. Cambridge: Cambridge UP, 1990.

Opland, Jeff. *Anglo-Saxon Oral Poetry: A Study of the Traditions*. New Haven, CT: Yale UP, 1980.

Orchard, Andy. *Pride and Prodigies: Studies in the Monsters of the Beowulf Manuscript*. Cambridge: Brewer, 1995.

Overing, Gillian R. *Language, Sign, and Gender in Beowulf*. Carbondale: Southern Illinois UP, 1990. Ch. 4 appears rev. in Baker, *Basic Readings*.

Page, R. I. "The Audience of *Beowulf* and the Vikings." Chase, *Dating*. 113–22.

Panzer, Friedrich. *Studien zur germanischen Sagengeschichte, I: Beowulf*. Munich: Beck, 1910.

Parks, Ward. *Verbal Dueling in Heroic Narrative: The Homeric and Old English Traditions*. Princeton, NJ: Princeton UP, 1990.

Pope, John C. "Beowulf's Old Age." *Philological Essays: Studies in Old and Middle English Language and Literature in Honour of Herbert Dean Meritt*. Ed. James L. Rosier. The Hague: Mouton, 1970. 55–64.

———. *The Rhythm of Beowulf*. 2nd ed. New Haven, CT: Yale UP, 1966.

Puhvel, Martin. *Beowulf and Celtic Tradition*. Waterloo, Ont.: Wilfrid Laurier UP, 1979.

Rauer, Christine. *Beowulf and the Dragon: Parallels and Analogues*. Cambridge: Brewer, 2000.

Raw, Barbara. "Royal Power and Royal Symbols in *Beowulf*." *The Age of Sutton Hoo: The Seventh Century in North-Western Europe*. Ed. M. O. H. Carver. Woodbridge: Boydell, 1992. 167–74.

Renoir, Alain. "Point of View and Design for Terror in *Beowulf*." *Neuphilologische Mitteilungen* 63 (1962) 91–105. Rep. in Fry, *Collection*.

Robinson, Fred C. "*Beowulf*." Godden, *Companion*. 142–59.

———. *Beowulf and the Appositive Style*. The Hodges Lectures. Knoxville: U of Tennessee P, 1985. Ch. 1 rep. in Donaldson/Howe; ch. 2 in Bloom.

———. "Elements of the Marvellous in the Characterization of *Beowulf*: A Reconsideration of the Textual Evidence." *Old English Studies in Honour of John C. Pope*. Ed. Robert B. Burlin and Edward B. Irving, Jr. Toronto: U of Toronto P, 1974. 119–37. Rep. in Baker, *Basic Readings*; Robinson, *Tomb*.

• ———. "The Tomb of Beowulf." Robinson, *Tomb*. 3–19.

Rogers, H. L. "Beowulf's Three Great Fights." *Review of English Studies* n.s. 6 (1955): 339–55. Rep. in Nicholson, *Anthology*.
Sawyer, P. H. *From Roman Britain to Norman England*. 2nd ed. New York: Routledge, 1998. (General history)
Scowcroft, R. Mark. "The Irish Analogues to *Beowulf*." *Speculum* 74 (1999): 22–64.
Shippey, T. A. *Beowulf*. Studies in English Literature. London: Edward Arnold, 1978.
Sisam, Kenneth. "Anglo-Saxon Royal Genealogies." *Proceedings of the British Academy* 39 (1953): 287–348.
———. *The Structure of Beowulf*. Oxford: Clarendon, 1965.
Stanley, Eric G. *"Beowulf." Continuations and Beginnings*. London: Thomas Nelson, 1966. 104–40. Rep. in Baker, *Basic Readings*.
———. "The Date of *Beowulf*: Some Doubts and No Conclusions." Chase, *Dating*. 197–211.
———. *In the Foreground: Beowulf*. Cambridge: Brewer, 1994.
• Tolkien, J. R. R. "*Beowulf*: The Monsters and the Critics." *Proceedings of the British Academy* 22 (1936): 245–95. Rep. in Bloom; Fulk, *Interpretations*; Fry, *Collection*; Nicholson, *Anthology*.
———. "Prefatory Remarks on Prose Translations of 'Beowulf'." In J. R. Clark Hall, trans., *Beowulf and the Finnesburg Fragment*. ix–xliii.
Vendler, Helen Hennessy. *Seamus Heaney*. London: HarperCollins, 1998.
• Webster, Leslie. "Archaeology and *Beowulf*." In Mitchell and Robinson, eds. *Beowulf: An Edition*. 183–94.
Whitelock, Dorothy. *The Audience of Beowulf*. Oxford: Clarendon, 1951.
———. *The Beginnings of English Society*. Rev. ed. Harmondsworth: Penguin, 1974. (General history)
Williams, David. *Cain and Beowulf: A Study in Secular Allegory*. Toronto: U of Toronto P, 1982.
Wormald, Patrick. "Bede, *Beowulf* and the Conversion of the Anglo-Saxon Aristocracy." *Bede and Anglo-Saxon England*. Ed. Robert T. Farrell. Oxford: British Archaeological Reports, 1978. 32–95.
———. *The Making of English Law: King Alfred to the Twelfth Century*. Oxford: Blackwell, 1999. (Legal history)

SELECTED WRITINGS OF SEAMUS HEANEY

Heaney, Seamus. *Preoccupations: Selected Prose, 1968–1978*. New York: Farrar, Straus and Giroux, 1980.
———. *Poems, 1965–1975*. New York: Farrar, Straus and Giroux, 1980.
———. *The Government of the Tongue: Selected Prose, 1978–1987*. New York: Farrar, Straus and Giroux, 1989.
———. *The Redress of Poetry*. New York: Farrar, Straus and Giroux, 1995.
———. *Opened Ground: Poems, 1966–1996*. New York: Farrar, Straus and Giroux, 1998.